My Heavenly Hockey Club

4

AI MORINAGA

Translated and adapted by Athena and Alethea Nibley
Lettered by North Market Street Graphics

BALLANTINE BOOKS • NEW YORK

My Heavenly Hockey Club volume 4 is a work of fiction. Names, characters, places, and incidents are the products of the author's imagination or are used fictitiously. Any resemblance to actual events, locales, or persons, living or dead, is entirely coincidental.

A Del Rey Manga/Kodansha Trade Paperback Original

Published in the United States by Del Rey Books, an imprint of The Random House Publishing Group, a division of Random House, Inc., New York.

DEL REY is a registered trademark and the Del Rey colophon is a trademark of Random House, Inc.

Publication rights arranged through Kodansha Ltd.

First published in Japan in 2006 by Kodansha Ltd., Tokyo, as *Gokuraku Seishun Hockeybu*.

ISBN 978-0-345-50032-8

Printed in the United States of America

www.delreymanga.com

9 8 7 6 5 4 3 2

Translator/Adapter—Athena and Alethea Nibley
Lettering—North Market Street Graphics

Contents

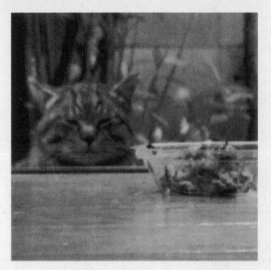

Bagel (a male so named because his tail is shaped like a bagel), whom I haven't seen lately, came back and is now shaped like a barrel. I think that, when it comes to animals, the fatter and furrier they are, the cuter they are. If I was an animal, I would be pretty cute, but regrettably, I am a human.

Honorifics Explained

Throughout the Del Rey Manga books, you will find Japanese honorifics left intact in the translations. For those not familiar with how the Japanese use honorifics and, more important, how they differ from American honorifics, we present this brief overview.

Politeness has always been a critical facet of Japanese culture. Ever since the feudal era, when Japan was a highly stratified society, use of honorifics—which can be defined as polite speech that indicates relationship or status—has played an essential role in the Japanese language. When addressing someone in Japanese, an honorific usually takes the form of a suffix attached to one's name (example: "Asuna-san"), is used as a title at the end of one's name, or appears in place of the name itself (example: "Negi-sensei," or simply "Sensei!").

Honorifics can be expressions of respect or endearment. In the context of manga and anime, honorifics give insight into the nature of the relationship between characters. Many English translations leave out these important honorifics and therefore distort the feel of the original Japanese. Because Japanese honorifics contain nuances that English honorifics lack, it is our policy at Del Rey not to translate them. Here, instead, is a guide to some of the honorifics you may encounter in Del Rey Manga.

-san: This is the most common honorific and is equivalent to Mr., Miss, Ms., or Mrs. It is the all-purpose honorific and can be used in any situation where politeness is required.

-sama: This is one level higher than "-san" and is used to confer great respect.

-dono: This comes from the word "tono," which means "lord." It is an even higher level than "-sama" and confers utmost respect.

-kun: This suffix is used at the end of boys' names to express familiarity or endearment. It is also sometimes used by men among friends, or when addressing someone younger or of a lower station.

-chan: This is used to express endearment, mostly toward girls. It is also used for little boys, pets, and even among lovers. It gives a sense of childish cuteness.

Bozu: This is an informal way to refer to a boy, similar to the English terms "kid" and "squirt."

Sempai/Senpai: This title suggests that the addressee is one's senior in a group or organization. It is most often used in a school setting, where underclassmen refer to their upperclassmen as "sempai." It can also be used in the workplace, such as when a newer employee addresses an employee who has seniority in the company.

Kohai: This is the opposite of "sempai" and is used toward underclassmen in school or newcomers in the workplace. It connotes that the addressee is of a lower station.

Sensei: Literally meaning "one who has come before," this title is used for teachers, doctors, or masters of any profession or art.

-[blank]: This is usually forgotten in these lists, but it is perhaps the most significant difference between Japanese and English. The lack of honorific means that the speaker has permission to address the person in a very intimate way. Usually, only family, spouses, or very close friends have this kind of permission. Known as *yobisute*, it can be gratifying when someone who has earned the intimacy starts to call one by one's name without an honorific. But when that intimacy hasn't been earned, it can be very insulting.

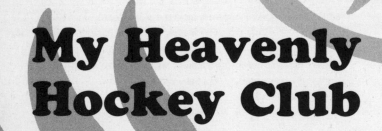

My Heavenly Hockey Club

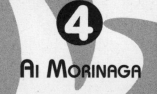

4

AI MORINAGA

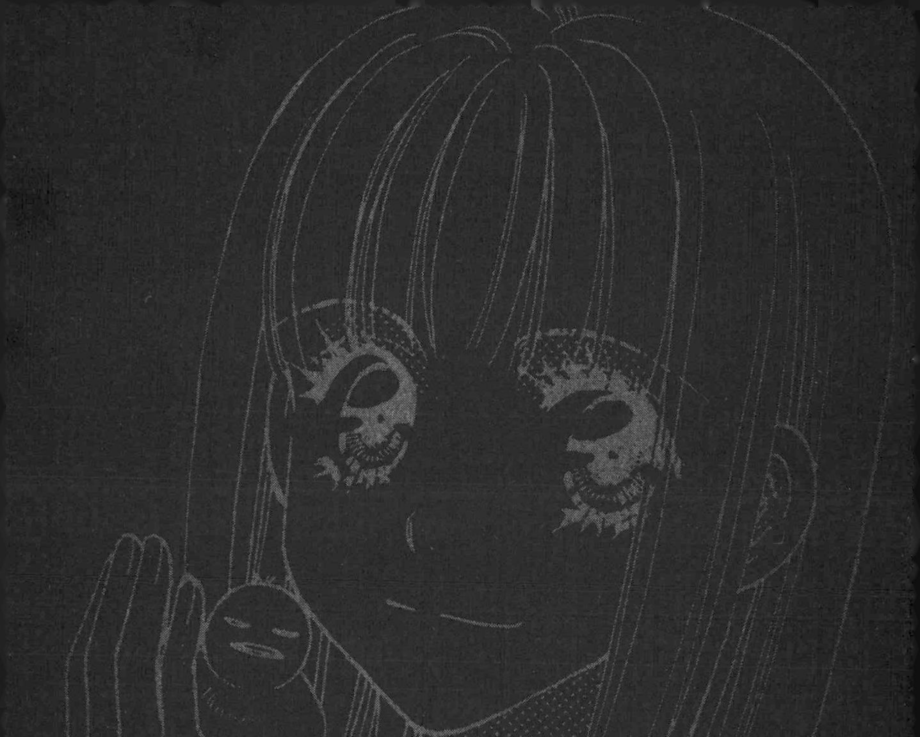

Contents

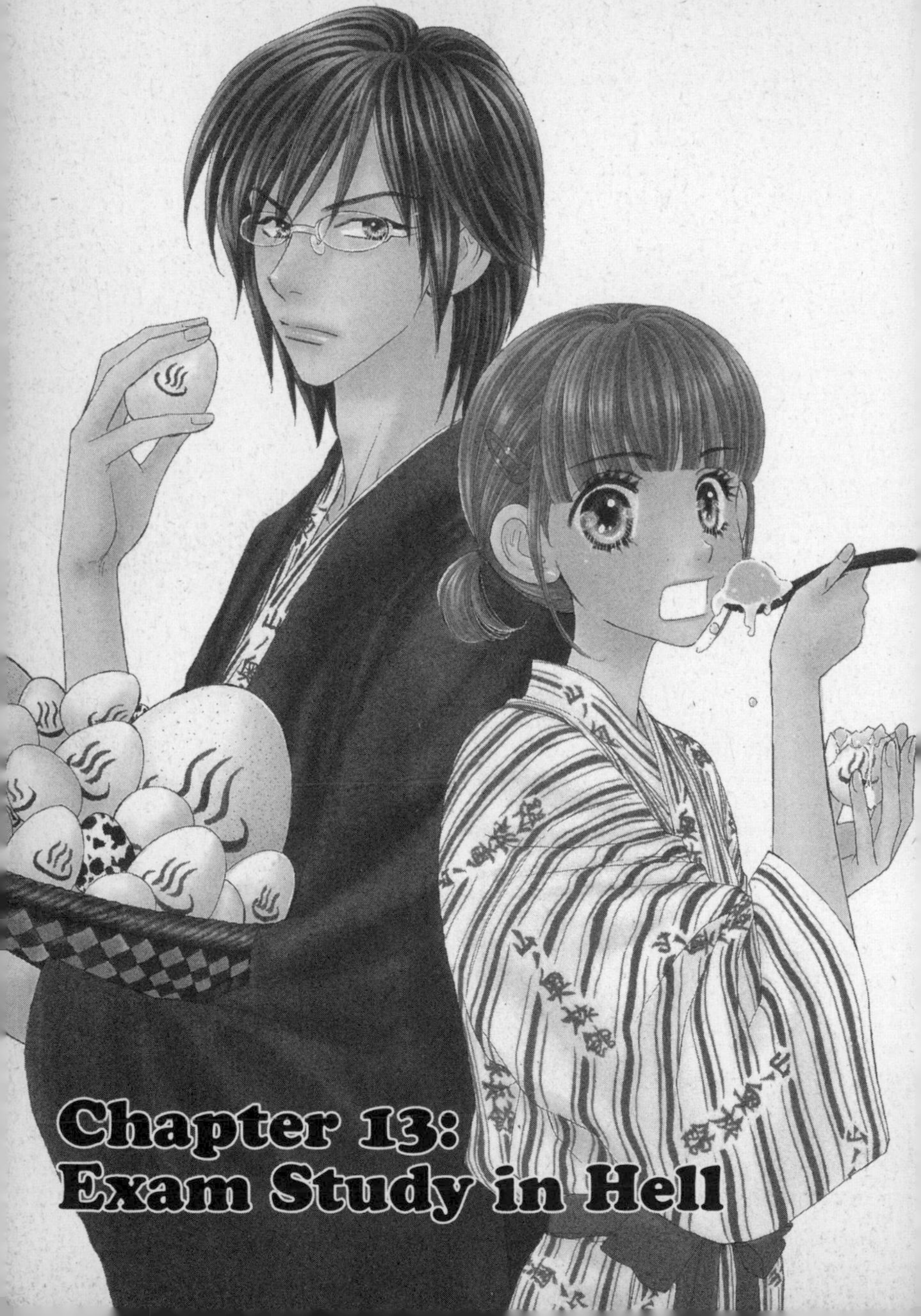
Chapter 13:
Exam Study in Hell

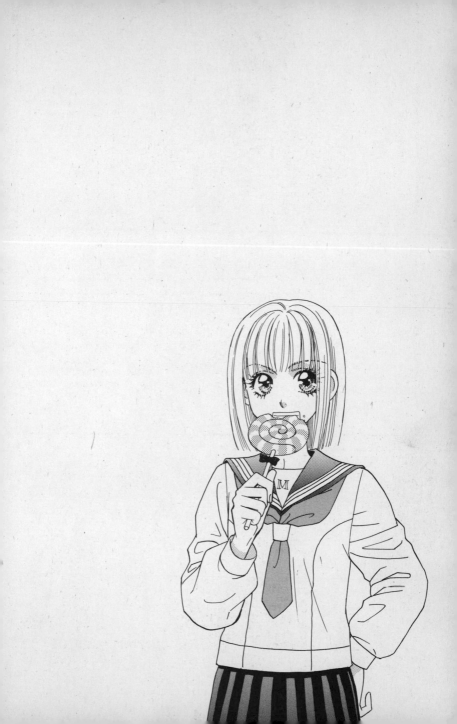

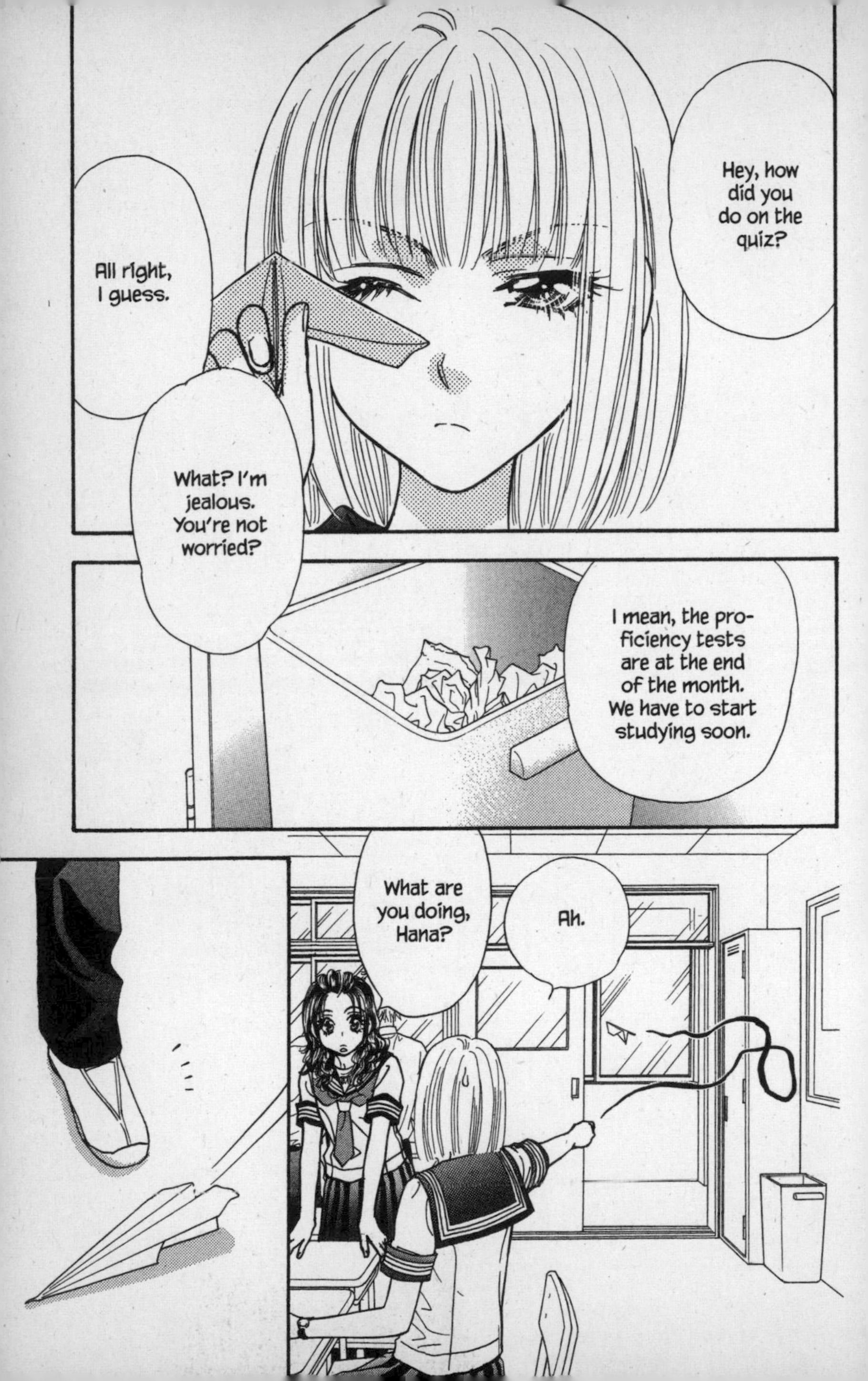
Hey, how did you do on the quiz?
All right, I guess.
What? I'm jealous. You're not worried?
I mean, the proficiency tests are at the end of the month. We have to start studying soon.
What are you doing, Hana?
Ah.

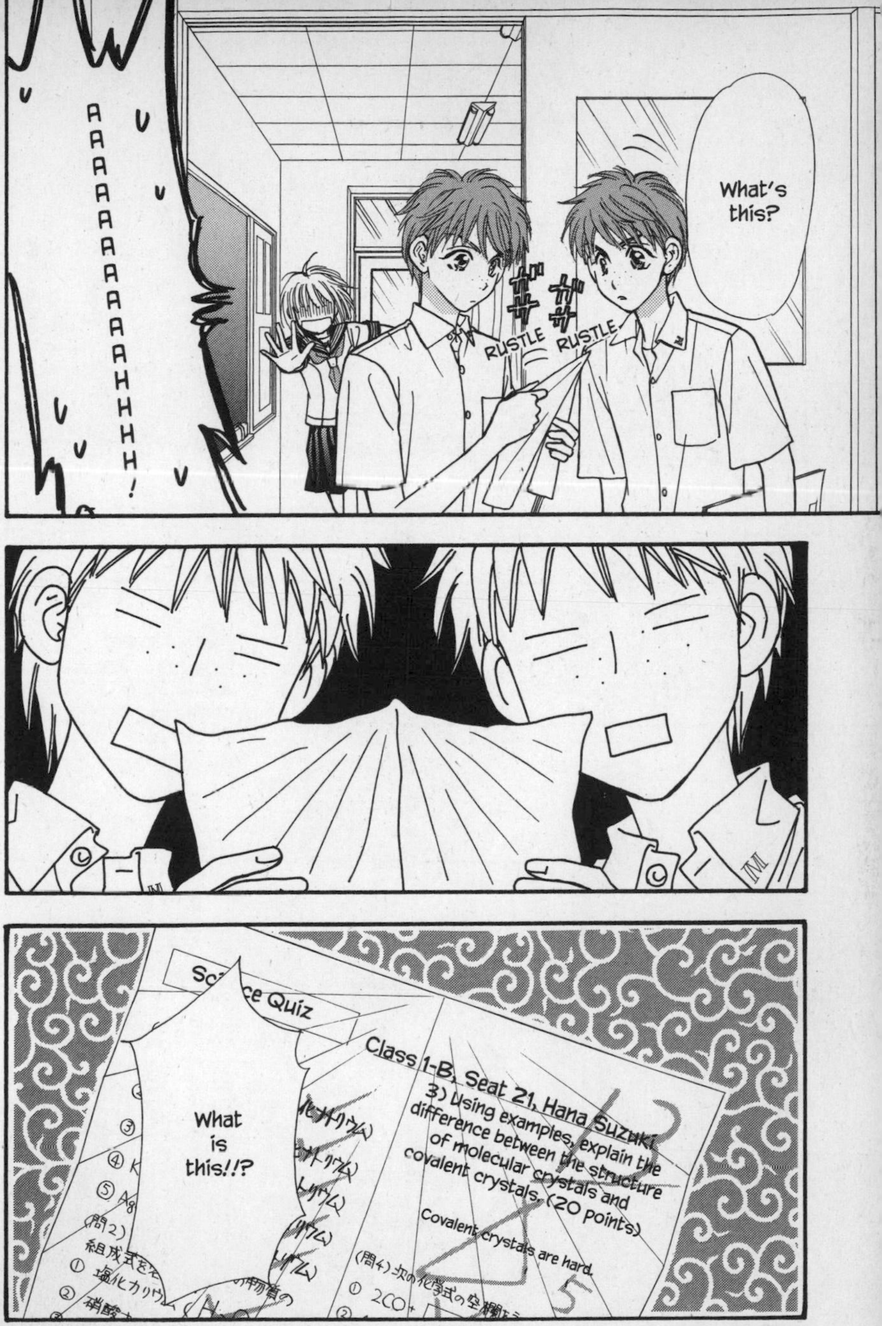
What's this?
RUSTLE RUSTLE
AAAAAAAAAAAAHHHH!
Class 1-B, Seat 21, Hana Suzuki
3) Using examples, explain the difference between the structure of molecular crystals and covalent crystals. (20 points)
Covalent crystals are hard.
What is this!!?

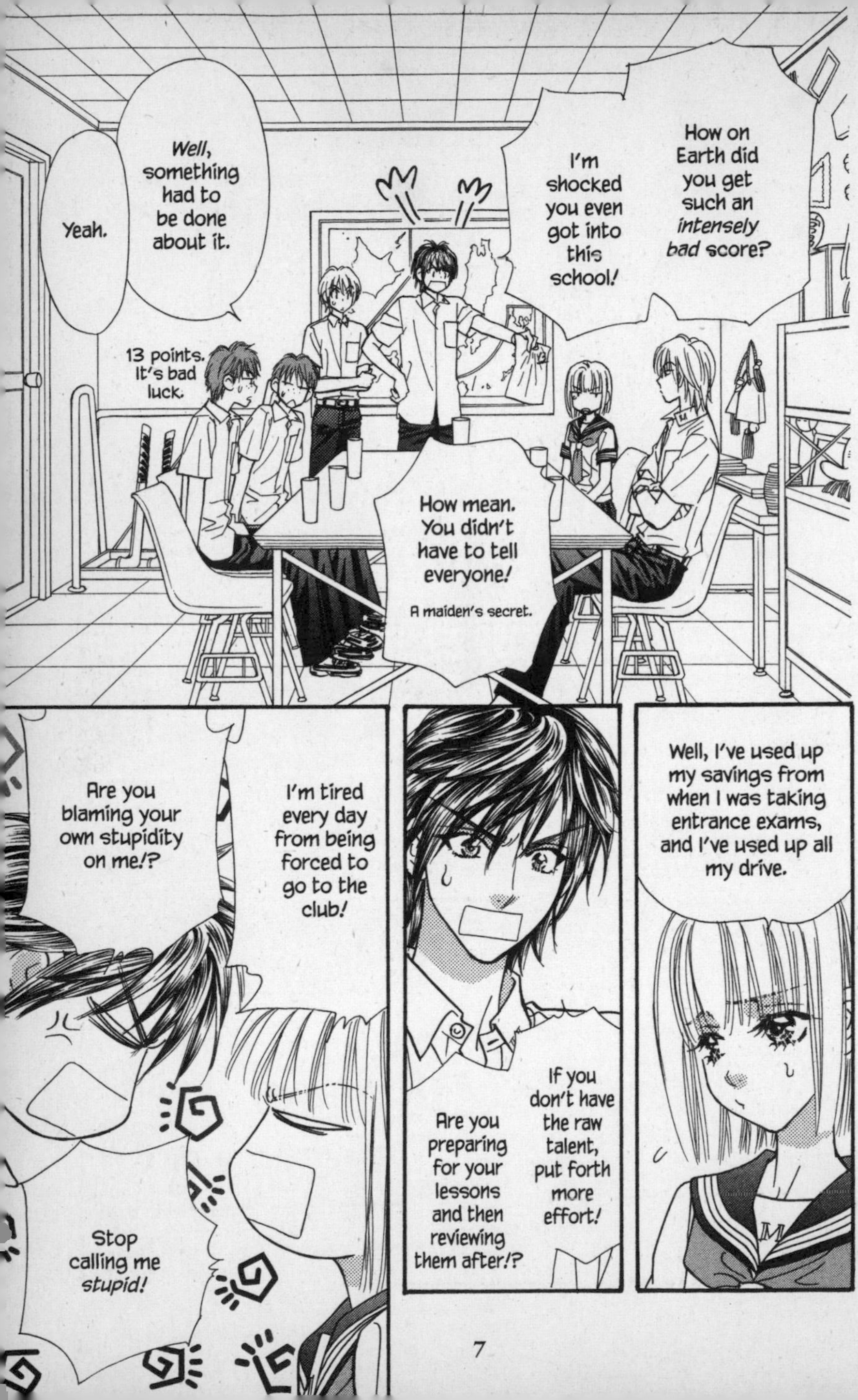
How on Earth did you get such an *intensely bad* score?
I'm shocked you even got into this school!
Well, something had to be done about it.
Yeah.
13 points. It's bad luck.
How mean. You didn't have to tell everyone!
A maiden's secret.
Well, I've used up my savings from when I was taking entrance exams, and I've used up all my drive.
If you don't have the raw talent, put forth more effort!
Are you preparing for your lessons and then reviewing them after!?
I'm tired every day from being forced to go to the club!
Are you blaming your own stupidity on me!?
Stop calling me *stupid!*

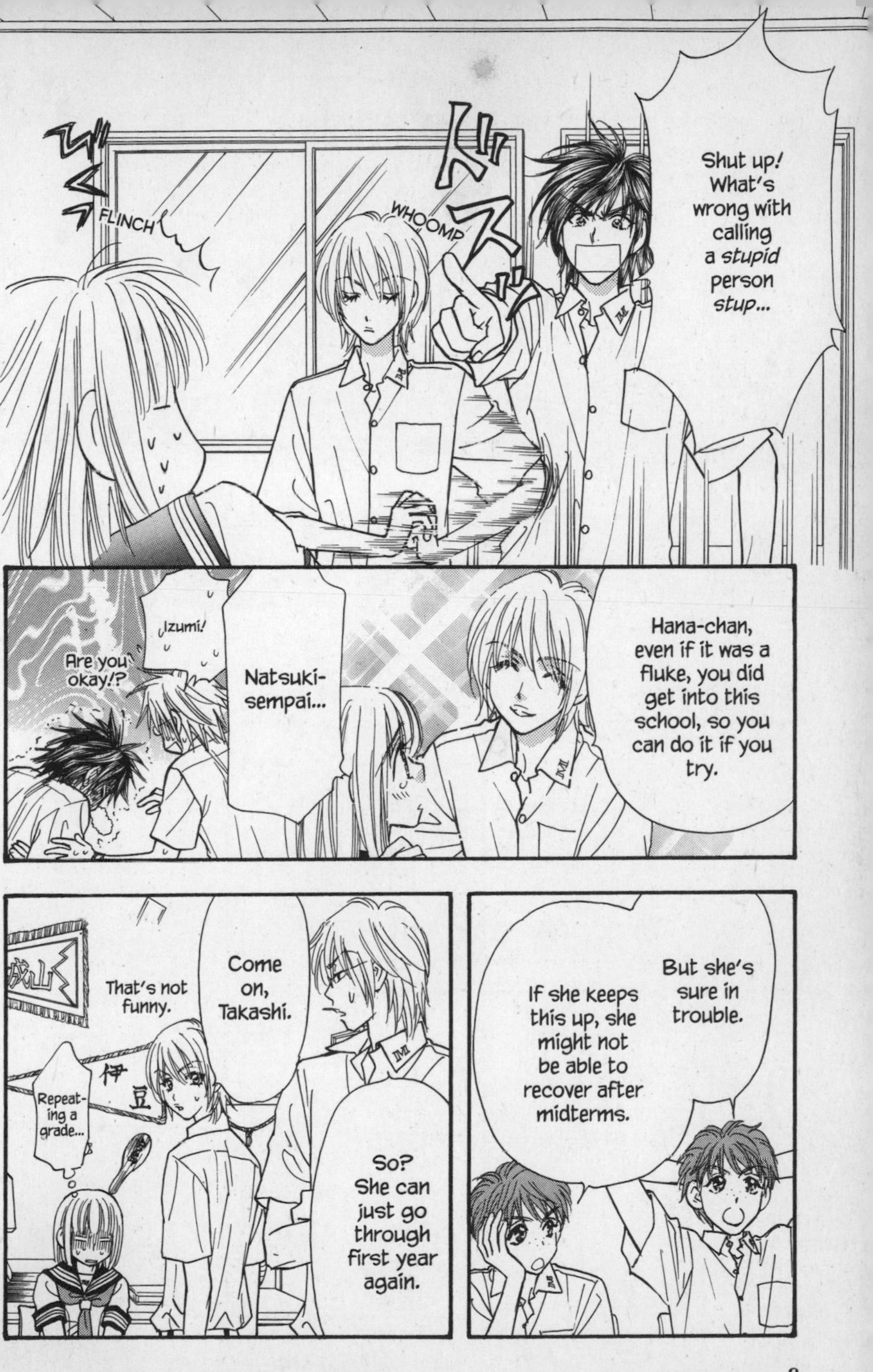
Shut up! What's wrong with calling a *stupid* person *stup...*
WHOOMP
FLINCH
Hana-chan, even if it was a fluke, you did get into this school, so you can do it if you try.
Natsuki-sempai...
Izumi!
Are you okay!?
But she's sure in trouble.
If she keeps this up, she might not be able to recover after midterms.
Come on, Takashi.
That's not funny.
So? She can just go through first year again.
Repeating a grade...

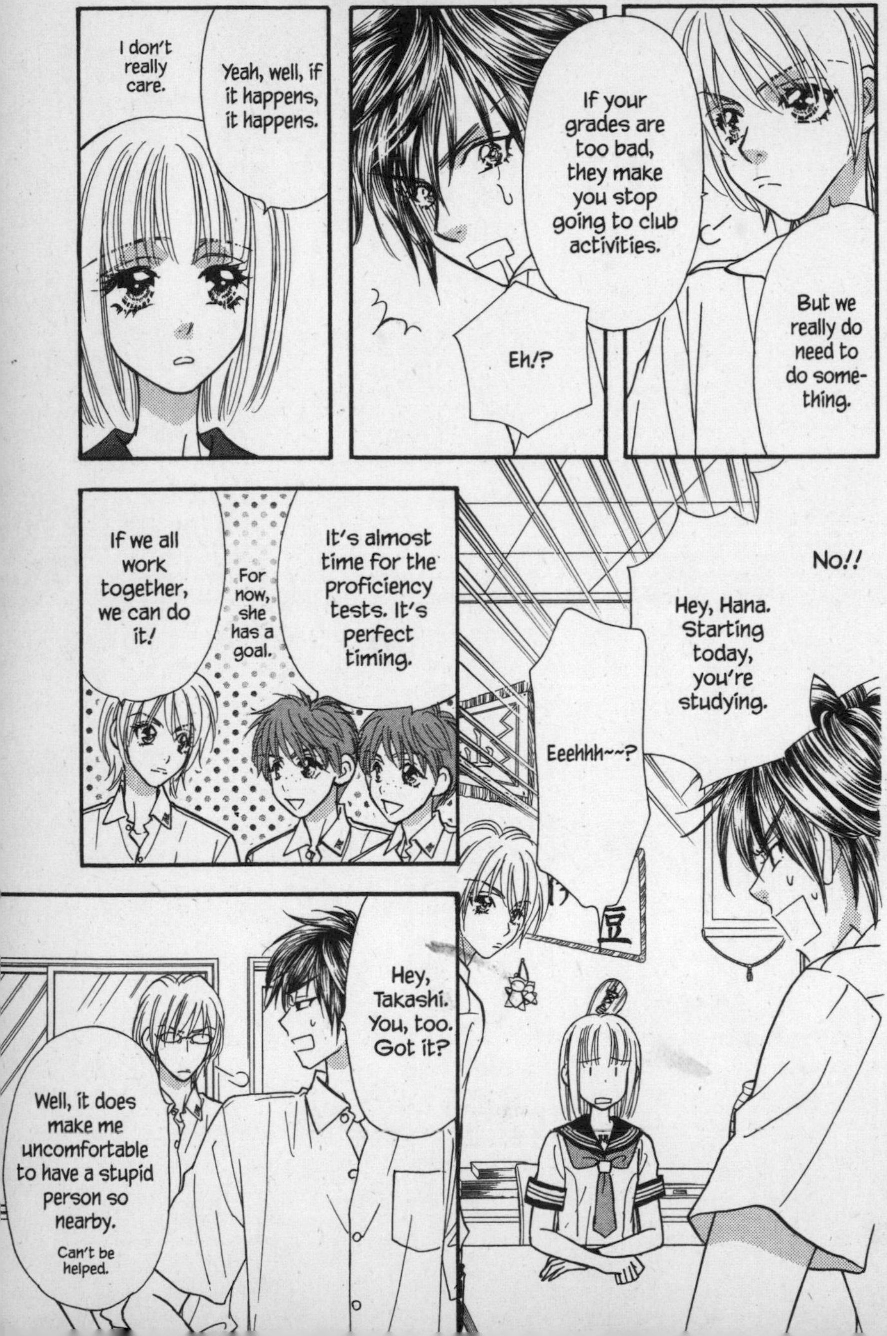
If your grades are too bad, they make you stop going to club activities.
But we really do need to do something.
Eh!?
Yeah, well, if it happens, it happens.
I don't really care.
No!!
Hey, Hana. Starting today, you're studying.
Eeehhh~~?
It's almost time for the proficiency tests. It's perfect timing.
For now, she has a goal.
If we all work together, we can do it!
Hey, Takashi. You, too. Got it?
Well, it does make me uncomfortable to have a stupid person so nearby.
Can't be helped.

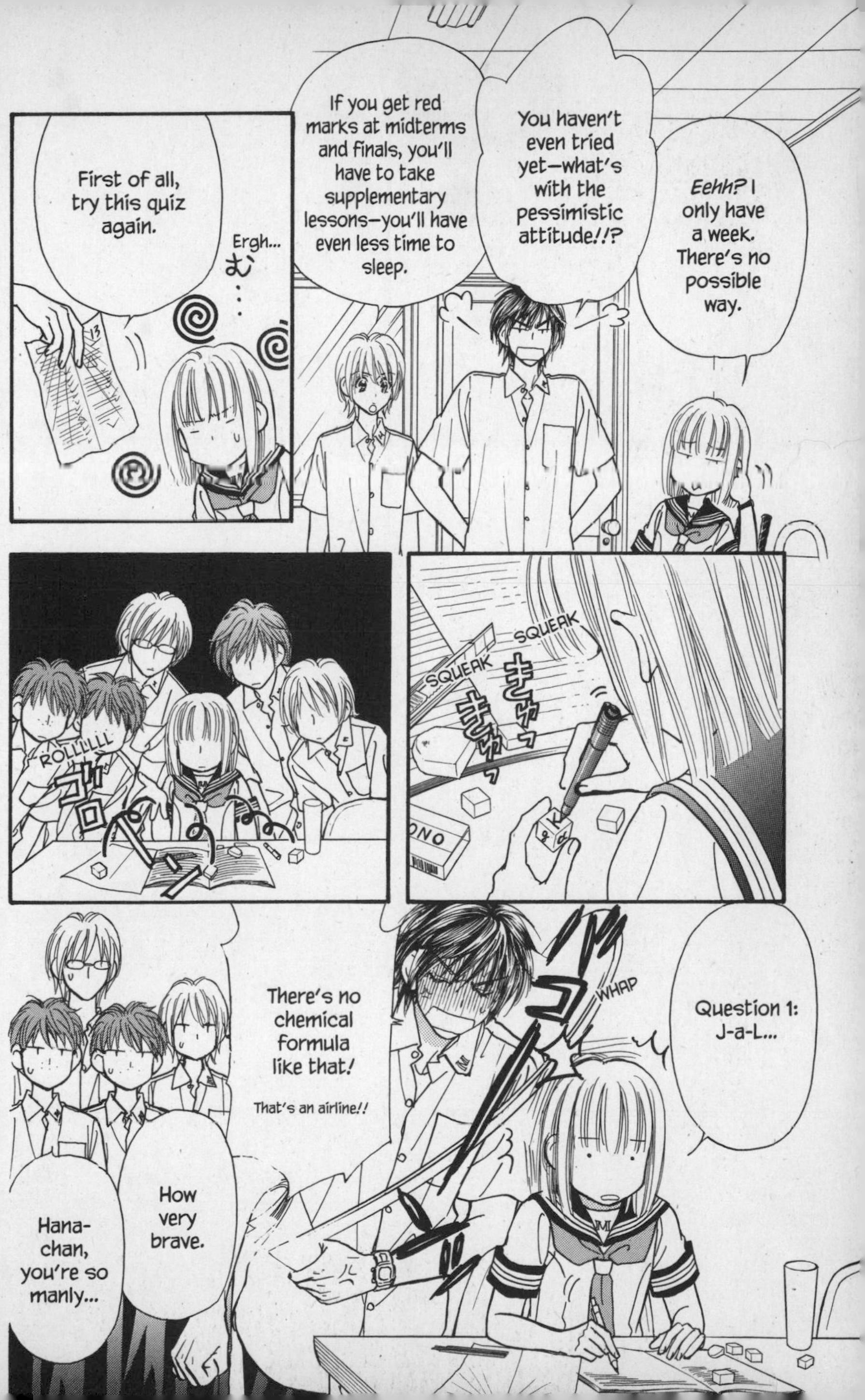
Eehh? I only have a week. There's no possible way.
You haven't even tried yet—what's with the pessimistic attitude!!?
If you get red marks at midterms and finals, you'll have to take supplementary lessons—you'll have even less time to sleep.
First of all, try this quiz again.
Ergh...
む…
SQUEAK
SQUEAK
ROLLLLLL
Question 1: J-a-L...
WHAP
There's no chemical formula like that!
That's an airline!!
How very brave.
Hana-chan, you're so manly...

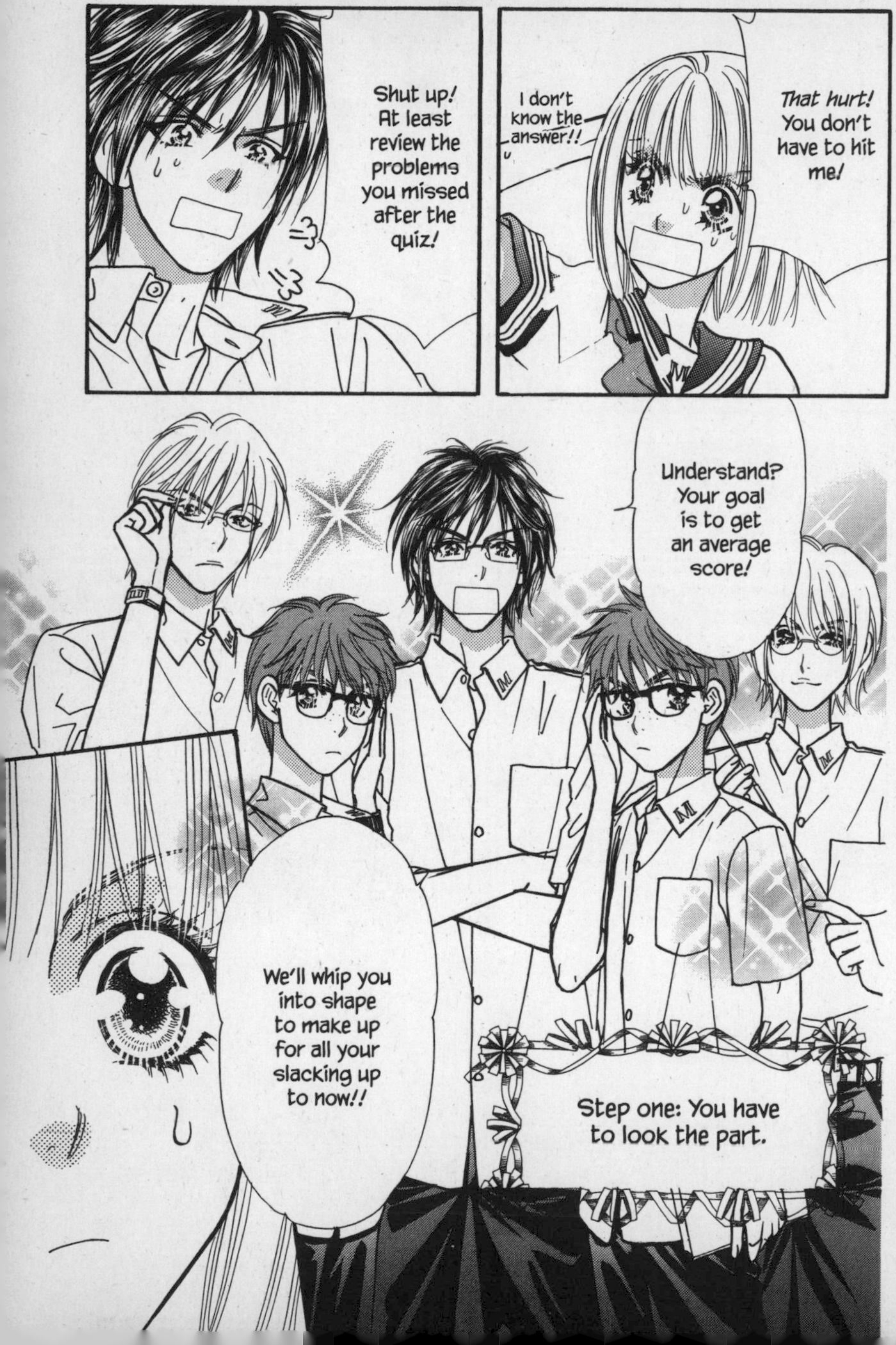
That hurt! You don't have to hit me!
I don't know the answer!!
Shut up! At least review the problems you missed after the quiz!
Understand? Your goal is to get an average score!
We'll whip you into shape to make up for all your slacking up to now!!
Step one: You have to look the part.

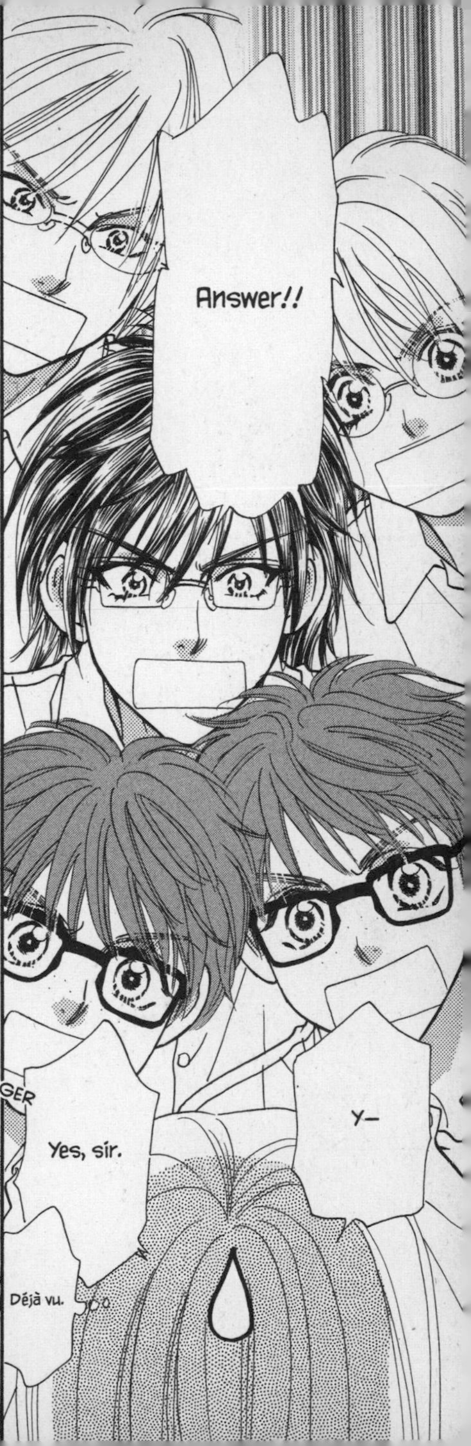
Answer!!
Y—
Yes, sir.
Déjà vu.

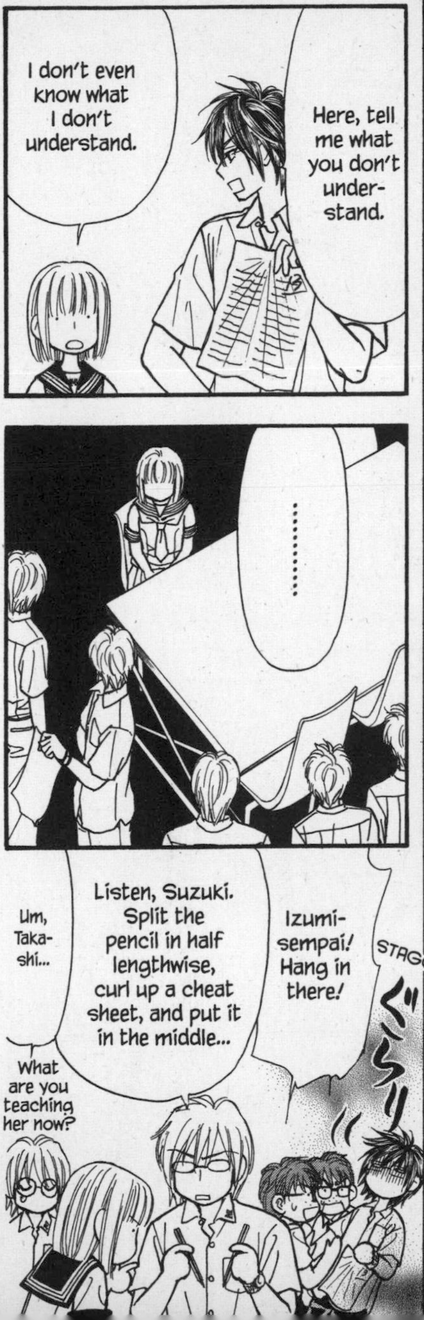
Here, tell me what you don't under-stand.
I don't even know what I don't understand.
......
STAGGER
ぐらり
Izumi-sempai! Hang in there!
Listen, Suzuki. Split the pencil in half lengthwise, curl up a cheat sheet, and put it in the middle...
Um, Taka-shi...
What are you teaching her now?

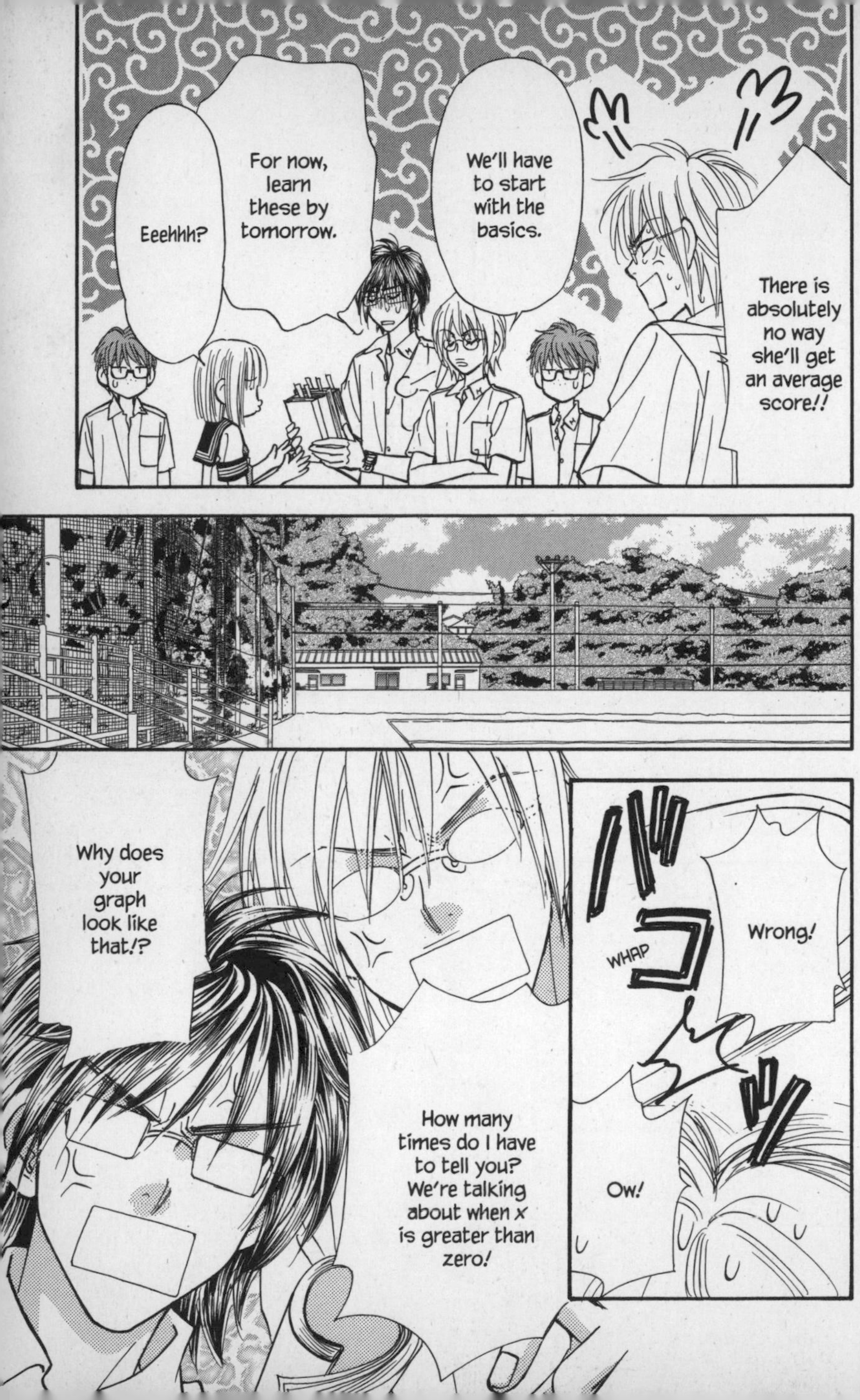
There is absolutely no way she'll get an average score!!
We'll have to start with the basics.
For now, learn these by tomorrow.
Eeehhh?
Wrong!
WHAP
Ow!
Why does your graph look like that!?
How many times do I have to tell you? We're talking about when x is greater than zero!

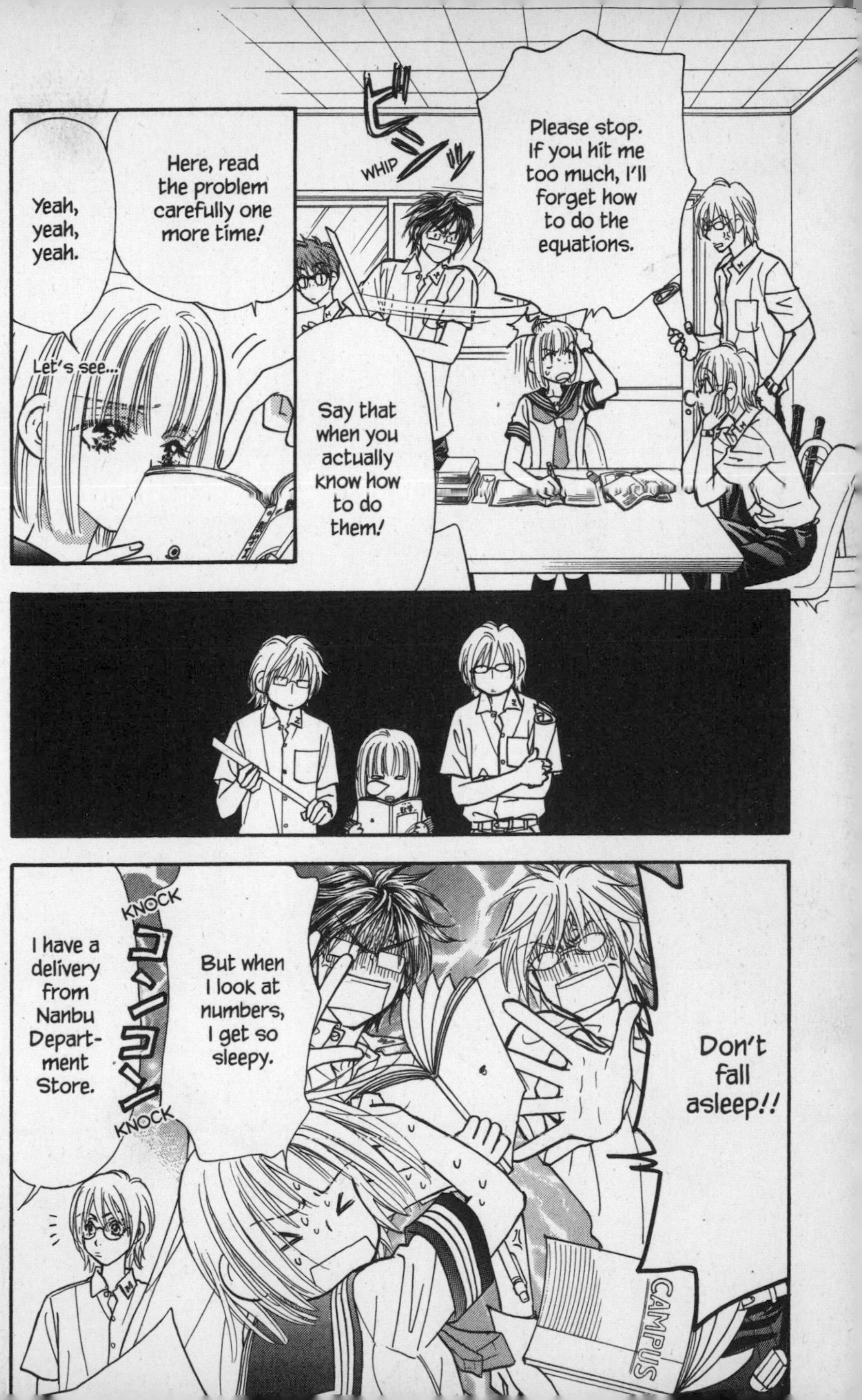
Please stop. If you hit me too much, I'll forget how to do the equations.
WHIP
Say that when you actually know how to do them!
Here, read the problem carefully one more time!
Yeah, yeah, yeah.
Let's see...
Don't fall asleep!!
But when I look at numbers, I get so sleepy.
KNOCK
KNOCK
I have a delivery from Nanbu Department Store.
CAMPUS

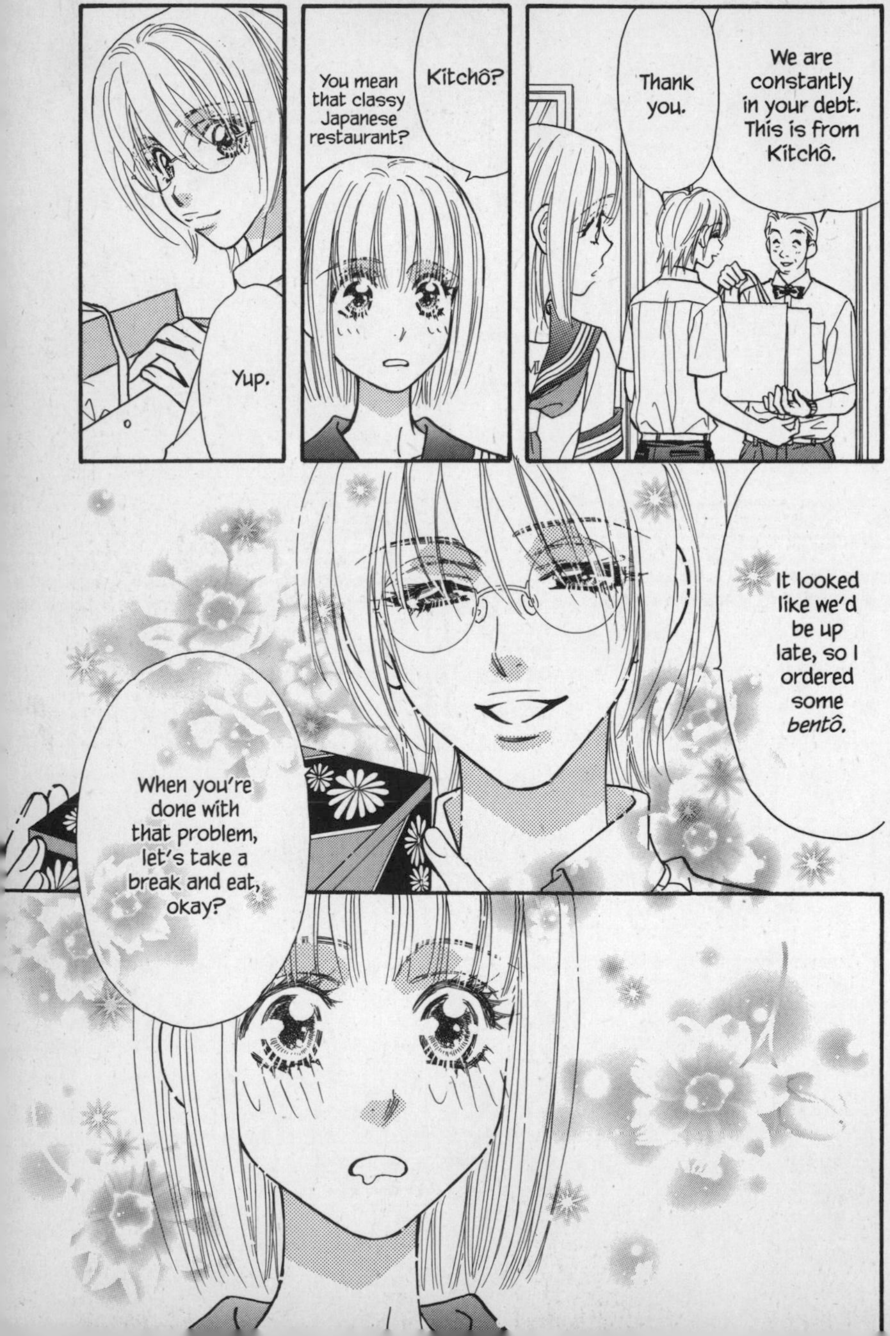
We are constantly in your debt. This is from Kitchô.
Thank you.
Kitchô?
You mean that classy Japanese restaurant?
Yup.
It looked like we'd be up late, so I ordered some *bentô.*
When you're done with that problem, let's take a break and eat, okay?

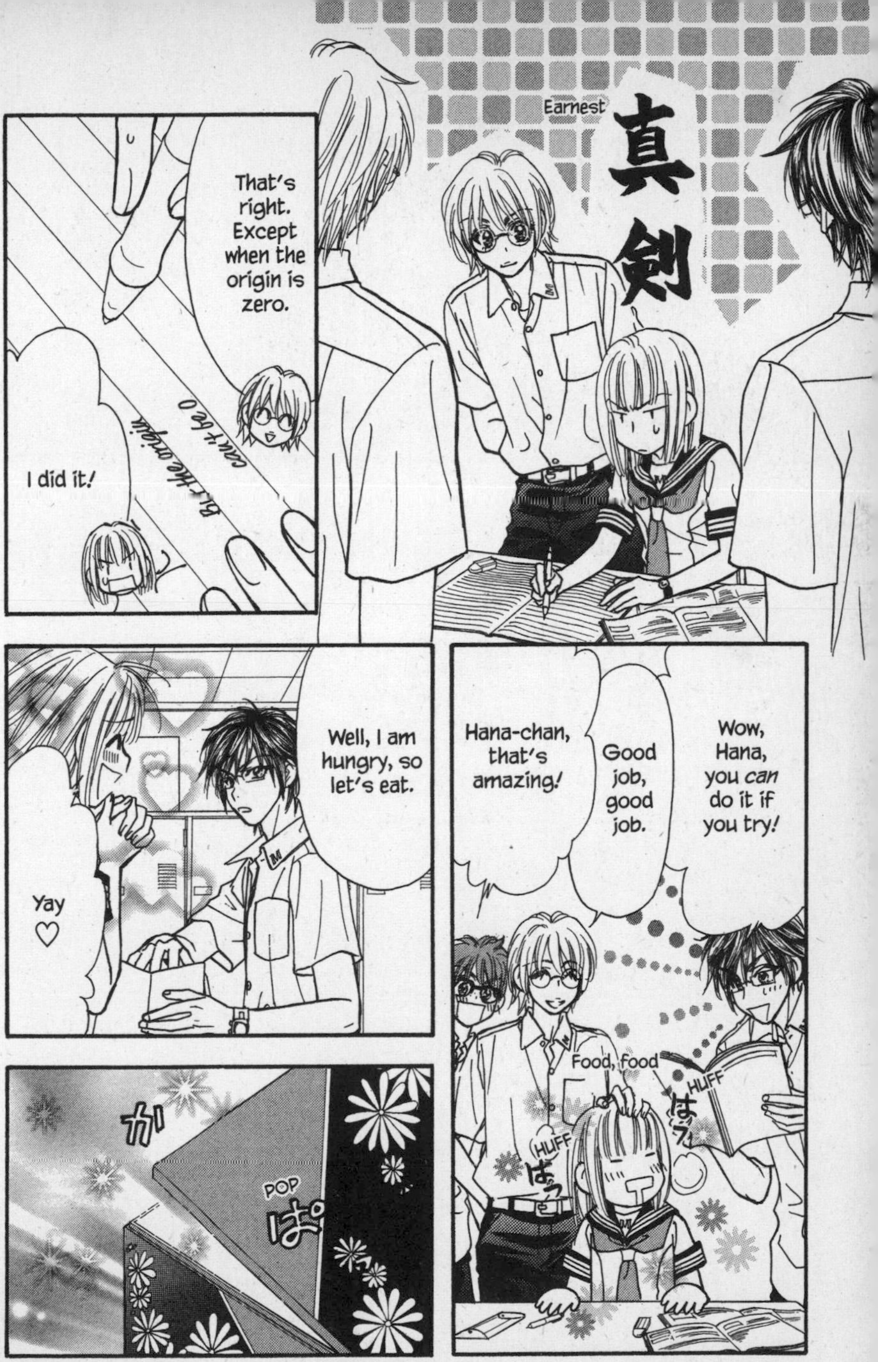
Earnest
真剣
That's right. Except when the origin is zero.
But the origin can't be 0
I did it!
Wow, Hana, you *can* do it if you try!
Good job, good job.
Hana-chan, that's amazing!
Food, food
HUFF
HUFF
Well, I am hungry, so let's eat.
Yay ♡
POP

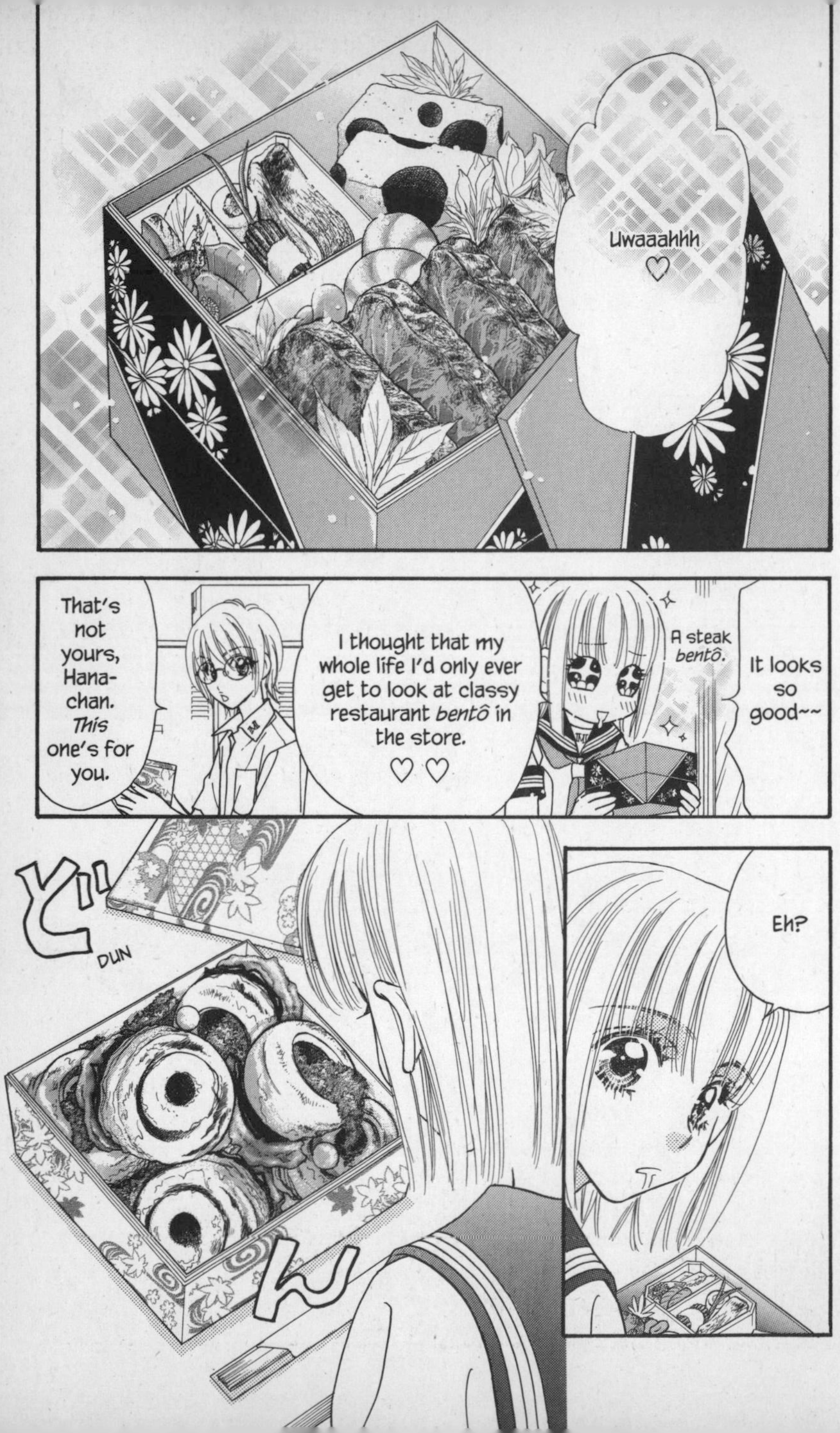
Uwaaahhh ♡
It looks so good~~
A steak *bentô*.
I thought that my whole life I'd only ever get to look at classy restaurant *bentô* in the store. ♡ ♡
That's not yours, Hana-chan. *This* one's for you.
Eh?
DUN

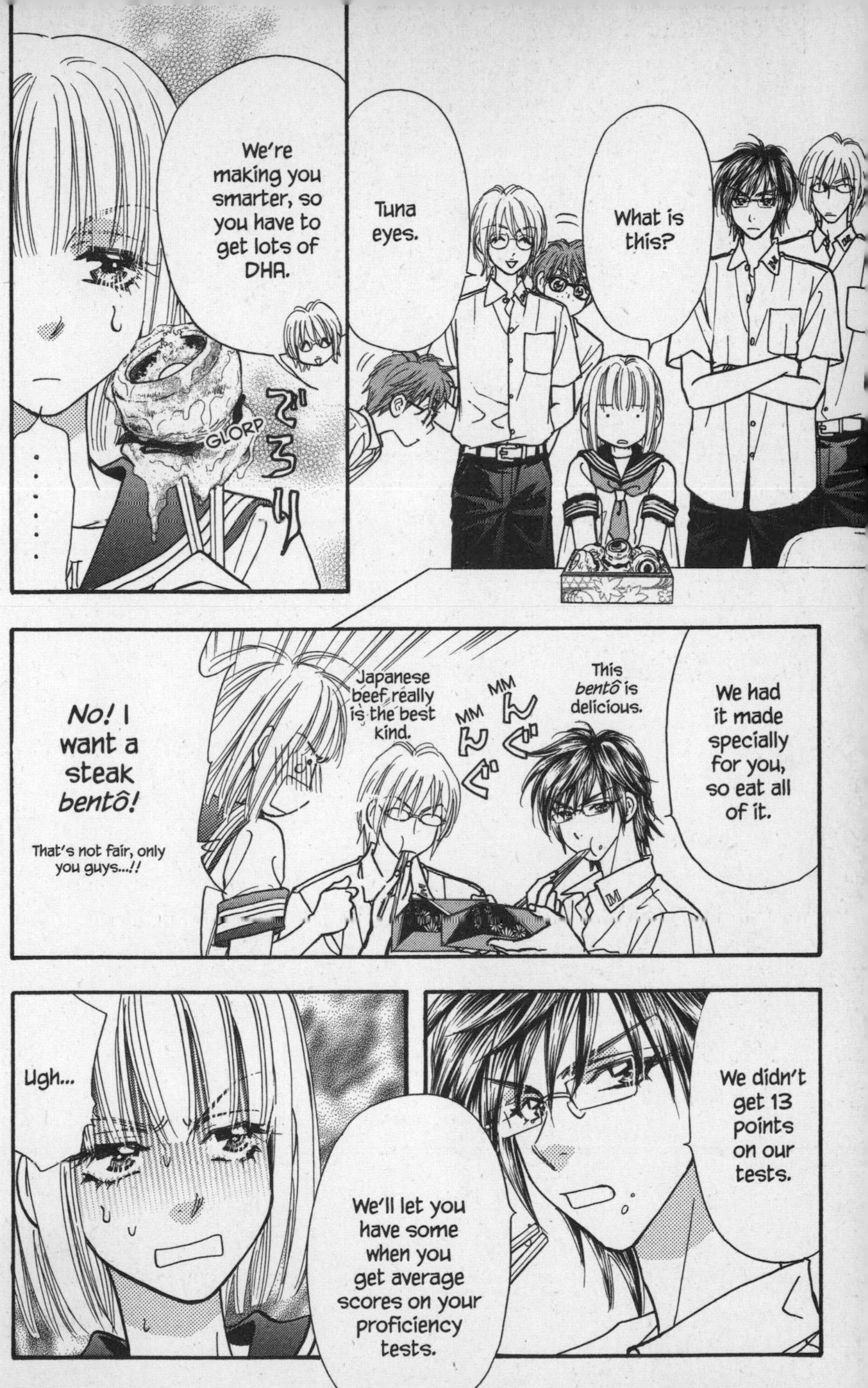
What is this?
Tuna eyes.
We're making you smarter, so you have to get lots of DHA.
GLORP
でろり
We had it made specially for you, so eat all of it.
This *bentô* is delicious.
MM
んぐ
MM
んぐ
Japanese beef really is the best kind.
No! I want a steak *bentô!*
That's not fair, only you guys...!!
We didn't get 13 points on our tests.
We'll let you have some when you get average scores on your proficiency tests.
Ugh...

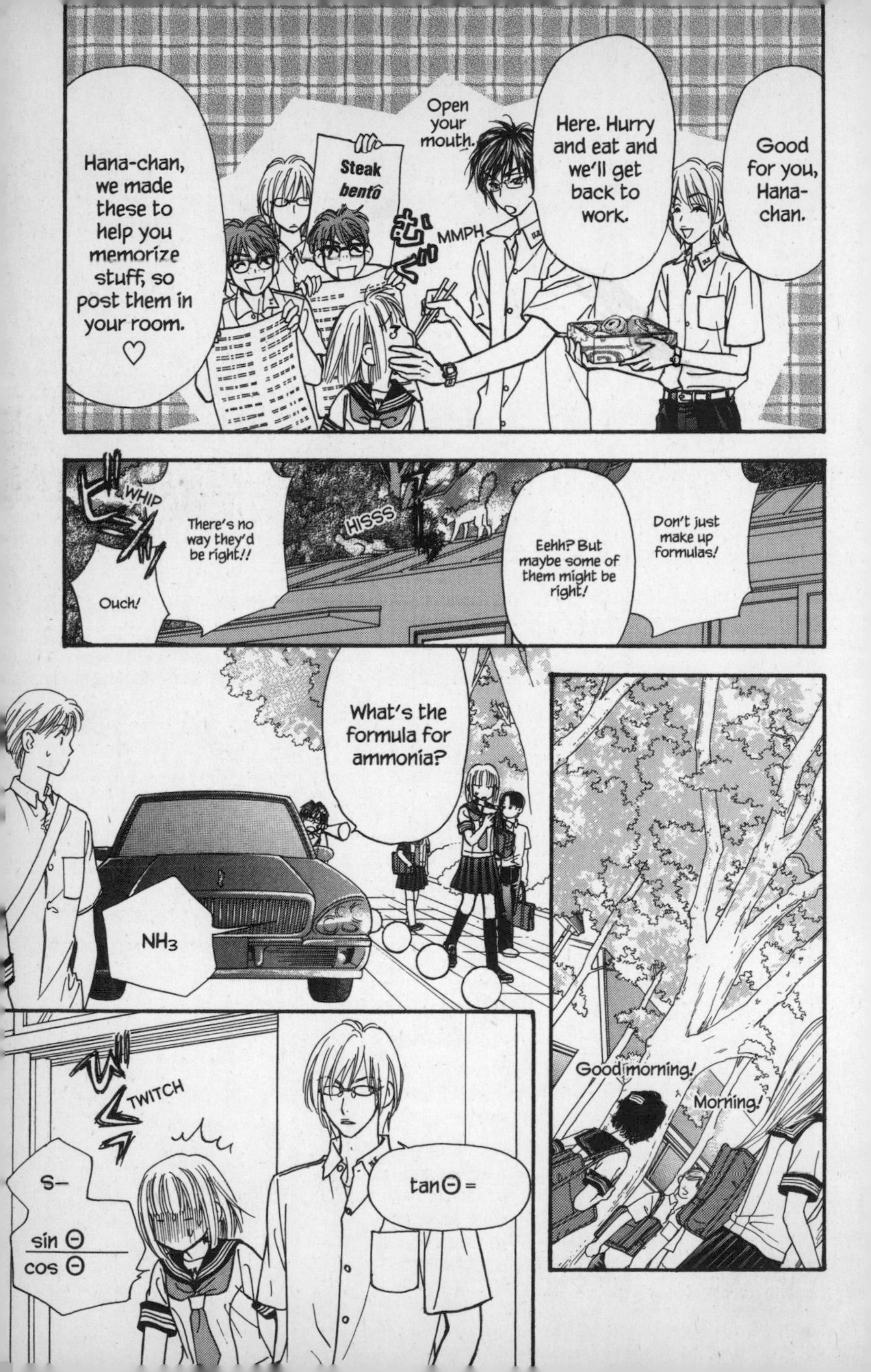
Good for you, Hana-chan.
Here. Hurry and eat and we'll get back to work.
Open your mouth.
MMPH
Steak bentô
Hana-chan, we made these to help you memorize stuff, so post them in your room. ♡
Don't just make up formulas!
Eehh? But maybe some of them might be right!
HISSS
There's no way they'd be right!!
WHIP
Ouch!
Morning!
Good morning!
What's the formula for ammonia?
NH_3
tan Θ =
TWITCH
S—
$\frac{\sin \Theta}{\cos \Theta}$

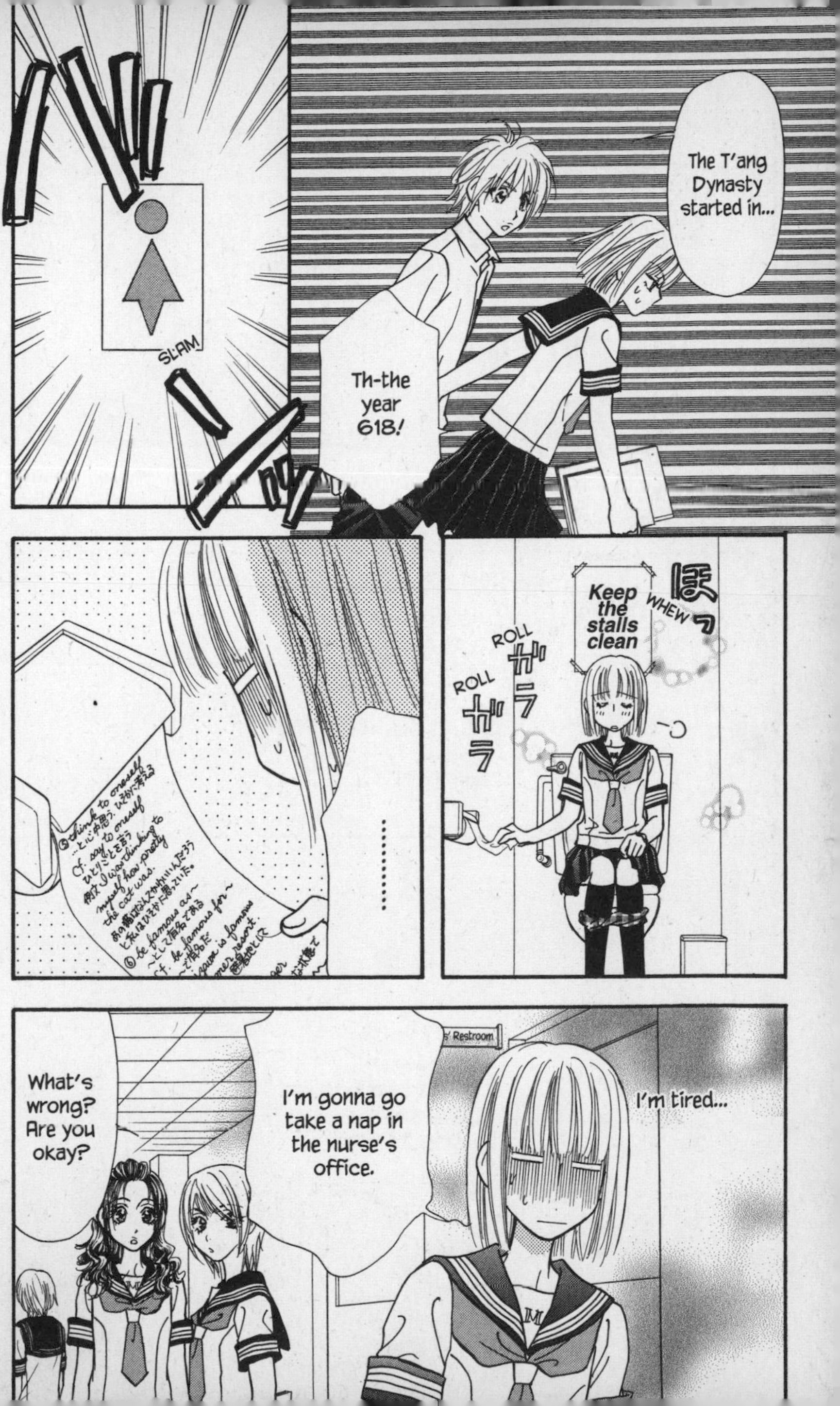
The T'ang Dynasty started in...
Th-the year 618!
SLAM
ほっ
WHEW
Keep the stalls clean
ROLL
ガラ
ROLL
ガラ
think to oneself
say to oneself
I was thinking to myself how pretty the cat was.
be famous as~
be famous for~
......
I'm tired...
I'm gonna go take a nap in the nurse's office.
What's wrong? Are you okay?

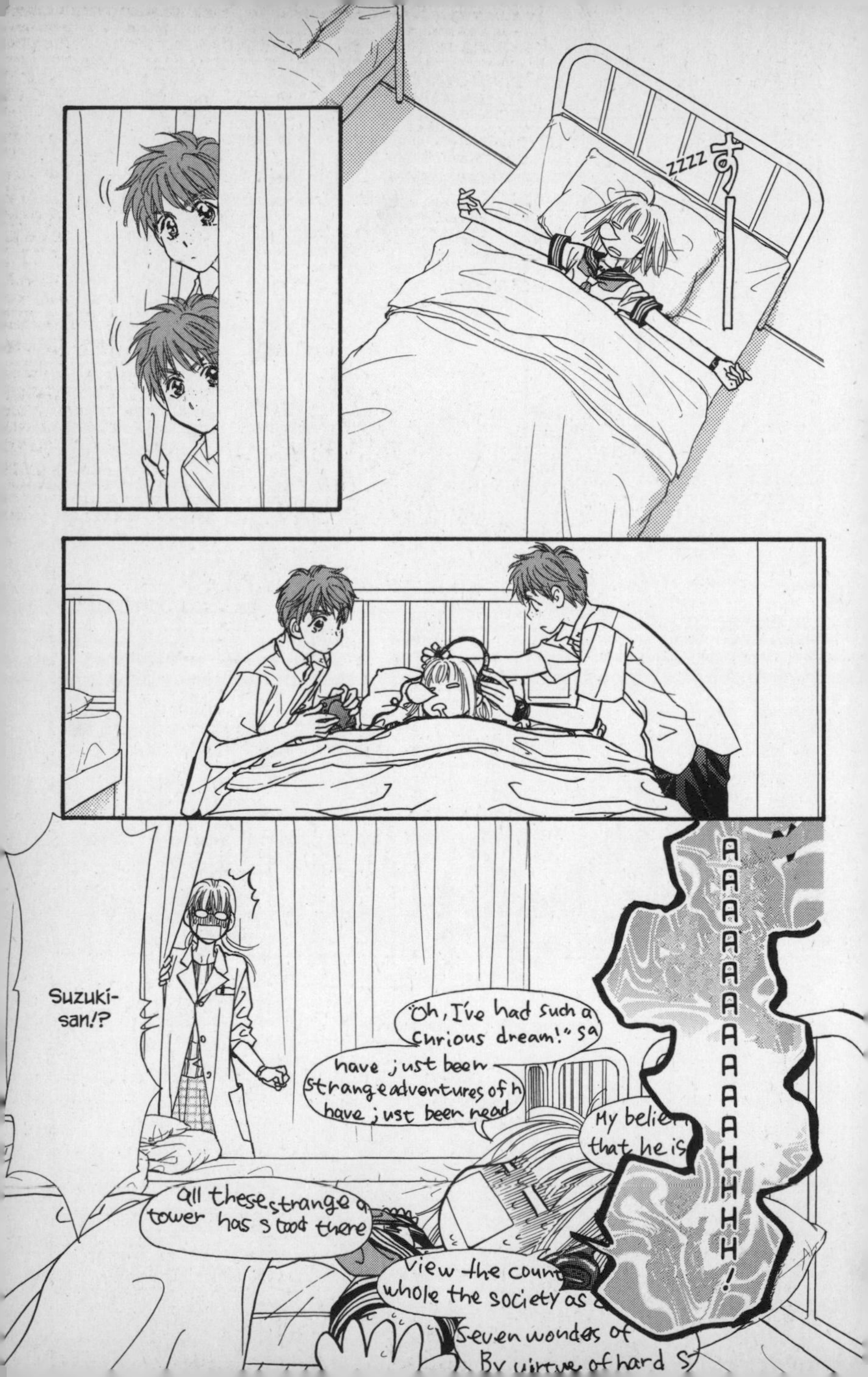
ZZZZ すー
AAAAAAAAAAAAAAHHHH!
"Oh, I've had such a curious dream!" sa
have just been
strange adventures of h
have just been read
My belie
that he is
all these strange a
tower has stood there
view the count
whole the society as a
Seven wonders of
By virtue of hard S
Suzuki-san!?

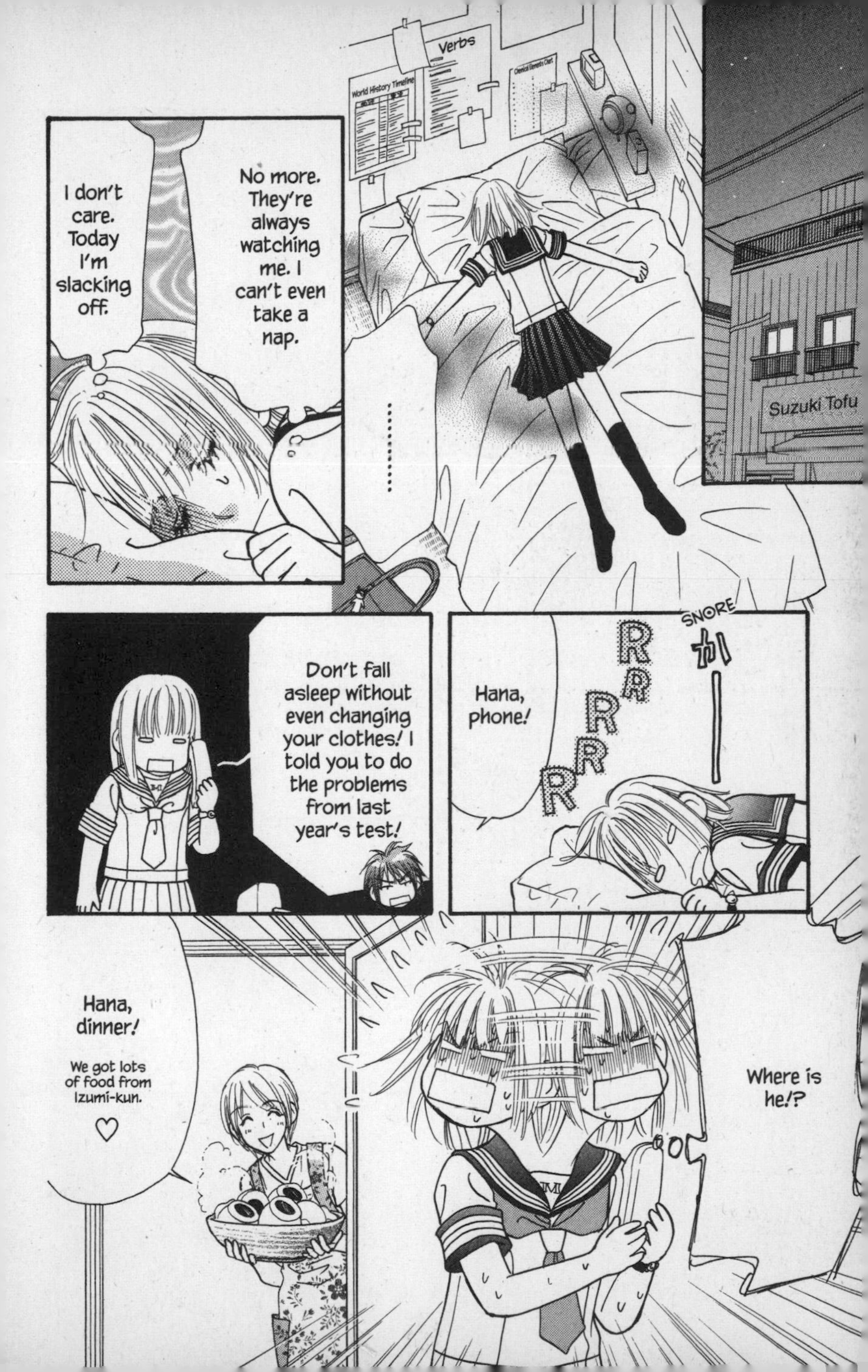
Suzuki Tofu
Verbs
World History Timeline
Chemical Elements Chart
......
No more. They're always watching me. I can't even take a nap.
I don't care. Today I'm slacking off.
SNORE
カー
RRRRR
Hana, phone!
Don't fall asleep without even changing your clothes! I told you to do the problems from last year's test!
Where is he!?
Hana, dinner!
We got lots of food from Izumi-kun. ♡

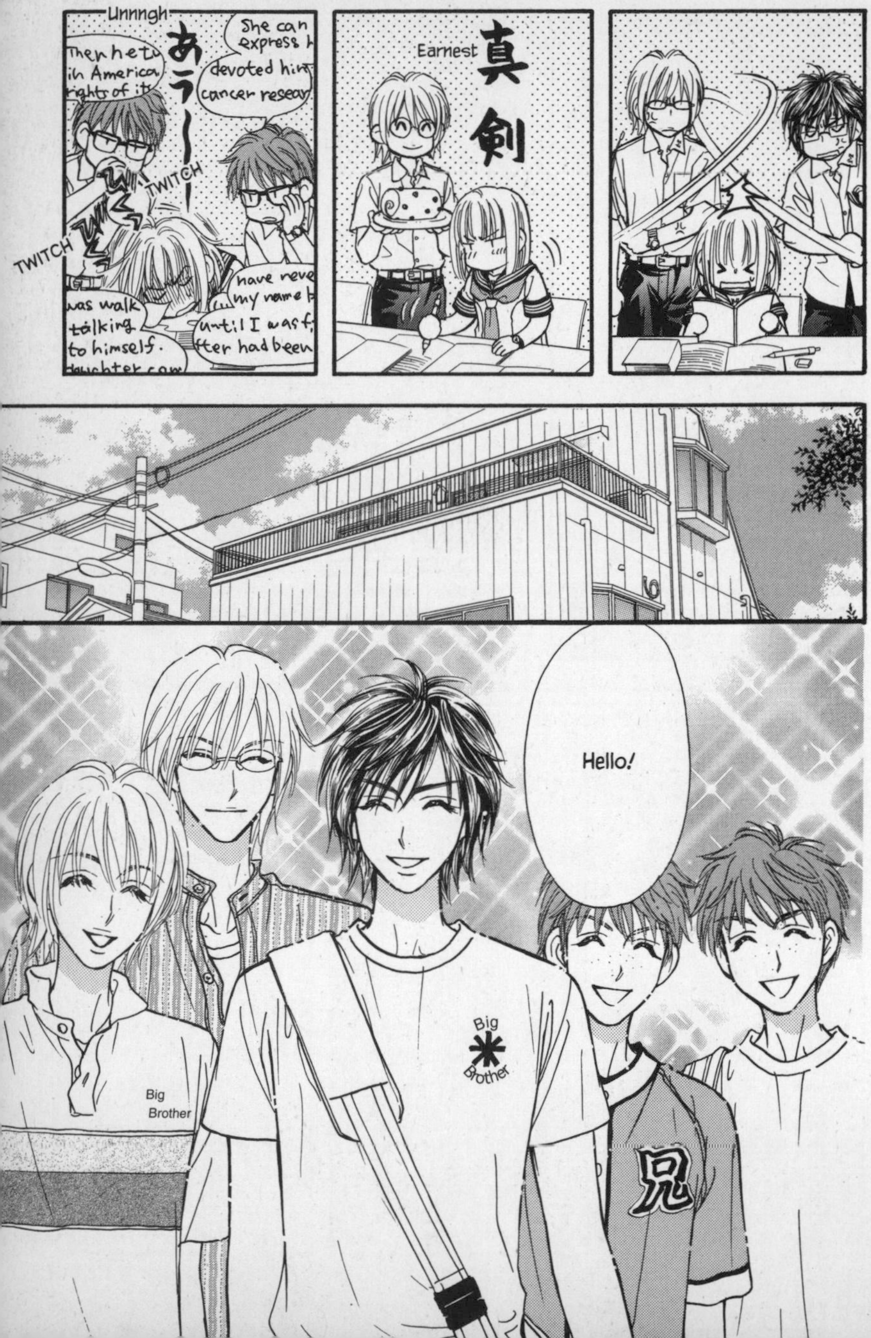
Earnest
真剣
Unnngh
あう〜
TWITCH
TWITCH
Hello!
Big Brother
Big Brother
兄

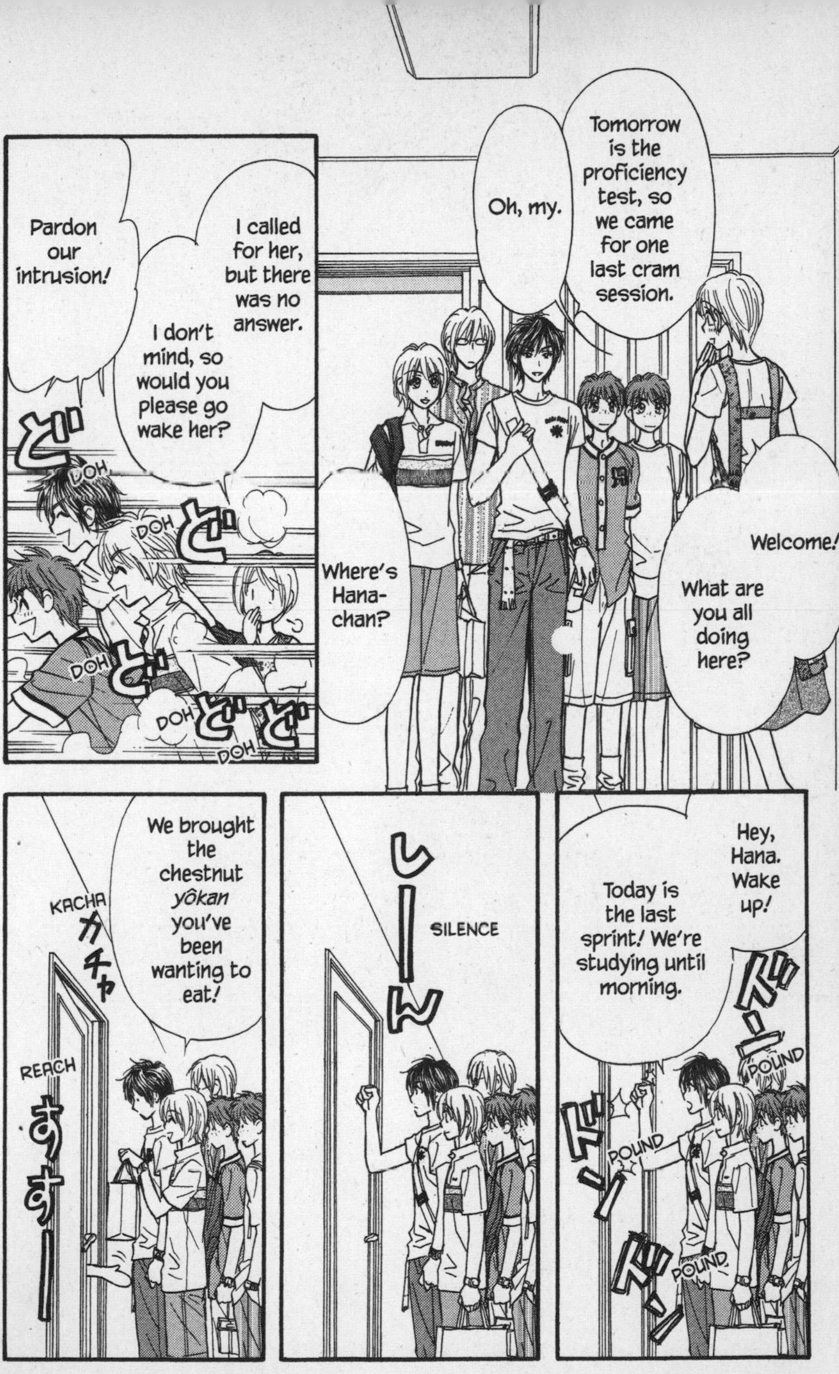
Tomorrow is the proficiency test, so we came for one last cram session.
Oh, my.
Welcome! What are you all doing here?
Where's Hana-chan?
I called for her, but there was no answer.
I don't mind, so would you please go wake her?
Pardon our intrusion!
ど DOH
ど DOH
ど DOH
ど DOH
ど DOH
Hey, Hana. Wake up!
Today is the last sprint! We're studying until morning.
ドー POUND
ドー POUND
ドー POUND
しーん
SILENCE
We brought the chestnut *yôkan* you've been wanting to eat!
カチャ
KACHA
すすー
REACH

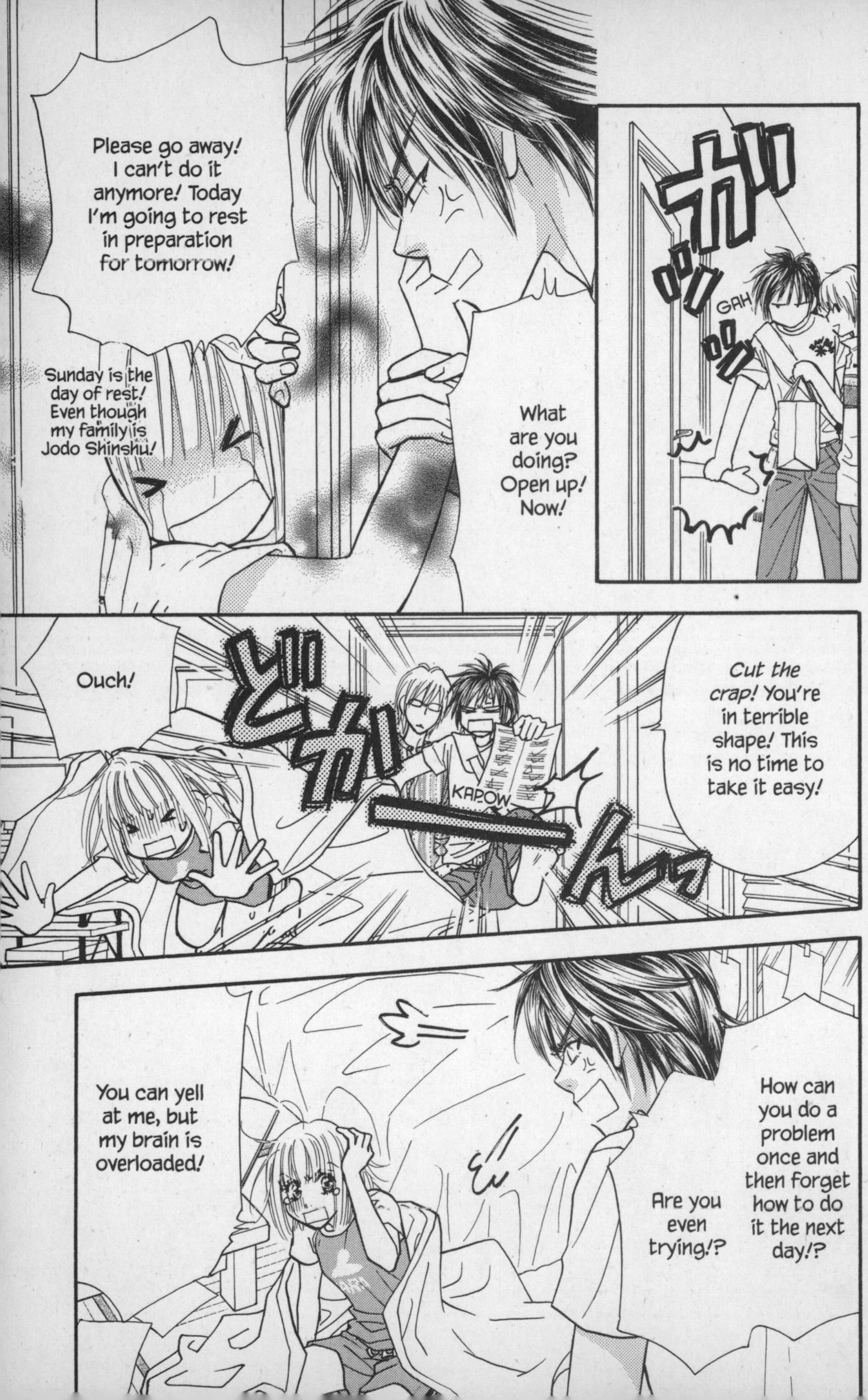
GAH
What are you doing? Open up! Now!
Please go away! I can't do it anymore! Today I'm going to rest in preparation for tomorrow!
Sunday is the day of rest! Even though my family is Jodo Shinshu!
Cut the crap! You're in terrible shape! This is no time to take it easy!
KAPOW
Ouch!
How can you do a problem once and then forget how to do it the next day!?
Are you even trying!?
You can yell at me, but my brain is overloaded!

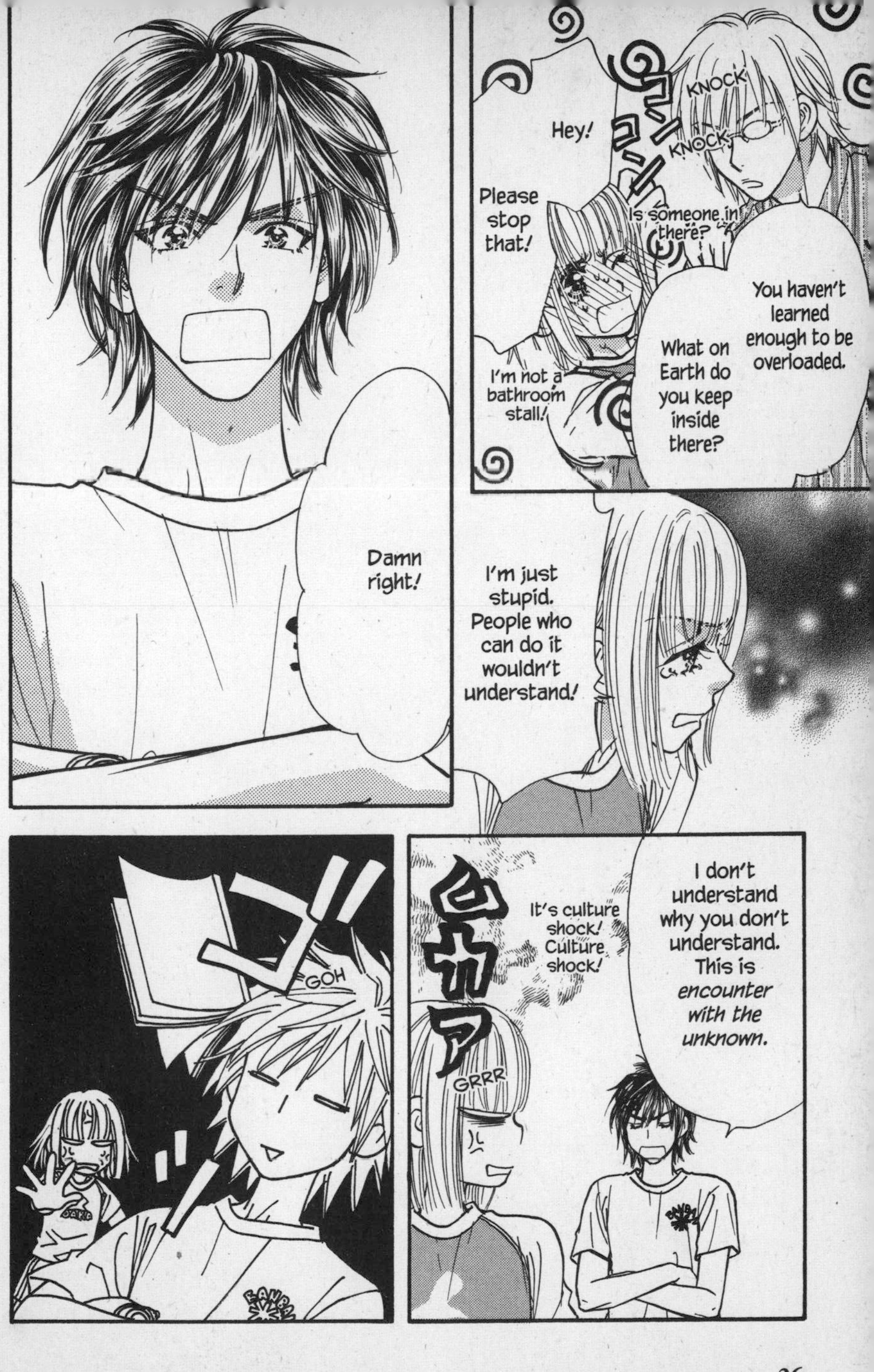
KNOCK
KNOCK
Hey!
Is someone in there?
Please stop that!
You haven't learned enough to be overloaded.
What on Earth do you keep inside there?
I'm not a bathroom stall!
I'm just stupid. People who can do it wouldn't understand!
Damn right!
I don't understand why you don't understand. This is *encounter with the unknown.*
It's culture shock! Culture shock!
GRRR
GOH

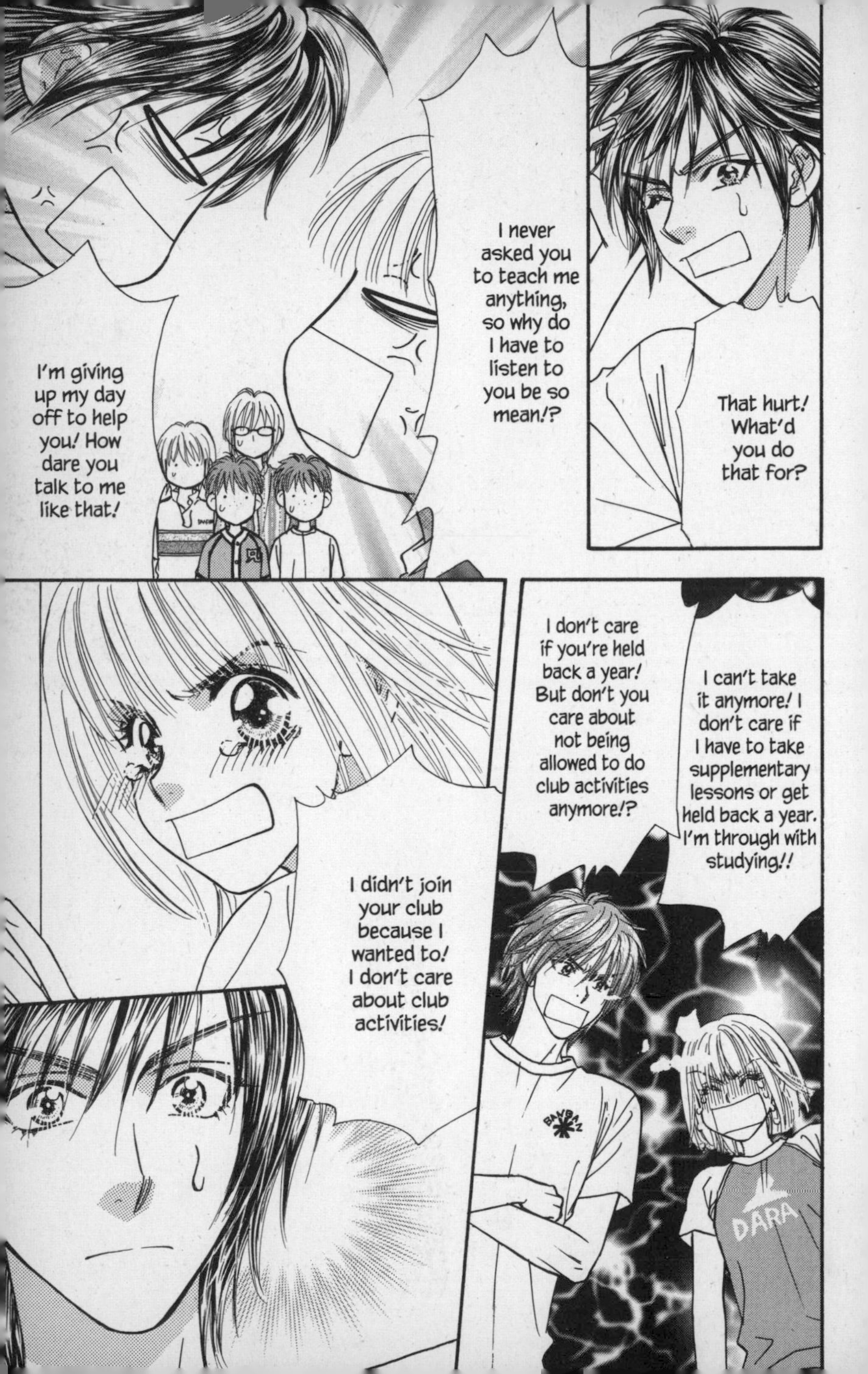
That hurt! What'd you do that for?
I never asked you to teach me anything, so why do I have to listen to you be so mean!?
I'm giving up my day off to help you! How dare you talk to me like that!
I can't take it anymore! I don't care if I have to take supplementary lessons or get held back a year. I'm through with studying!!
I don't care if you're held back a year! But don't you care about not being allowed to do club activities anymore!?
I didn't join your club because I wanted to! I don't care about club activities!
SANBAN
DARA

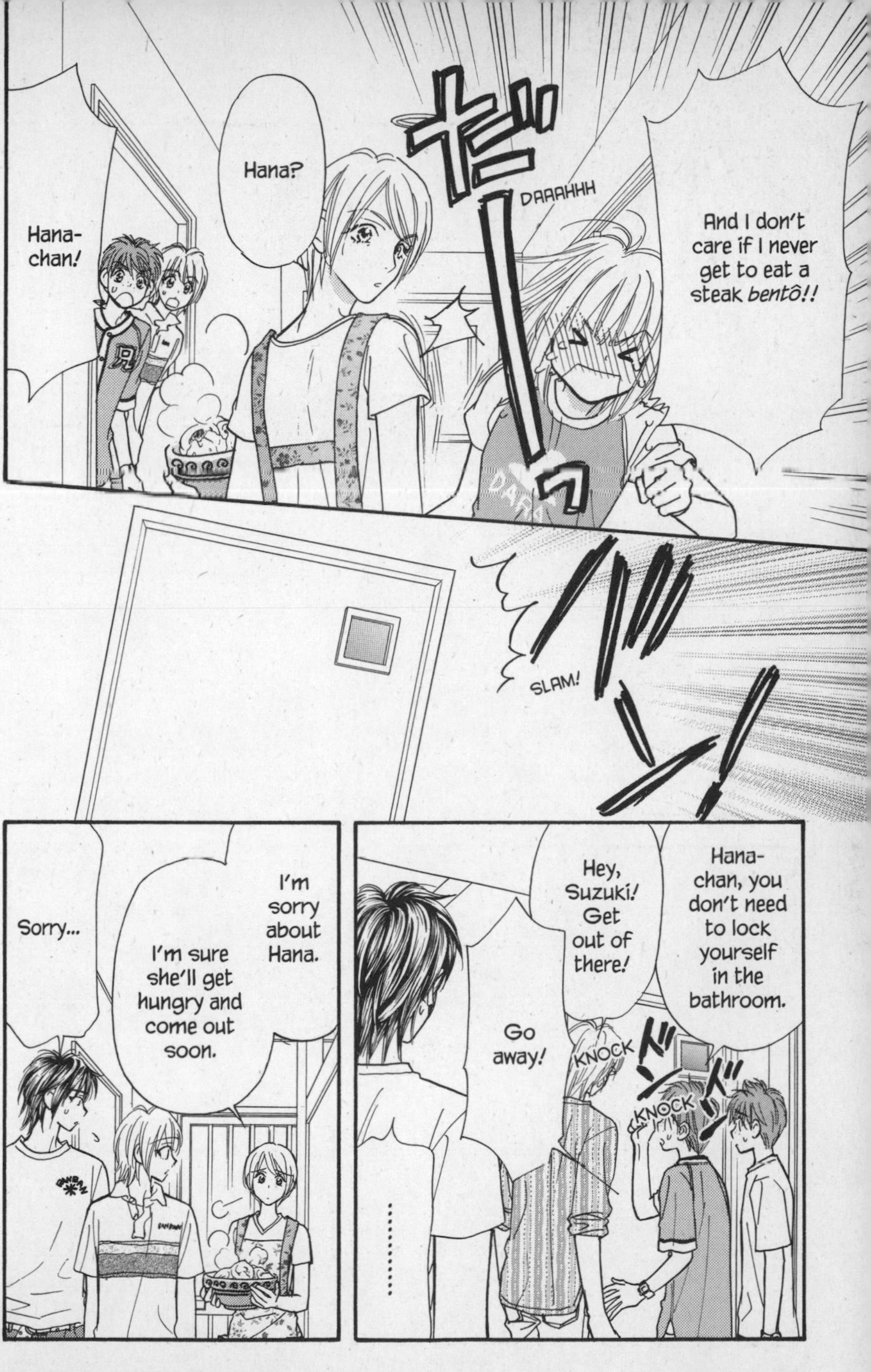
And I don't care if I never get to eat a steak *bentô*!!
DAAAHHH
Hana?
Hana-chan!
SLAM!
Hana-chan, you don't need to lock yourself in the bathroom.
Hey, Suzuki! Get out of there!
KNOCK
KNOCK
Go away!
......
I'm sorry about Hana.
I'm sure she'll get hungry and come out soon.
Sorry...

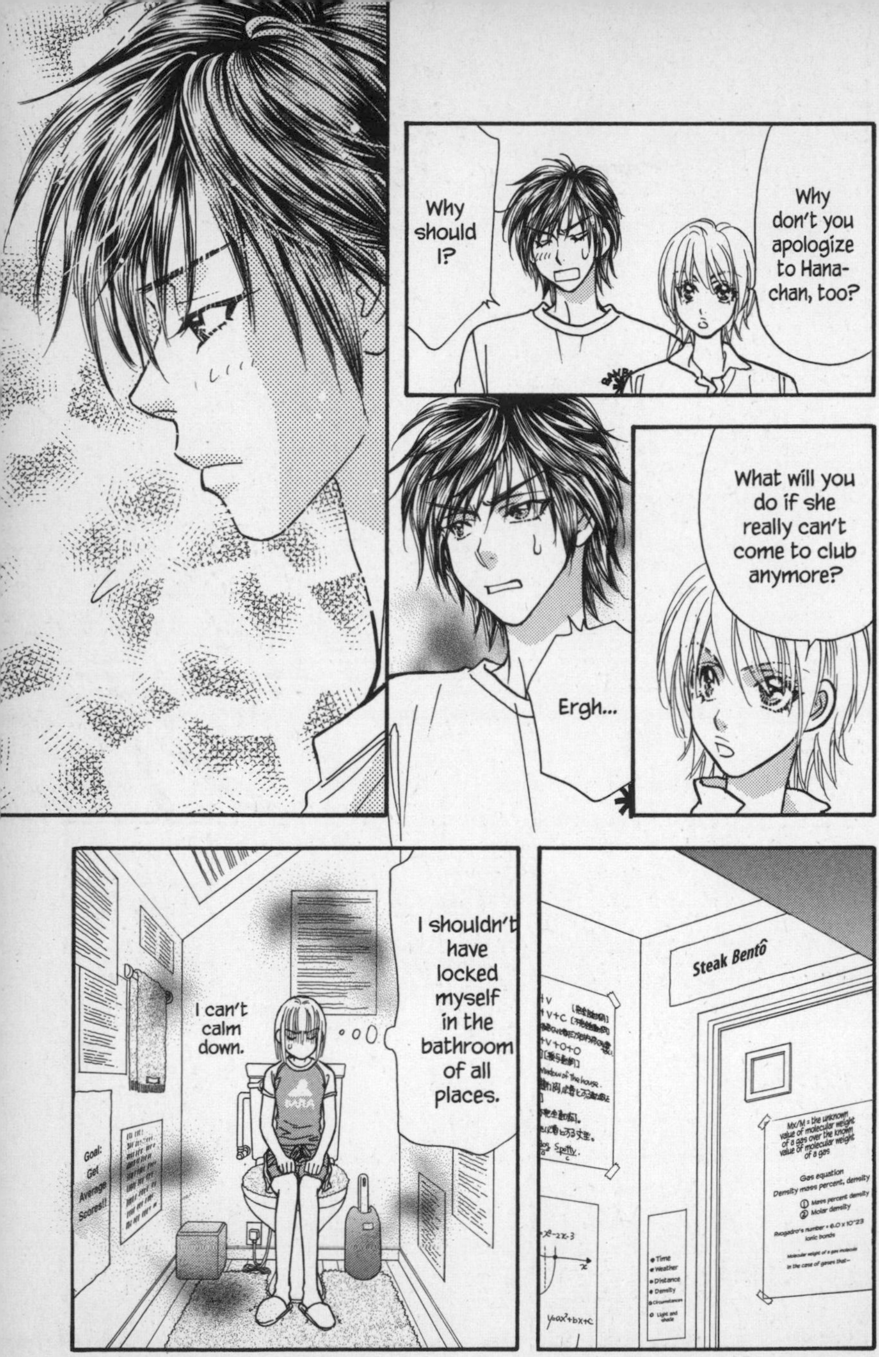
Why don't you apologize to Hana-chan, too?
Why should I?
What will you do if she really can't come to club anymore?
Ergh...
Steak Bentô
Mx/M = the unknown value of molecular weight of a gas over the known value of molecular weight of a gas
Gas equation
Density mass percent, density
① Mass percent density
② Molar density
Avogadro's number = 6.0 x 10^23
Ionic bonds
Time
Weather
Distance
Density
Light and shade
I shouldn't have locked myself in the bathroom of all places.
I can't calm down.
Goal: Get Average Scores!!

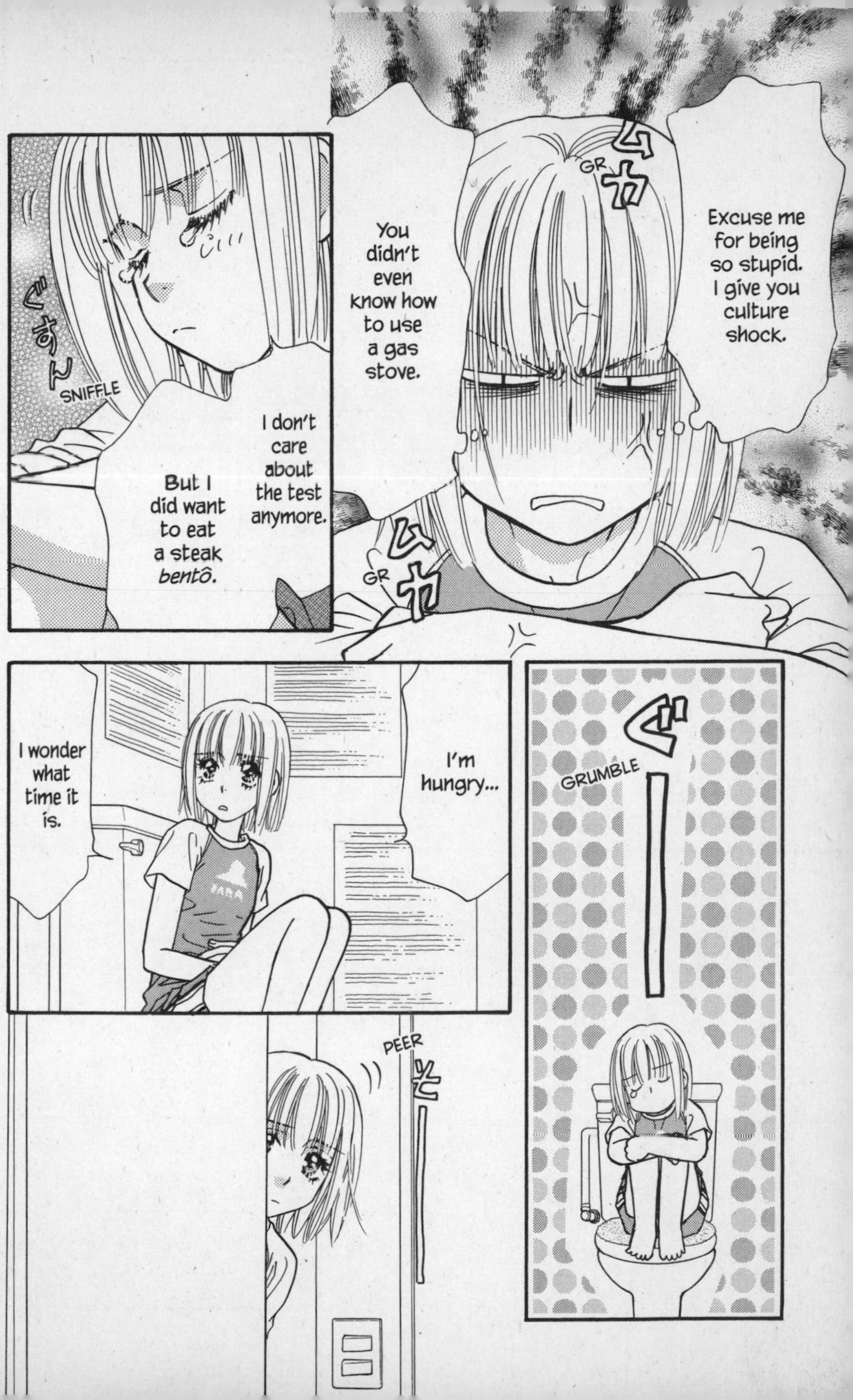
ムカ
GR
Excuse me for being so stupid. I give you culture shock.
You didn't even know how to use a gas stove.
ムカ
GR
ぐすん
SNIFFLE
I don't care about the test anymore.
But I did want to eat a steak *bentô*.
ぐー
GRUMBLE
I'm hungry...
I wonder what time it is.
PEER

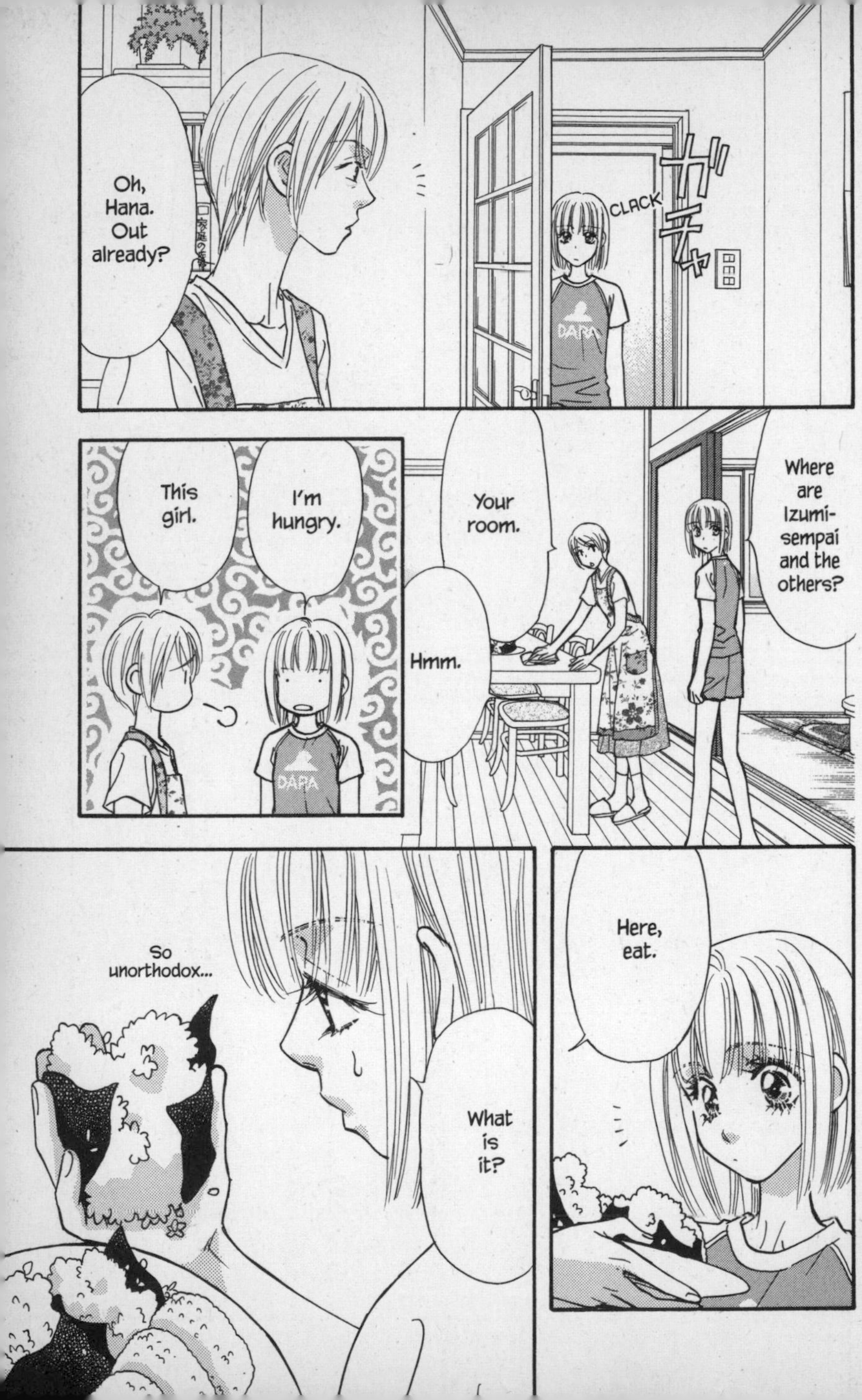
ガチャ
CLACK
Oh, Hana. Out already?
Where are Izumi-sempai and the others?
Your room.
Hmm.
I'm hungry.
This girl.
Here, eat.
What is it?
So unorthodox...

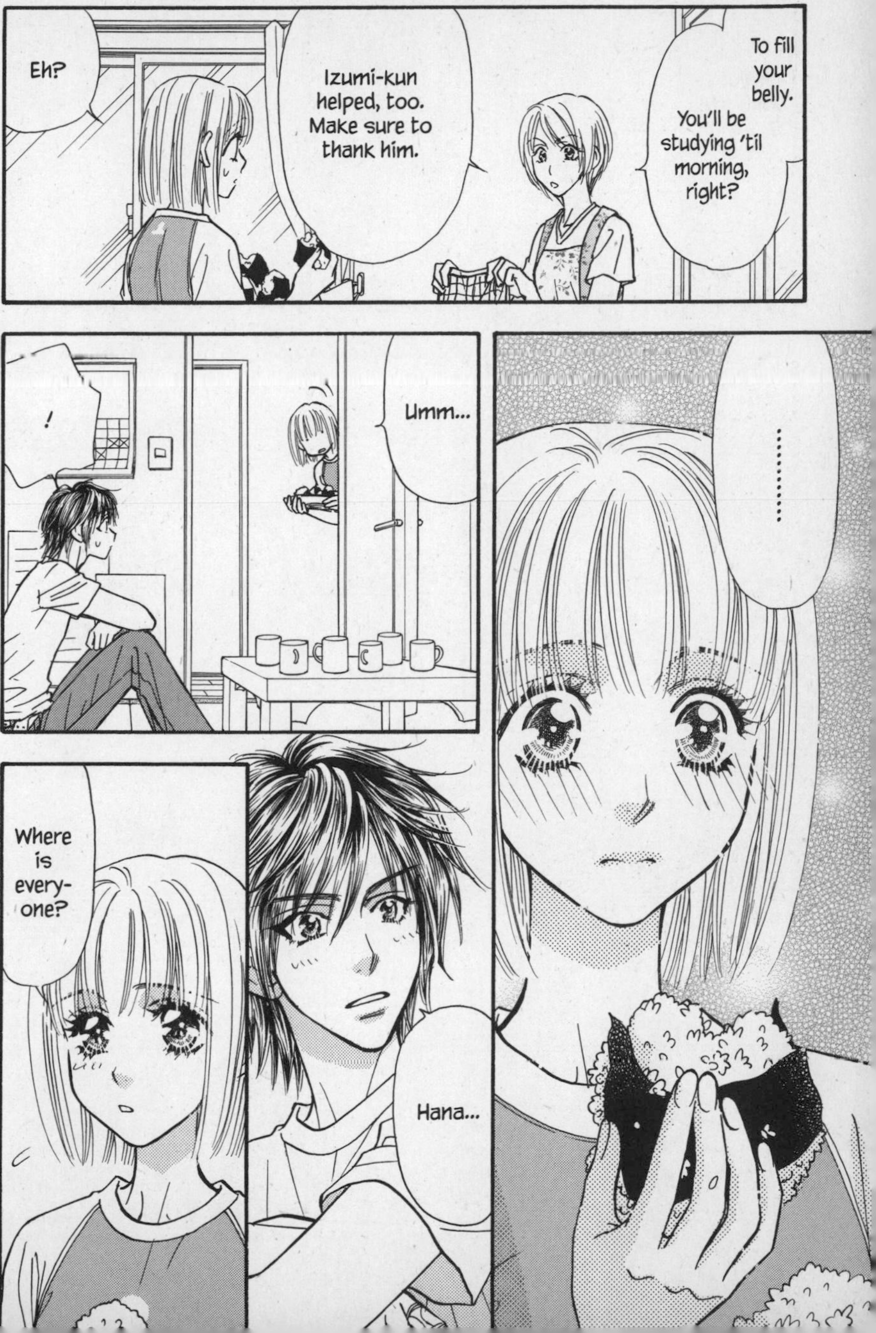
To fill your belly.
You'll be studying 'til morning, right?
Izumi-kun helped, too. Make sure to thank him.
Eh?
......
Umm...
!
Hana...
Where is everyone?

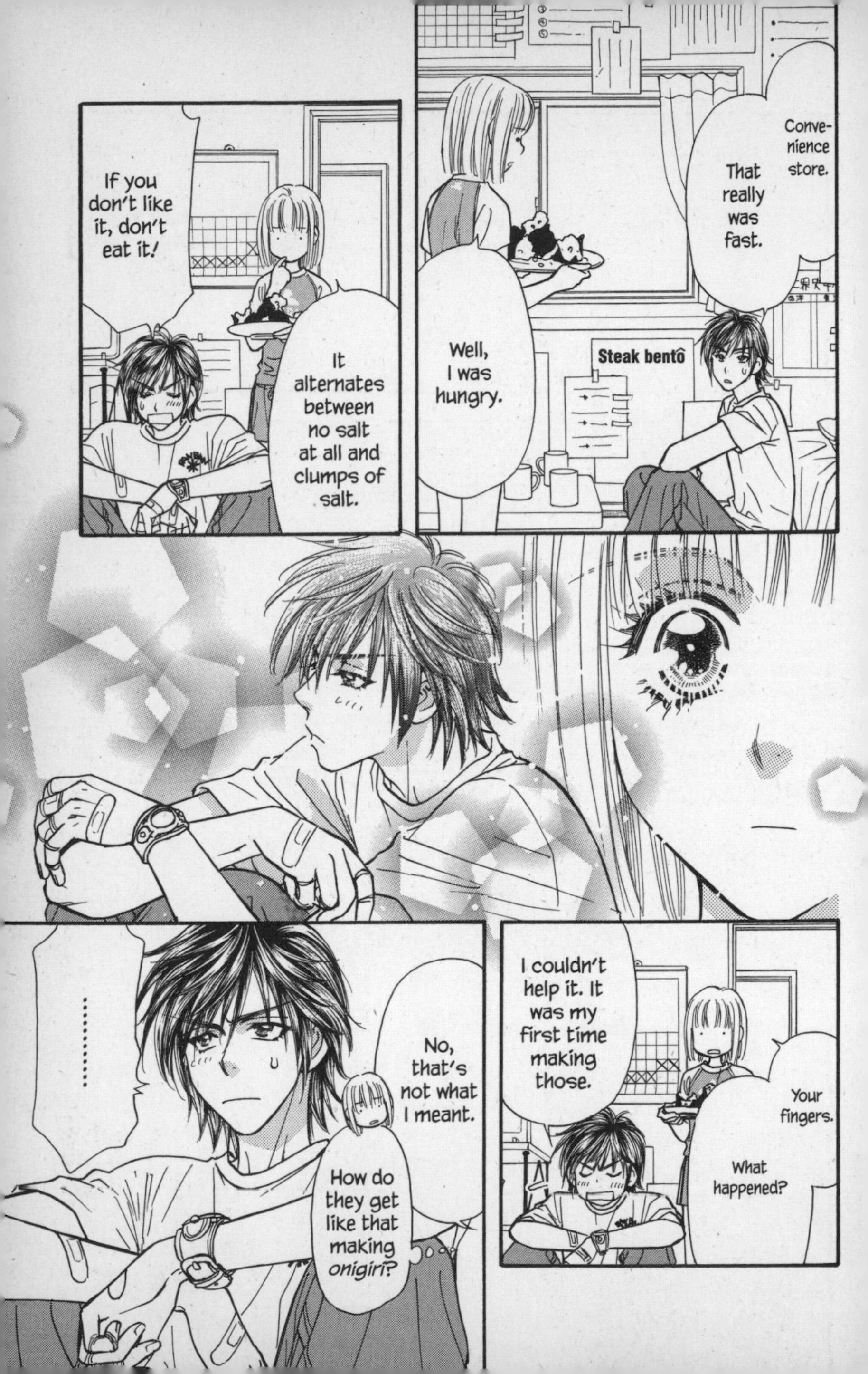
Convenience store.
That really was fast.
Steak bentô
Well, I was hungry.
It alternates between no salt at all and clumps of salt.
If you don't like it, don't eat it!
Your fingers.
What happened?
I couldn't help it. It was my first time making those.
No, that's not what I meant.
How do they get like that making *onigiri*?
......

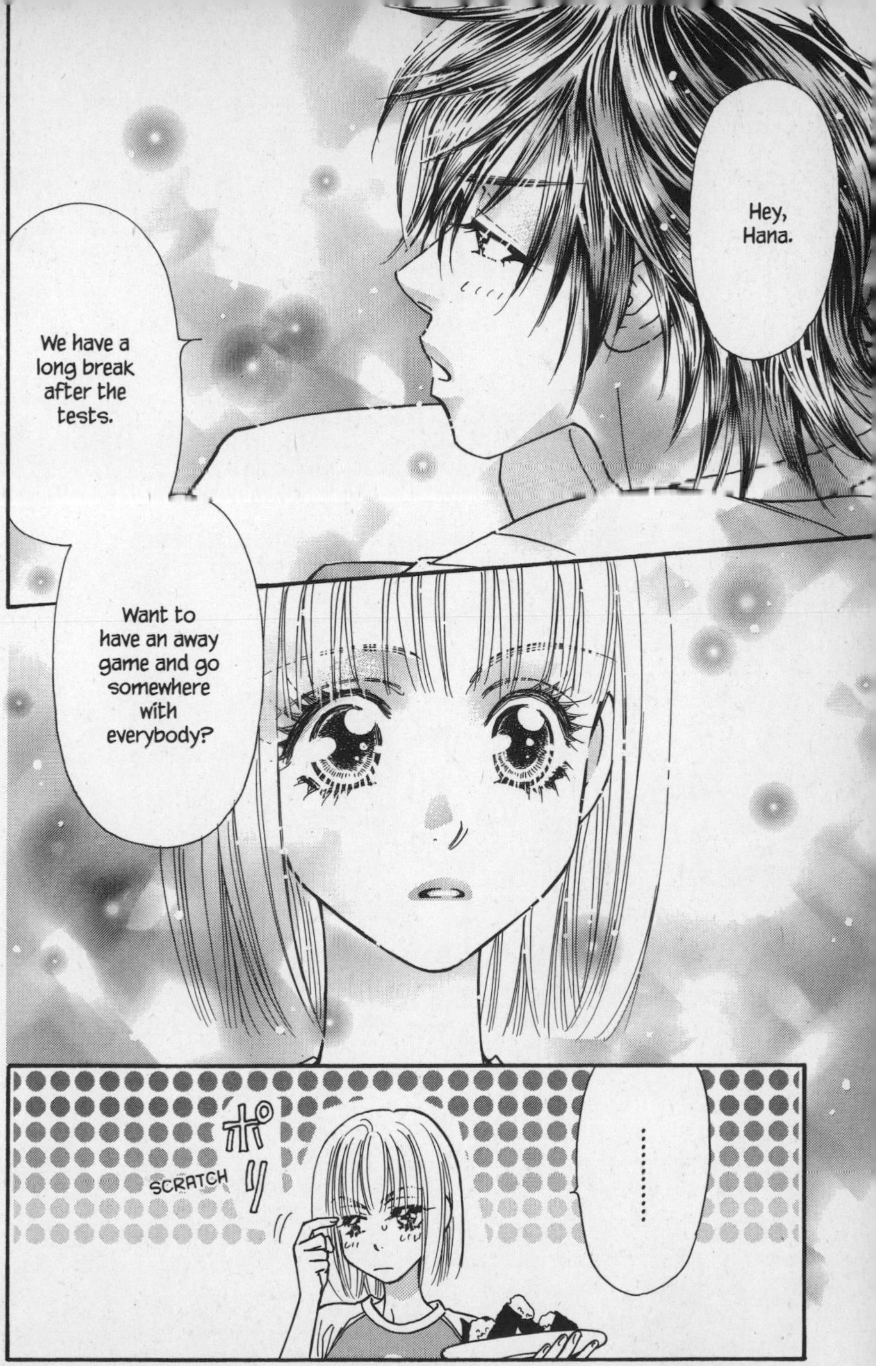
Hey, Hana.
We have a long break after the tests.
Want to have an away game and go somewhere with everybody?
......
ポリ
SCRATCH

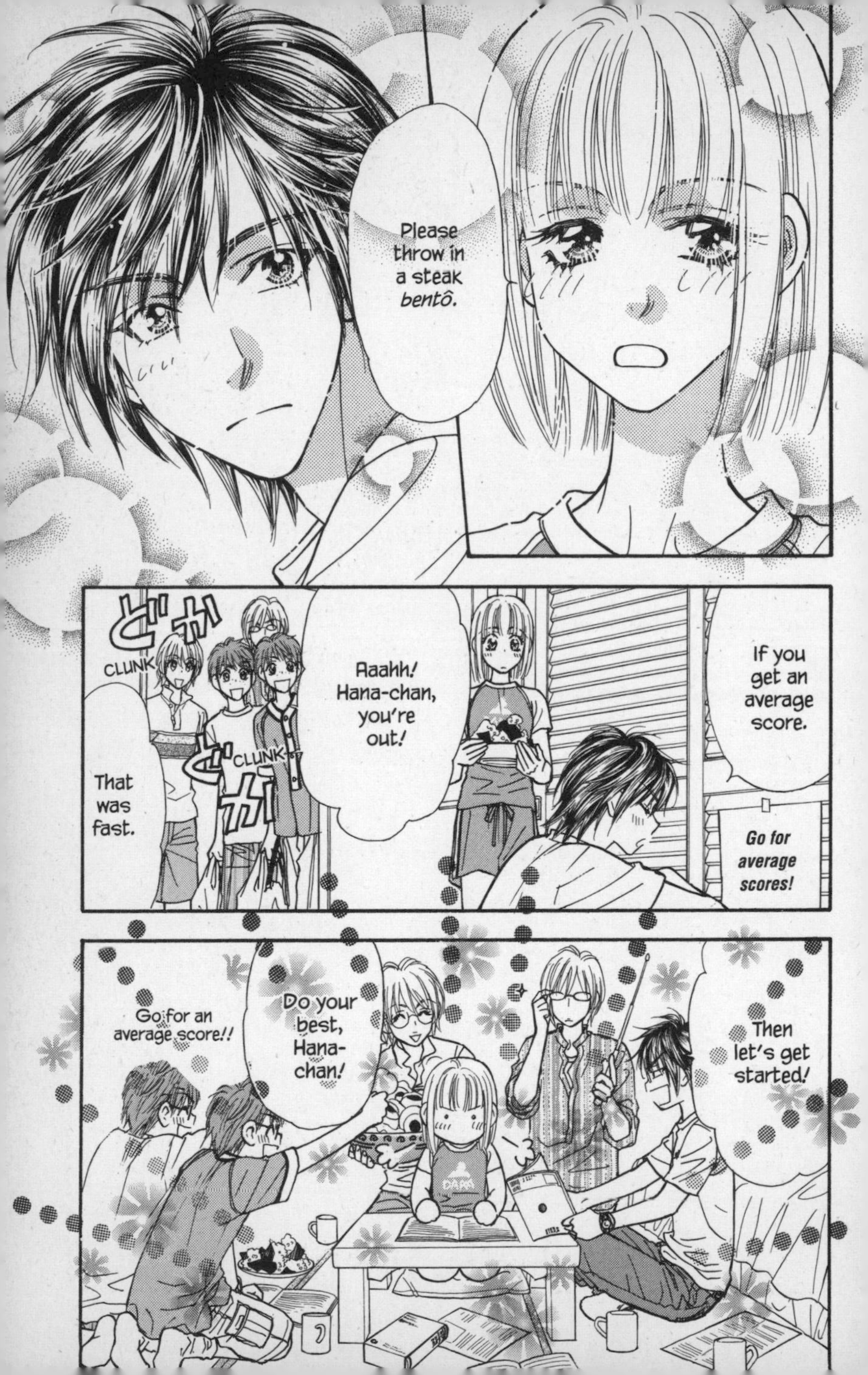
Please throw in a steak *bentô*.
If you get an average score.
Go for average scores!
Aaahh! Hana-chan, you're out!
CLUNK
CLUNK
That was fast.
Then let's get started!
Do your best, Hana-chan!
Go for an average score!!

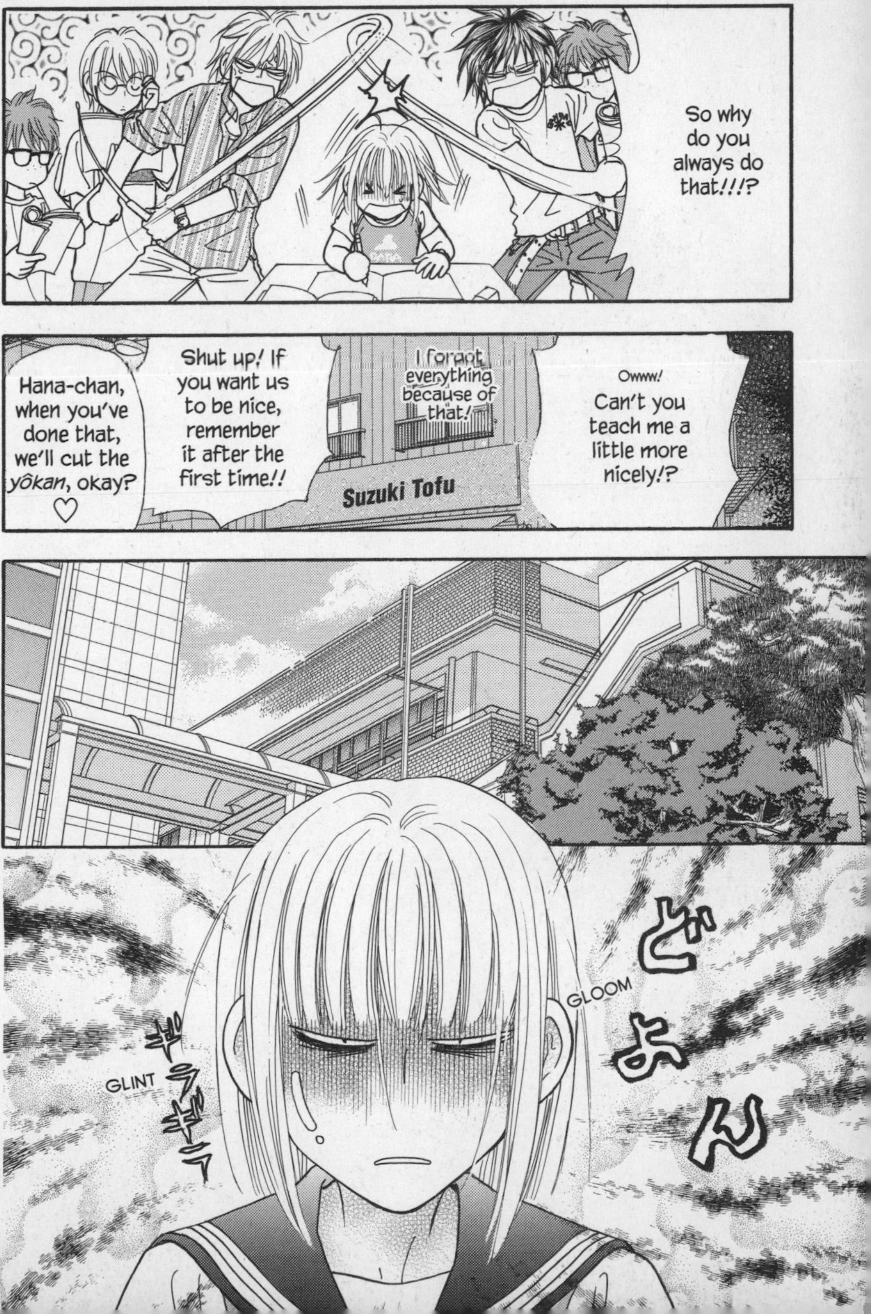
So why do you always do that!!!?
Owww!
Can't you teach me a little more nicely!?
I forgot everything because of that!
Suzuki Tofu
Shut up! If you want us to be nice, remember it after the first time!!
Hana-chan, when you've done that, we'll cut the *yôkan*, okay? ♡
どよん
GLOOM
ギラギラ
GLINT

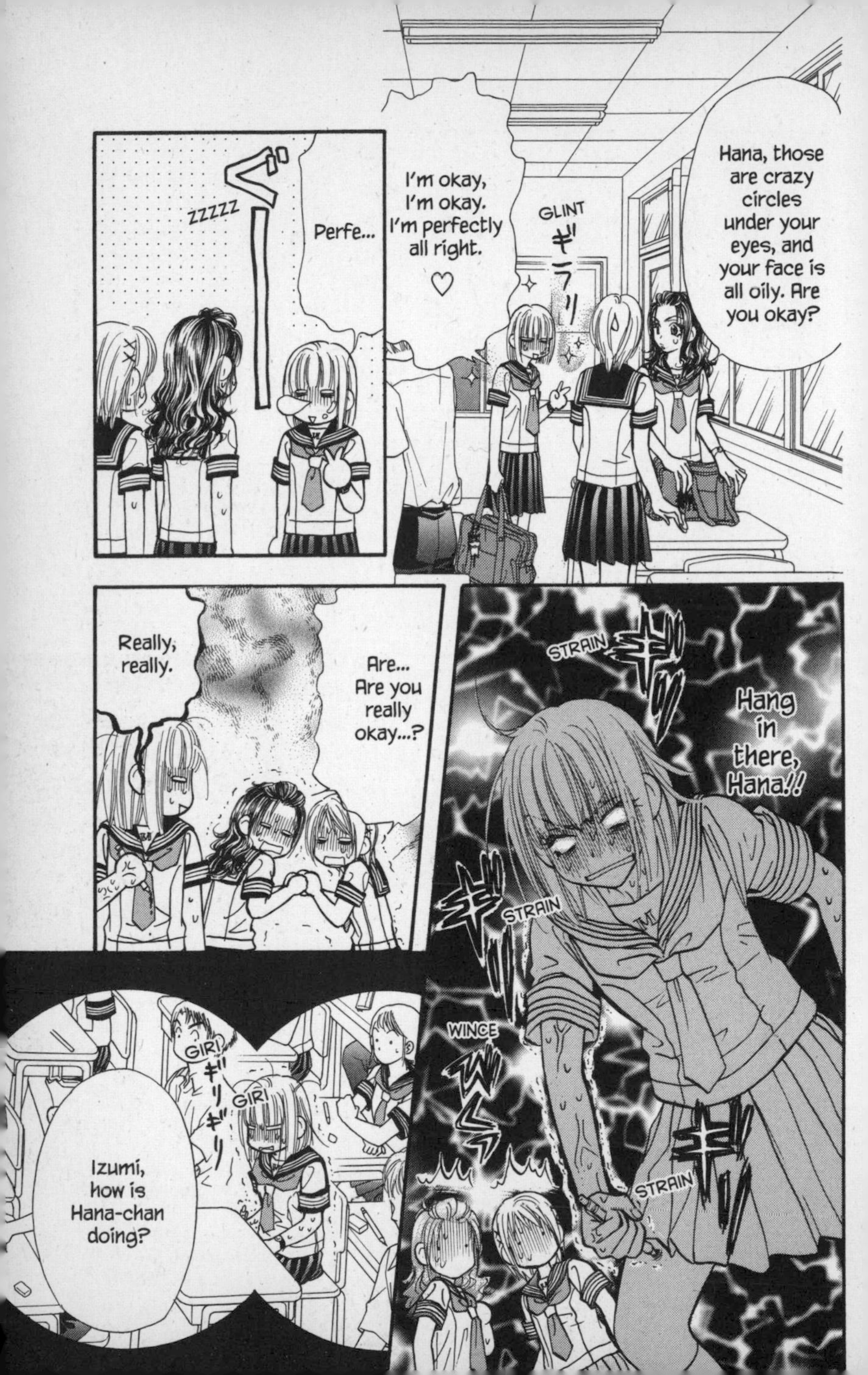
Hana, those are crazy circles under your eyes, and your face is all oily. Are you okay?
GLINT
I'm okay, I'm okay. I'm perfectly all right. ♡
Perfe...
ZZZZZ
STRAIN
Hang in there, Hana!!
STRAIN
WINCE
STRAIN
Are... Are you really okay...?
Really, really.
GIRI
GIRI
Izumi, how is Hana-chan doing?

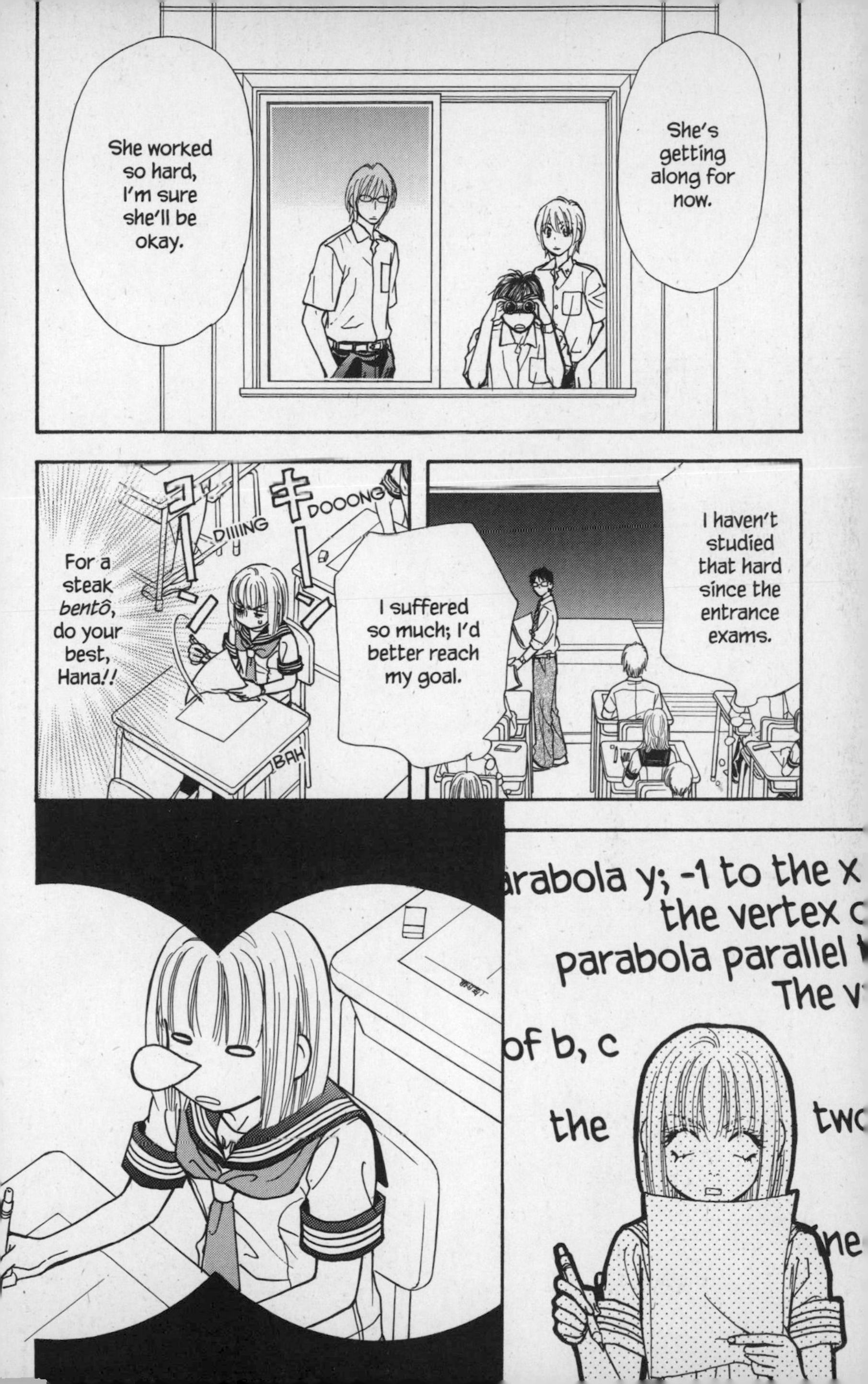
She's getting along for now.
She worked so hard, I'm sure she'll be okay.
I haven't studied that hard since the entrance exams.
I suffered so much; I'd better reach my goal.
DOOONG
DIIIING
For a steak *bentô*, do your best, Hana!!
BAH
arabola y; -1 to the x
the vertex
parabola parallel
The
of b, c
the
tw
ne

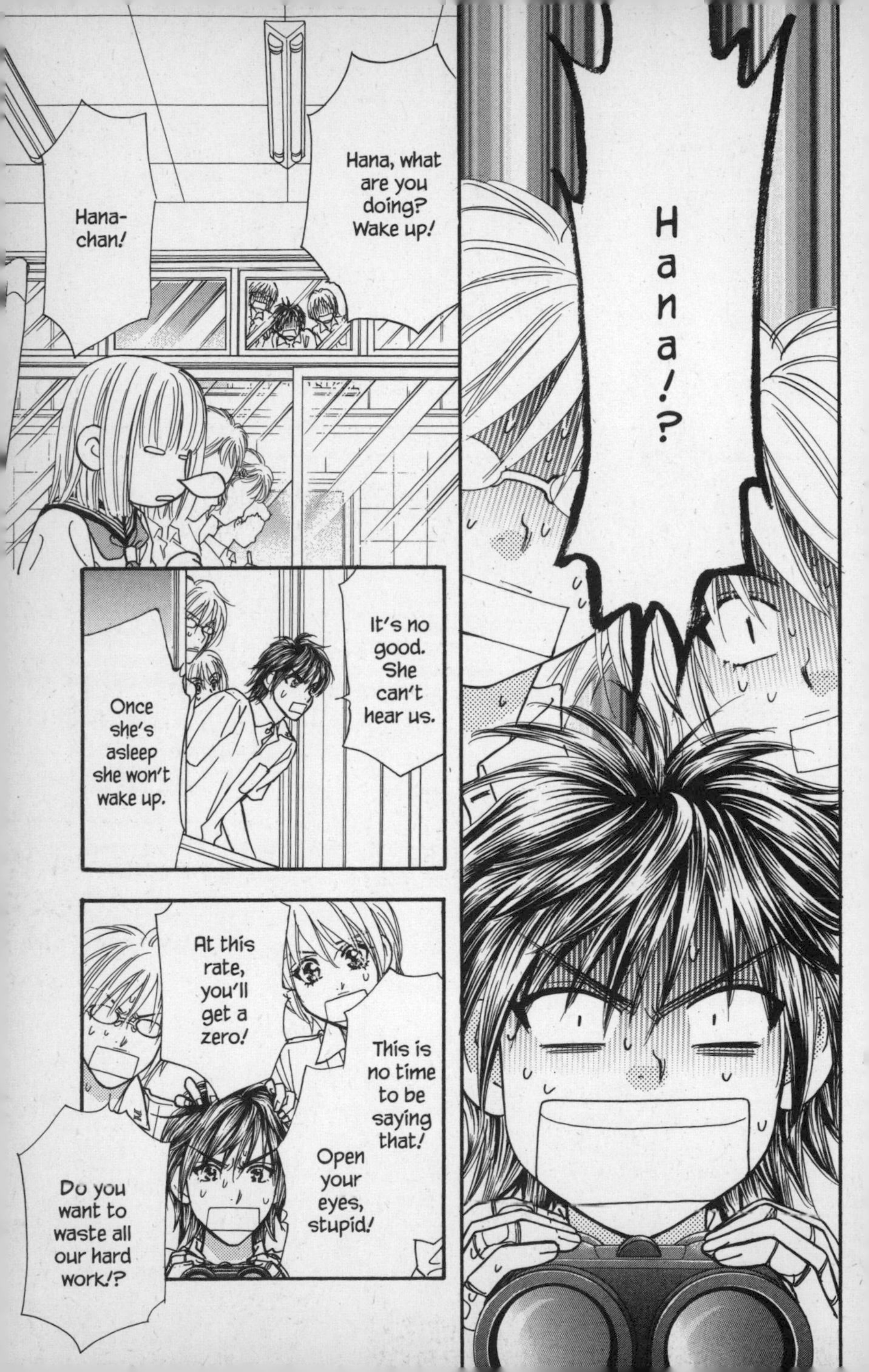
Hana!?
Hana, what are you doing? Wake up!
Hana-chan!
It's no good. She can't hear us.
Once she's asleep she won't wake up.
At this rate, you'll get a zero!
This is no time to be saying that!
Open your eyes, stupid!
Do you want to waste all our hard work!?

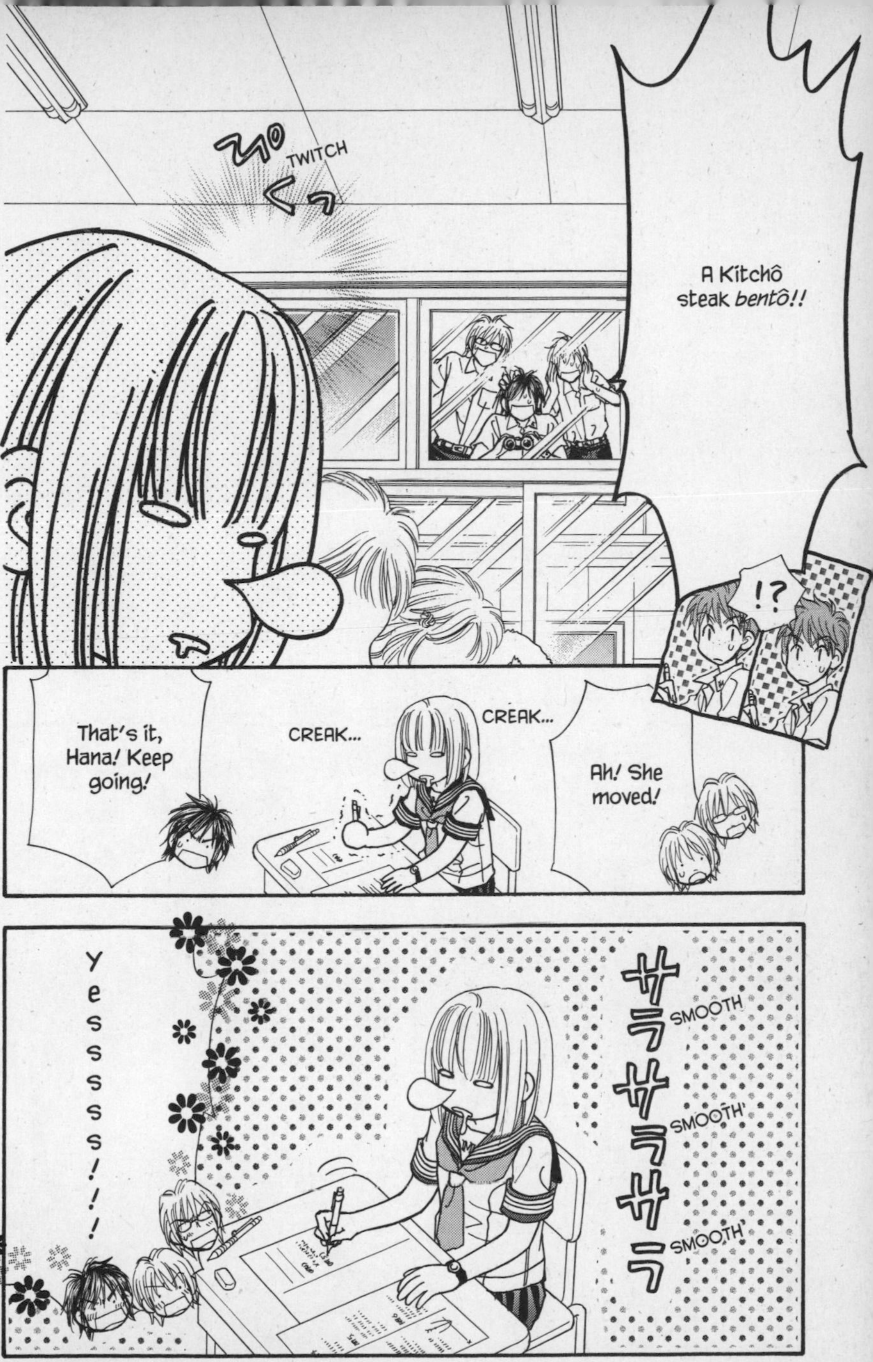
A Kitchô steak *bentô*!!
!?
TWITCH
Ah! She moved!
CREAK...
CREAK...
That's it, Hana! Keep going!
サラサラサラ
SMOOTH
SMOOTH
SMOOTH
Yessss!!!

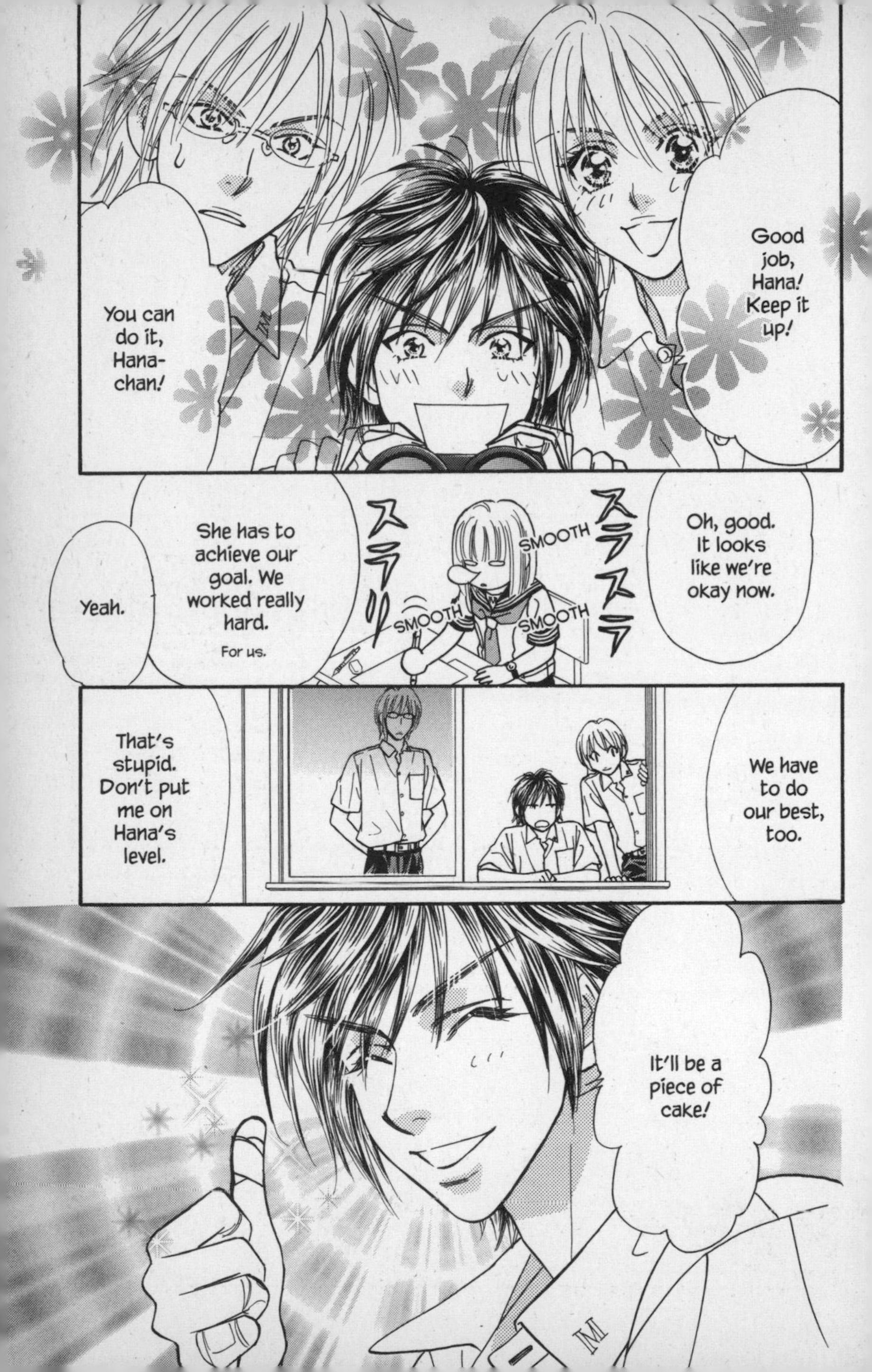
Good job, Hana! Keep it up!
You can do it, Hana-chan!
Oh, good. It looks like we're okay now.
SMOOTH
SMOOTH
SMOOTH
She has to achieve our goal. We worked really hard.
For us.
Yeah.
We have to do our best, too.
That's stupid. Don't put me on Hana's level.
It'll be a piece of cake!

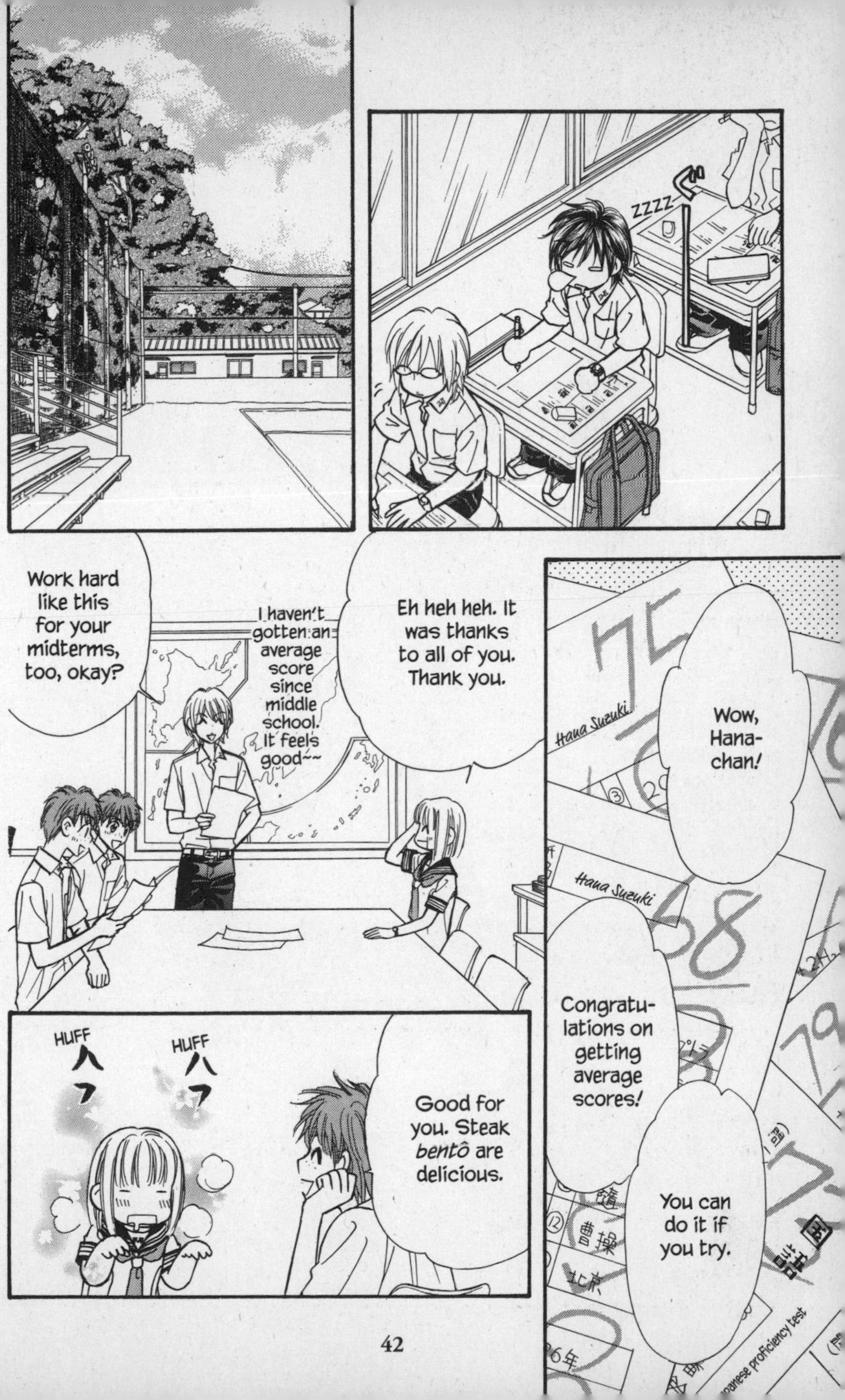
ZZZZ
Hana Suzuki
Wow, Hana-chan!
Hana Suzuki
Congratulations on getting average scores!
You can do it if you try.
Eh heh heh. It was thanks to all of you. Thank you.
I haven't gotten an average score since middle school. It feels good~~
Work hard like this for your midterms, too, okay?
Good for you. Steak *bentô* are delicious.
HUFF
HUFF

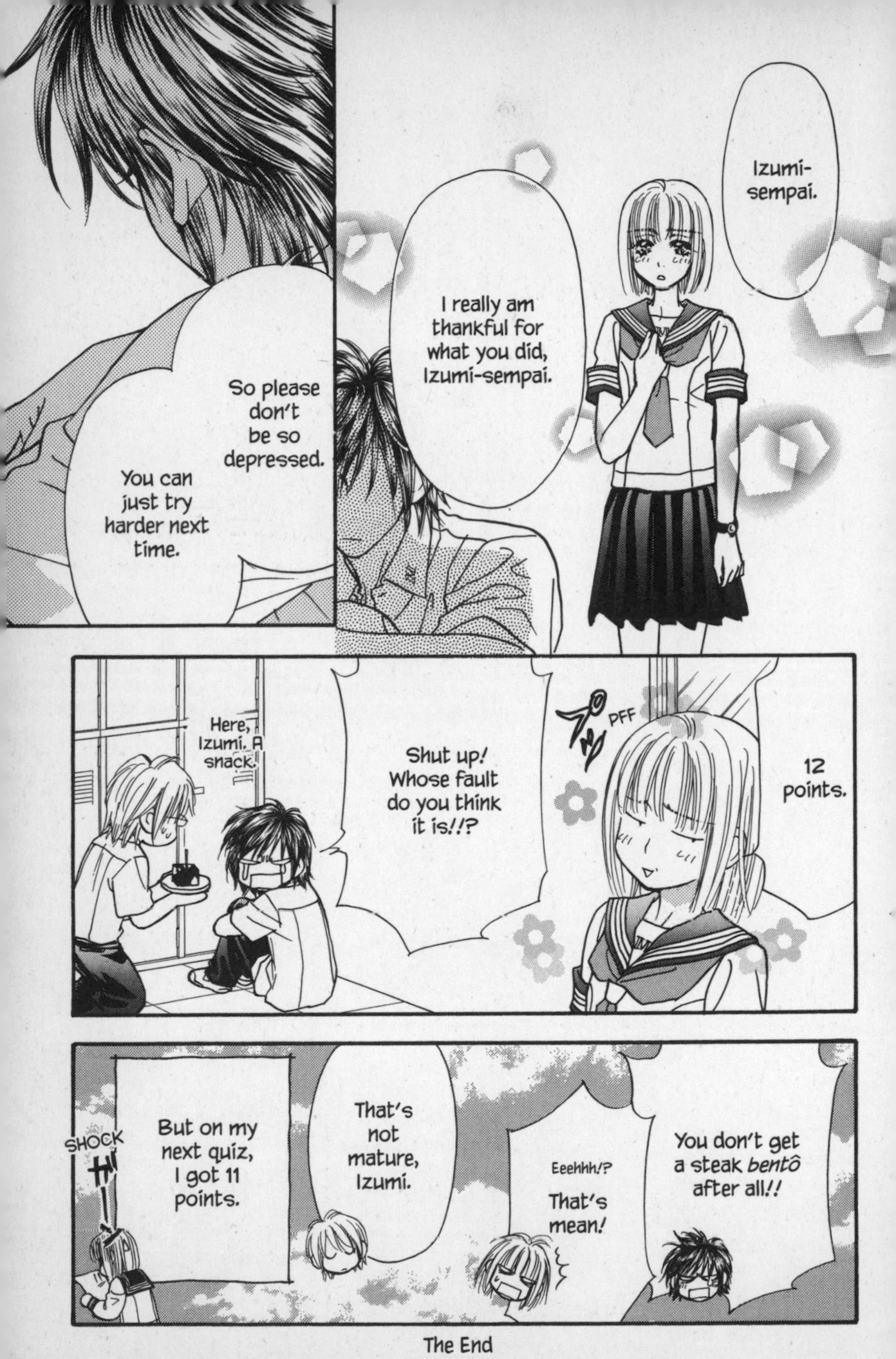
Izumi-sempai.
I really am thankful for what you did, Izumi-sempai.
So please don't be so depressed.
You can just try harder next time.
12 points.
PFF
Shut up! Whose fault do you think it is!!?
Here, Izumi. A snack.
You don't get a steak *bentô* after all!!
Eeehhh!?
That's mean!
That's not mature, Izumi.
But on my next quiz, I got 11 points.
SHOCK

The End

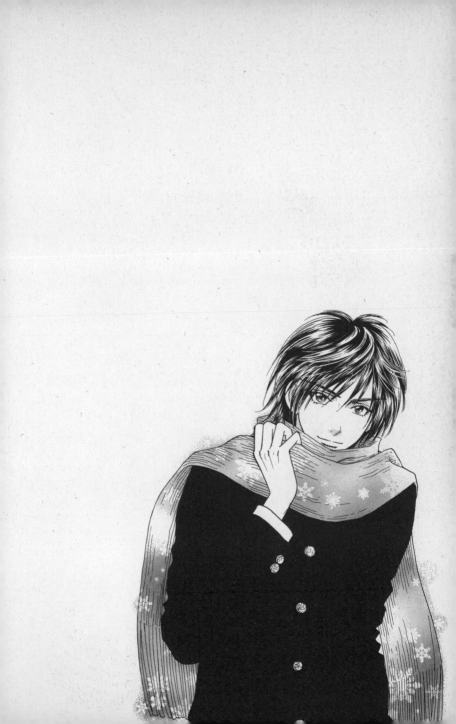

Chapter 14: Searching for Love

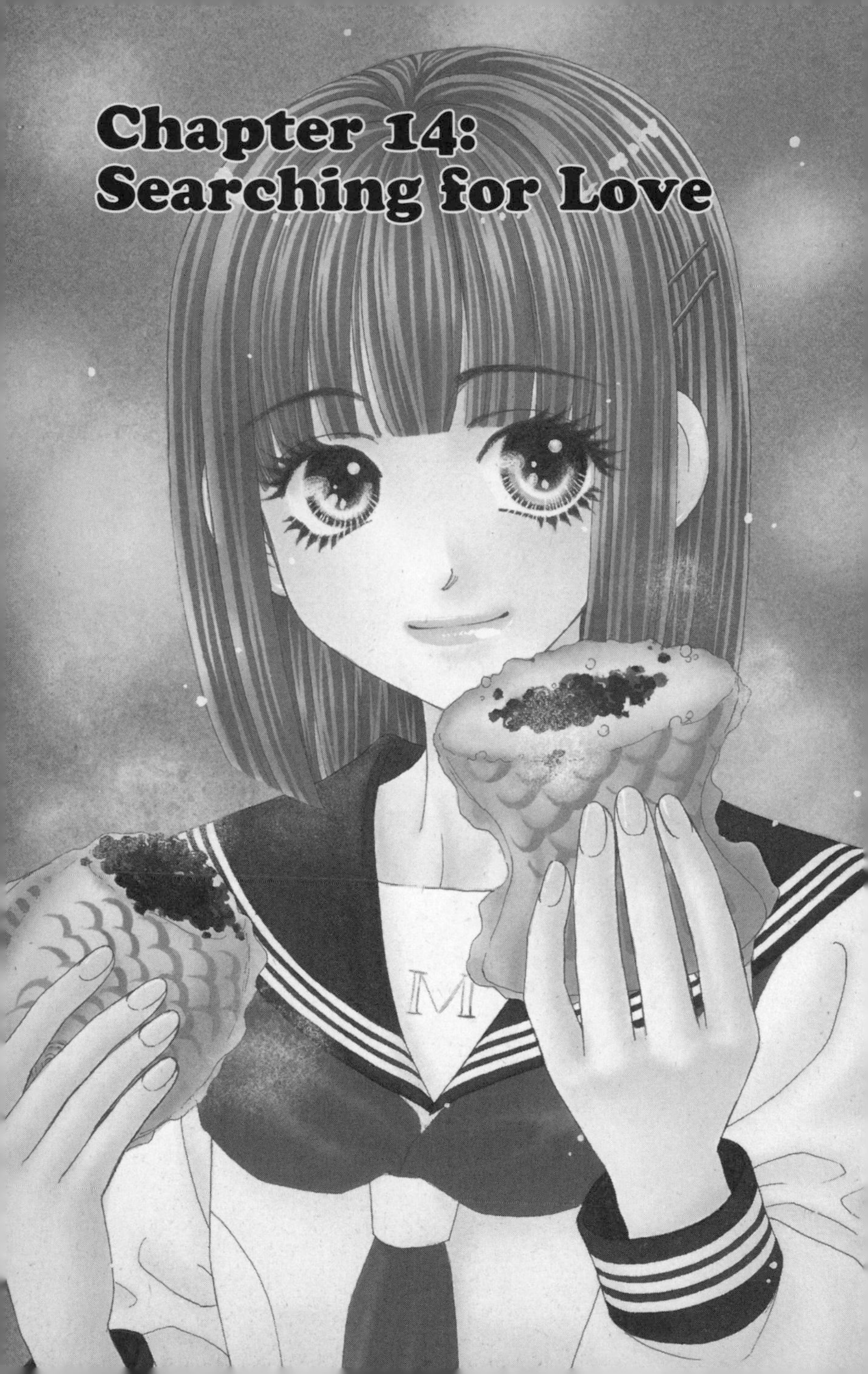

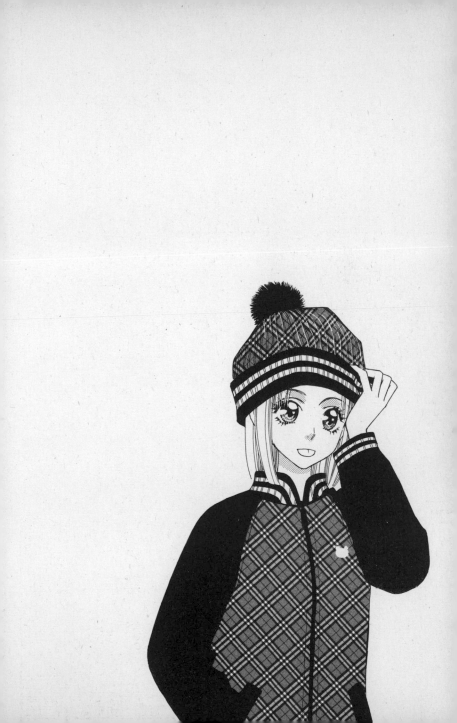

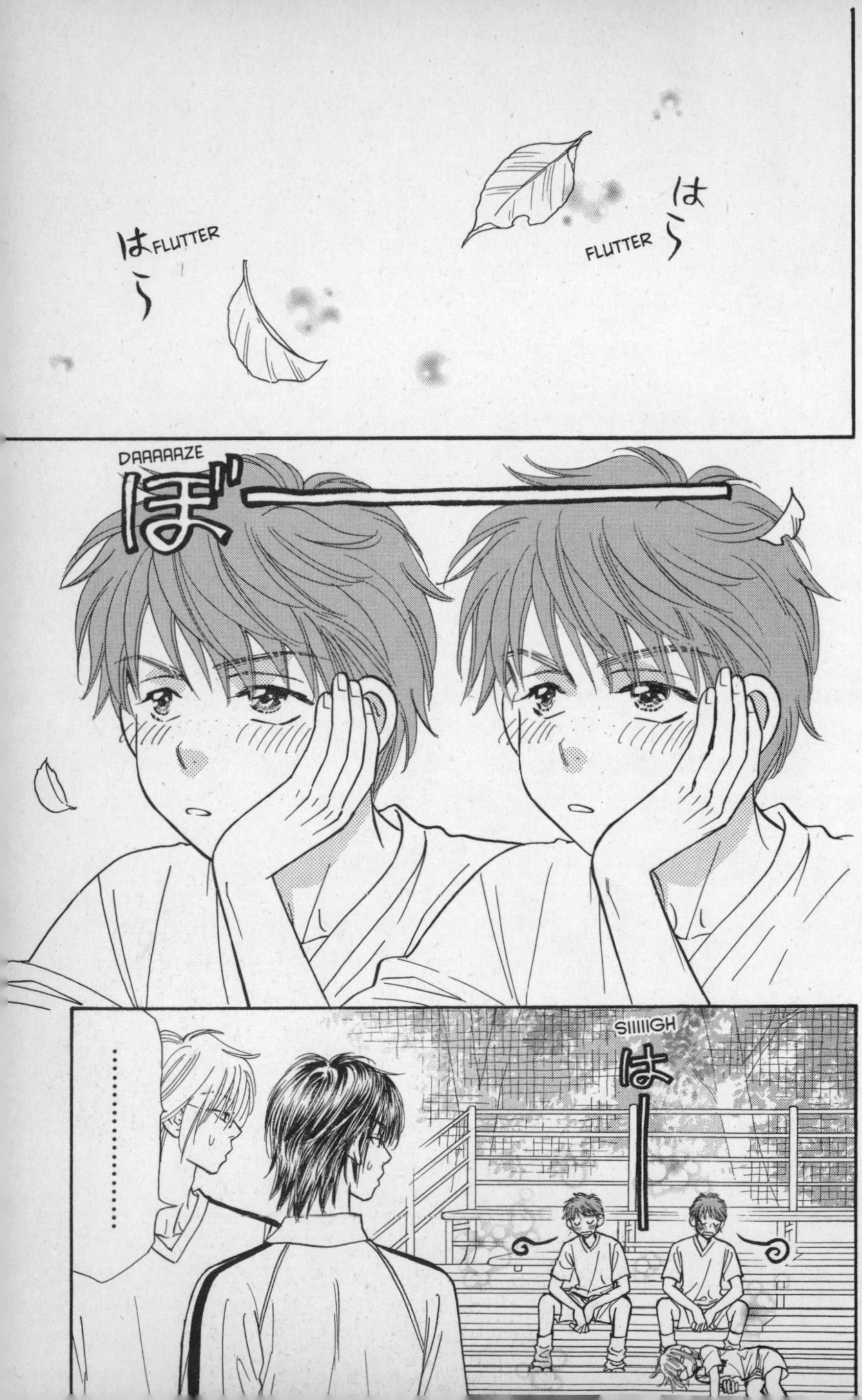

はら
FLUTTER
はら
FLUTTER
DAAAAAZE
ぼー
SIIIIGH
はー
……

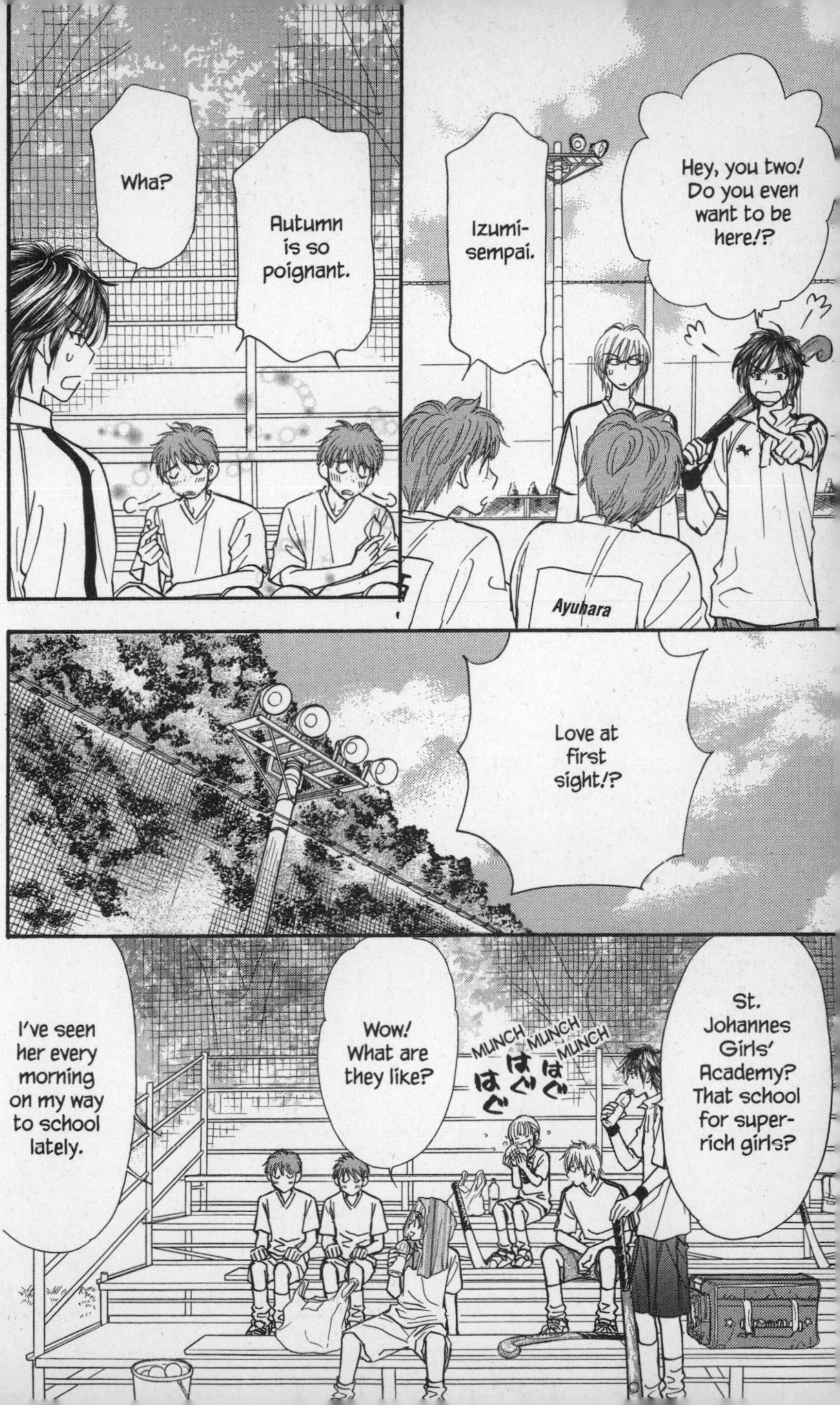
Hey, you two! Do you even want to be here!?
Ayuhara
Izumi-sempai.
Autumn is so poignant.
Wha?
Love at first sight!?
St. Johannes Girls' Academy? That school for super-rich girls?
MUNCH MUNCH MUNCH
はぐ はぐ はぐ
Wow! What are they like?
I've seen her every morning on my way to school lately.

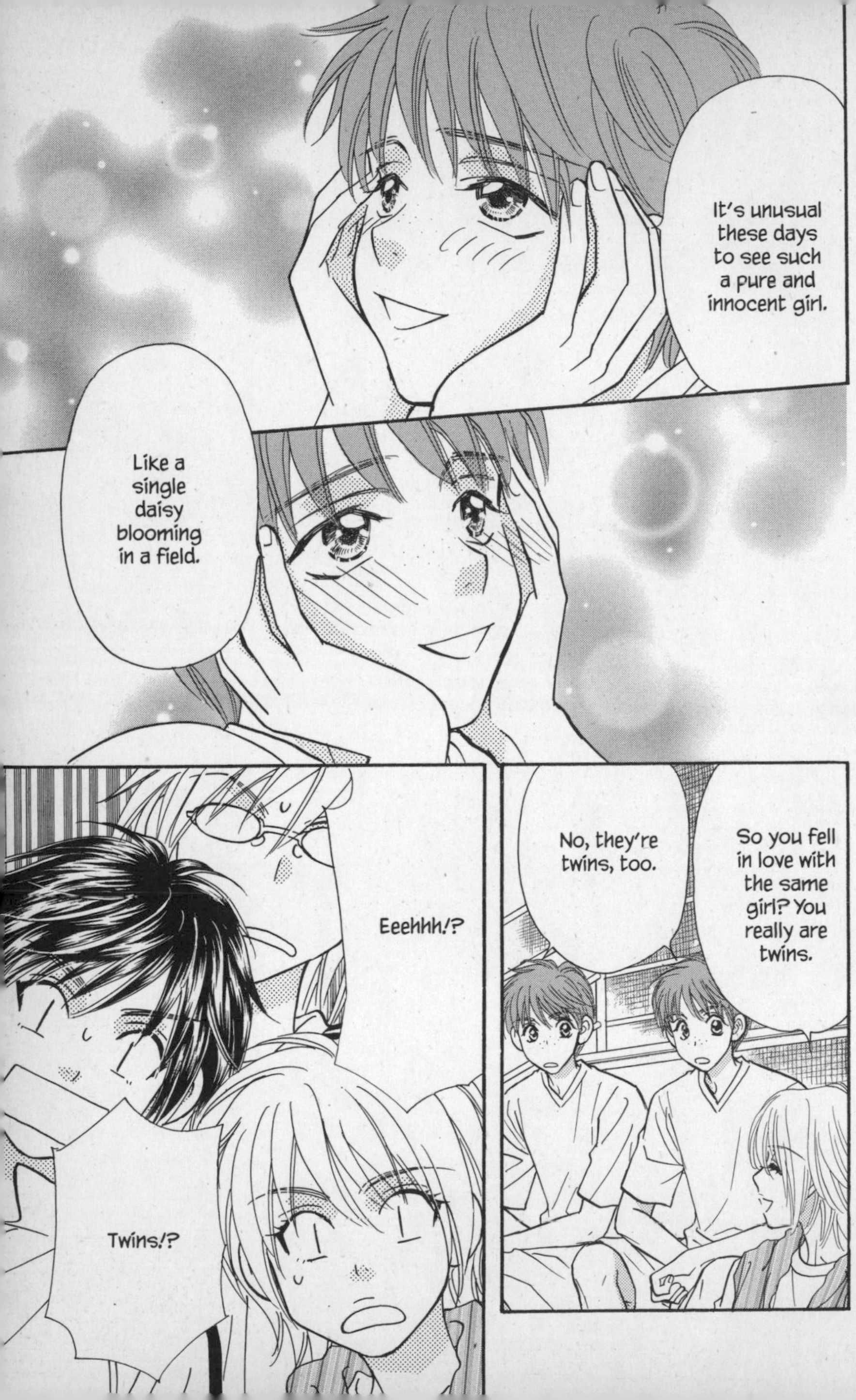
It's unusual these days to see such a pure and innocent girl.
Like a single daisy blooming in a field.
So you fell in love with the same girl? You really are twins.
No, they're twins, too.
Eeehhh!?
Twins!?

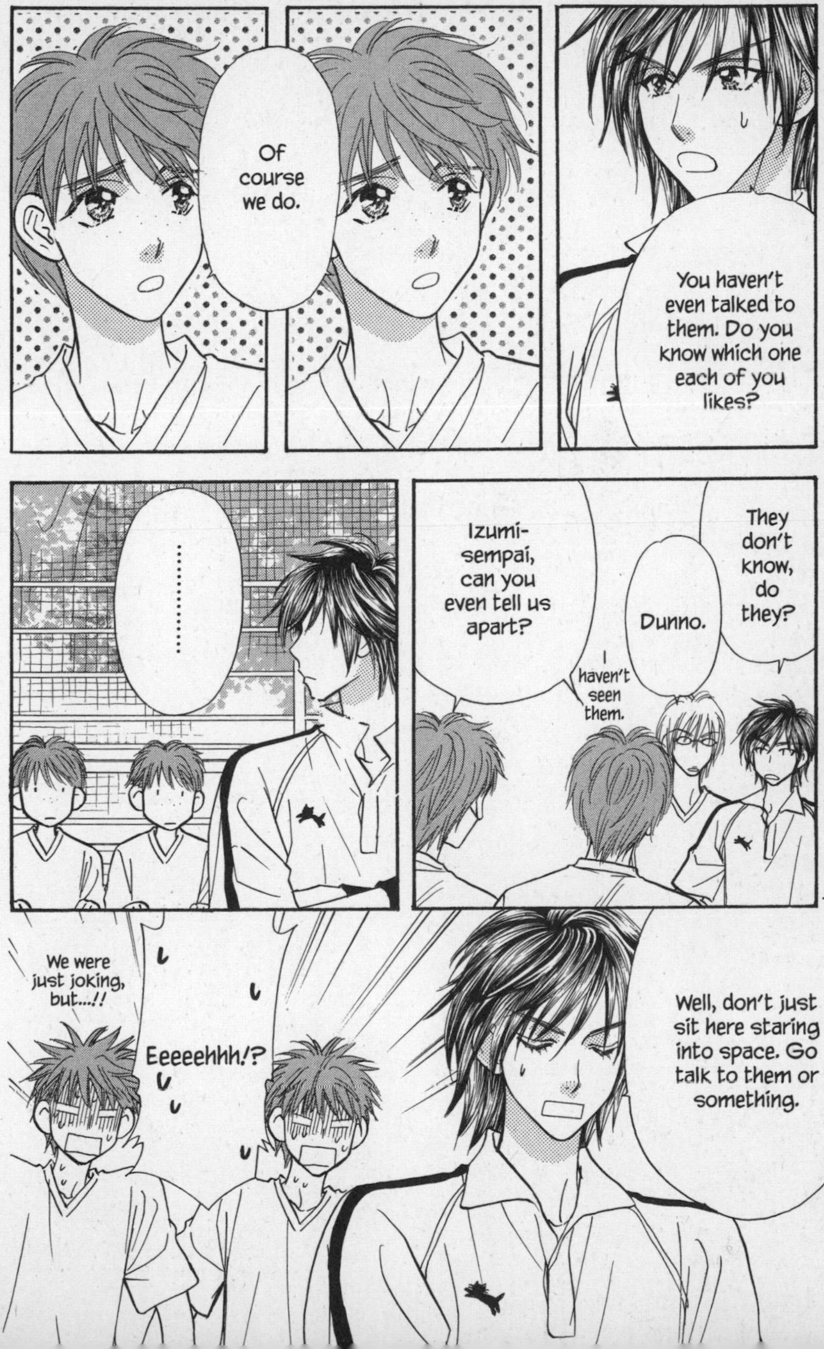
You haven't even talked to them. Do you know which one each of you likes?
Of course we do.
They don't know, do they?
Dunno.
I haven't seen them.
Izumi-sempai, can you even tell us apart?
......
Well, don't just sit here staring into space. Go talk to them or something.
Eeeeehhh!?
We were just joking, but...!!

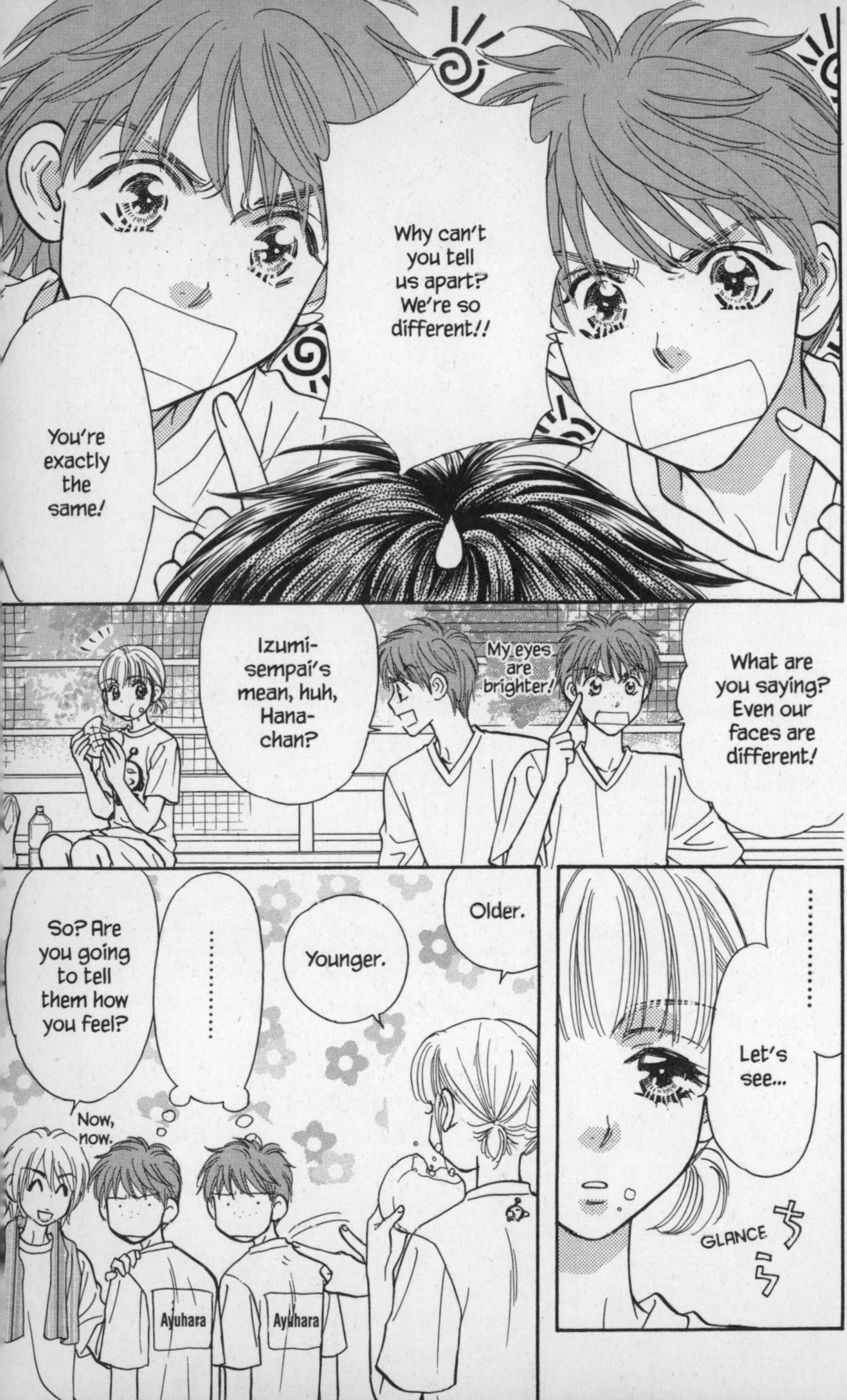
Why can't you tell us apart? We're so different!!
You're exactly the same!
What are you saying? Even our faces are different!
My eyes are brighter!
Izumi-sempai's mean, huh, Hana-chan?
......
Let's see...
GLANCE
Older.
Younger.
......
So? Are you going to tell them how you feel?
Now, now.
Ayuhara
Ayuhara

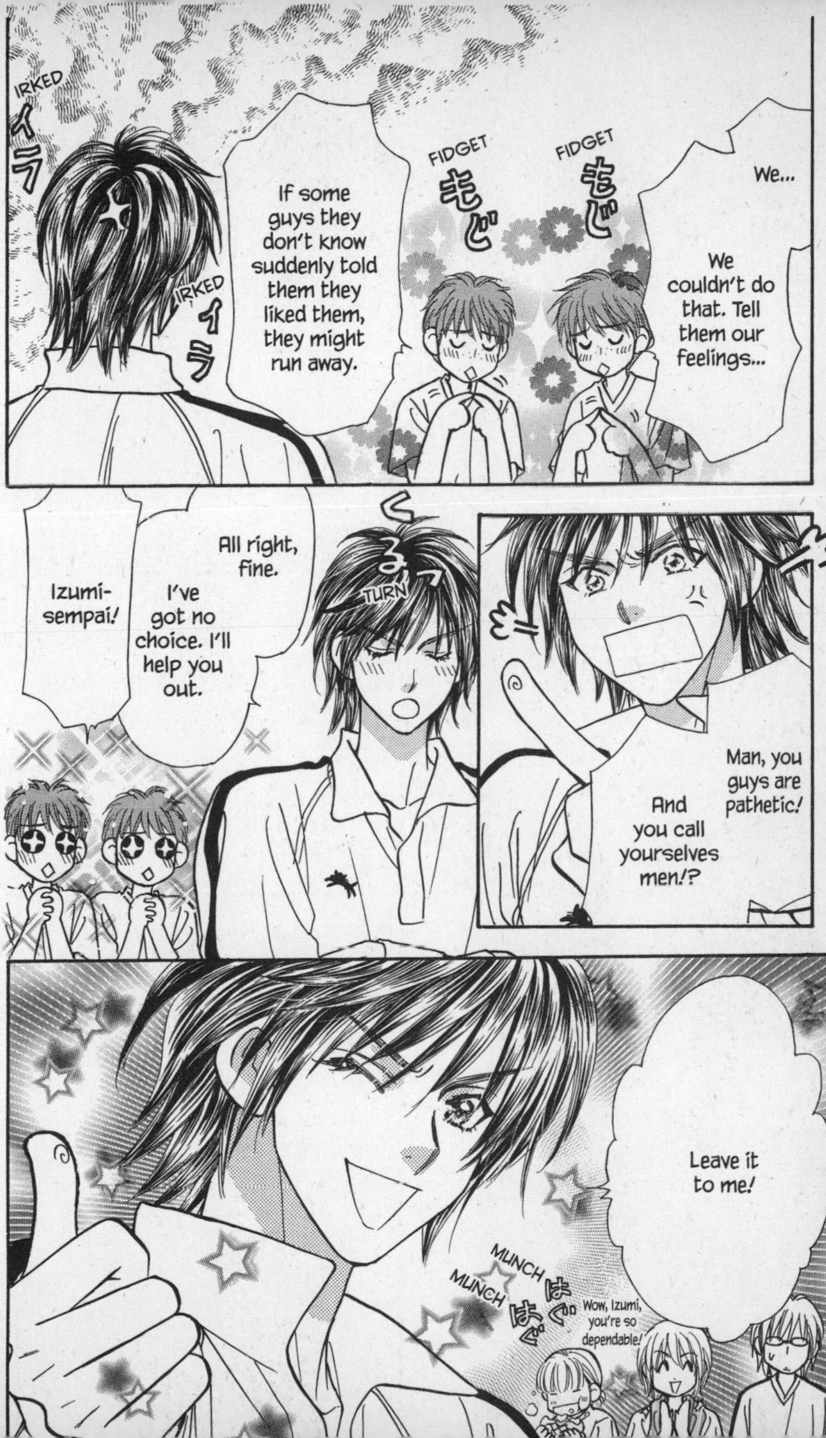
We...
We couldn't do that. Tell them our feelings...
FIDGET もじ
FIDGET もじ
If some guys they don't know suddenly told them they liked them, they might run away.
IRKED イラ
IRKED イラ
Man, you guys are pathetic!
And you call yourselves men!?
くるっ TURN
All right, fine.
I've got no choice. I'll help you out.
Izumi-sempai!
Leave it to me!
.....
Wow, Izumi, you're so dependable!
MUNCH はぐ
MUNCH はぐ

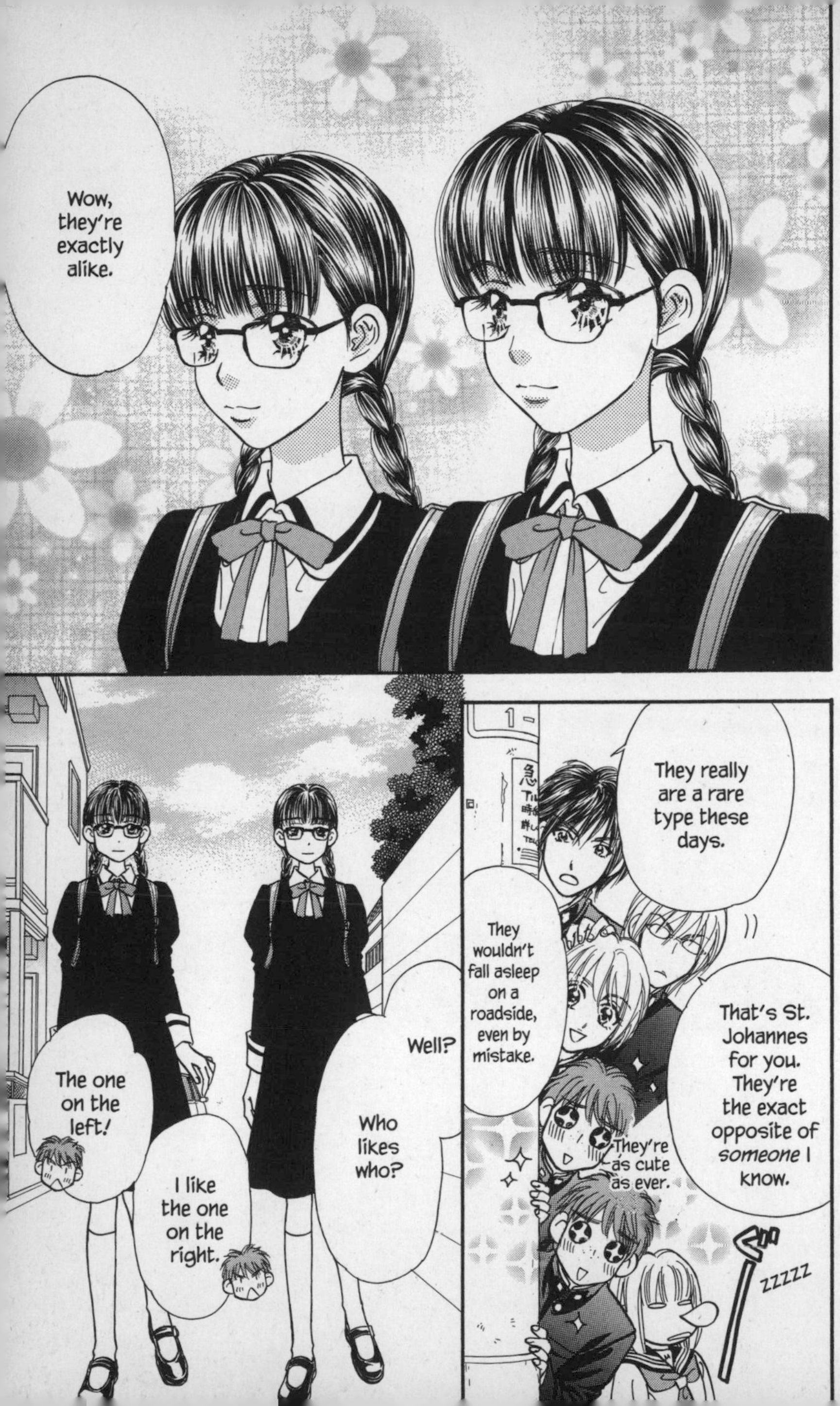

Wow, they're exactly alike.
They really are a rare type these days.
They wouldn't fall asleep on a roadside, even by mistake.
That's St. Johannes for you. They're the exact opposite of *someone* I know.
They're as cute as ever.
ZZZZZ
Well?
Who likes who?
I like the one on the right.
The one on the left!

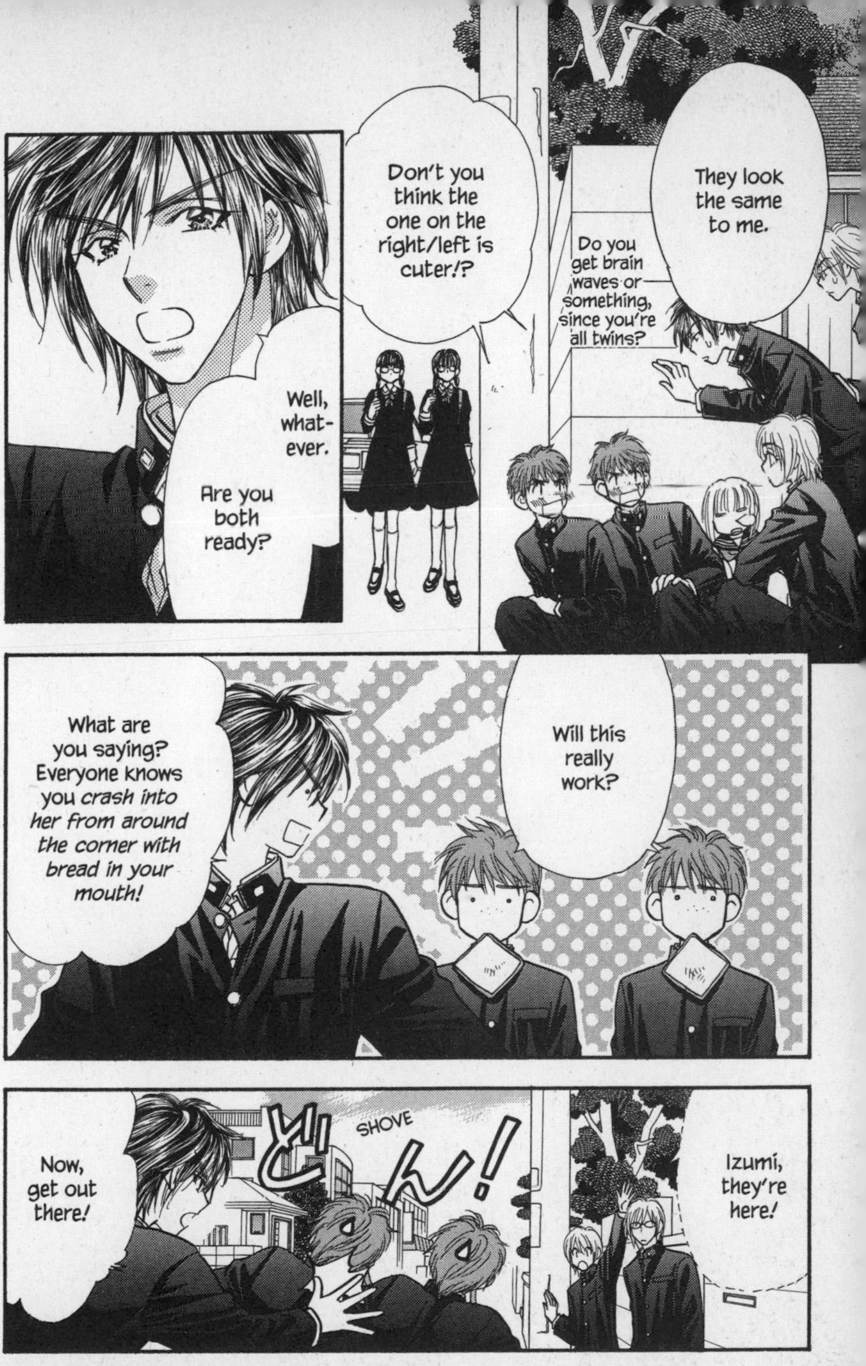
They look the same to me.
Do you get brain waves or something, since you're all twins?
Don't you think the one on the right/left is cuter!?
Well, whatever.
Are you both ready?
Will this really work?
What are you saying? Everyone knows you *crash into her from around the corner with bread in your mouth!*
Izumi, they're here!
SHOVE
Now, get out there!

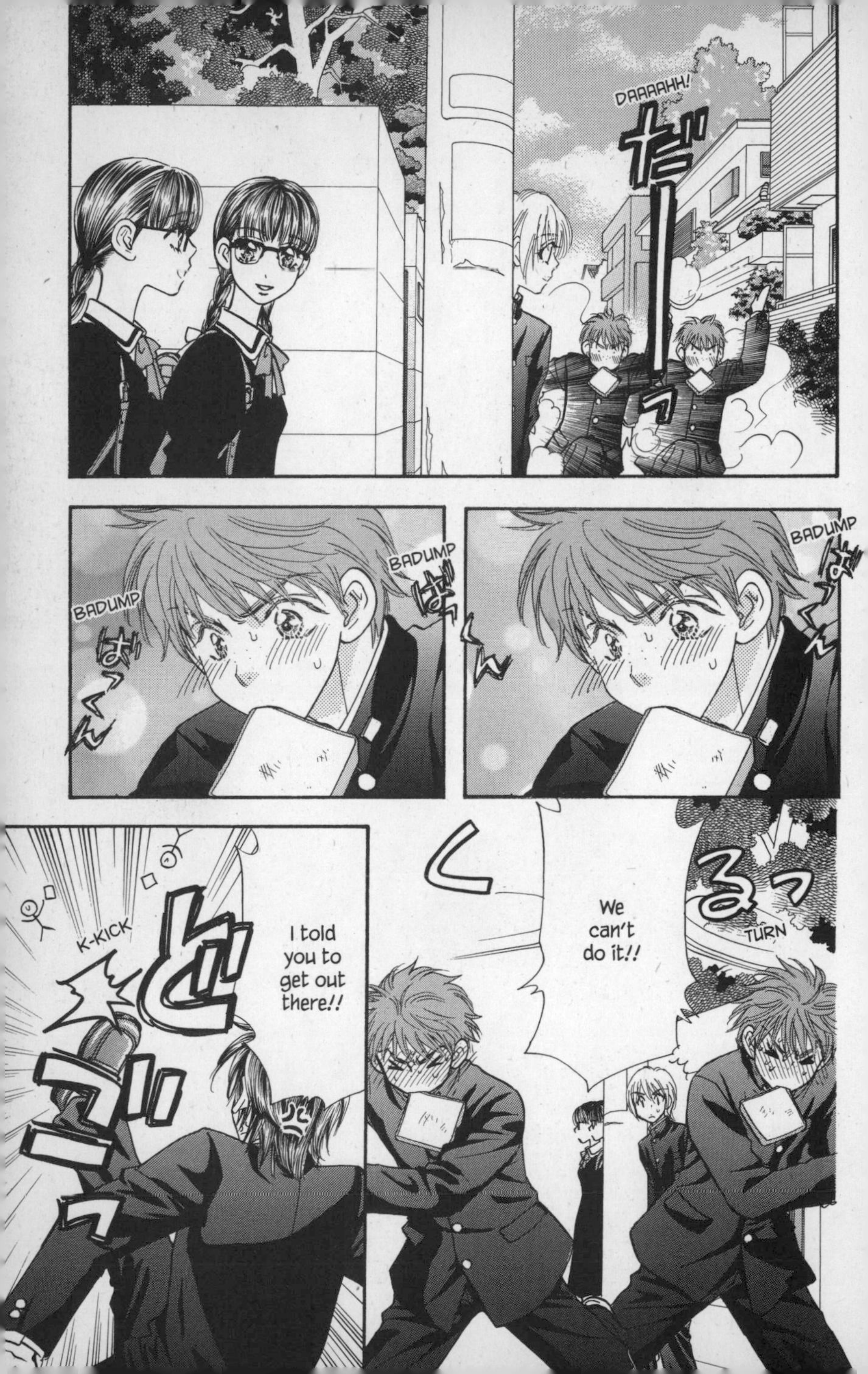
DAAAAHH!
BADUMP
BADUMP
BADUMP
TURN
We can't do it!!
I told you to get out there!!
K-KICK

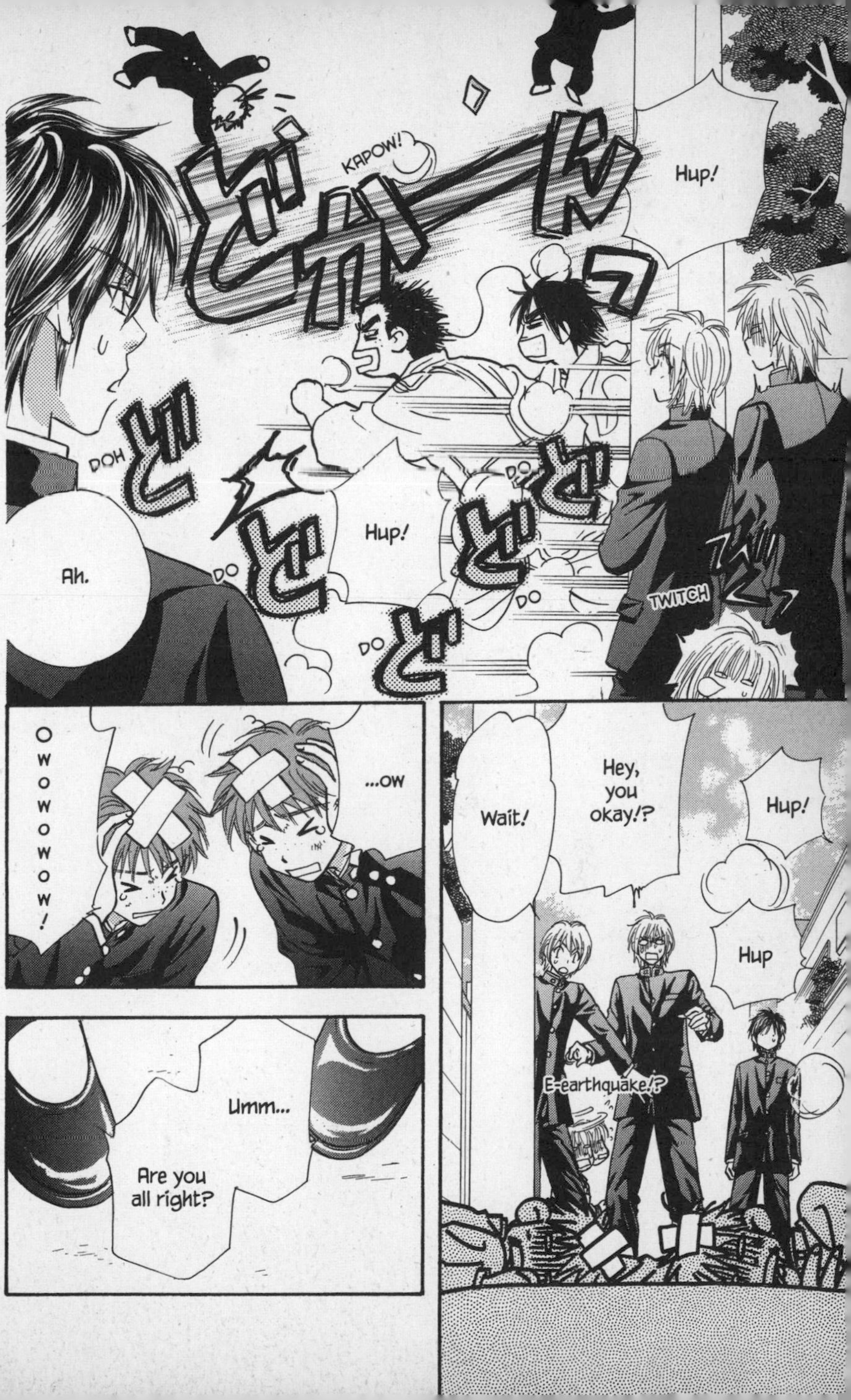
Hup!
KAPOW!
TWITCH
DO
DO
DO
Hup!
DO
DOH
Ah.
Hup!
Hey, you okay!?
Wait!
Hup
E-earthquake!?
...OW
OWOWOWOWOW!
Umm...
Are you all right?

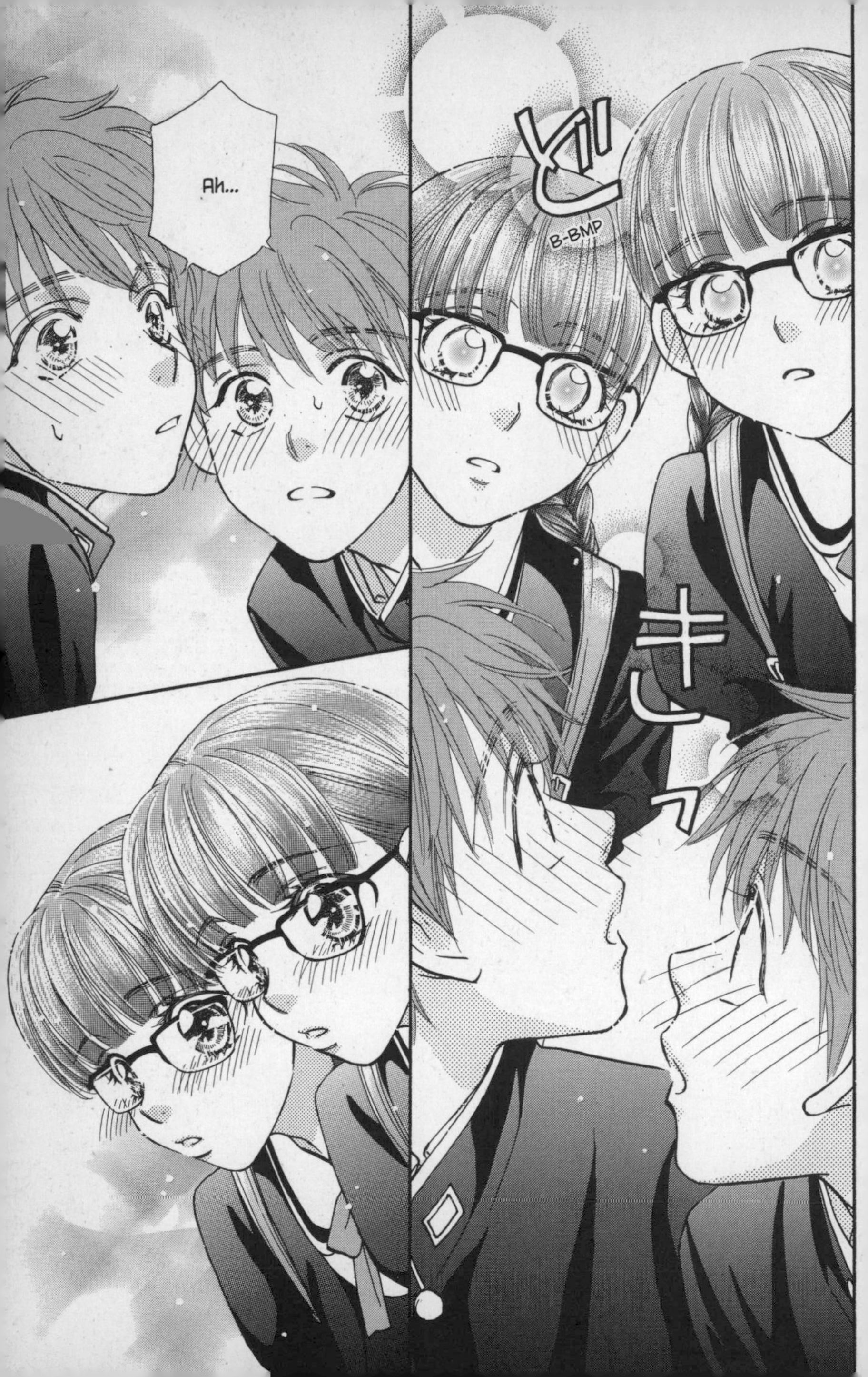
B-BMP
Ah...

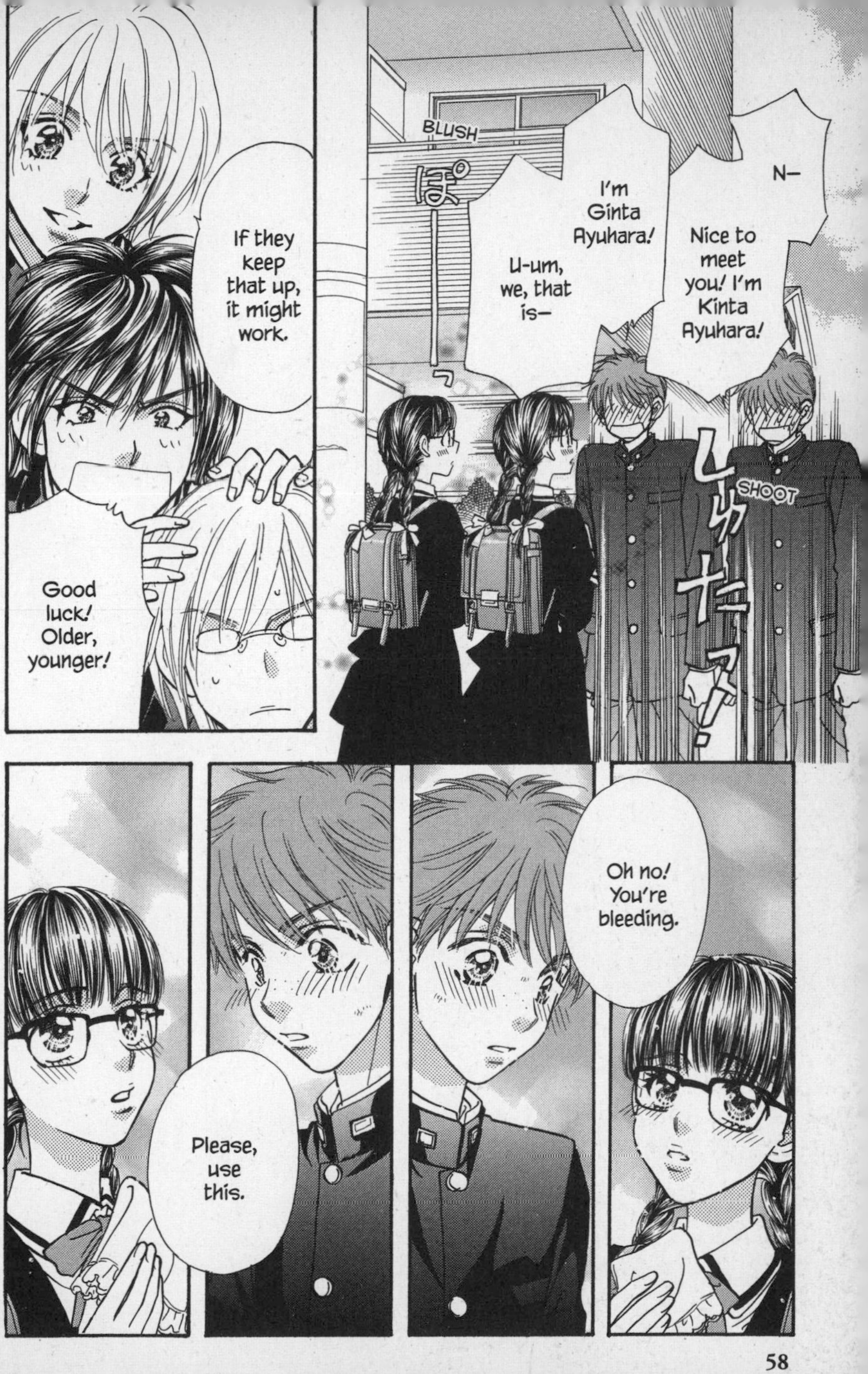
N—
Nice to meet you! I'm Kinta Ayuhara!
I'm Ginta Ayuhara!
U-um, we, that is—
BLUSH
SHOOT
If they keep that up, it might work.
Good luck! Older, younger!
Oh no! You're bleeding.
Please, use this.

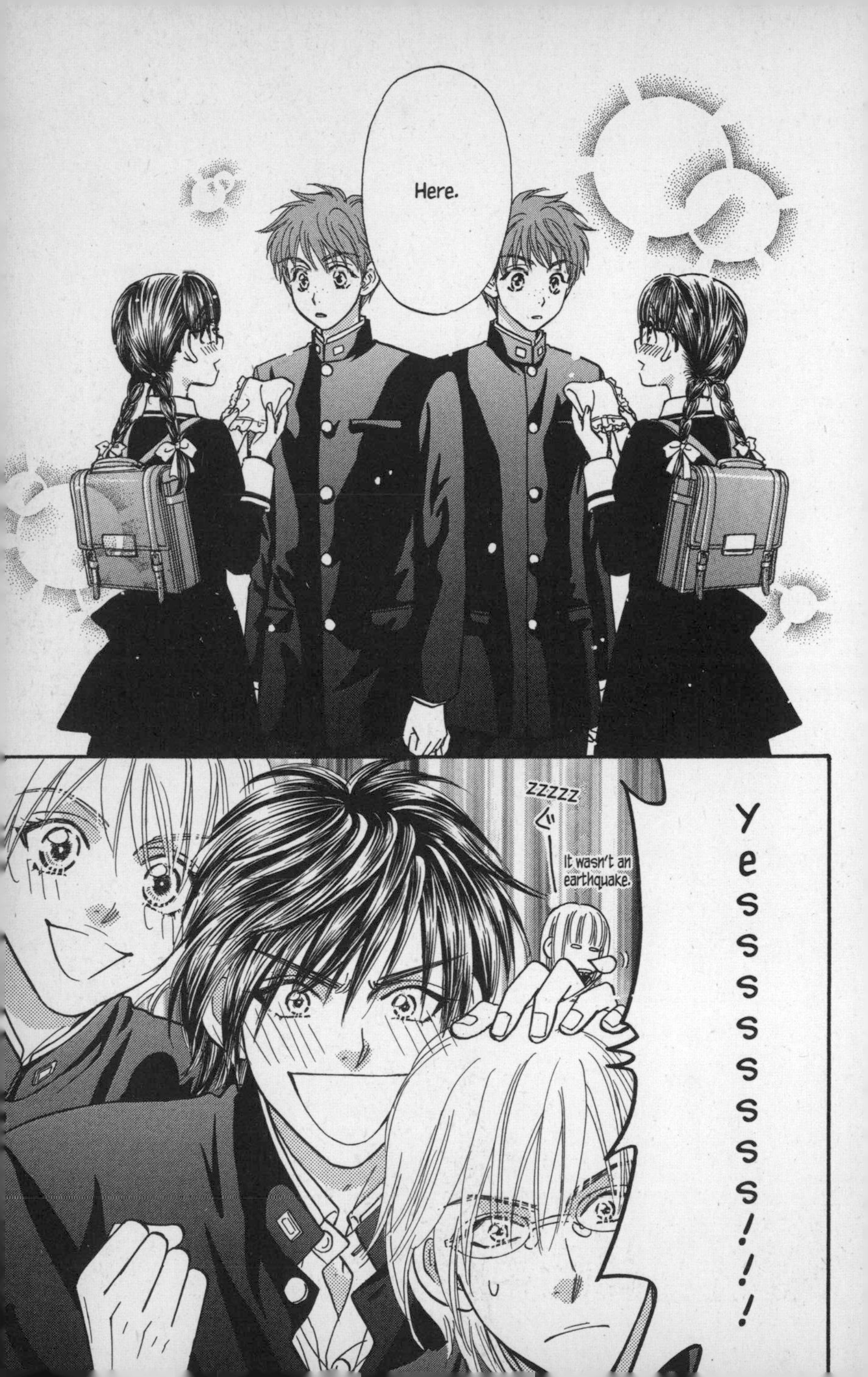
Here.
Yessssssss!!!
ZZZZZ
ぐー
It wasn't an earthquake.

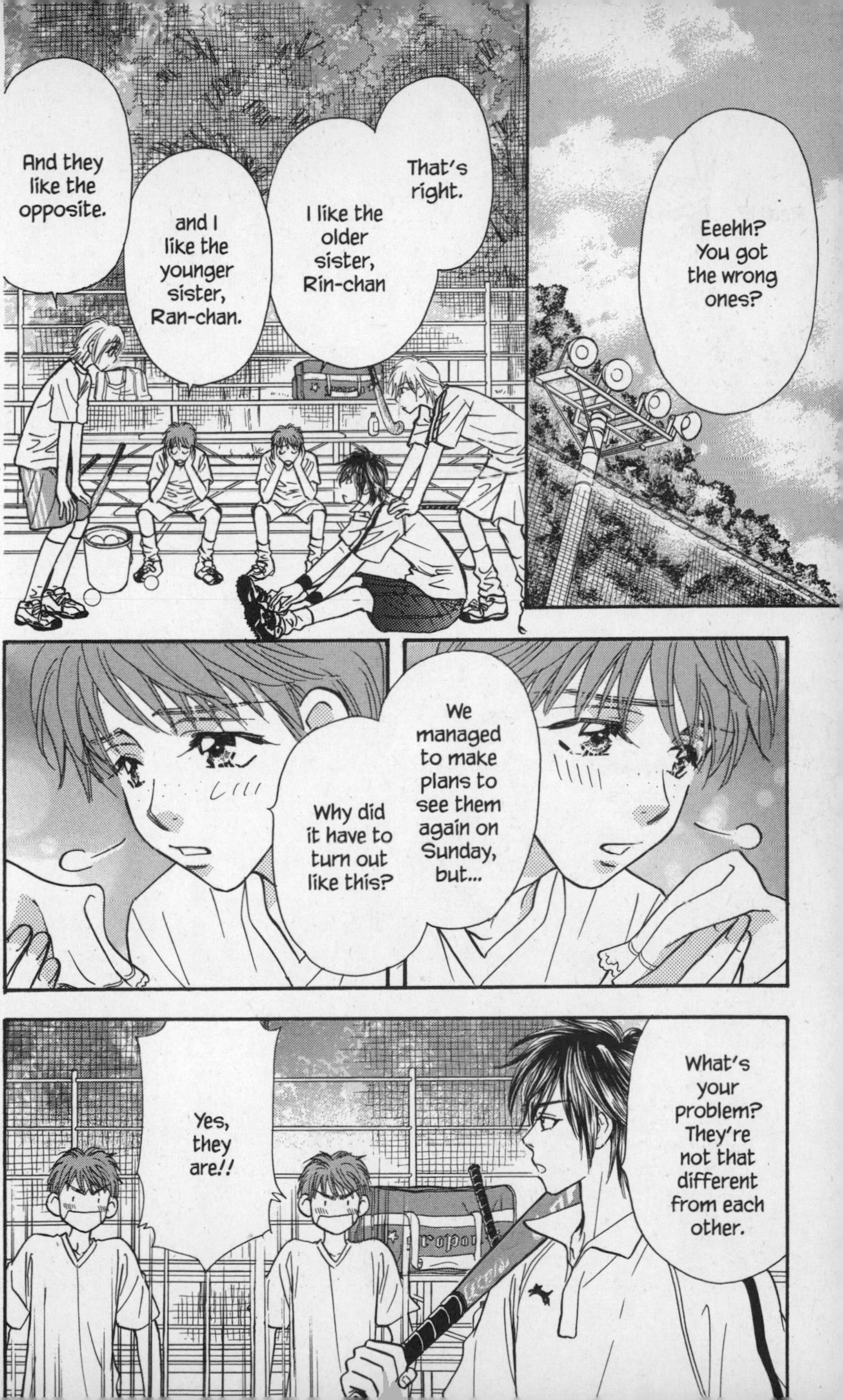
Eeehh? You got the wrong ones?
That's right.
I like the older sister, Rin-chan
and I like the younger sister, Ran-chan.
And they like the opposite.
We managed to make plans to see them again on Sunday, but...
Why did it have to turn out like this?
What's your problem? They're not that different from each other.
Yes, they are!!

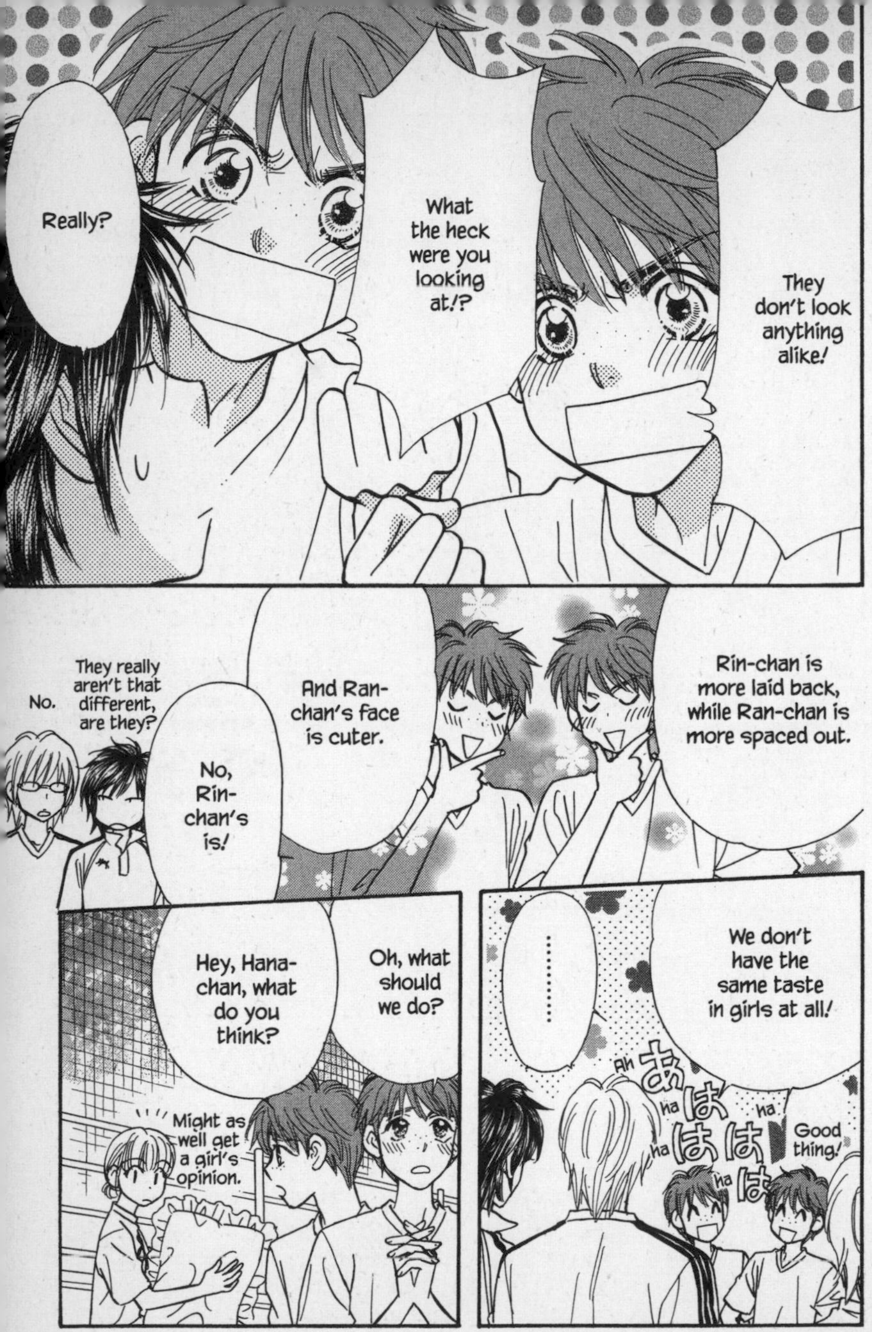
They don't look anything alike!
What the heck were you looking at!?
Really?
Rin-chan is more laid back, while Ran-chan is more spaced out.
And Ran-chan's face is cuter.
No, Rin-chan's is!
They really aren't that different, are they?
No.
We don't have the same taste in girls at all!
......
あははははは
Ah ha ha ha ha
Good thing!
Oh, what should we do?
Hey, Hana-chan, what do you think?
Might as well get a girl's opinion.

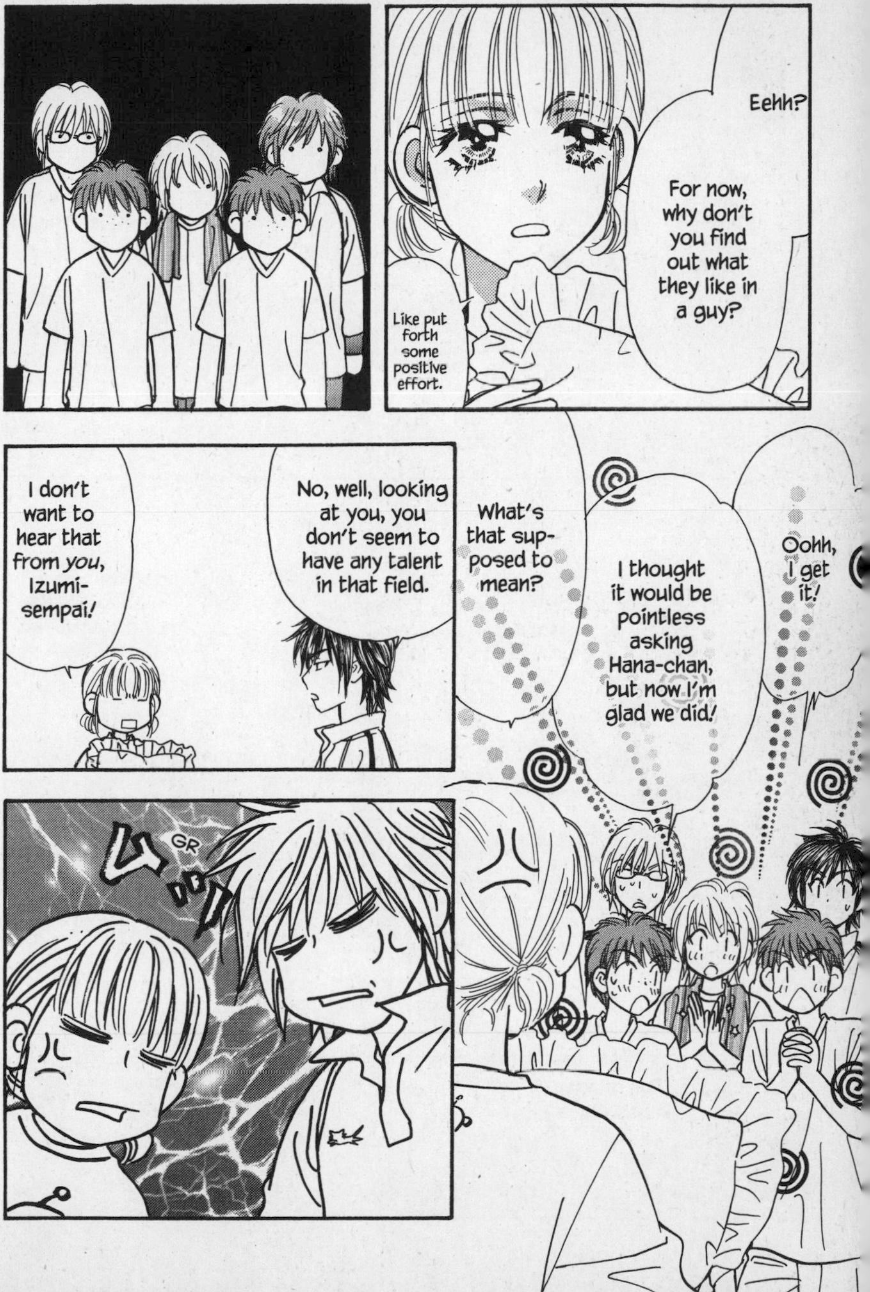
Eehh?
For now, why don't you find out what they like in a guy?
Like put forth some positive effort.
Oohh, I get it!
I thought it would be pointless asking Hana-chan, but now I'm glad we did!
What's that sup-posed to mean?
No, well, looking at you, you don't seem to have any talent in that field.
I don't want to hear that from *you*, Izumi-sempai!
GR

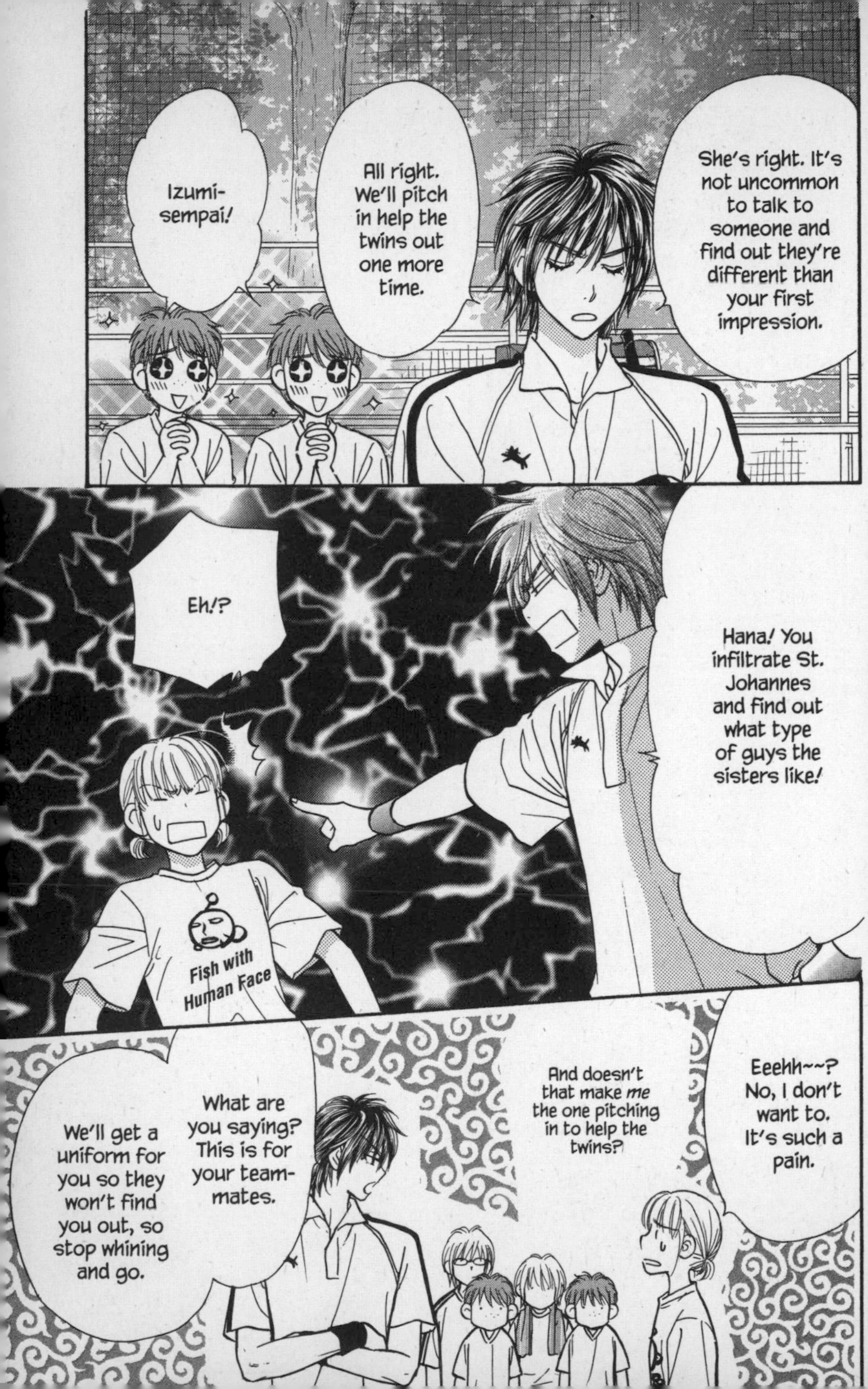
She's right. It's not uncommon to talk to someone and find out they're different than your first impression.
All right. We'll pitch in help the twins out one more time.
Izumi-sempai!
Hana! You infiltrate St. Johannes and find out what type of guys the sisters like!
Eh!?
Fish with Human Face
Eeehh~~? No, I don't want to. It's such a pain.
And doesn't that make *me* the one pitching in to help the twins?
What are you saying? This is for your team-mates.
We'll get a uniform for you so they won't find you out, so stop whining and go.

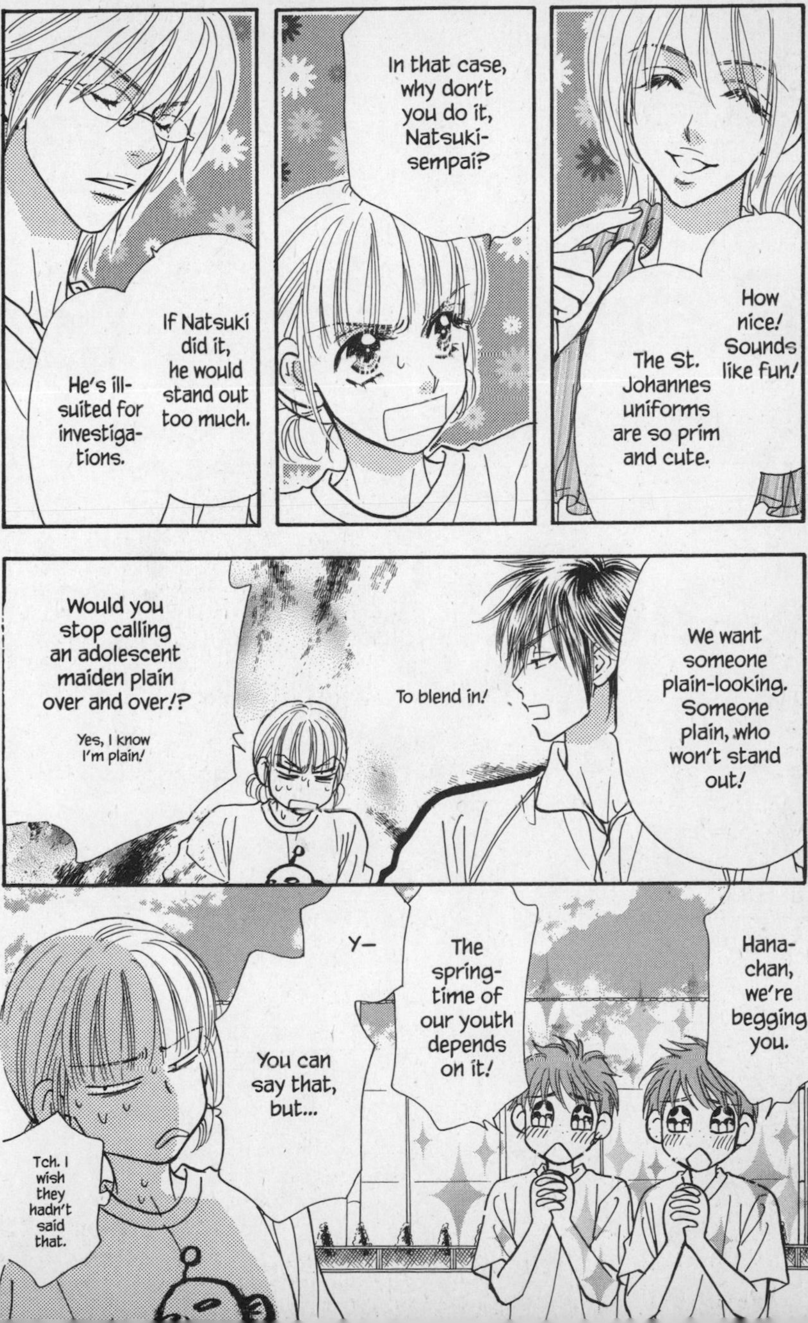
How nice! Sounds like fun!
The St. Johannes uniforms are so prim and cute.
In that case, why don't you do it, Natsuki-sempai?
If Natsuki did it, he would stand out too much.
He's ill-suited for investigations.
We want someone plain-looking. Someone plain, who won't stand out!
To blend in!
Would you stop calling an adolescent maiden plain over and over!?
Yes, I know I'm plain!
Hana-chan, we're begging you.
The springtime of our youth depends on it!
Y—
You can say that, but...
Tch. I wish they hadn't said that.

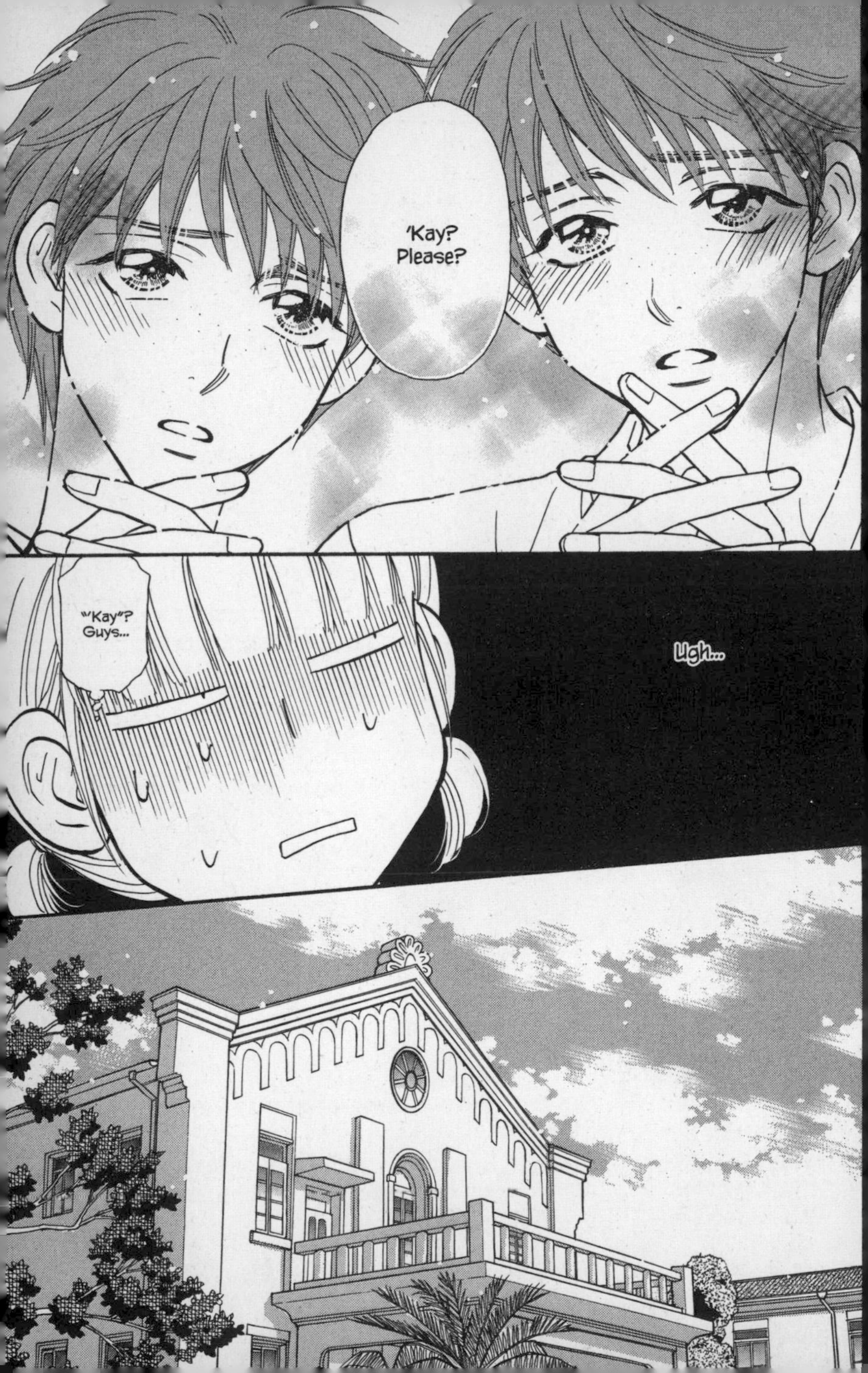
'Kay? Please?
"Kay"? Guys...
Ugh...

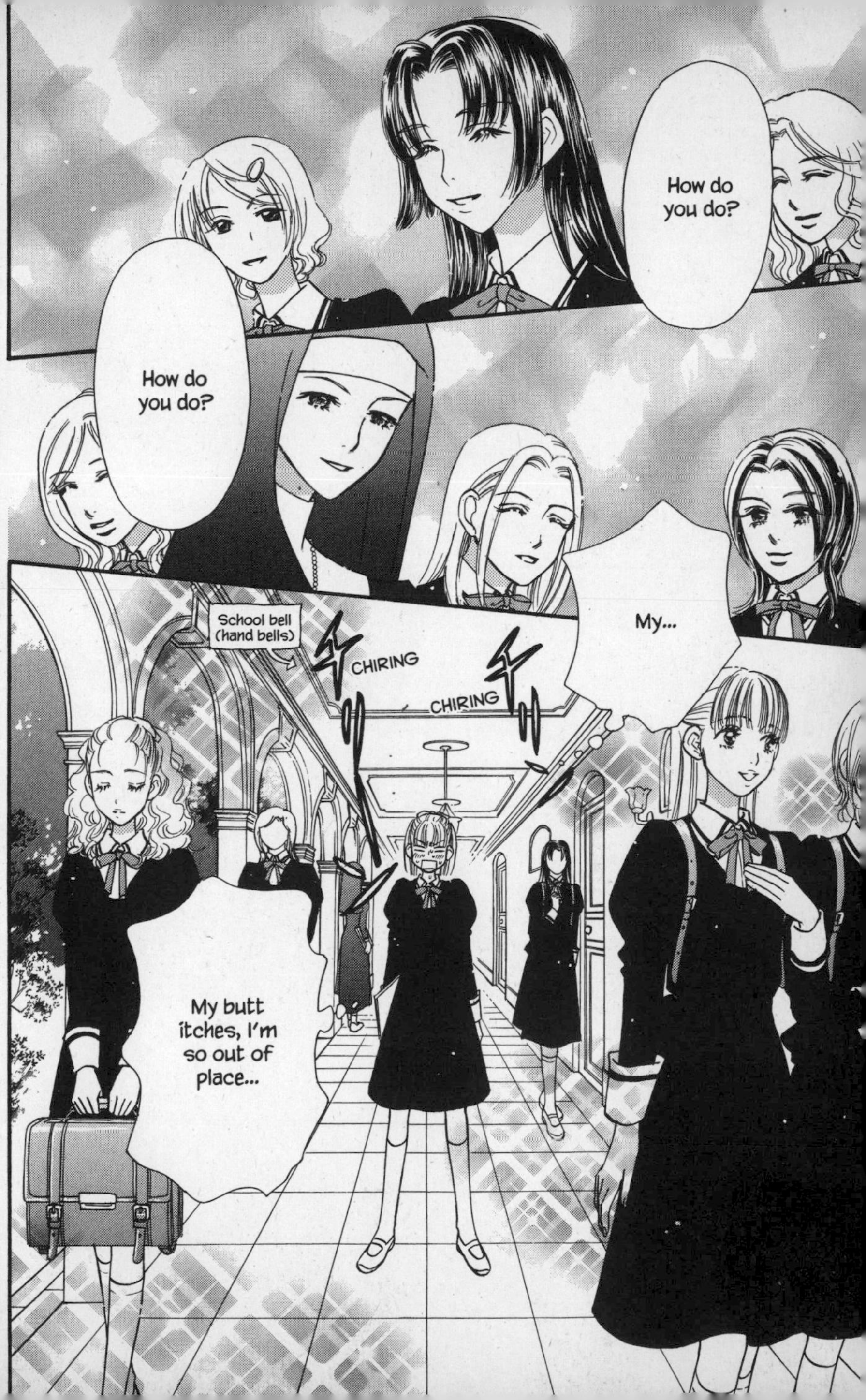
How do you do?
How do you do?
My...
School bell (hand bells)
CHIRING
CHIRING
My butt itches, I'm so out of place...

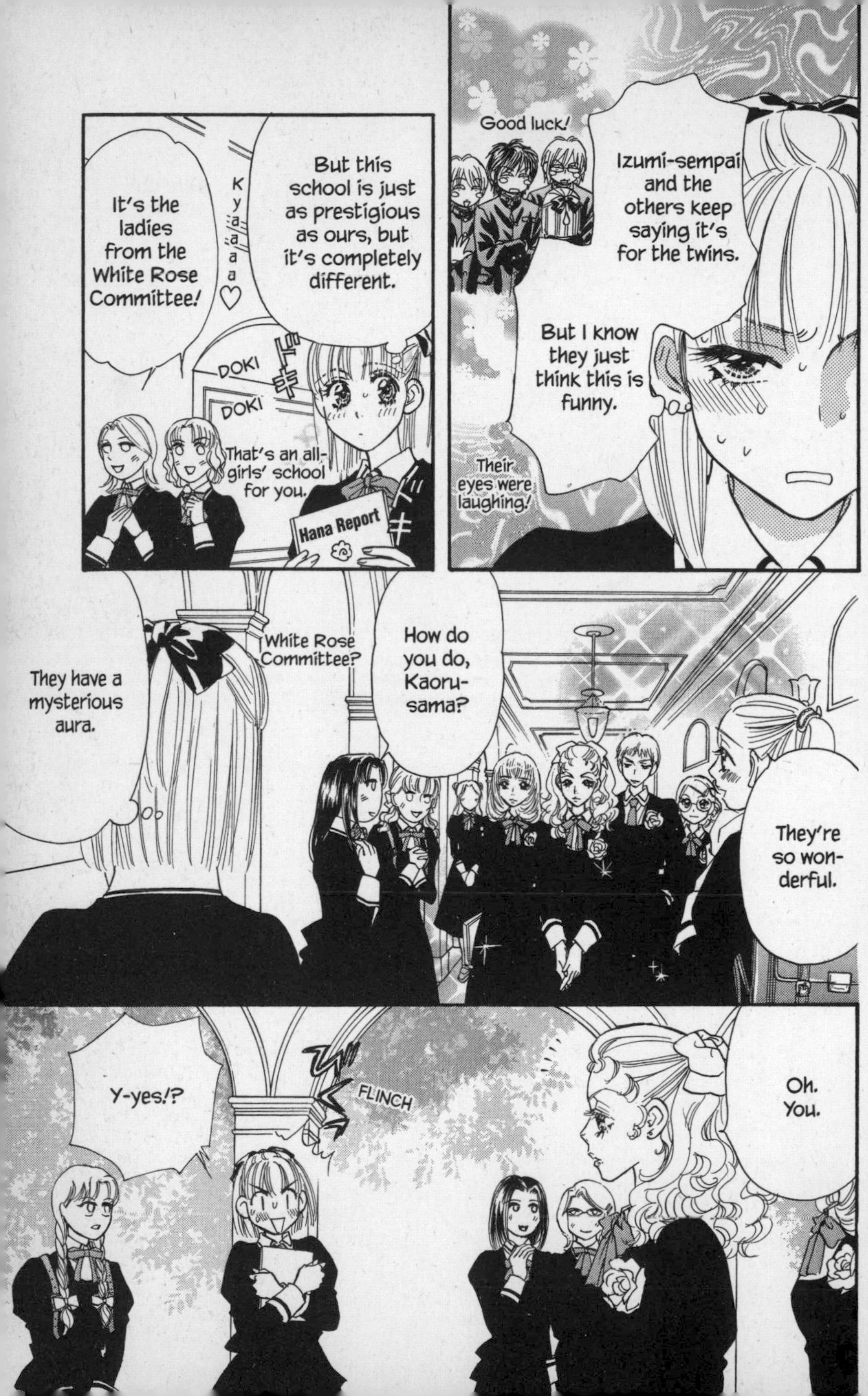
Izumi-sempai and the others keep saying it's for the twins.
Good luck!
But I know they just think this is funny.
Their eyes were laughing!
But this school is just as prestigious as ours, but it's completely different.
Kyaaaa ♡
It's the ladies from the White Rose Committee!
DOKI
DOKI
That's an all-girls' school for you.
Hana Report
They're so wonderful.
How do you do, Kaoru-sama?
White Rose Committee?
They have a mysterious aura.
Oh. You.
FLINCH
Y-yes!?

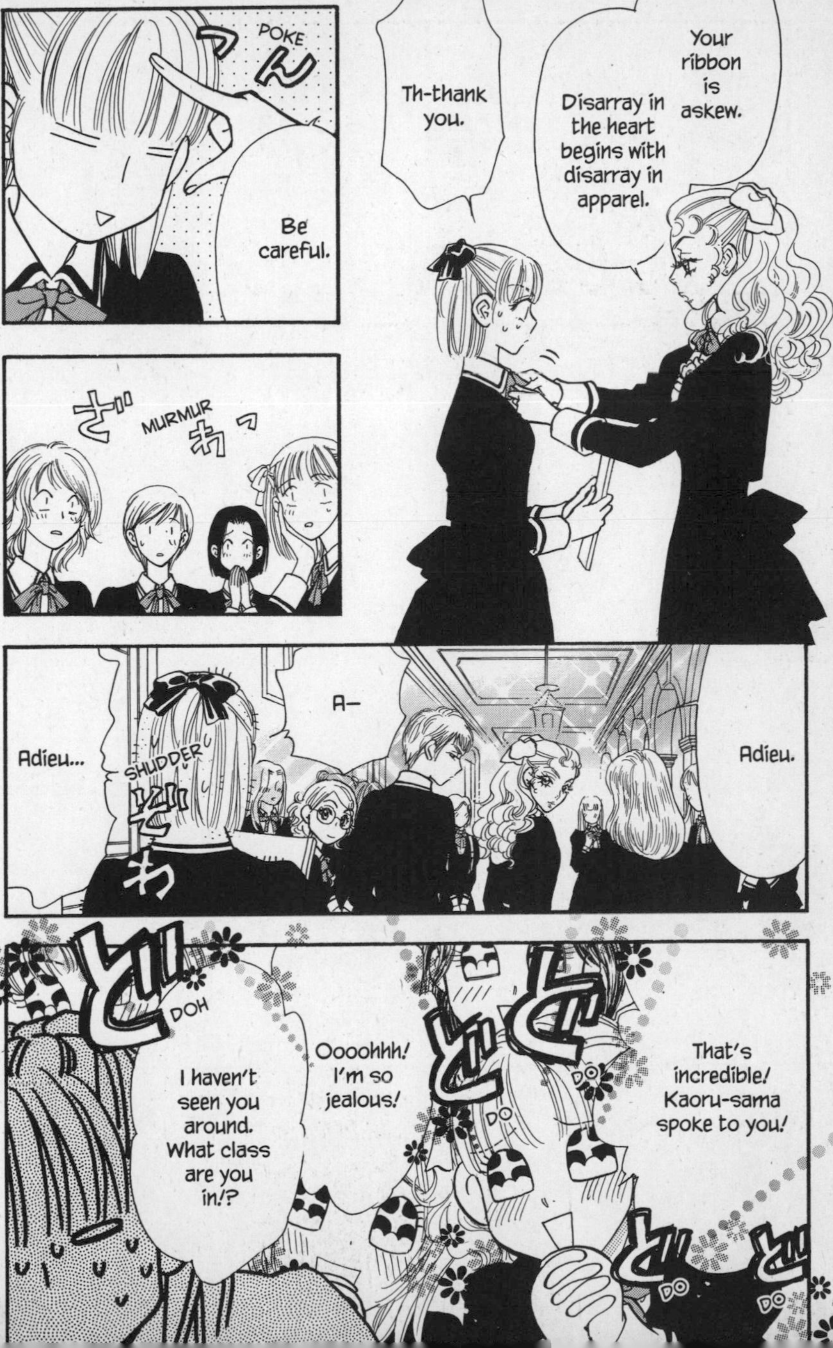
Your ribbon is askew.
Disarray in the heart begins with disarray in apparel.
Th-thank you.
POKE
Be careful.
MURMUR
Adieu.
A–
SHUDDER
Adieu...
That's incredible! Kaoru-sama spoke to you!
DO
DO
DO
DO
Oooohhh! I'm so jealous!
I haven't seen you around. What class are you in!?
DOH

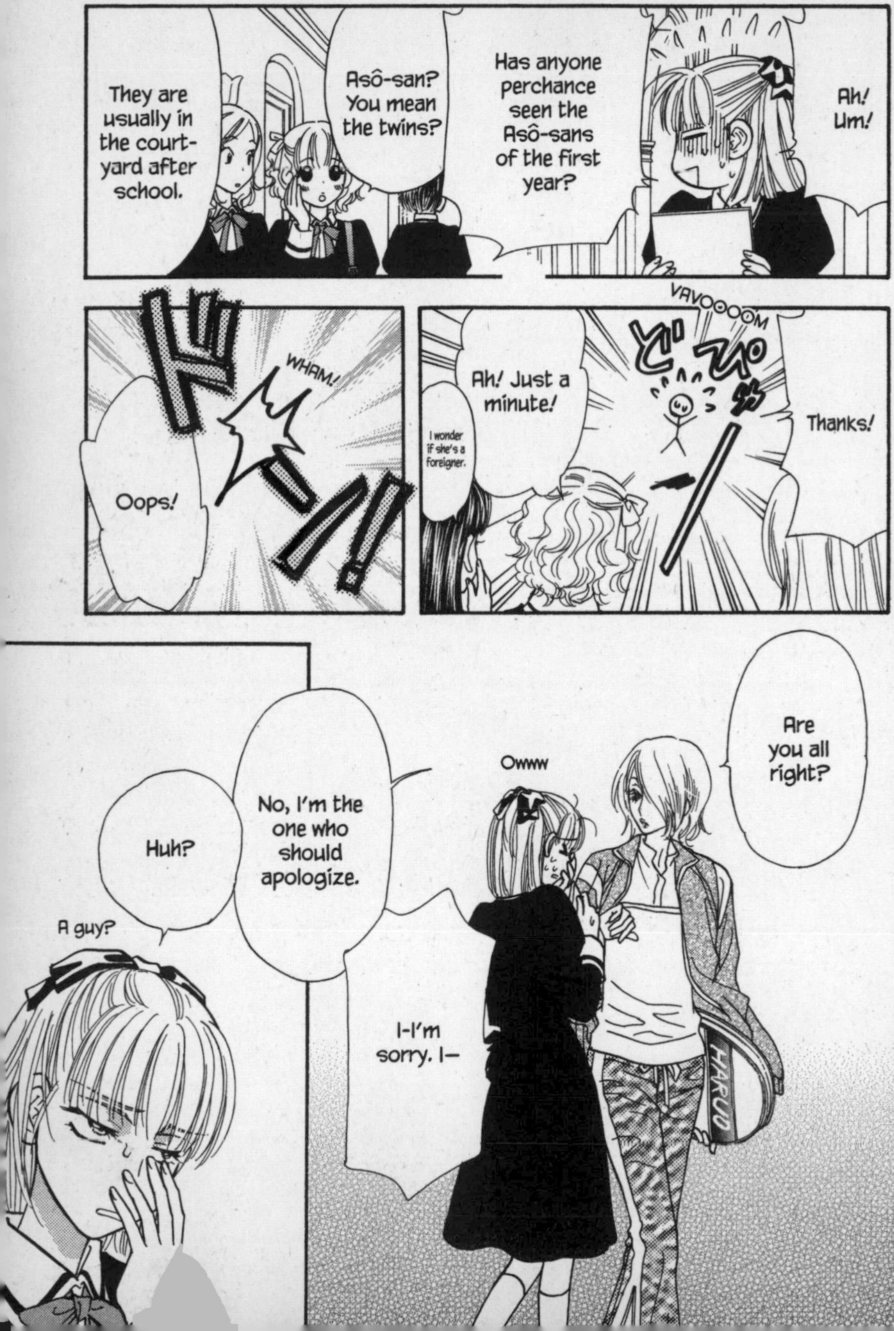
Ah! Um!
Has anyone perchance seen the Asô-sans of the first year?
Asô-san? You mean the twins?
They are usually in the court-yard after school.
VAVOOOOOM
Thanks!
Ah! Just a minute!
I wonder if she's a foreigner.
WHAM!
Oops!
Are you all right?
Owww
HARUO
I-I'm sorry. I–
No, I'm the one who should apologize.
Huh?
A guy?

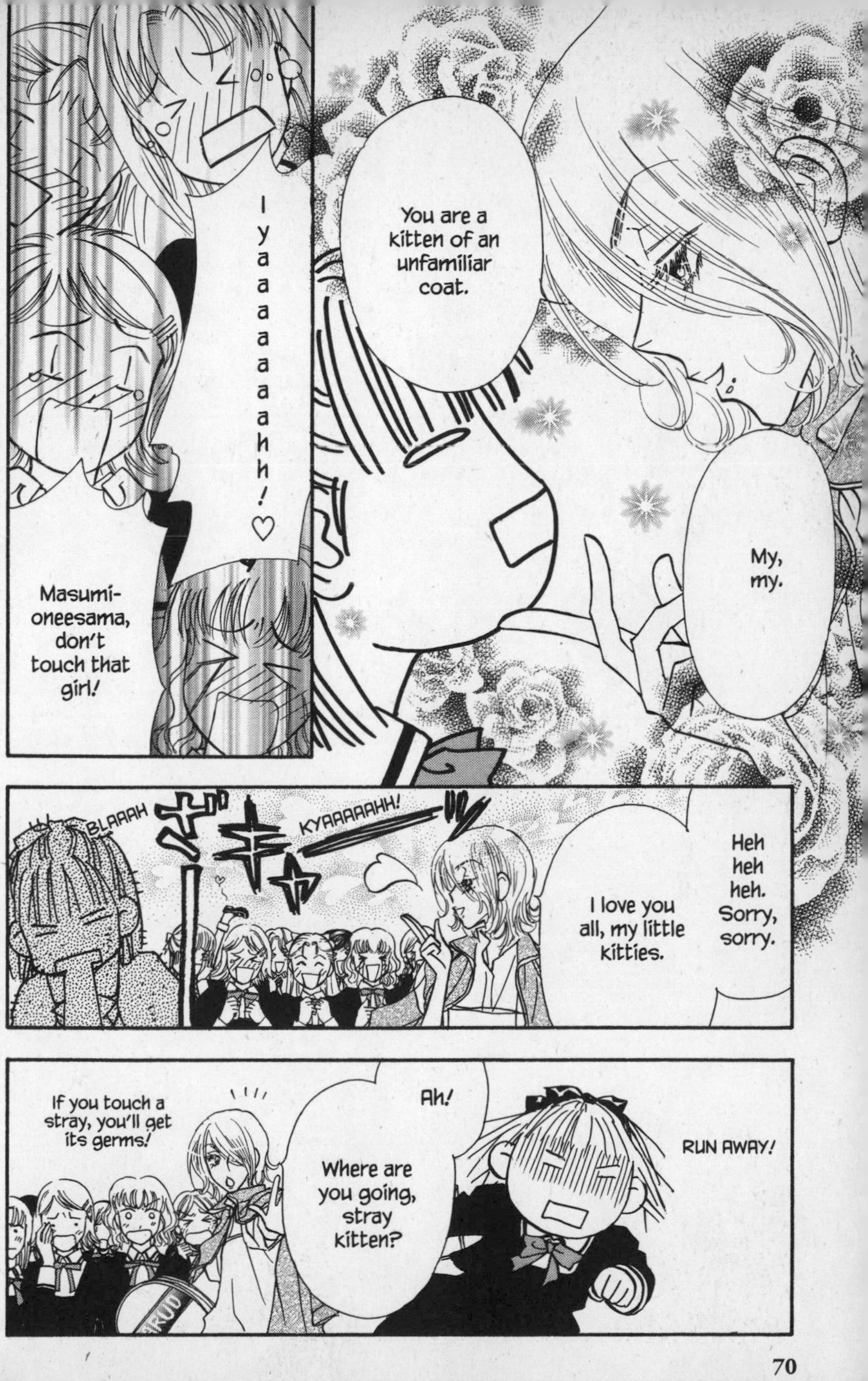
My, my.
You are a kitten of an unfamiliar coat.
Iyaaaaaaaahh!♡
Masumi-oneesama, don't touch that girl!
Heh heh heh. Sorry, sorry.
I love you all, my little kitties.
KYAAAAAAHH!
BLAAAH
RUN AWAY!
Ah!
Where are you going, stray kitten?
If you touch a stray, you'll get its germs!

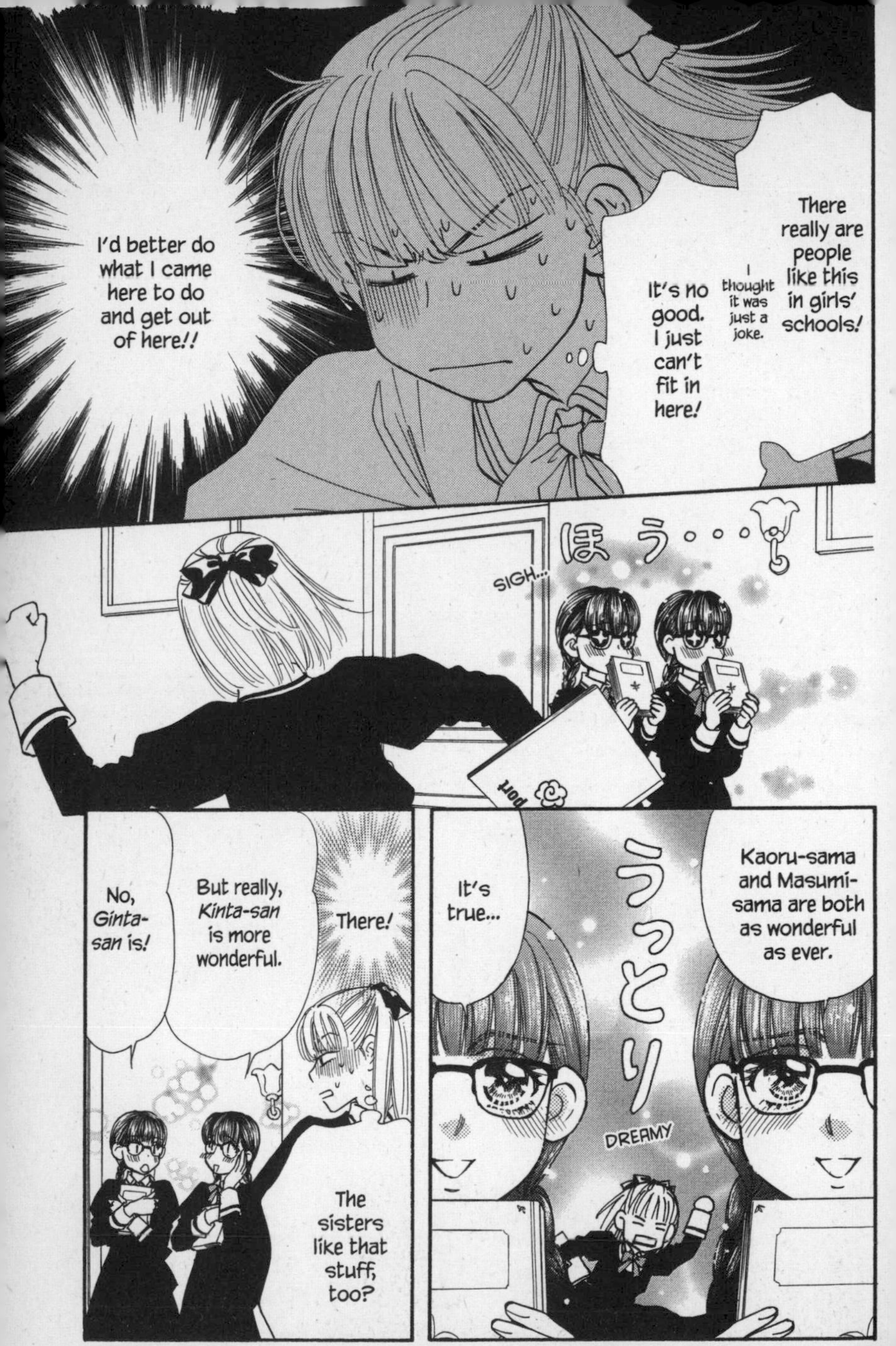

There really are people like this in girls' schools!
I thought it was just a joke.
It's no good. I just can't fit in here!
I'd better do what I came here to do and get out of here!!
ほう・・・
SIGH...
Kaoru-sama and Masumi-sama are both as wonderful as ever.
It's true...
うっとり
DREAMY
There!
But really, *Kinta-san* is more wonderful.
No, *Ginta-san* is!
The sisters like that stuff, too?

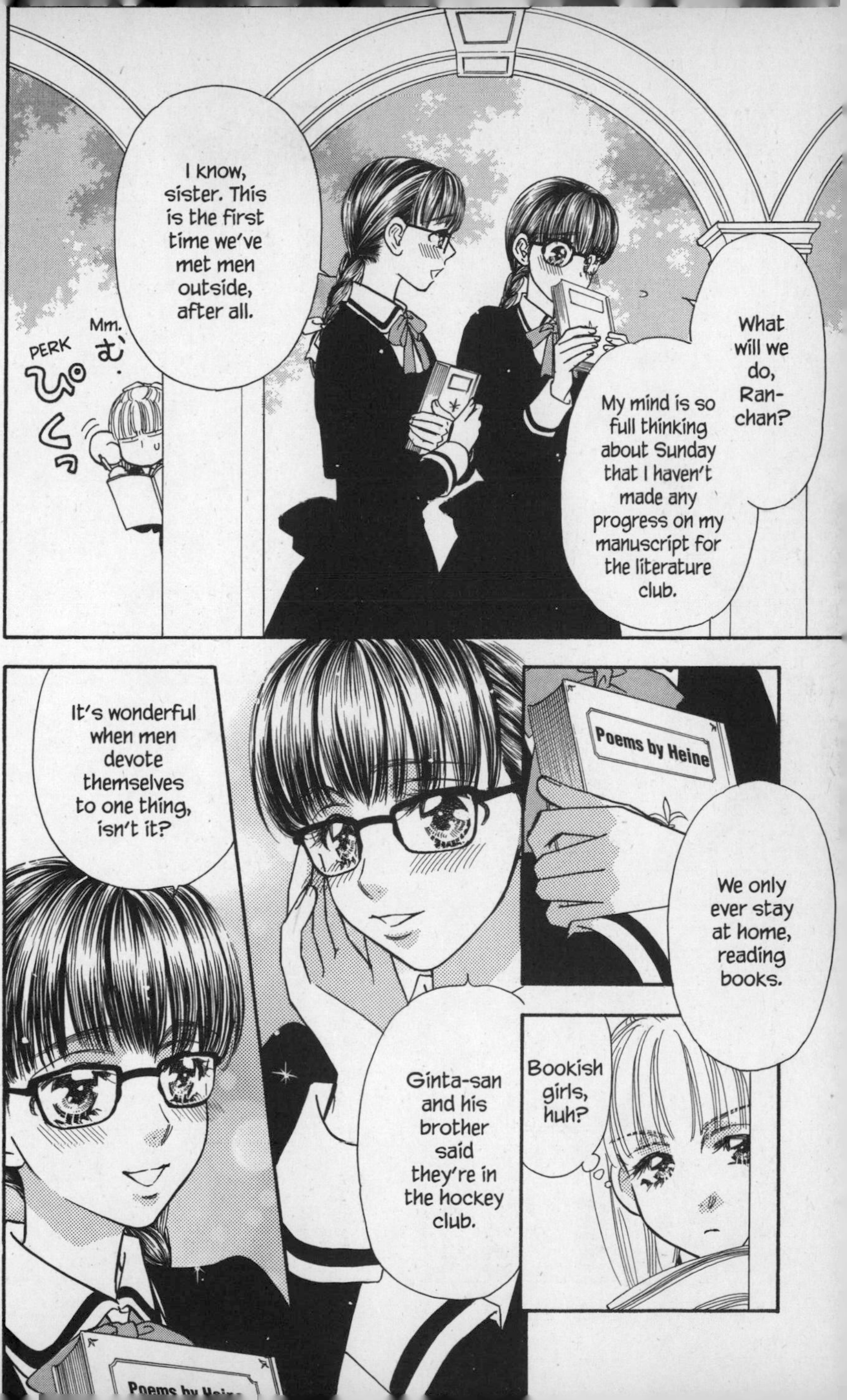
What will we do, Ran-chan?
My mind is so full thinking about Sunday that I haven't made any progress on my manuscript for the literature club.
I know, sister. This is the first time we've met men outside, after all.
Mm.
PERK
Poems by Heine
We only ever stay at home, reading books.
Bookish girls, huh?
Ginta-san and his brother said they're in the hockey club.
It's wonderful when men devote themselves to one thing, isn't it?

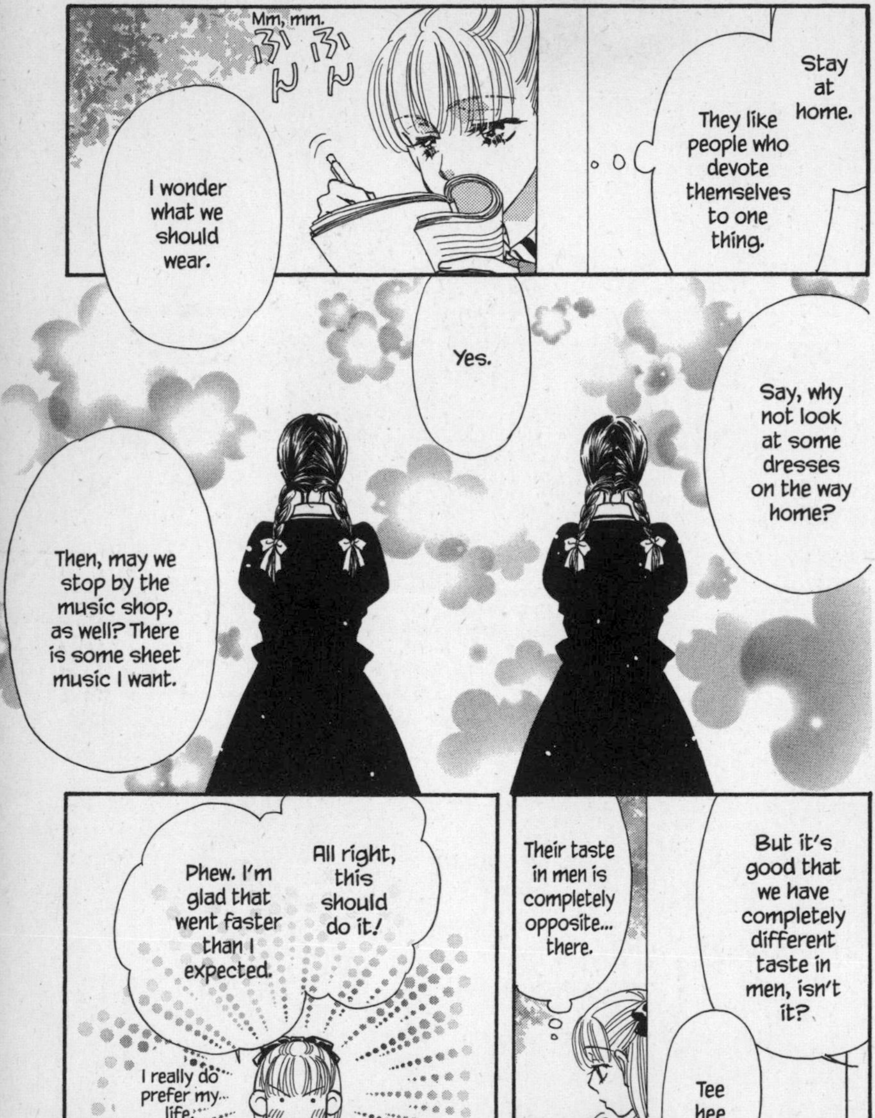

Stay at home.
They like people who devote themselves to one thing.
Mm, mm.
ふんふん
I wonder what we should wear.
Say, why not look at some dresses on the way home?
Yes.
Then, may we stop by the music shop, as well? There is some sheet music I want.
But it's good that we have completely different taste in men, isn't it?
Their taste in men is completely opposite... there.
Tee hee hee.
All right, this should do it!
Phew. I'm glad that went faster than I expected.
I really do prefer my life.
Hana Report

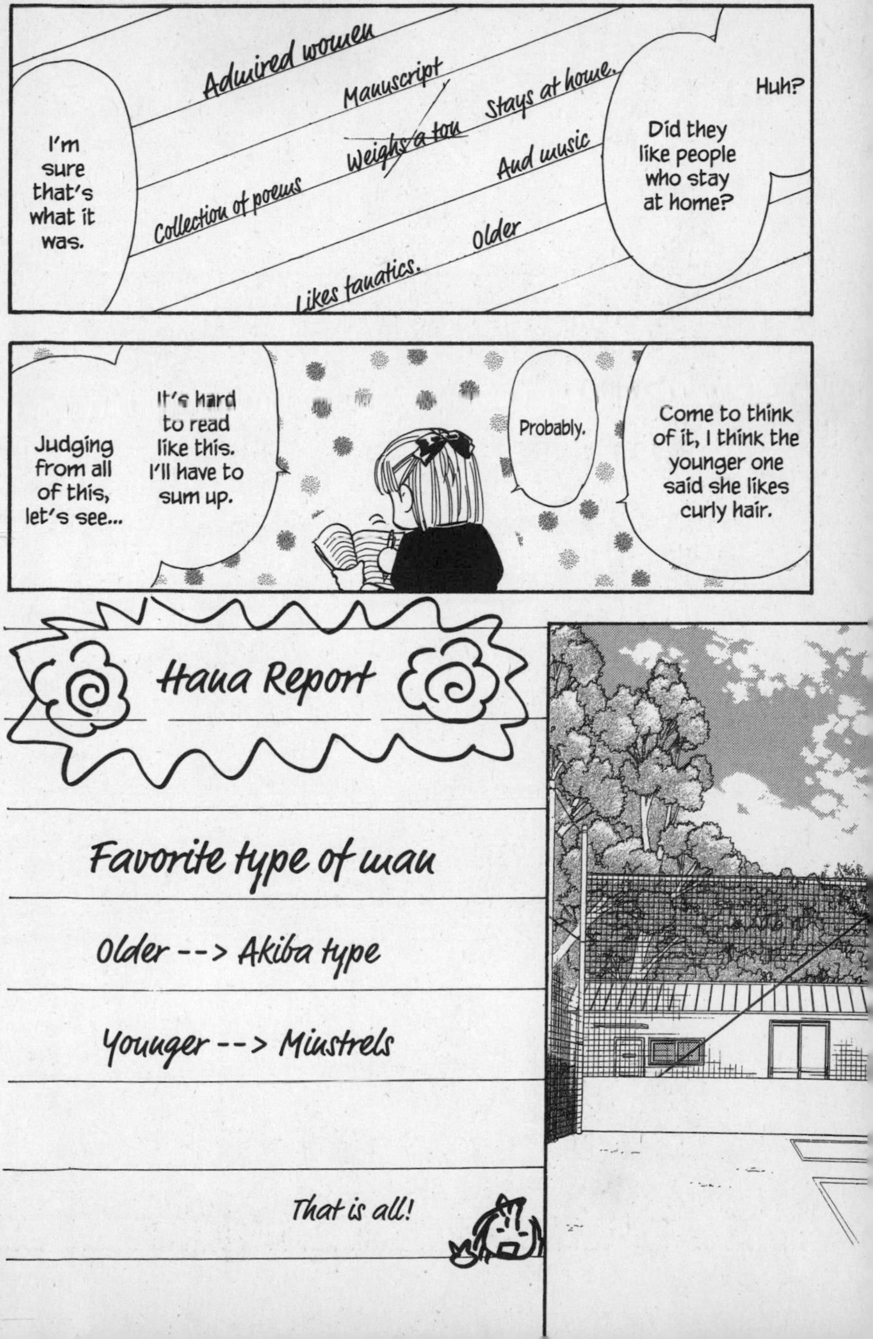
Huh?
Did they like people who stay at home?
Stays at home.
And music
Older
Admired women
Manuscript
Weighs a ton
Collection of poems
Likes fanatics.
I'm sure that's what it was.
Come to think of it, I think the younger one said she likes curly hair.
Probably.
It's hard to read like this. I'll have to sum up.
Judging from all of this, let's see...
Hana Report
Favorite type of man
Older --> Akiba type
Younger --> Minstrels
That is all!

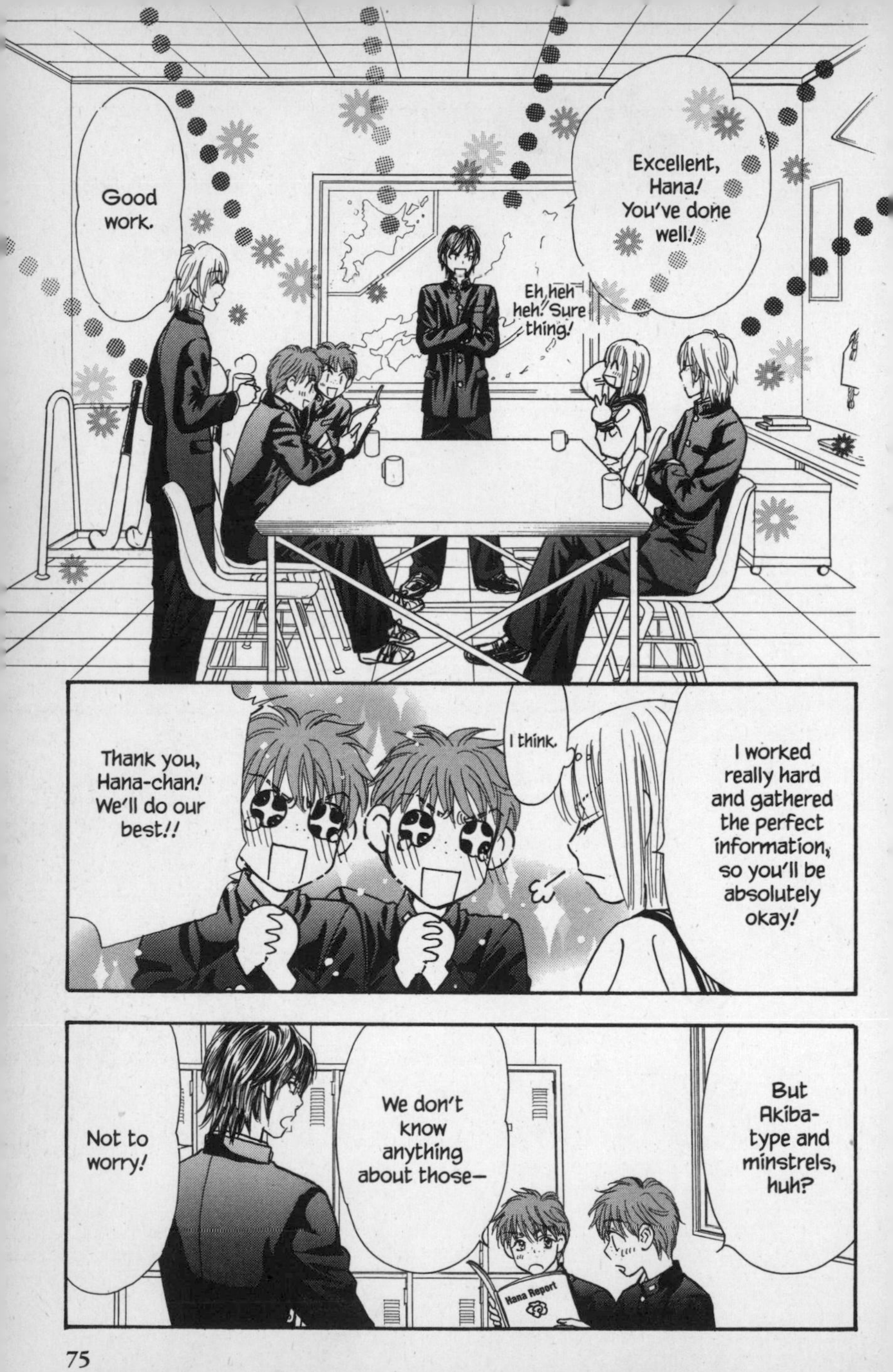
Excellent, Hana! You've done well!
Eh heh heh! Sure thing!
Good work.
I worked really hard and gathered the perfect information, so you'll be absolutely okay!
I think.
Thank you, Hana-chan! We'll do our best!!
But Akiba-type and minstrels, huh?
We don't know anything about those—
Not to worry!
Hana Report

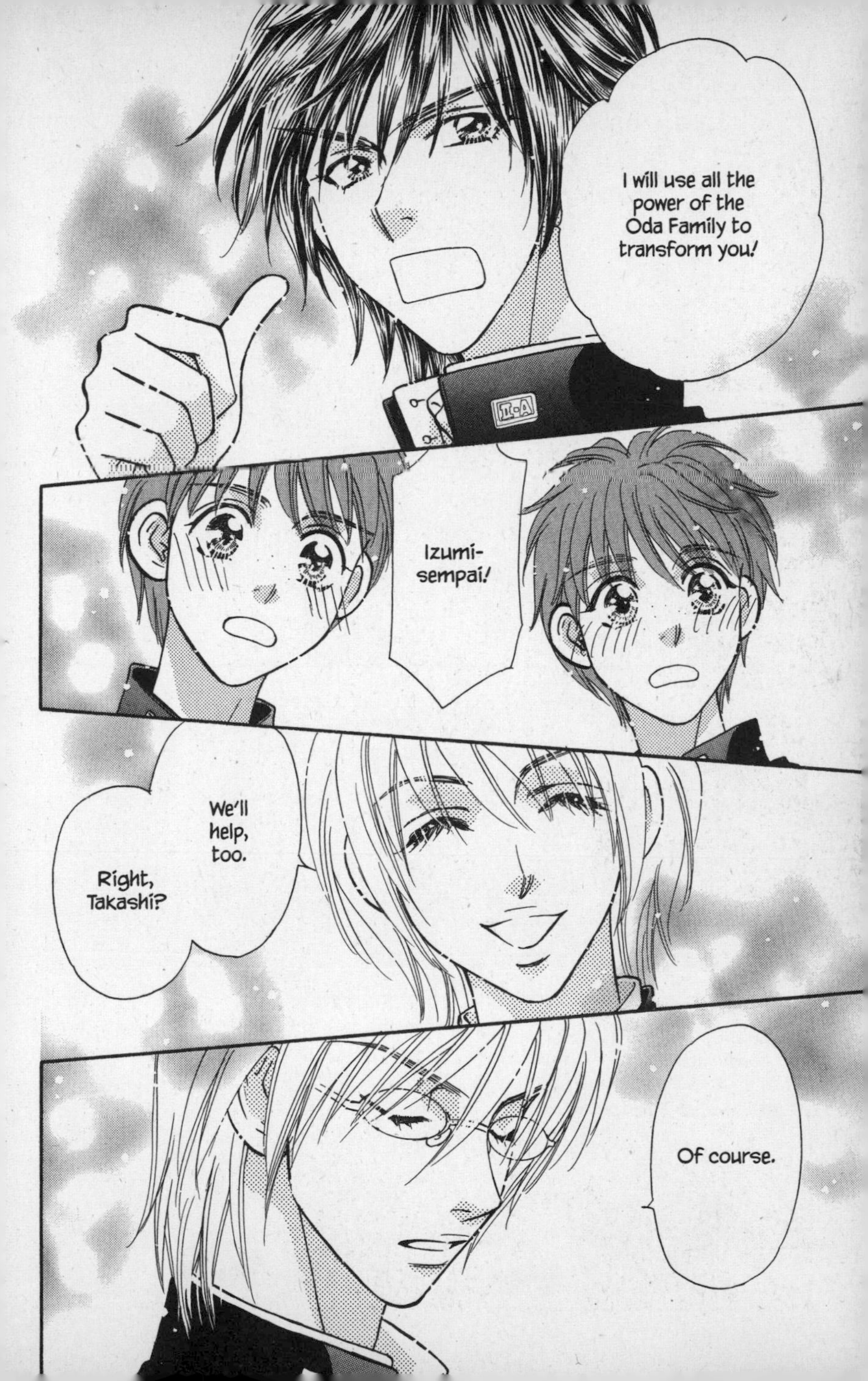
I will use all the power of the Oda Family to transform you!
Izumi-sempai!
We'll help, too.
Right, Takashi?
Of course.

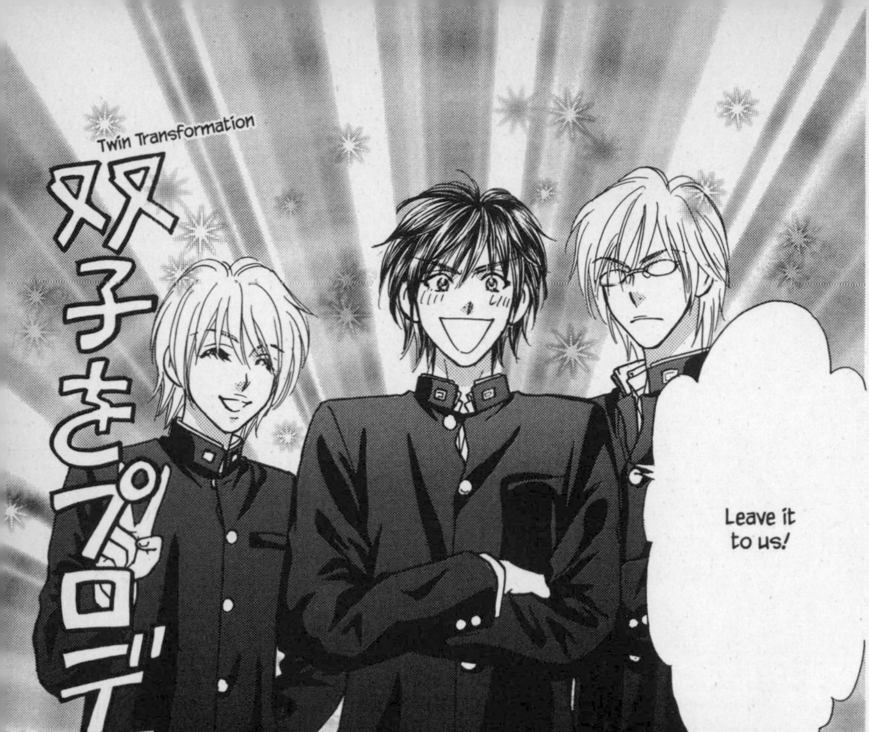
Twin Transformation
双子をプロデュース
Leave it to us!

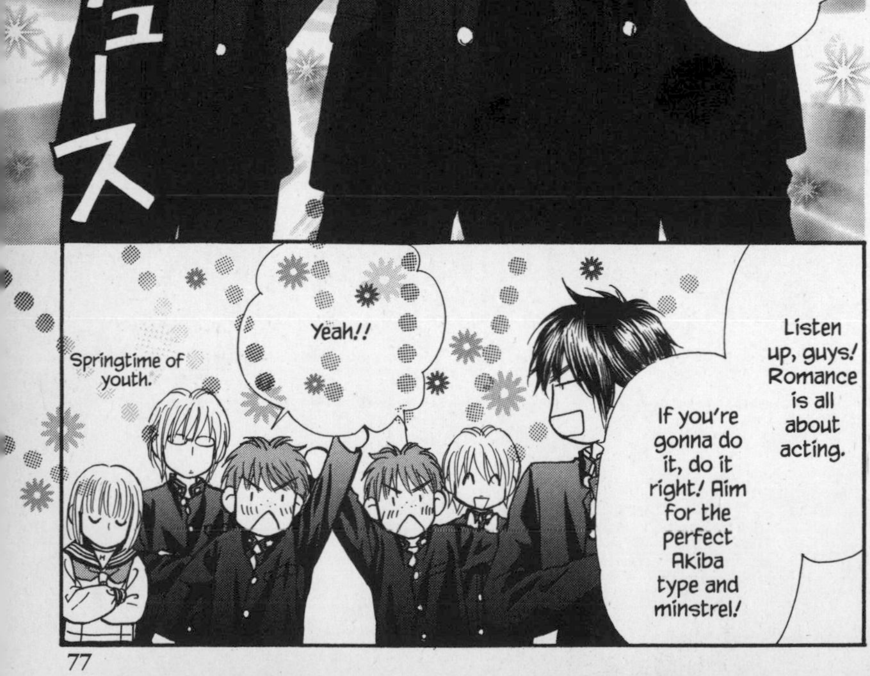
Listen up, guys! Romance is all about acting.
If you're gonna do it, do it right! Aim for the perfect Akiba type and minstrel!
Yeah!!
Springtime of youth.

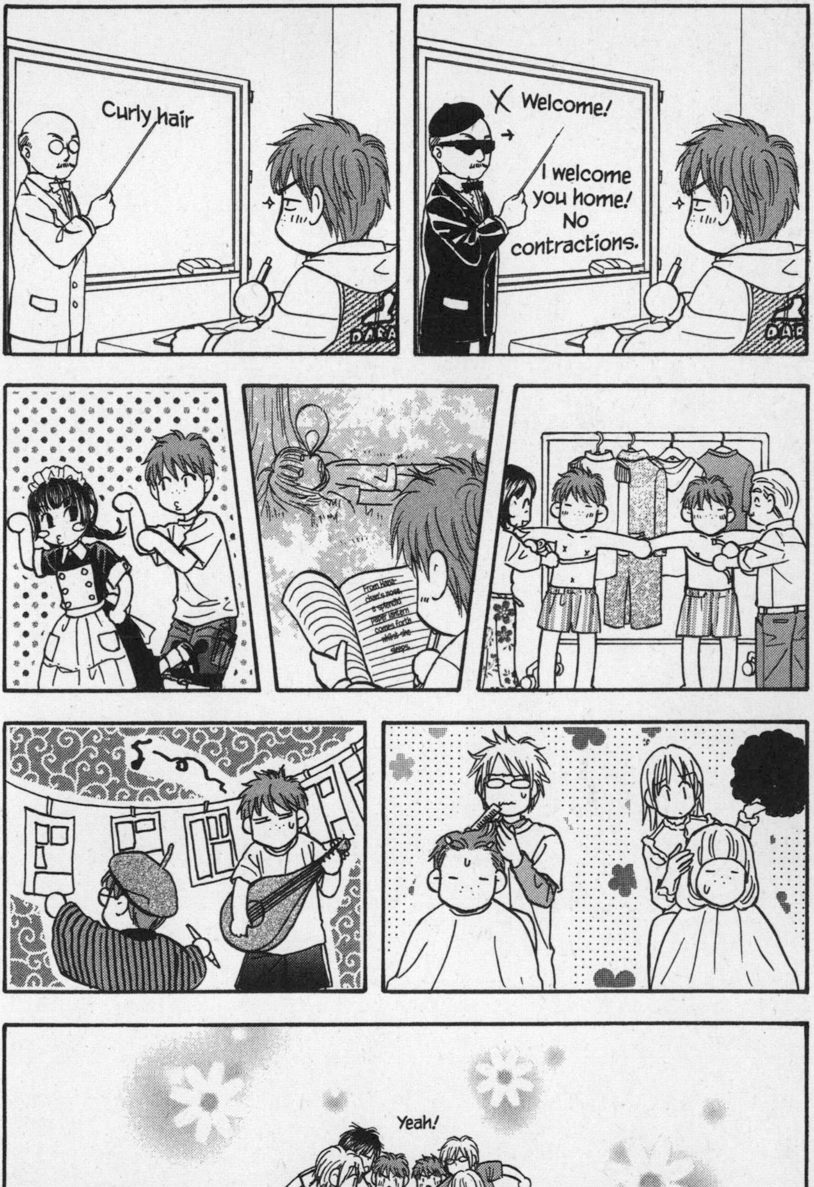
X Welcome!
→ I welcome you home! No contractions.
Curly hair
From Hana-chan's nose, a splendid paper lantern comes forth whilst she sleeps.
Yeah!

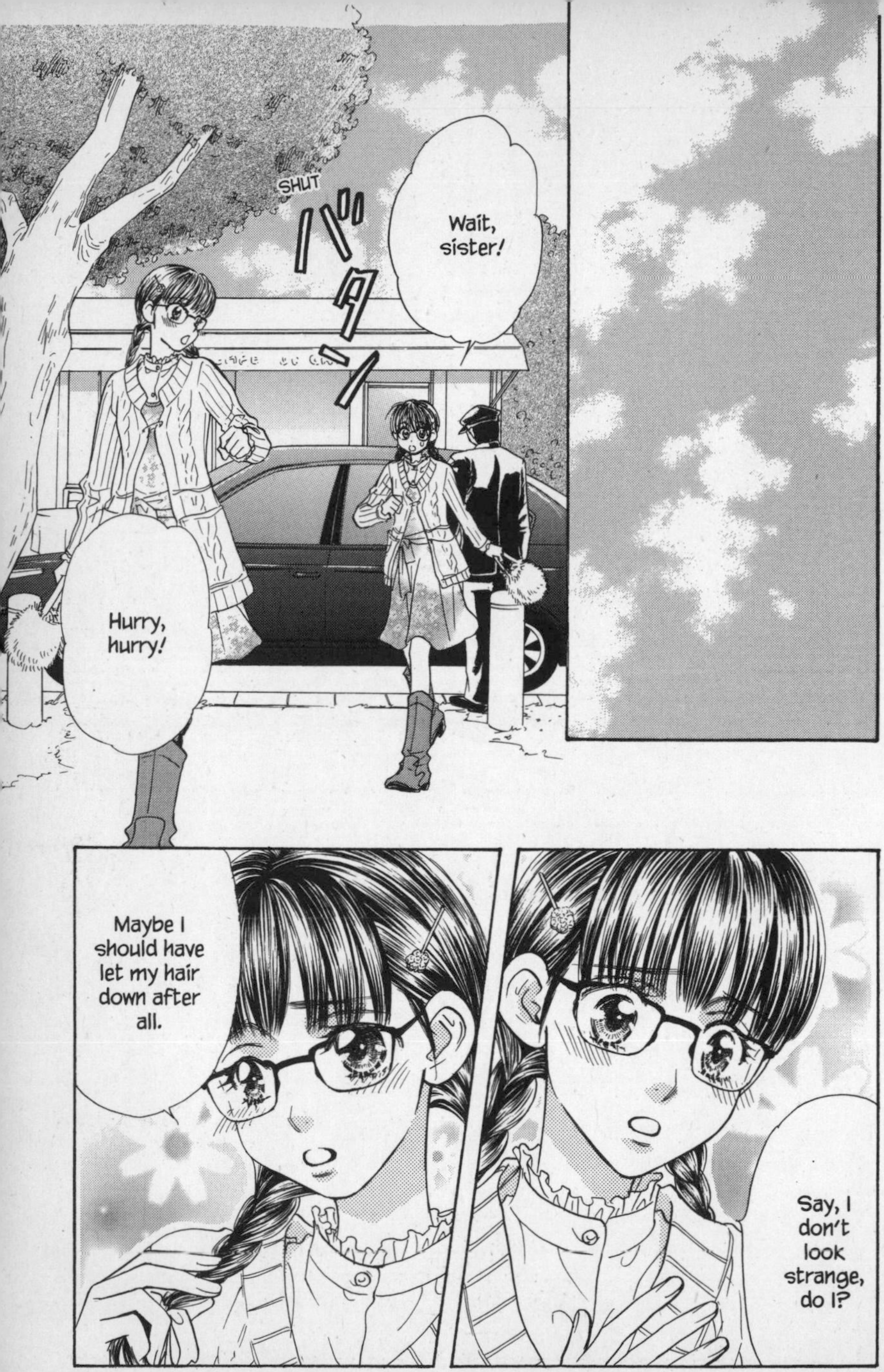
Wait, sister!
SHUT
Hurry, hurry!
Say, I don't look strange, do I?
Maybe I should have let my hair down after all.

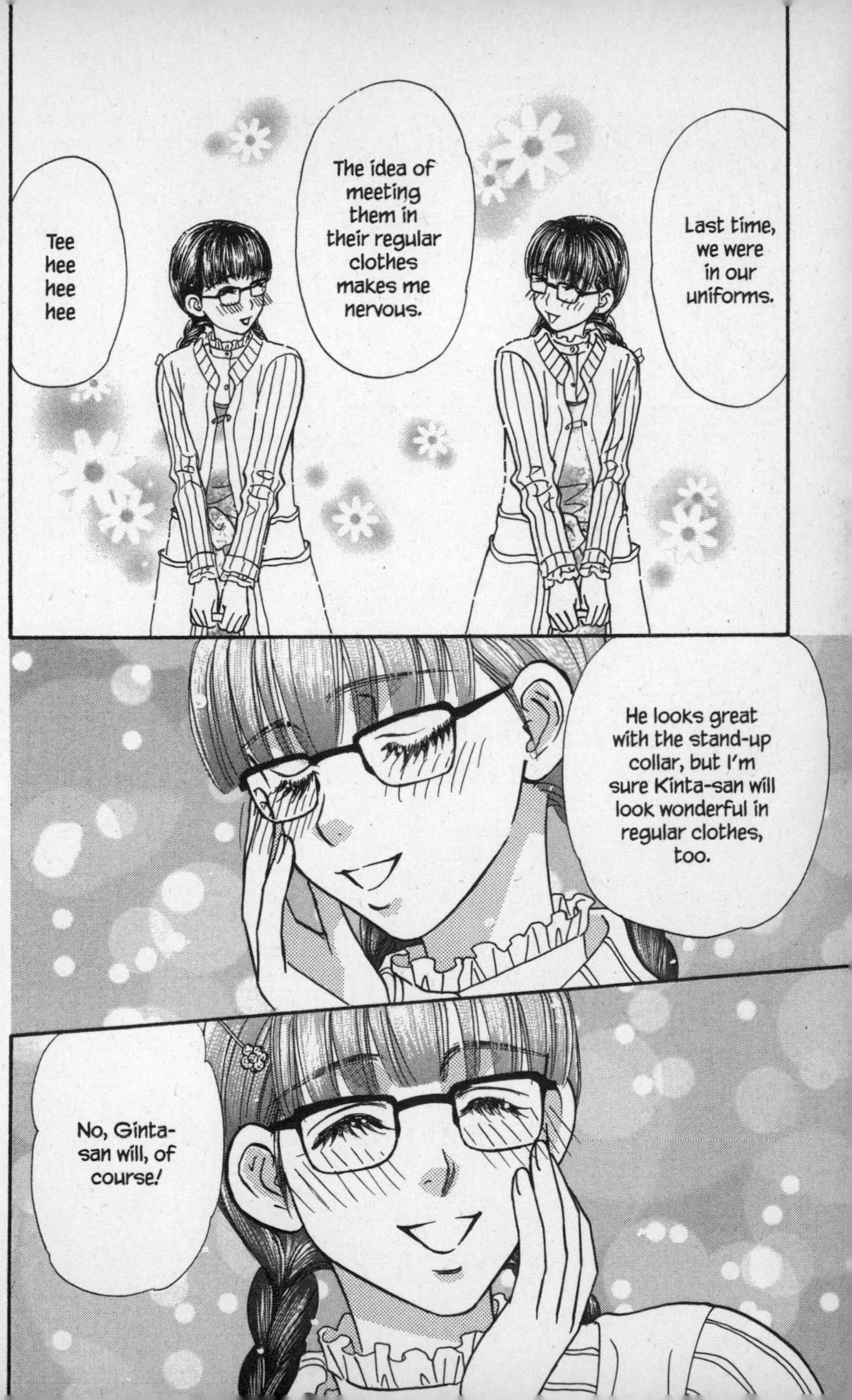
Last time, we were in our uniforms.
The idea of meeting them in their regular clothes makes me nervous.
Tee hee hee hee
He looks great with the stand-up collar, but I'm sure Kinta-san will look wonderful in regular clothes, too.
No, Ginta-san will, of course!

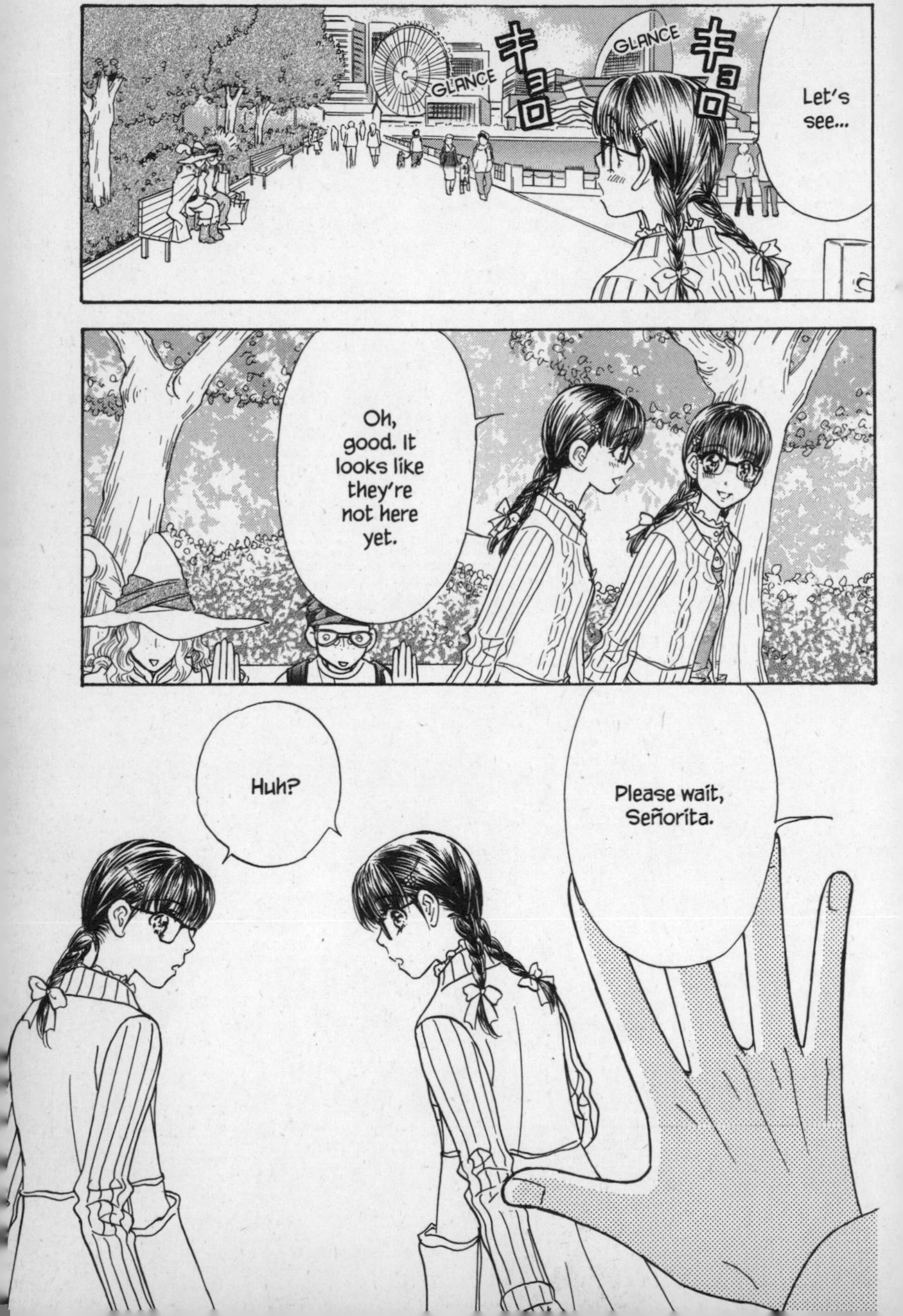
Let's see...
キョロ
GLANCE
キョロ
GLANCE
Oh, good. It looks like they're not here yet.
Please wait, Señorita.
Huh?

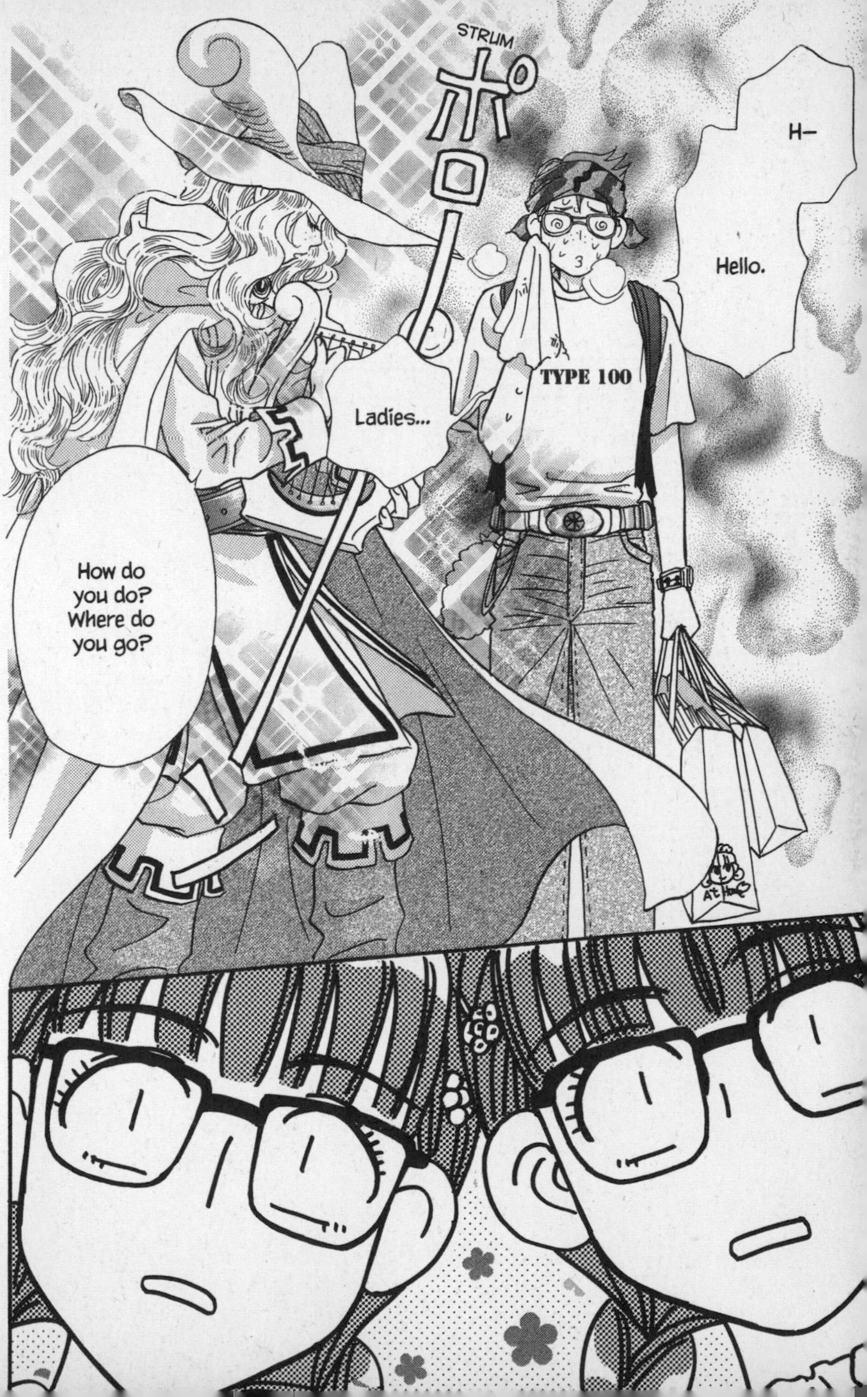
STRUM
ポロー
H—
Hello.
Ladies...
How do you do? Where do you go?
TYPE 100
At Home

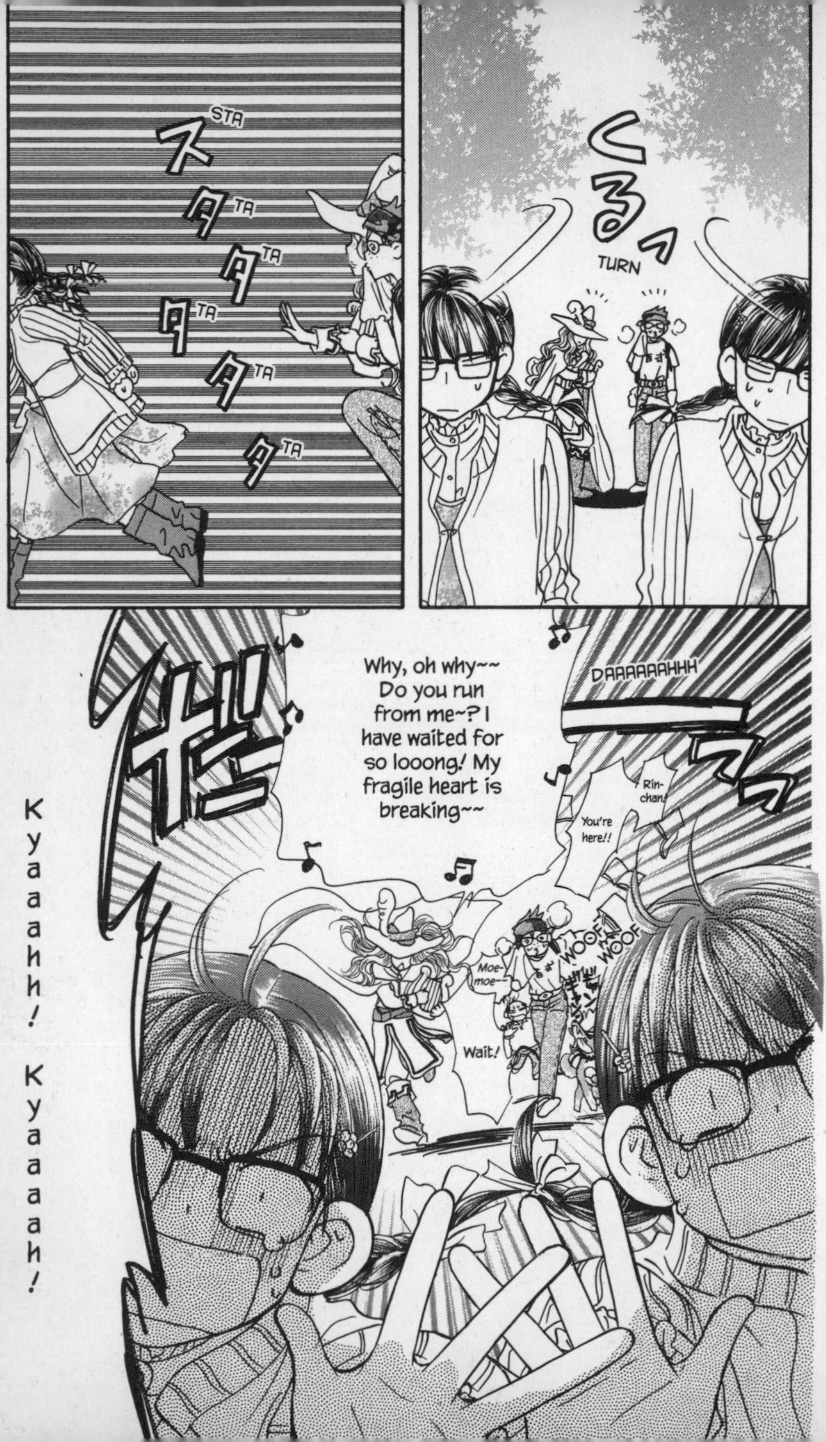
くる
TURN
STA
TA
TA
TA
TA
TA
DAAAAAAHHH
Rin-chan!
You're here!!
Why, oh why~~ Do you run from me~? I have waited for so looong! My fragile heart is breaking~~
Moe-moe~~
Wait!
WOOF WOOF
Kyaaaahh! Kyaaaaaah!

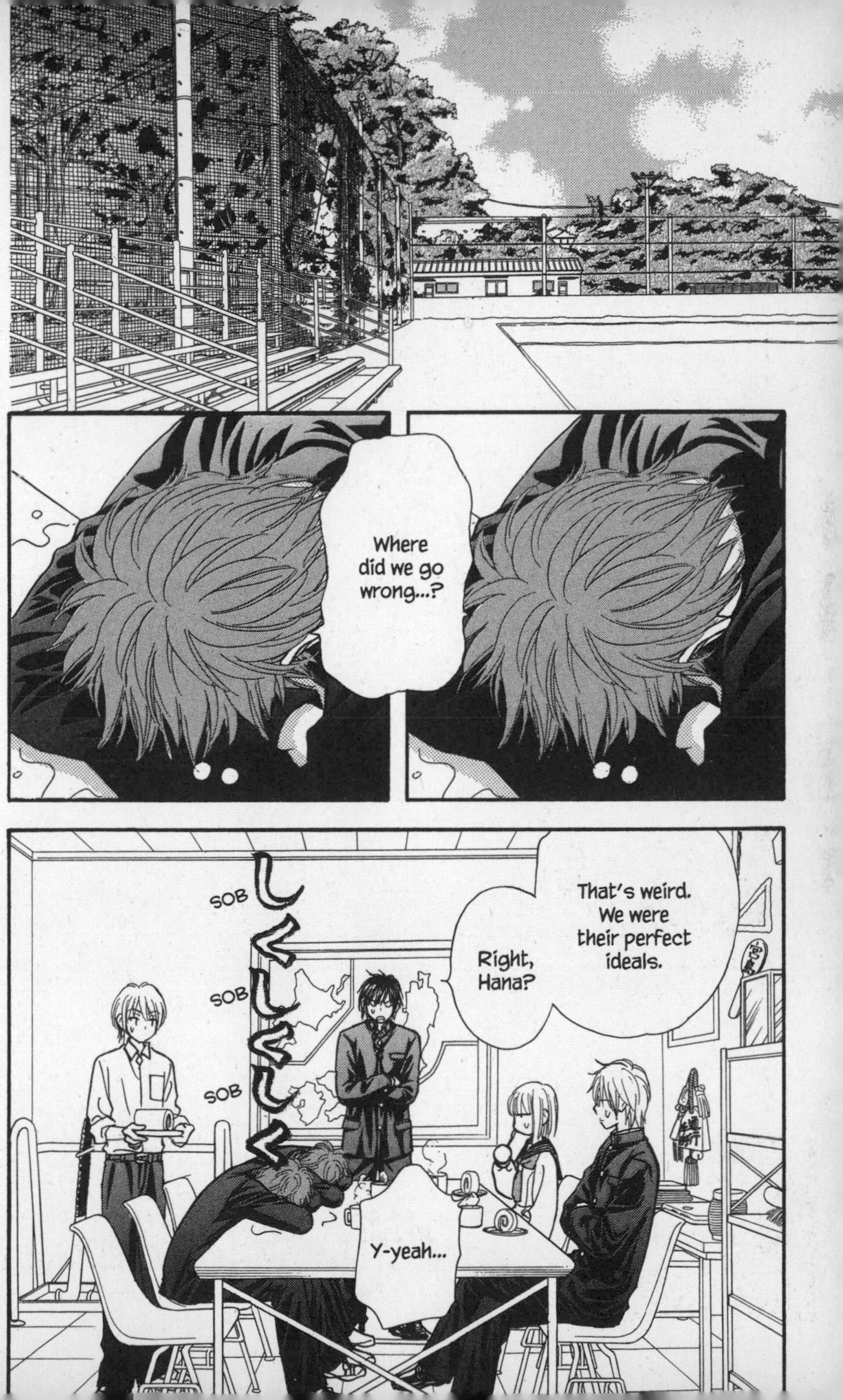
Where did we go wrong...?
That's weird. We were their perfect ideals.
Right, Hana?
SOB
SOB
SOB
Y-yeah...

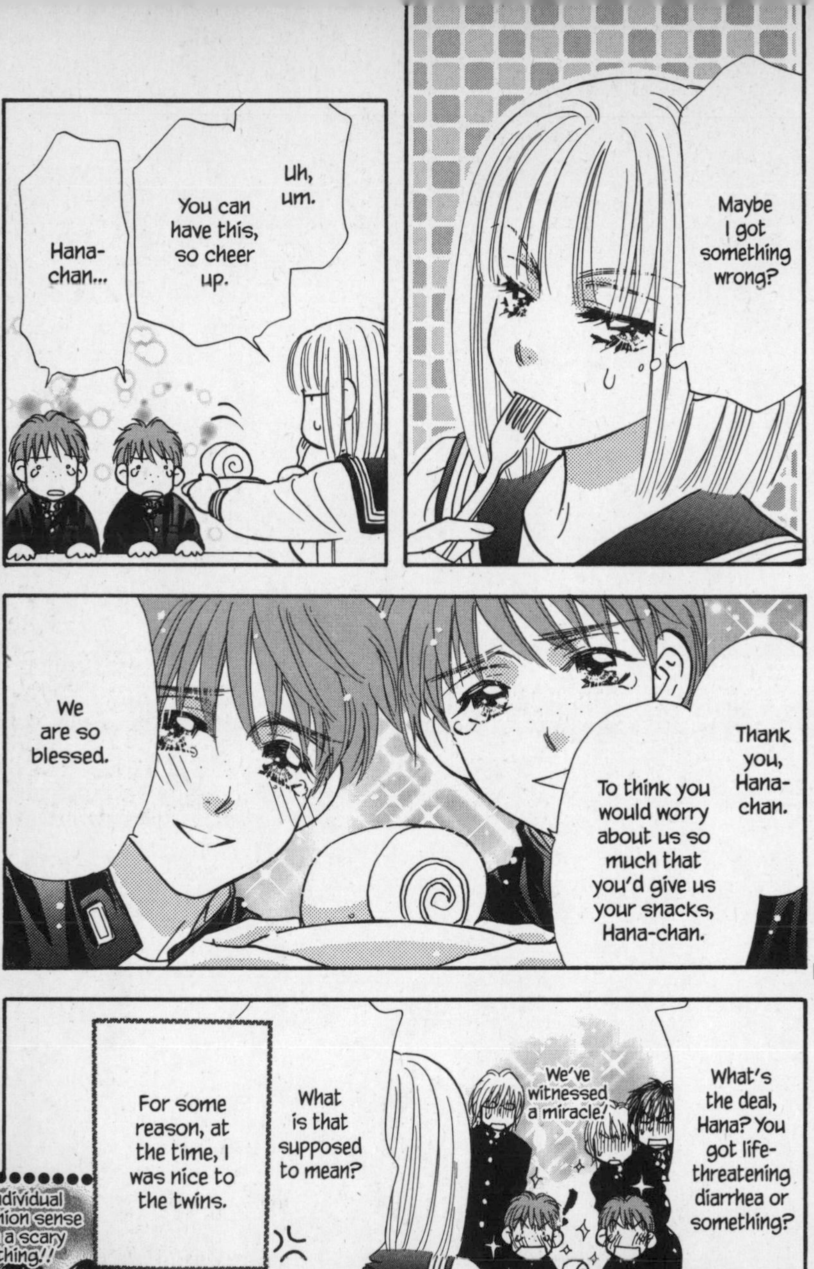
Maybe I got something wrong?
Uh, um.
You can have this, so cheer up.
Hana-chan...
Thank you, Hana-chan.
To think you would worry about us so much that you'd give us your snacks, Hana-chan.
We are so blessed.
What's the deal, Hana? You got life-threatening diarrhea or something?
We've witnessed a miracle!
What is that supposed to mean?
For some reason, at the time, I was nice to the twins.

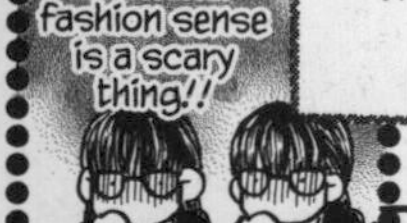
Individual fashion sense is a scary thing!!

The End

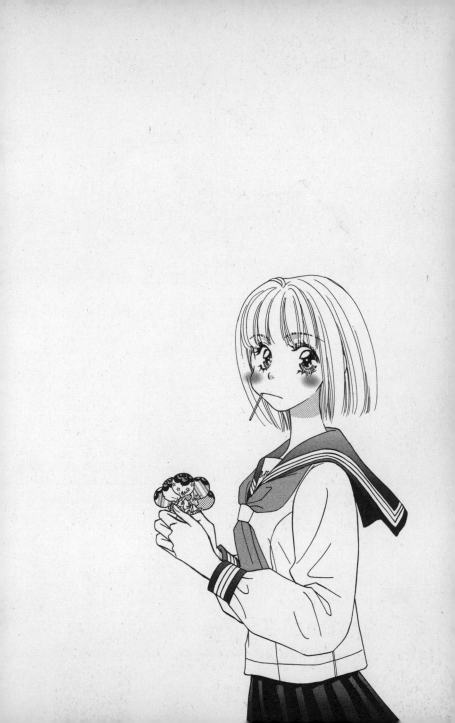

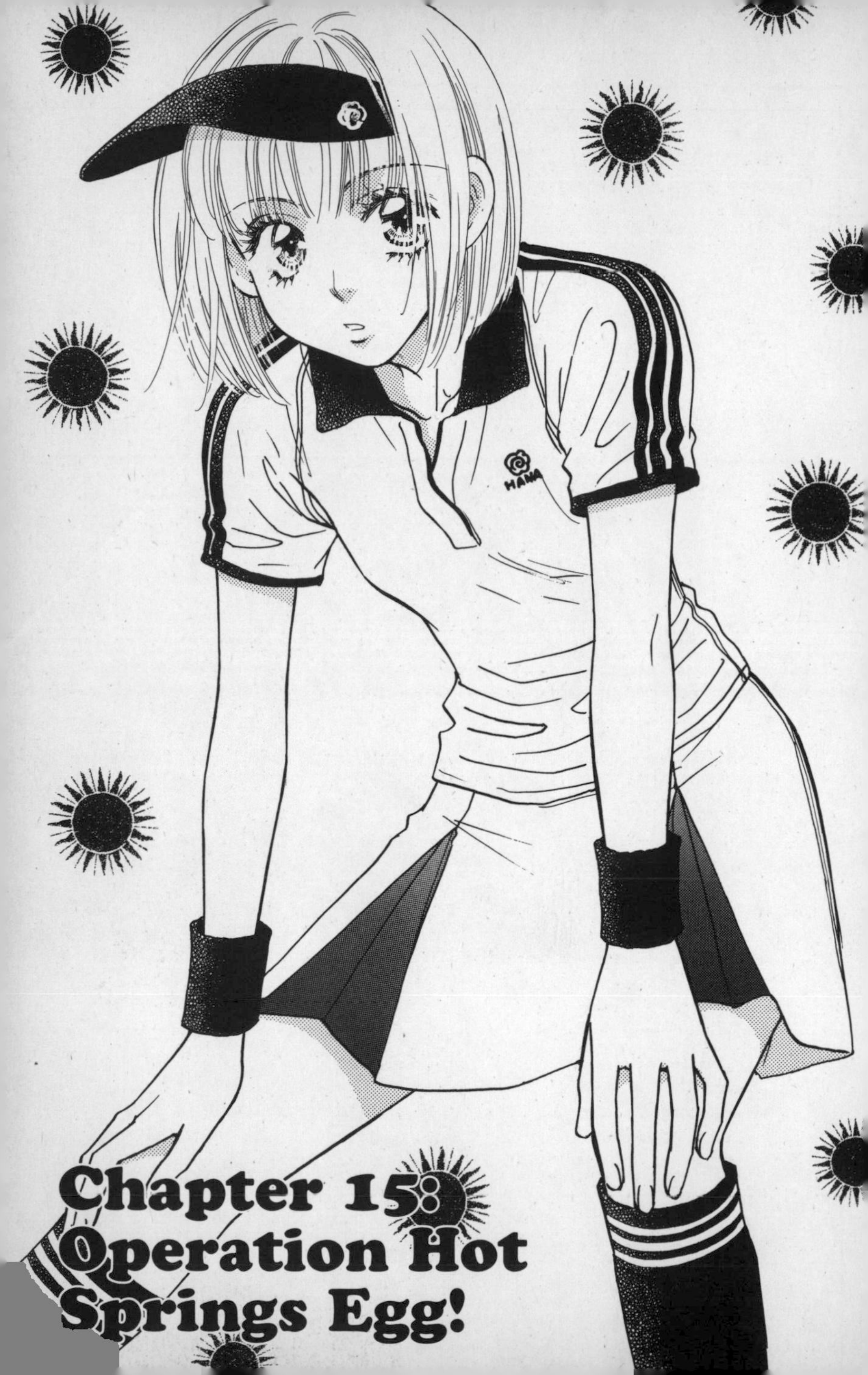
HANA

Chapter 15: Operation Hot Springs Egg!

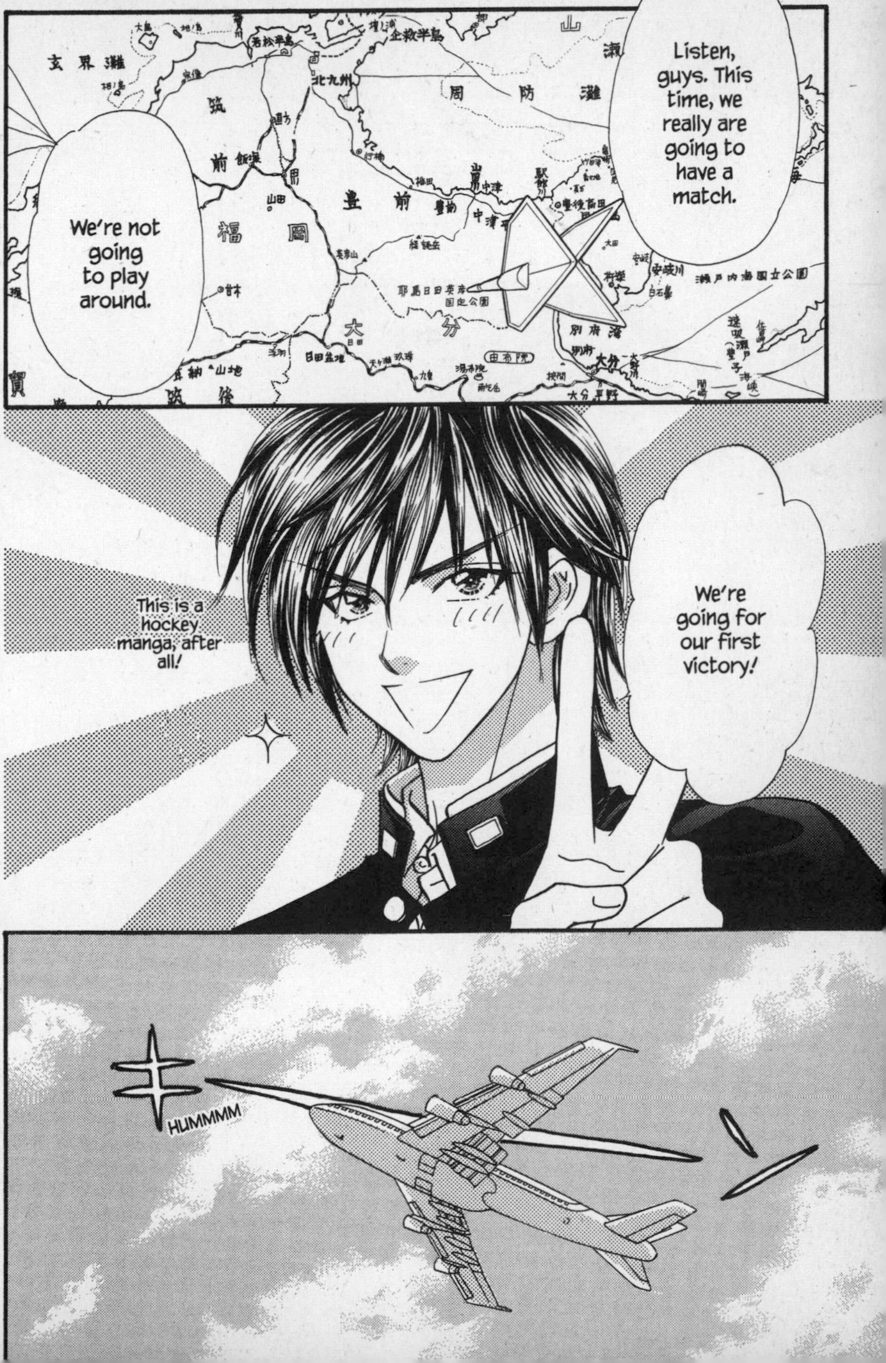
Listen, guys. This time, we really are going to have a match.
We're not going to play around.
玄界灘
周防灘
北九州
豊前
福岡
大分
We're going for our first victory!
This is a hockey manga, after all!
HUMMMM

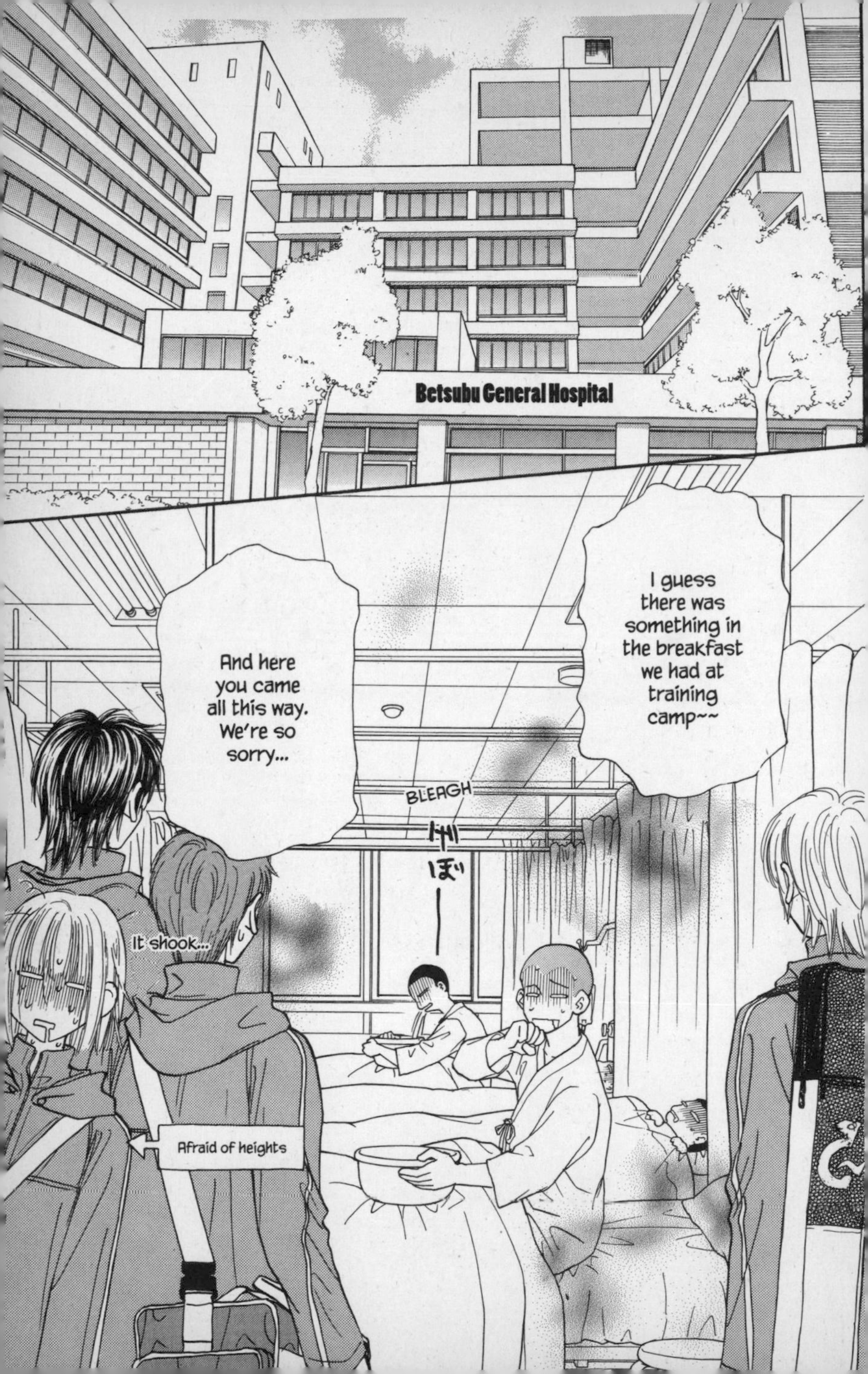
Betsubu General Hospital
I guess there was something in the breakfast we had at training camp~~
And here you came all this way. We're so sorry...
BLEAGH
It shook...
Afraid of heights

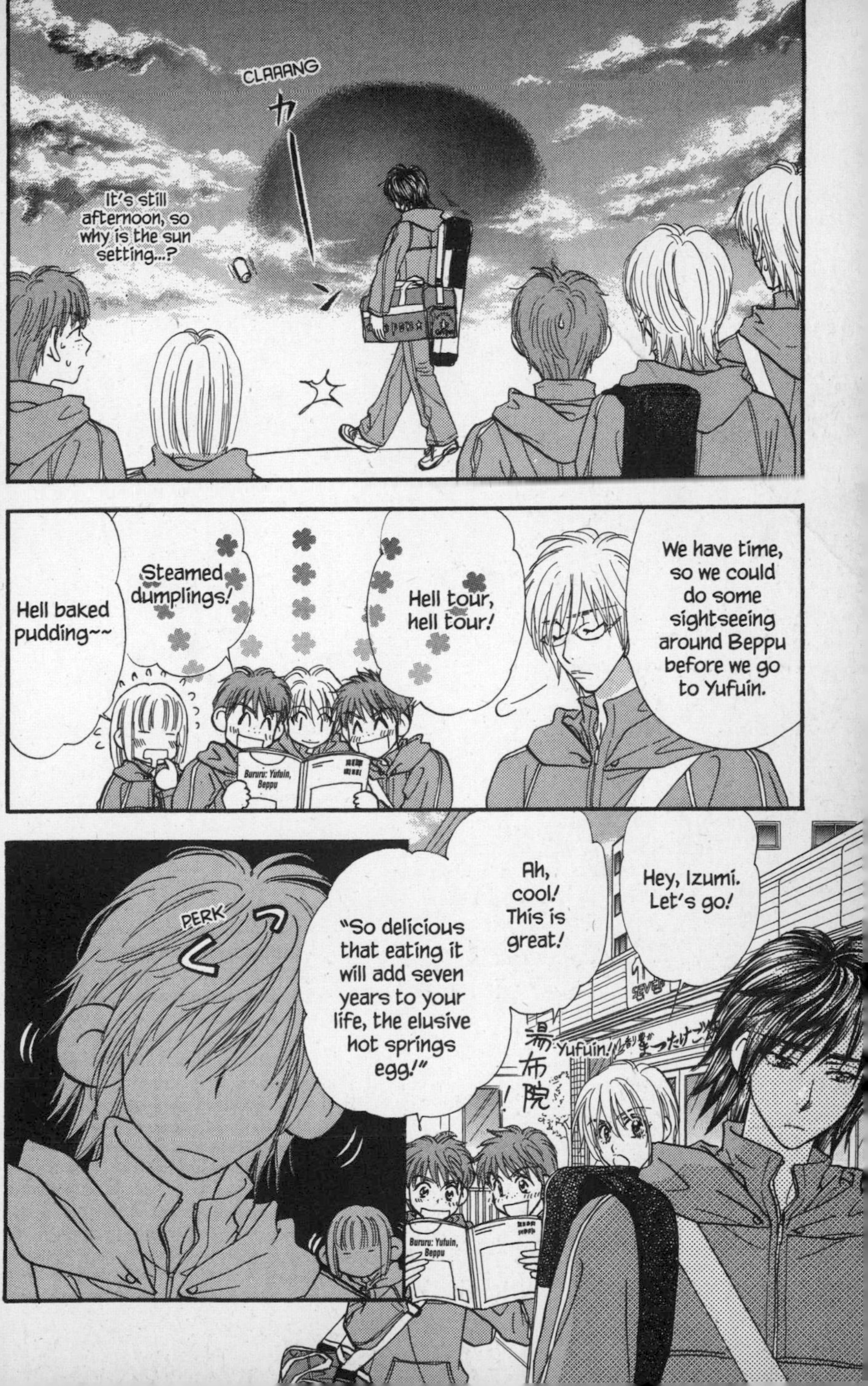
CLAAANG
It's still afternoon, so why is the sun setting...?
We have time, so we could do some sightseeing around Beppu before we go to Yufuin.
Hell tour, hell tour!
Steamed dumplings!
Hell baked pudding~~
Bururu: Yufuin, Beppu
Hey, Izumi. Let's go!
Ah, cool! This is great!
Yufuin!
"So delicious that eating it will add seven years to your life, the elusive hot springs egg!"
PERK
Bururu: Yufuin, Beppu

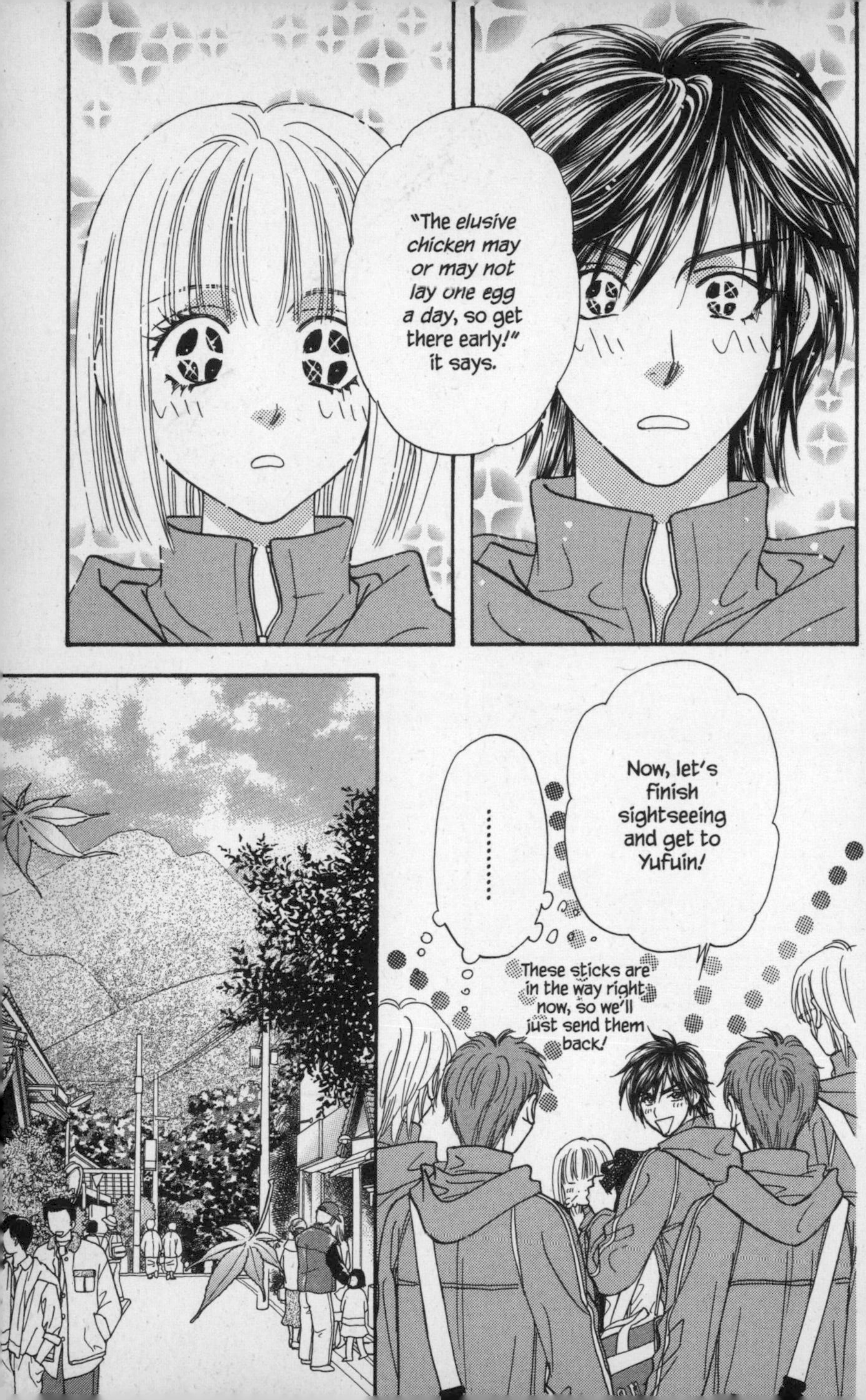
"The *elusive* chicken may or may not lay one egg a day, so get there early!" it says.
Now, let's finish sightseeing and get to Yufuin!
....
These sticks are in the way right now, so we'll just send them back!

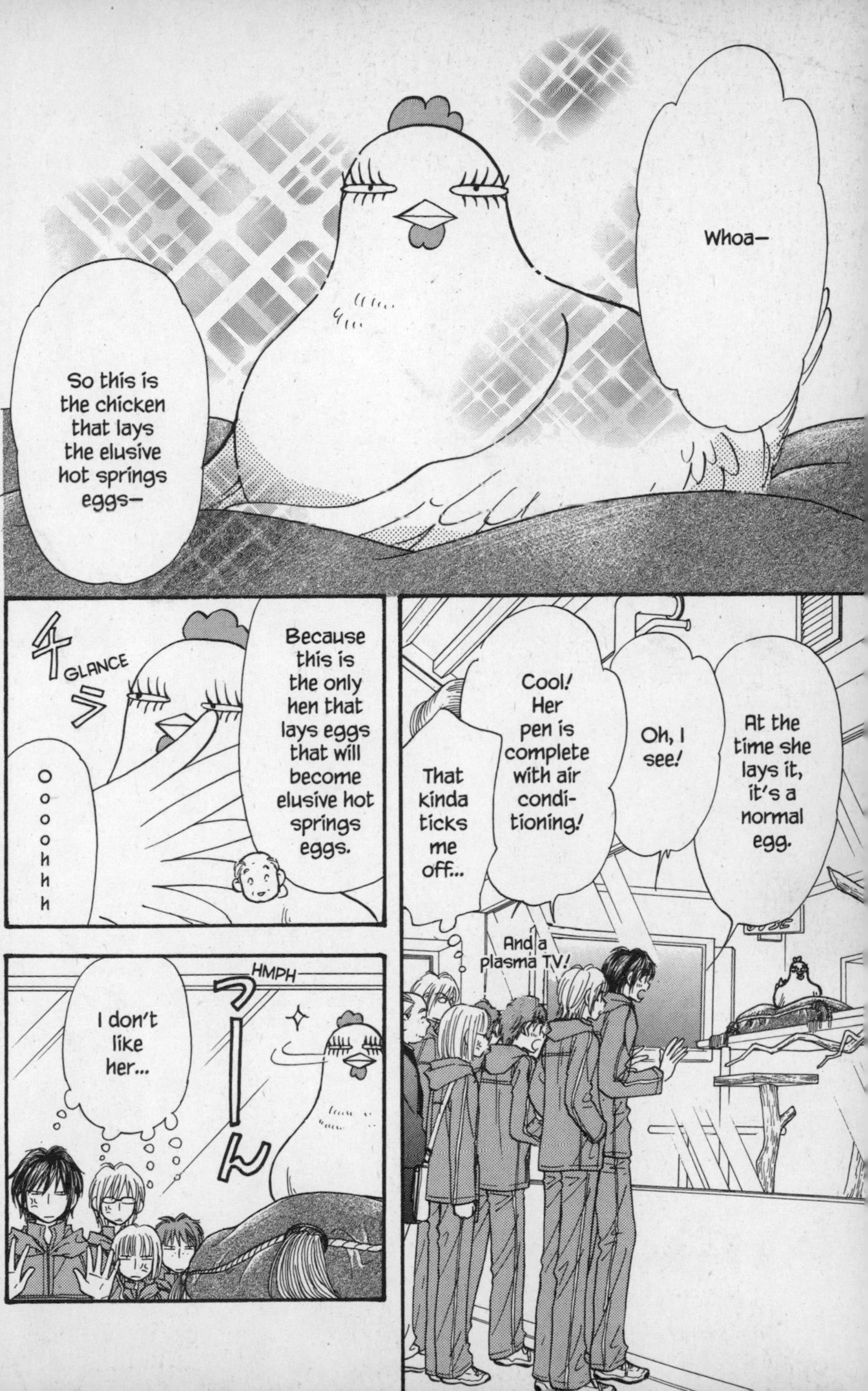
Whoa—
So this is the chicken that lays the elusive hot springs eggs—
At the time she lays it, it's a normal egg.
Oh, I see!
Cool! Her pen is complete with air conditioning!
That kinda ticks me off...
And a plasma TV!
Because this is the only hen that lays eggs that will become elusive hot springs eggs.
GLANCE
Ooooohhh
HMPH
I don't like her...

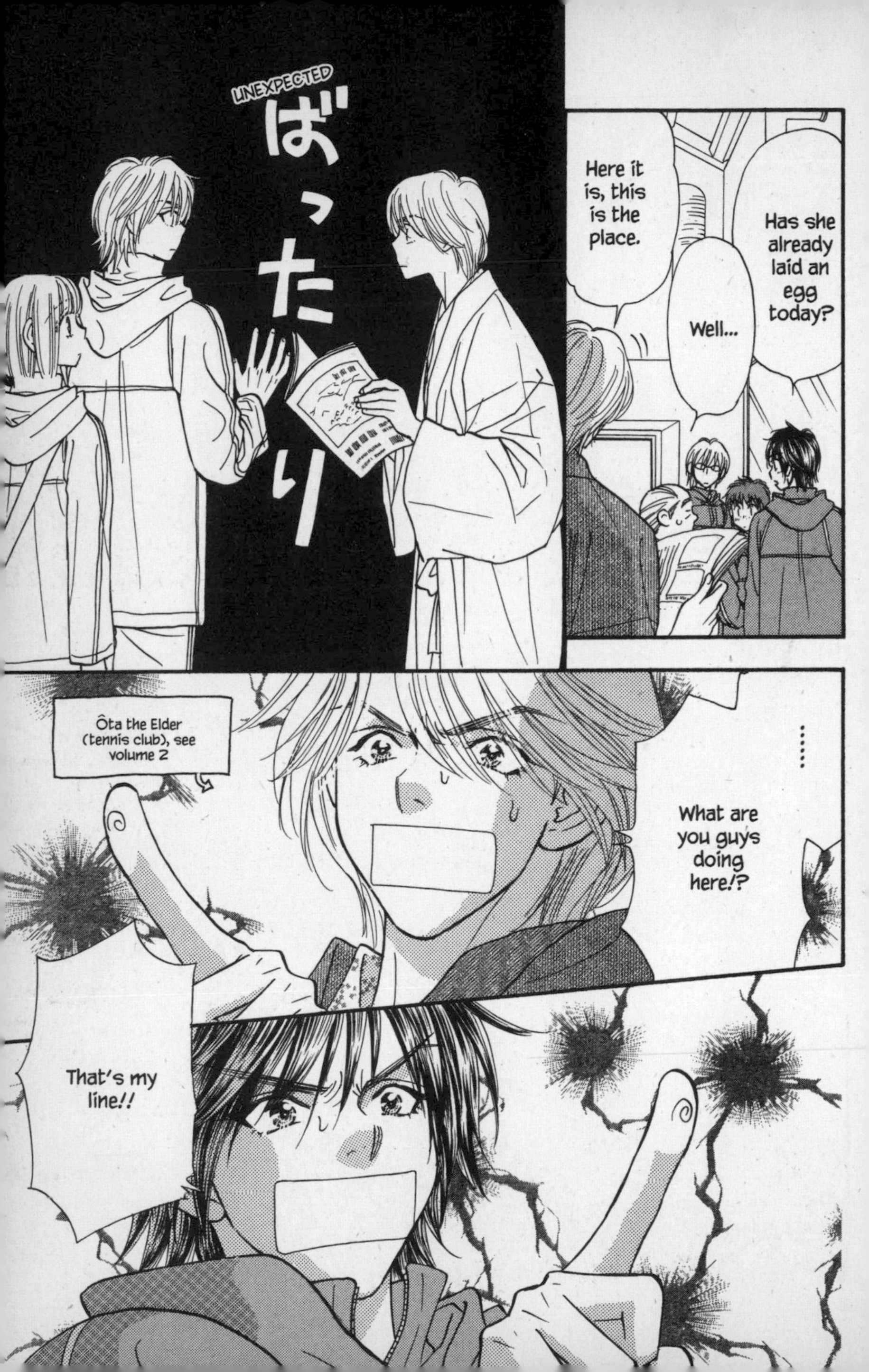
Here it is, this is the place.
Has she already laid an egg today?
Well...
UNEXPECTED
ばったり
......
What are you guys doing here!?
Ôta the Elder (tennis club), see volume 2
That's my line!!

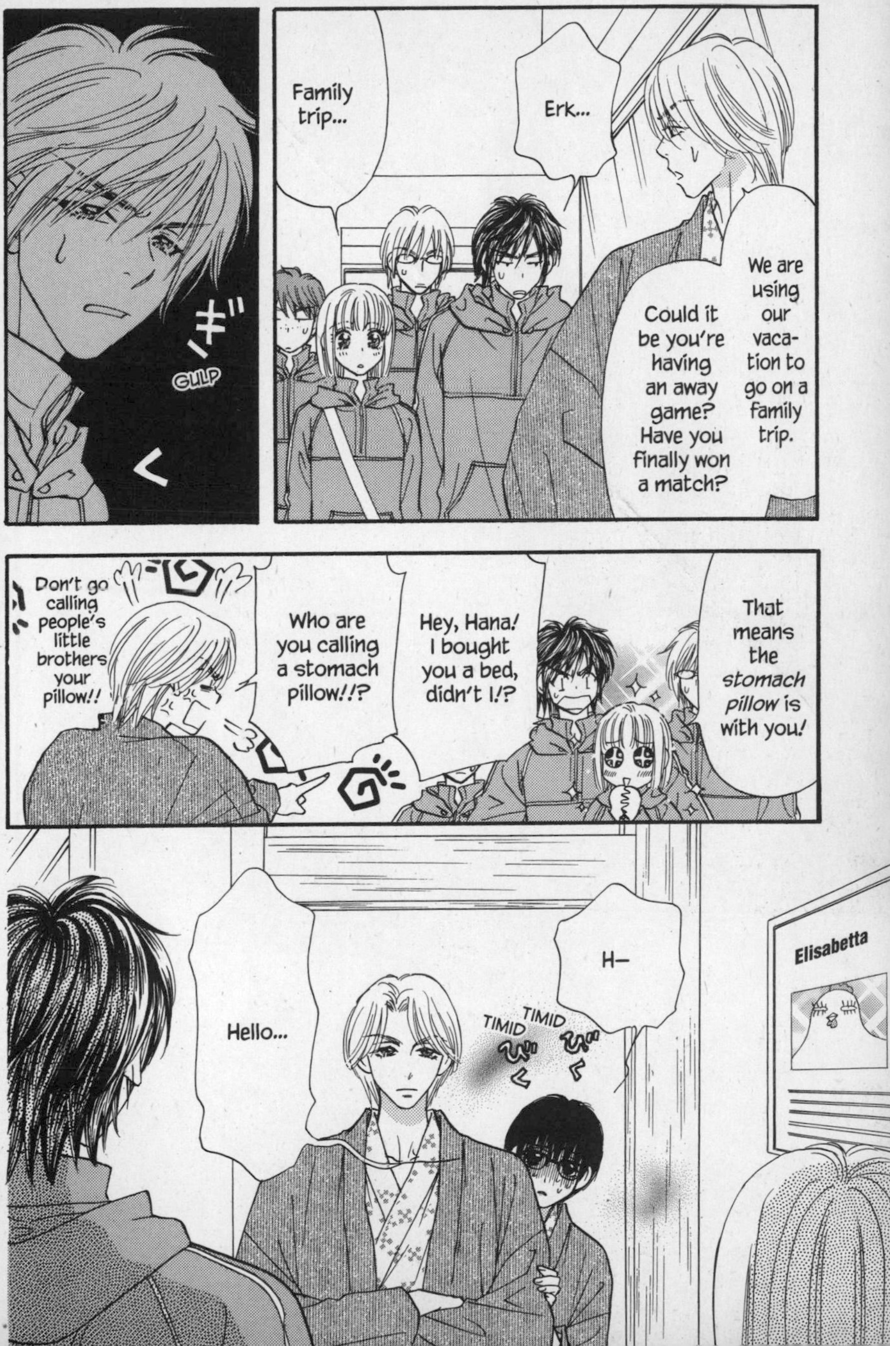
We are using our vacation to go on a family trip.
Could it be you're having an away game? Have you finally won a match?
Erk...
Family trip...
GULP
That means the stomach pillow is with you!
Hey, Hana! I bought you a bed, didn't I!?
Who are you calling a stomach pillow!!?
Don't go calling people's little brothers your pillow!!
Elisabetta
H—
TIMID TIMID
Hello...

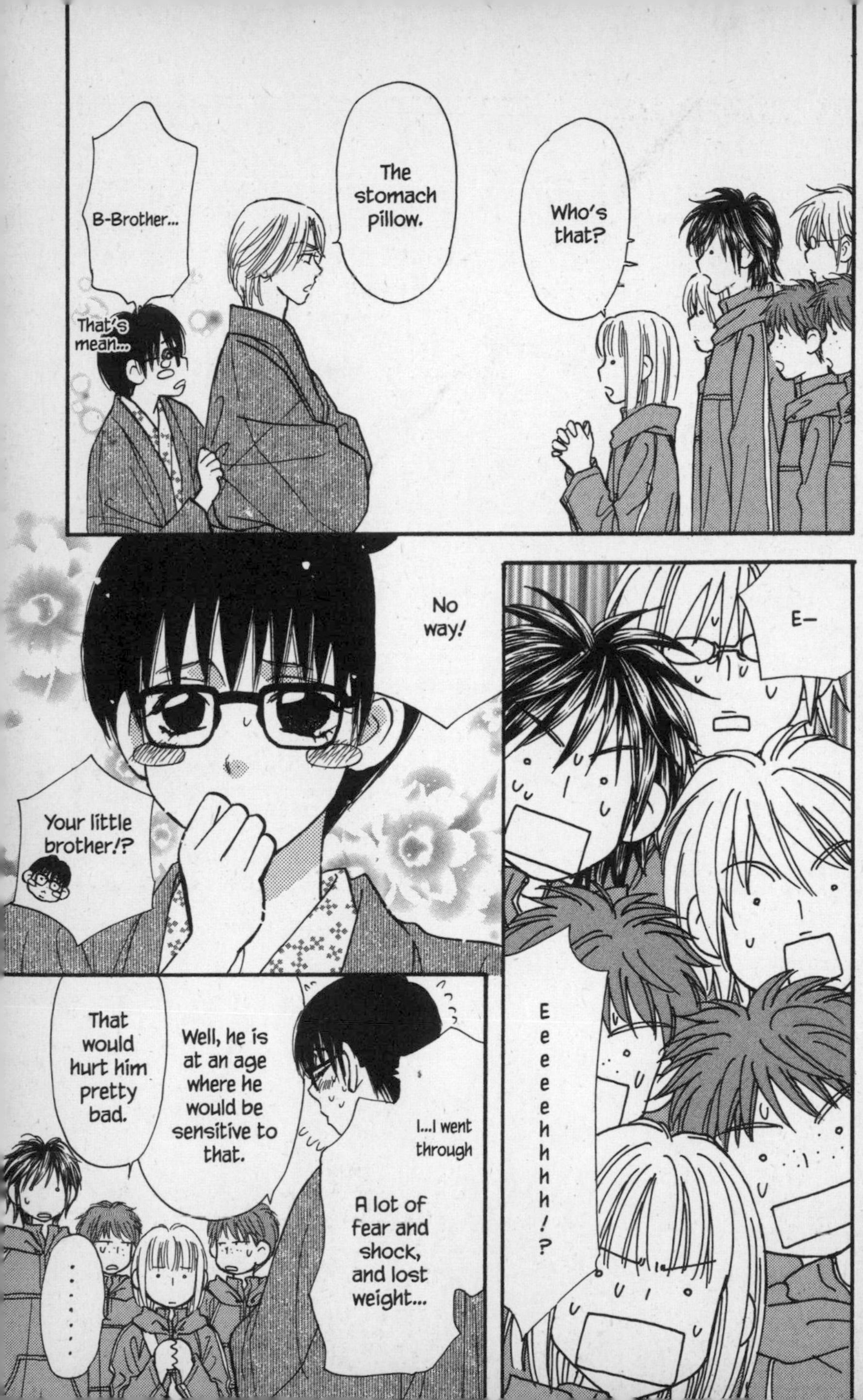
Who's that?
The stomach pillow.
B-Brother...
That's mean...
E—
Eeeeehhhh!?
No way!
Your little brother!?
I...I went through
A lot of fear and shock, and lost weight...
Well, he is at an age where he would be sensitive to that.
That would hurt him pretty bad.
......

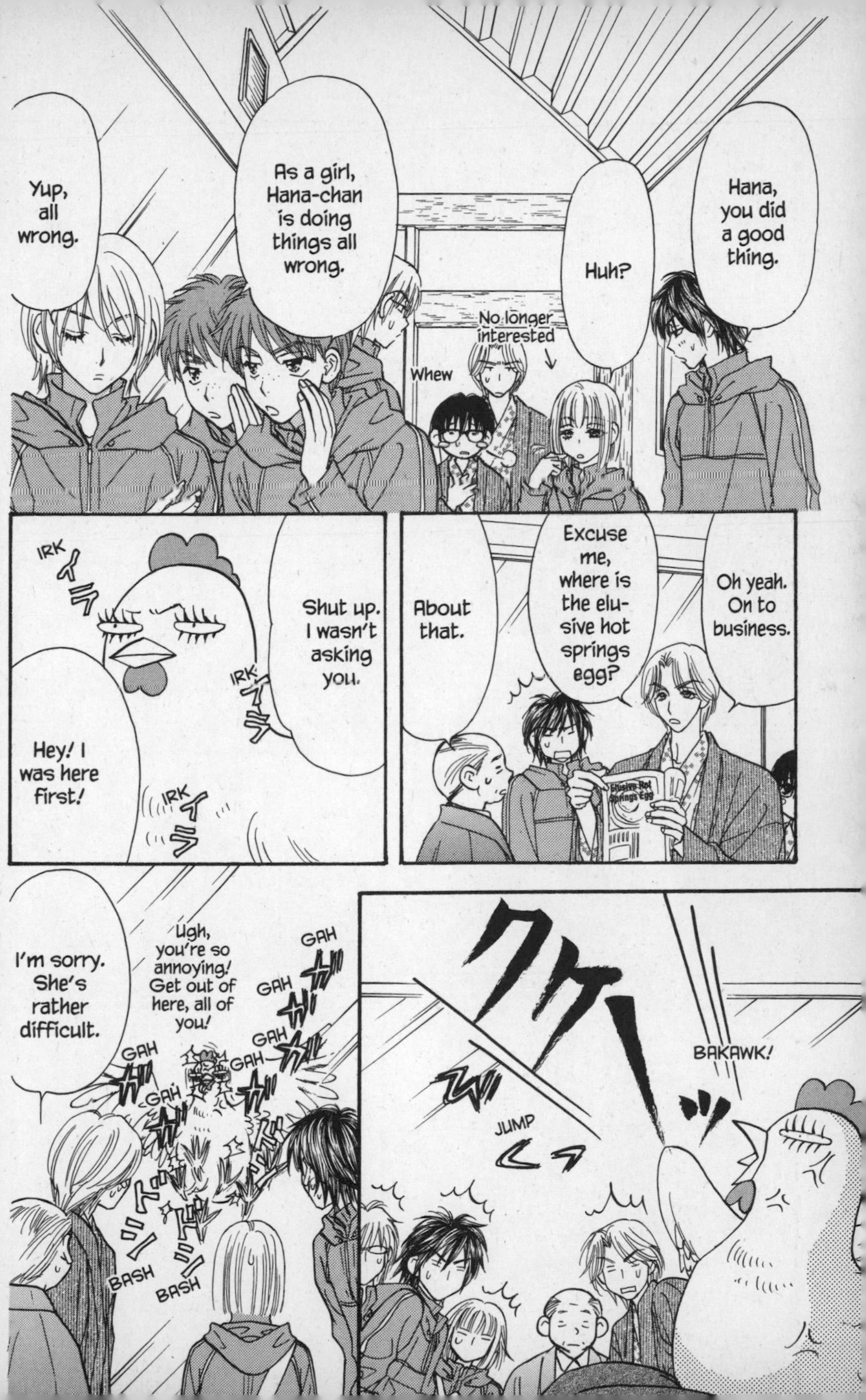
Hana, you did a good thing.
Huh?
No longer interested
Whew
As a girl, Hana-chan is doing things all wrong.
Yup, all wrong.
Oh yeah. On to business.
Excuse me, where is the elusive hot springs egg?
Elusive Hot Springs Egg
About that.
IRK
Shut up. I wasn't asking you.
IRK
Hey! I was here first!
IRK
BAKAWK!
JUMP
Ugh, you're so annoying! Get out of here, all of you!
GAH
GAH
GAH
GAH
GAH
GAH
BASH
BASH
I'm sorry. She's rather difficult.

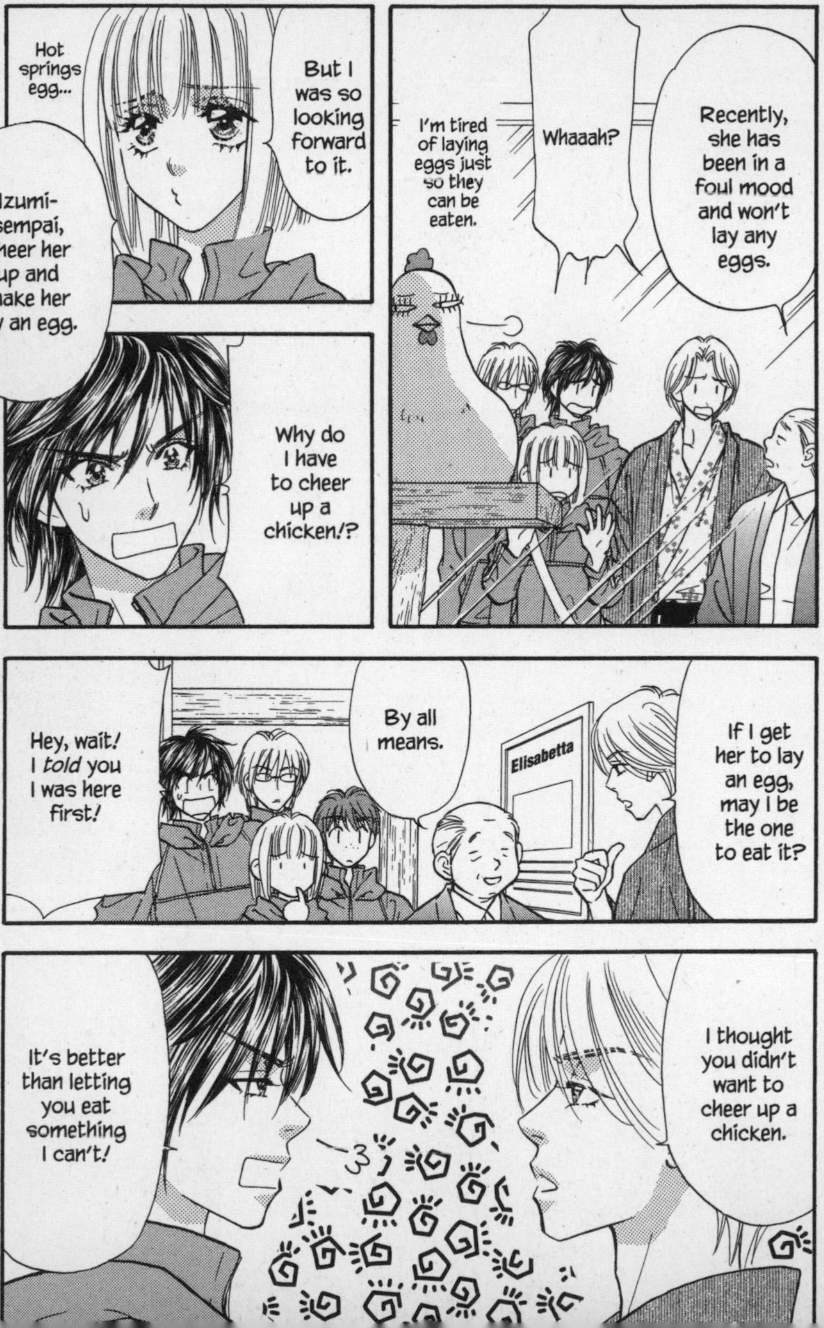
Recently, she has been in a foul mood and won't lay any eggs.
Whaaah?
I'm tired of laying eggs just so they can be eaten.
But I was so looking forward to it.
Hot springs egg...
Izumi-sempai, cheer her up and make her lay an egg.
Why do I have to cheer up a chicken!?
If I get her to lay an egg, may I be the one to eat it?
Elisabetta
By all means.
Hey, wait! I *told* you I was here first!
I thought you didn't want to cheer up a chicken.
It's better than letting you eat something I can't!

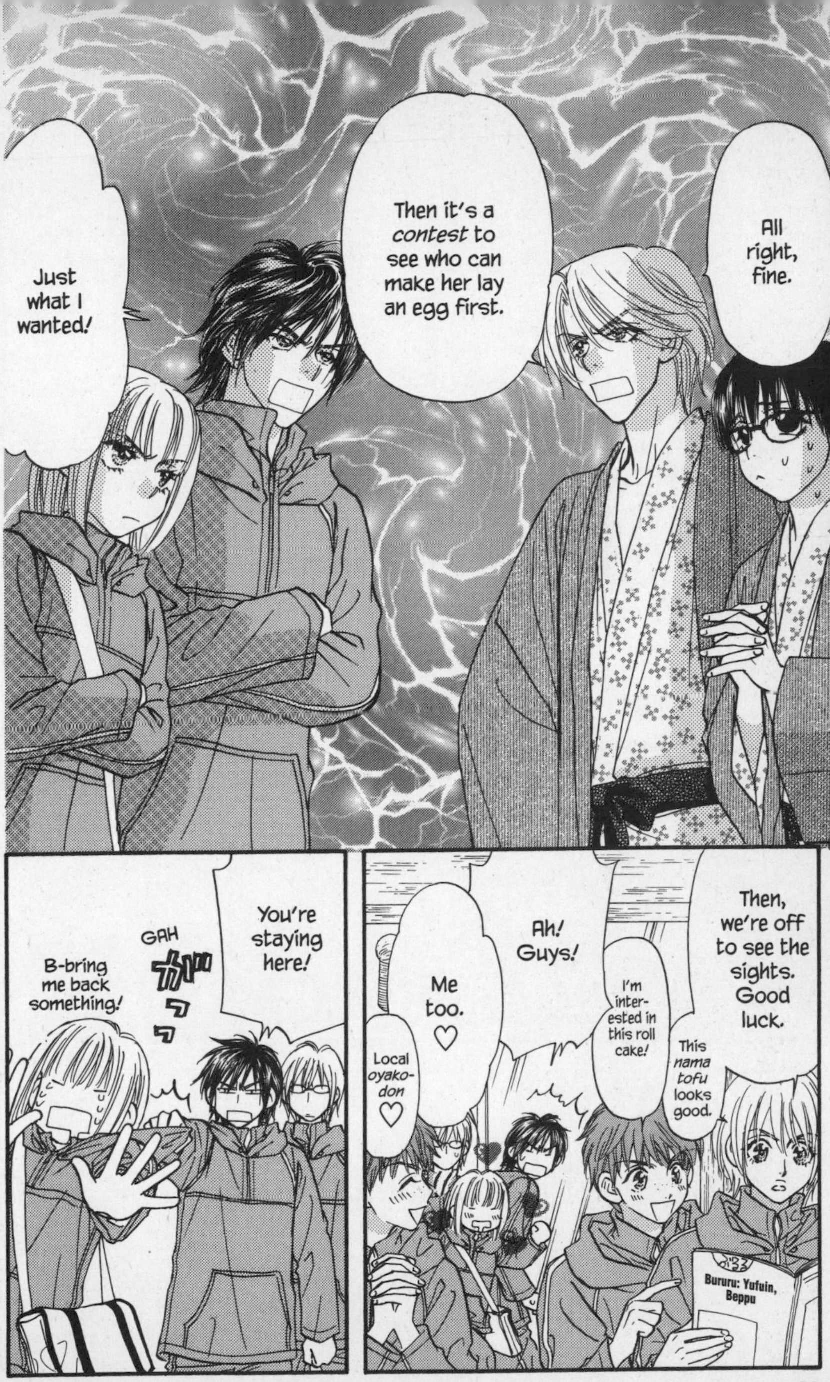
All right, fine.
Then it's a *contest* to see who can make her lay an egg first.
Just what I wanted!
Then, we're off to see the sights. Good luck.
This *nama tofu* looks good.
I'm interested in this roll cake!
Ah! Guys!
Me too. ♡
Local *oyako-don* ♡
Bururu: Yufuin, Beppu
You're staying here!
GAH
B-bring me back something!

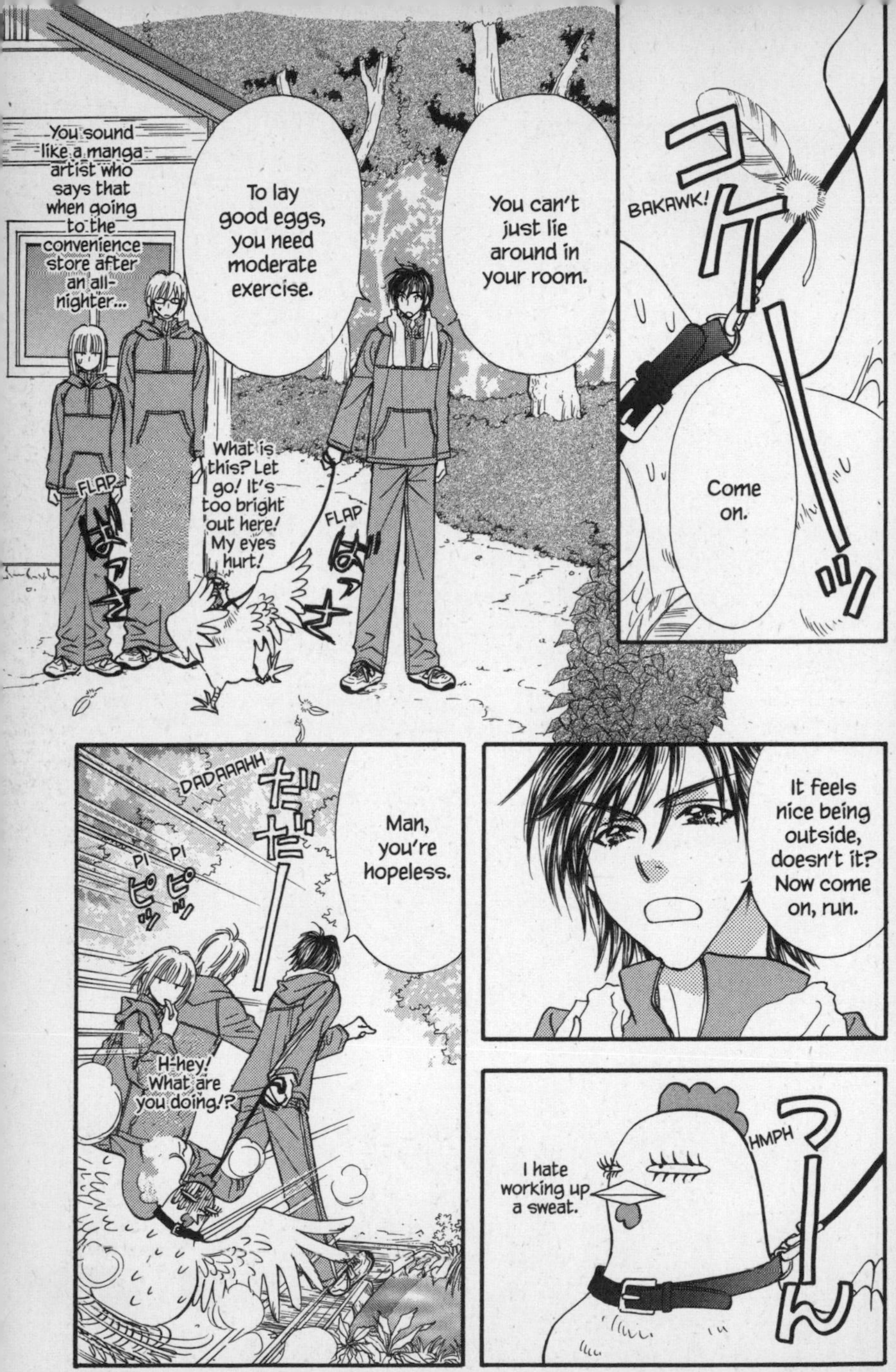
BAKAWK!
Come on.
You can't just lie around in your room.
To lay good eggs, you need moderate exercise.
You sound like a manga artist who says that when going to the convenience store after an all-nighter...
What is this? Let go! It's too bright out here! My eyes hurt!
FLAP
FLAP
It feels nice being outside, doesn't it? Now come on, run.
HMPH
I hate working up a sweat.
Man, you're hopeless.
DADAAAHH
PI
PI
H-hey! What are you doing!?

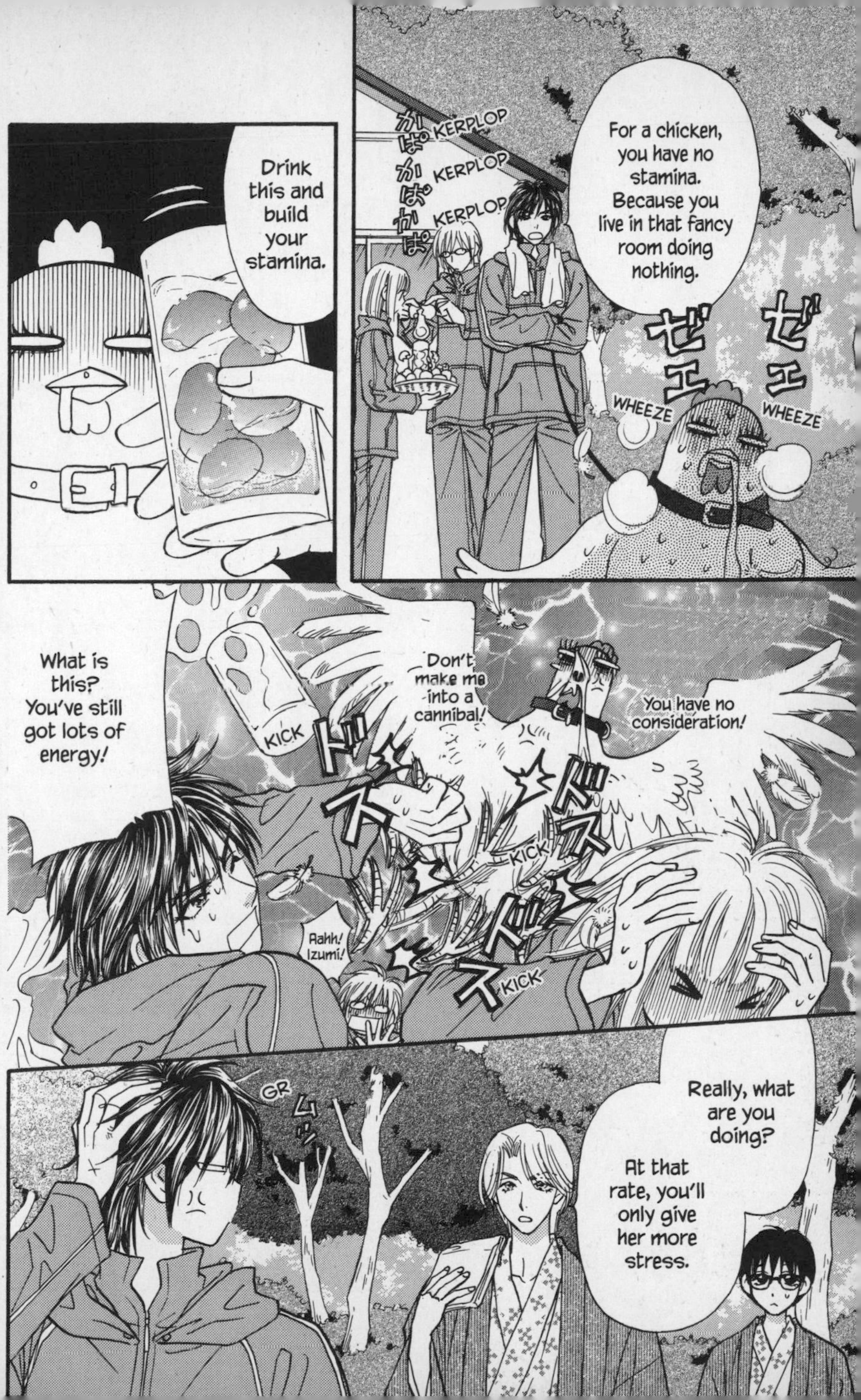
For a chicken, you have no stamina. Because you live in that fancy room doing nothing.
かぽ KERPLOP
かぽ KERPLOP
かぽ KERPLOP
ゼェ WHEEZE
ゼェ WHEEZE
Drink this and build your stamina.
You have no consideration!
Don't make me into a cannibal!
ドス KICK
ドス KICK
ドス KICK
What is this? You've still got lots of energy!
Aahh! Izumi!
Really, what are you doing?
At that rate, you'll only give her more stress.
ムッ GR

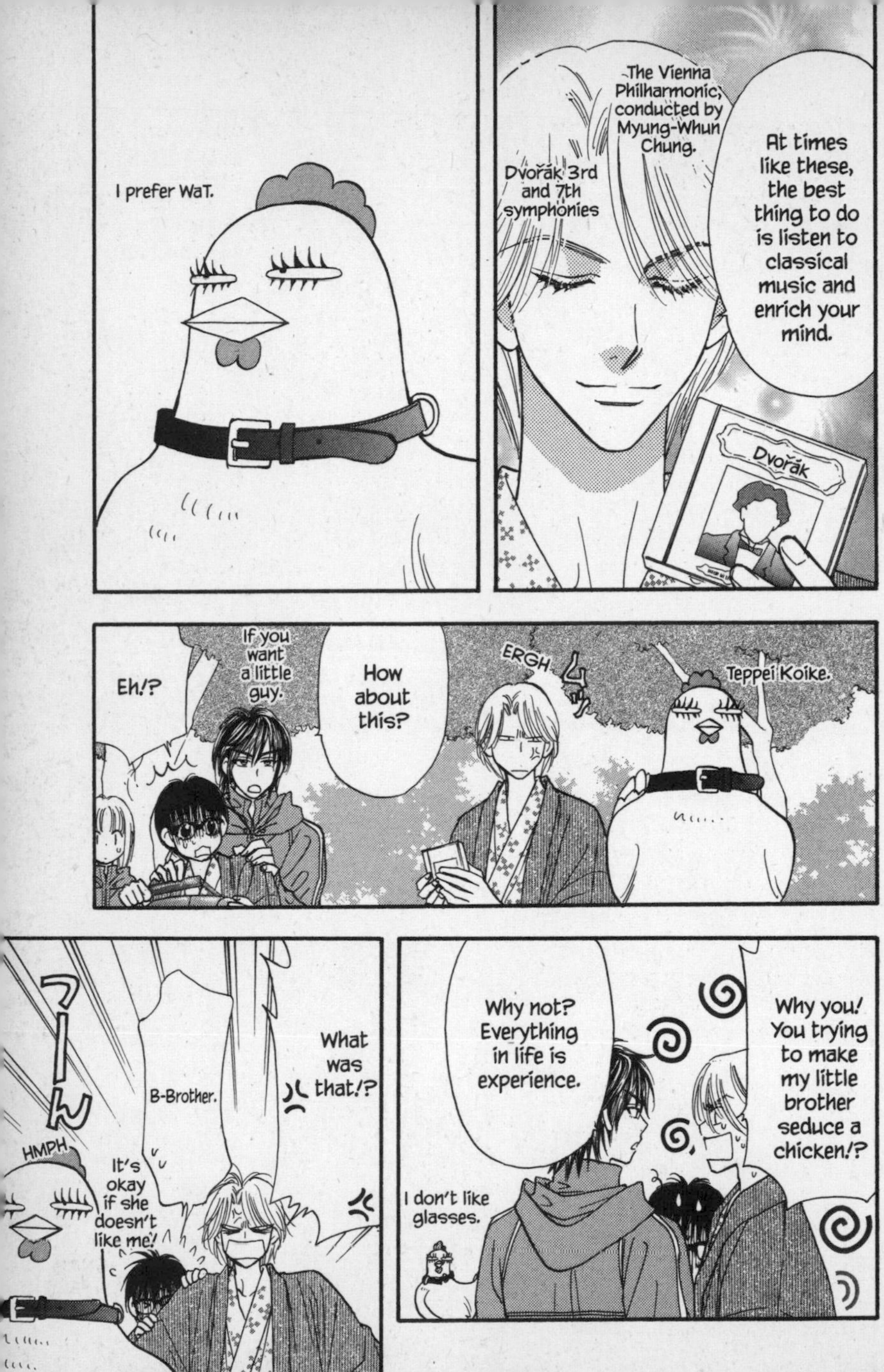
At times like these, the best thing to do is listen to classical music and enrich your mind.
The Vienna Philharmonic; conducted by Myung-Whun Chung.
Dvořák 3rd and 7th symphonies
Dvořák
I prefer WaT.
Teppei Koike.
ERGH
How about this?
If you want a little guy.
Eh!?
Why you! You trying to make my little brother seduce a chicken!?
Why not? Everything in life is experience.
I don't like glasses.
What was that!?
B-Brother.
It's okay if she doesn't like me!
HMPH

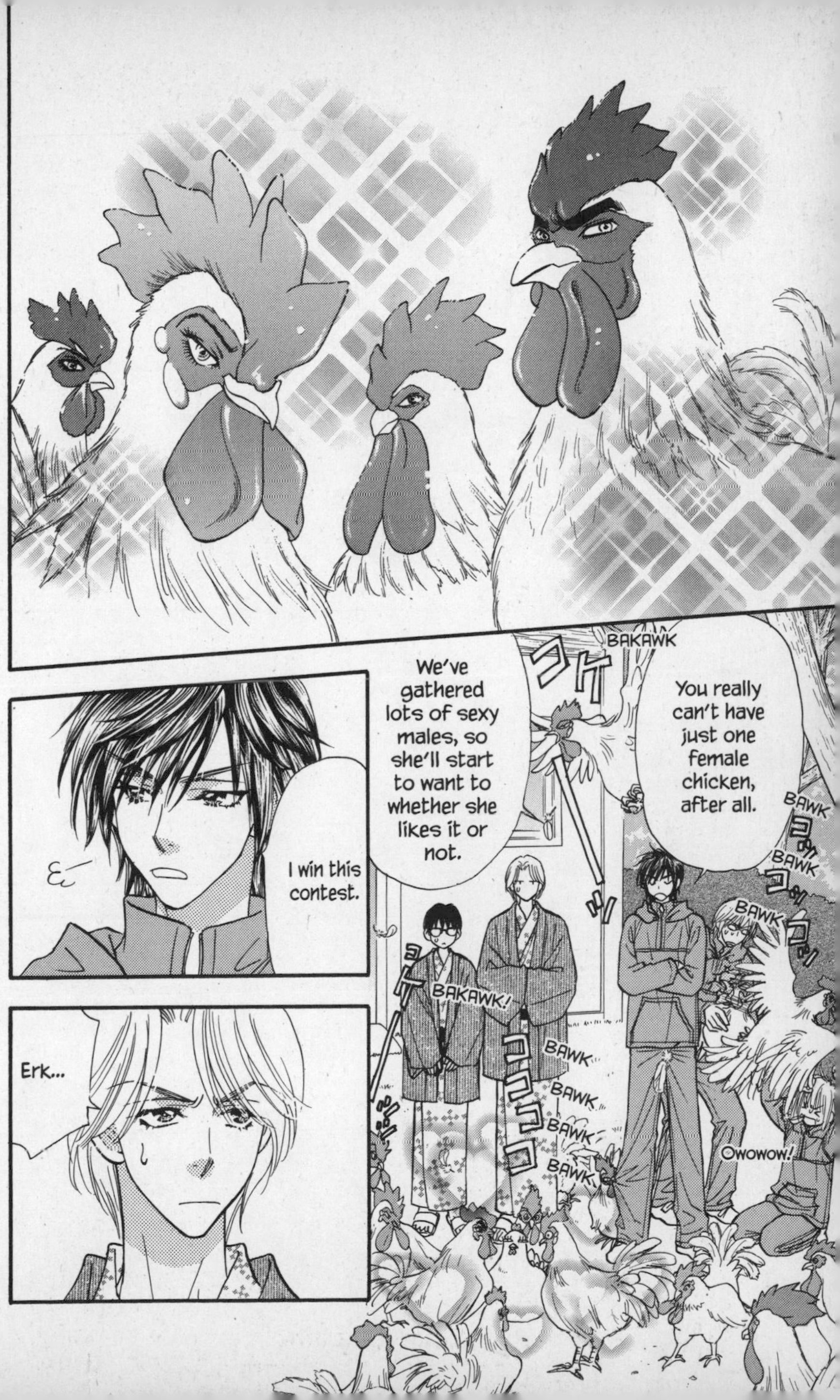
BAKAWK
You really can't have just one female chicken, after all.
We've gathered lots of sexy males, so she'll start to want to whether she likes it or not.
BAWK
BAWK
BAWK
BAKAWK!
BAWK
BAWK
BAWK
BAWK
Owowow!
I win this contest.
Erk...

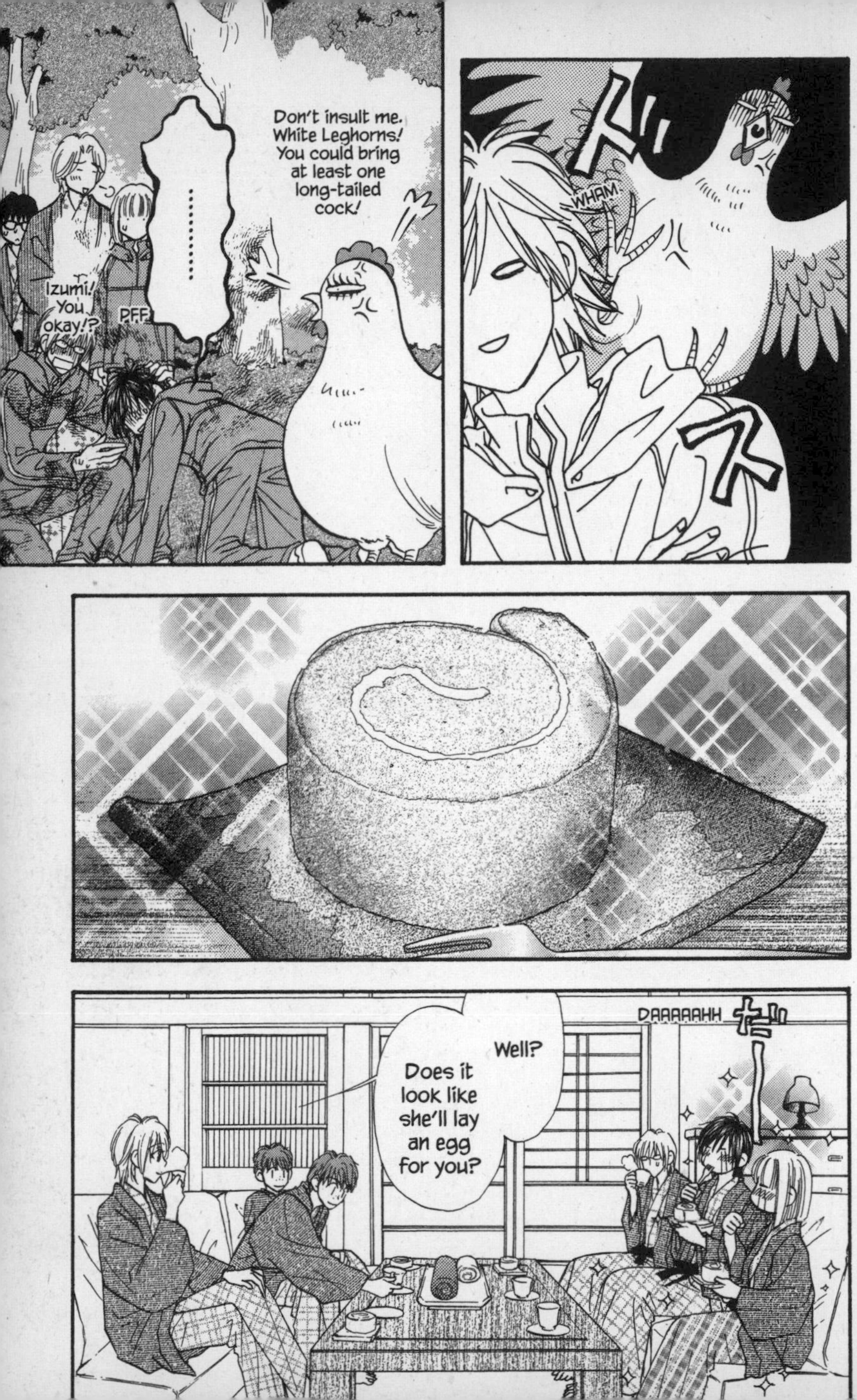
WHAM
Don't insult me. White Leghorns! You could bring at least one long-tailed cock!
......
PFF
Izumi! You okay!?
DAAAAAHH
Well?
Does it look like she'll lay an egg for you?

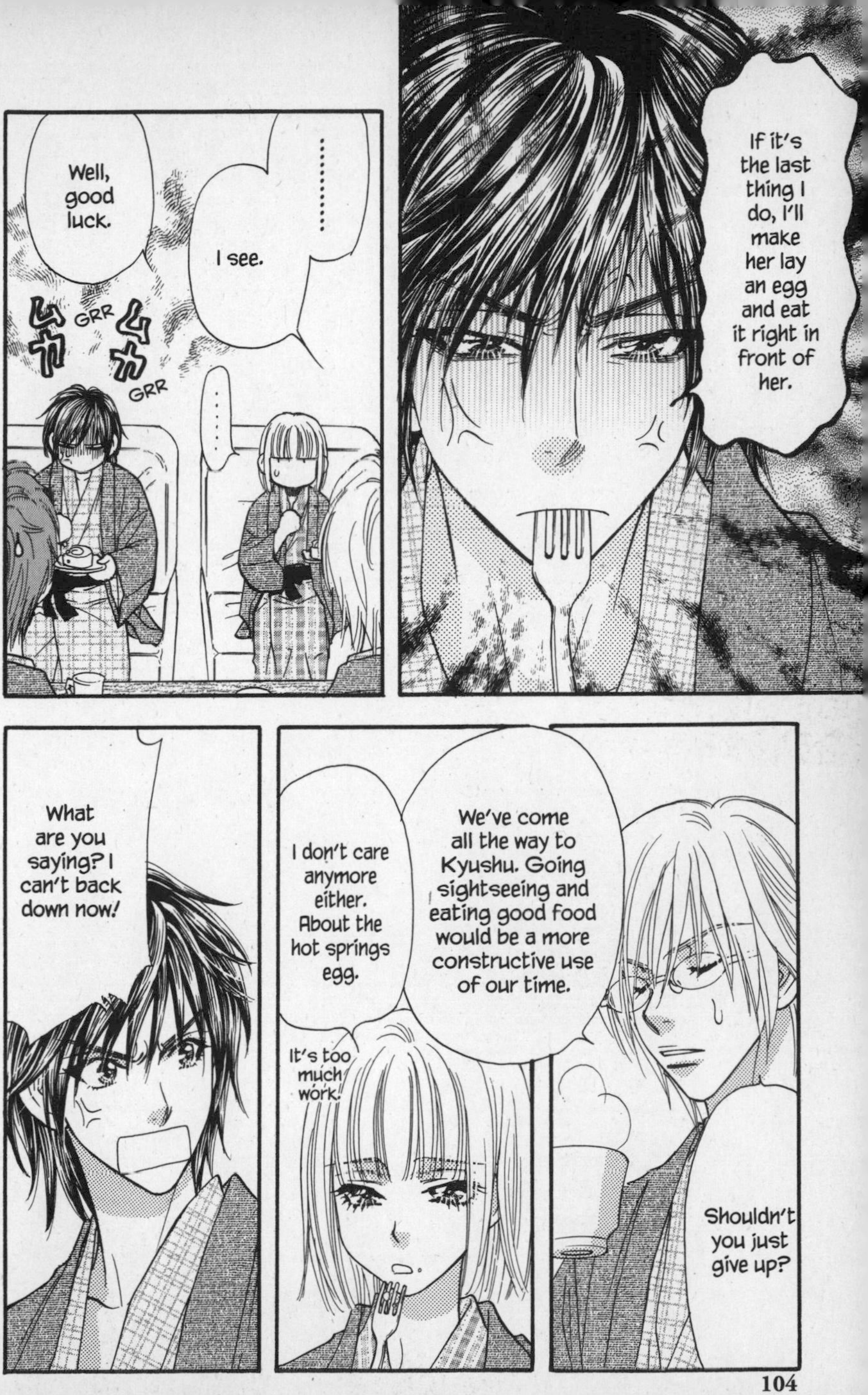
If it's the last thing I do, I'll make her lay an egg and eat it right in front of her.
......
I see.
Well, good luck.
GRR
GRR
......
We've come all the way to Kyushu. Going sightseeing and eating good food would be a more constructive use of our time.
Shouldn't you just give up?
I don't care anymore either. About the hot springs egg.
It's too much work!
What are you saying? I can't back down now!

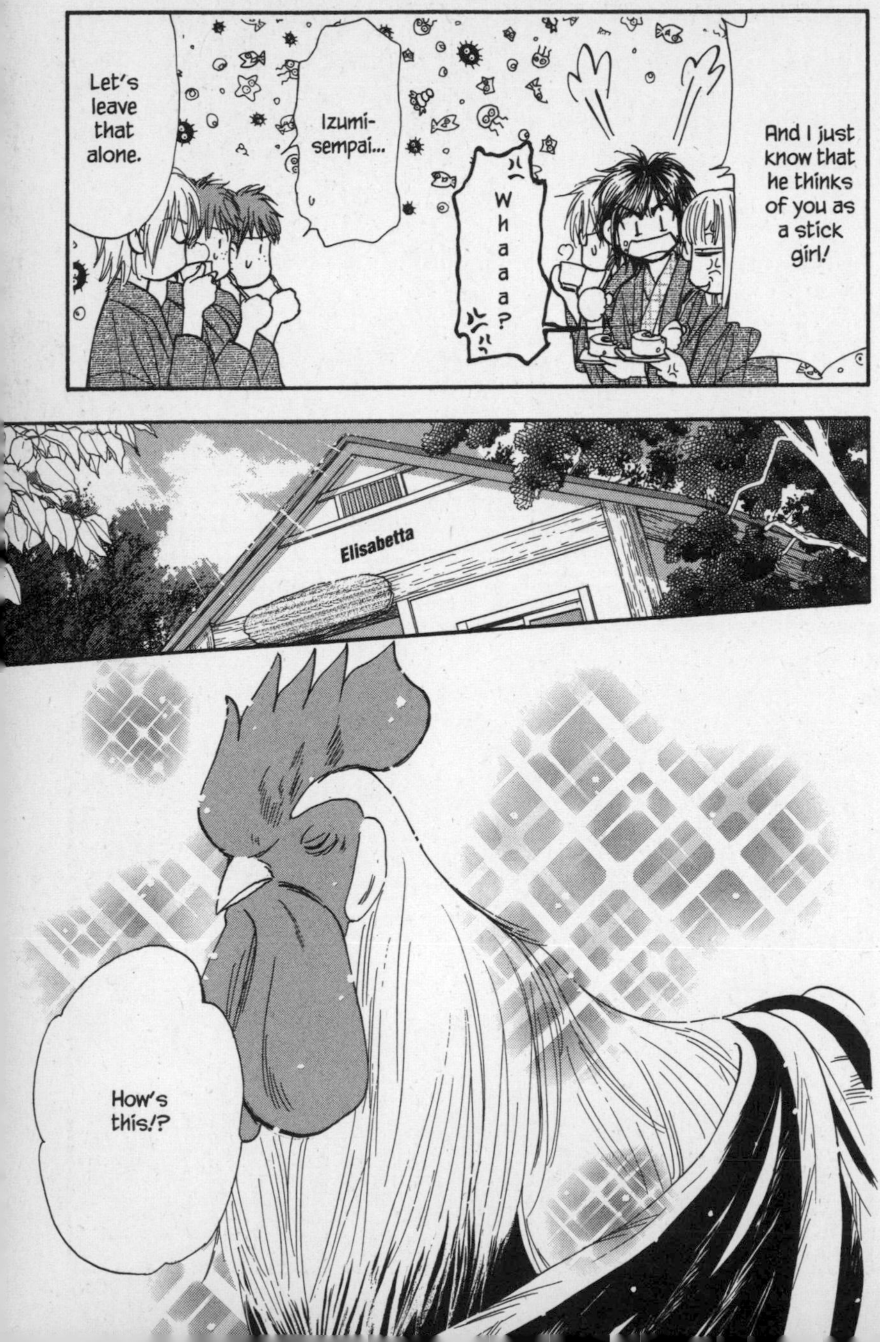
And I just know that he thinks of you as a stick girl!
Whaaaa?
Izumi-sempai...
Let's leave that alone.
Elisabetta
How's this!?

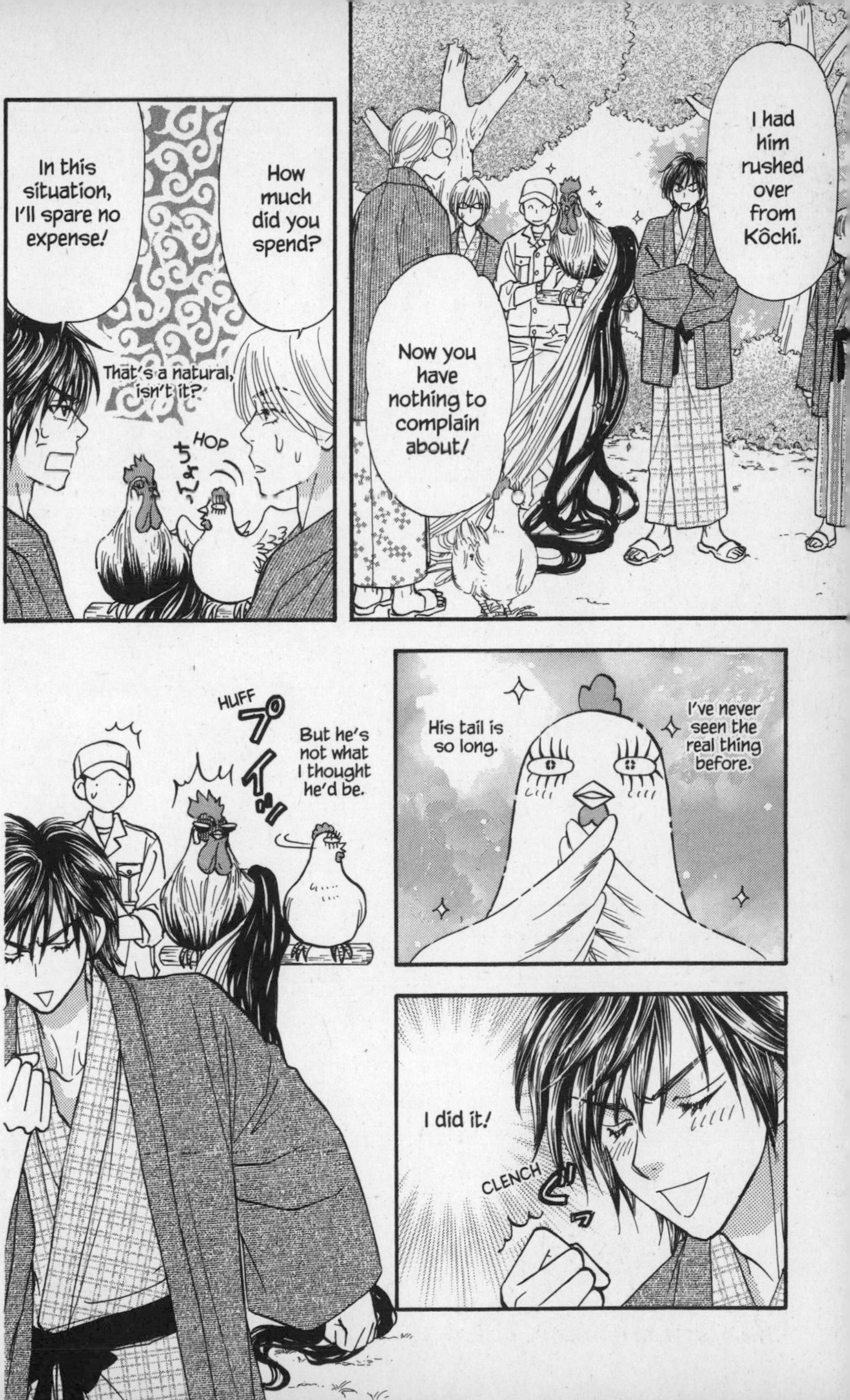
I had him rushed over from Kôchi.
Now you have nothing to complain about!
How much did you spend?
In this situation, I'll spare no expense!
That's a natural, isn't it?
HOP
I've never seen the real thing before.
His tail is so long.
I did it!
CLENCH
But he's not what I thought he'd be.
HUFF

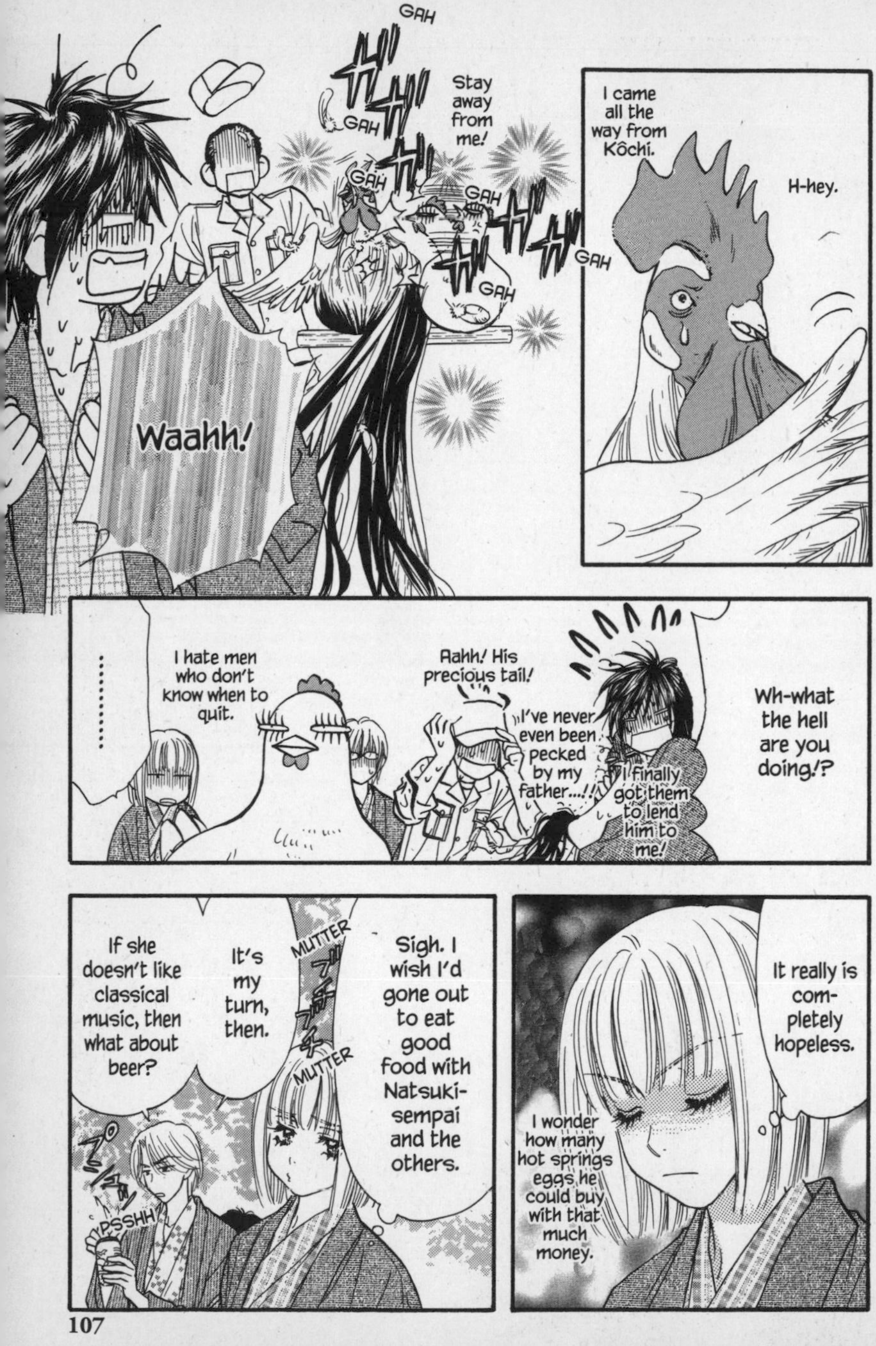

H-hey.
I came all the way from Kôchi.
GAH
GAH
Stay away from me!
GAH
GAH
GAH
GAH
Waahh!
Wh-what the hell are you doing!?
I finally got them to lend him to me!
I've never even been pecked by my father...!!
Aahh! His precious tail!
I hate men who don't know when to quit.
....
It really is com-pletely hopeless.
I wonder how many hot springs eggs he could buy with that much money.
Sigh. I wish I'd gone out to eat good food with Natsuki-sempai and the others.
MUTTER
MUTTER
It's my turn, then.
If she doesn't like classical music, then what about beer?
PSSHH

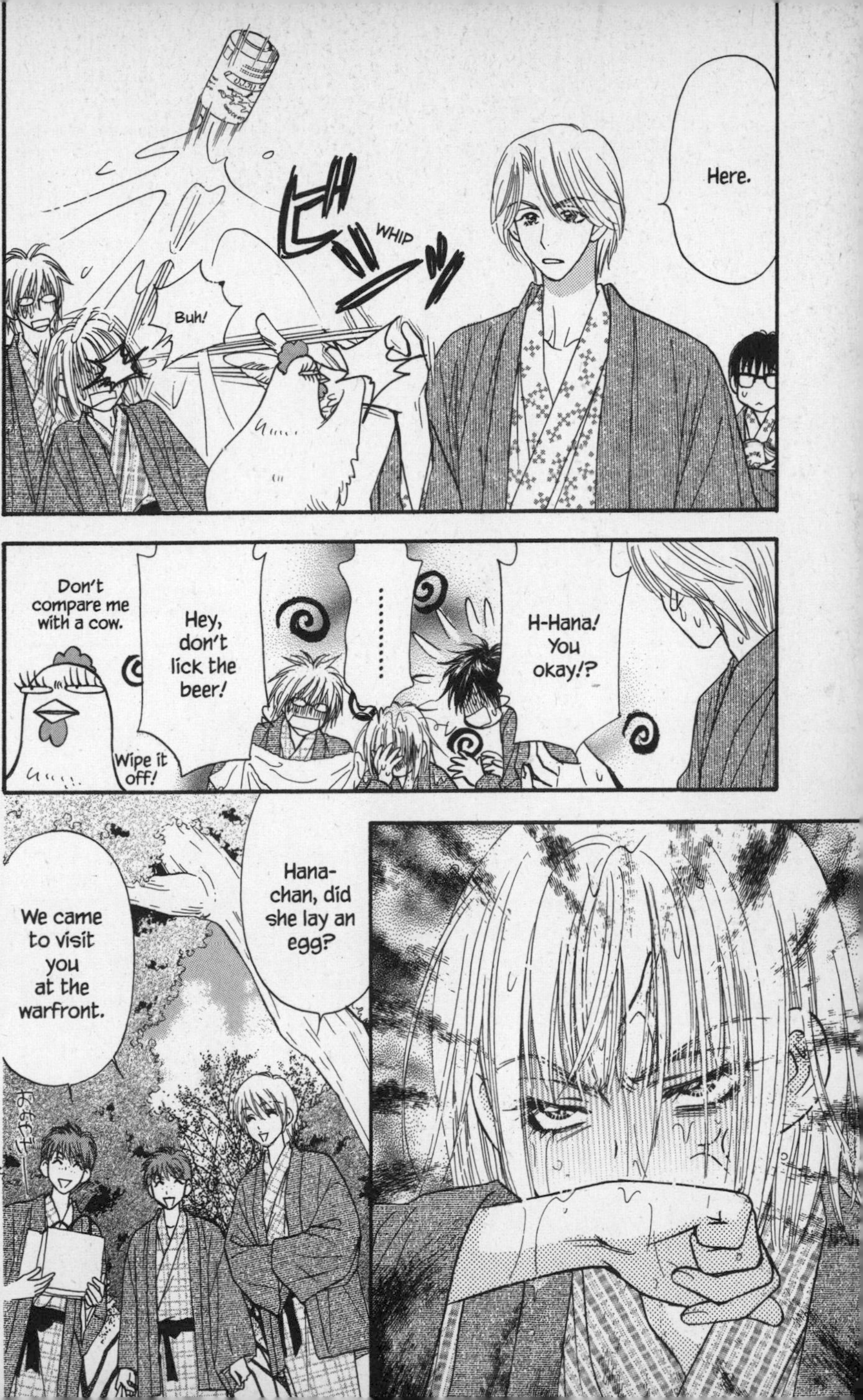
Here.
WHIP
Buh!
H-Hana! You okay!?
......
Hey, don't lick the beer!
Don't compare me with a cow.
Wipe it off!
Hana-chan, did she lay an egg?
We came to visit you at the warfront.

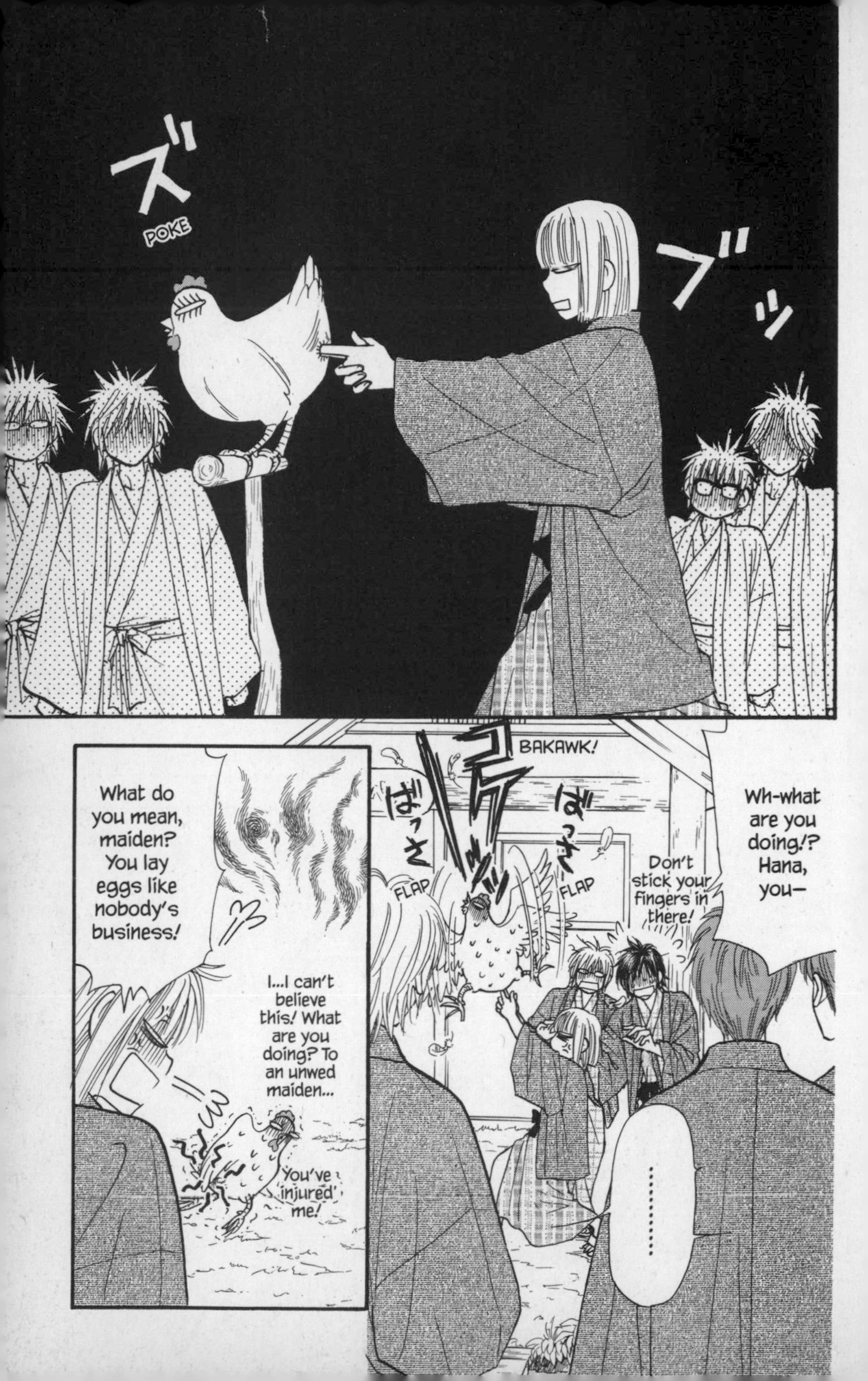
ブッ
ズ
POKE
Wh-what are you doing!? Hana, you—
Don't stick your fingers in there!
BAKAWK!
ばっさ
FLAP
ばっさ
FLAP
......
What do you mean, maiden? You lay eggs like nobody's business!
I...I can't believe this! What are you doing? To an unwed maiden...
You've injured me!

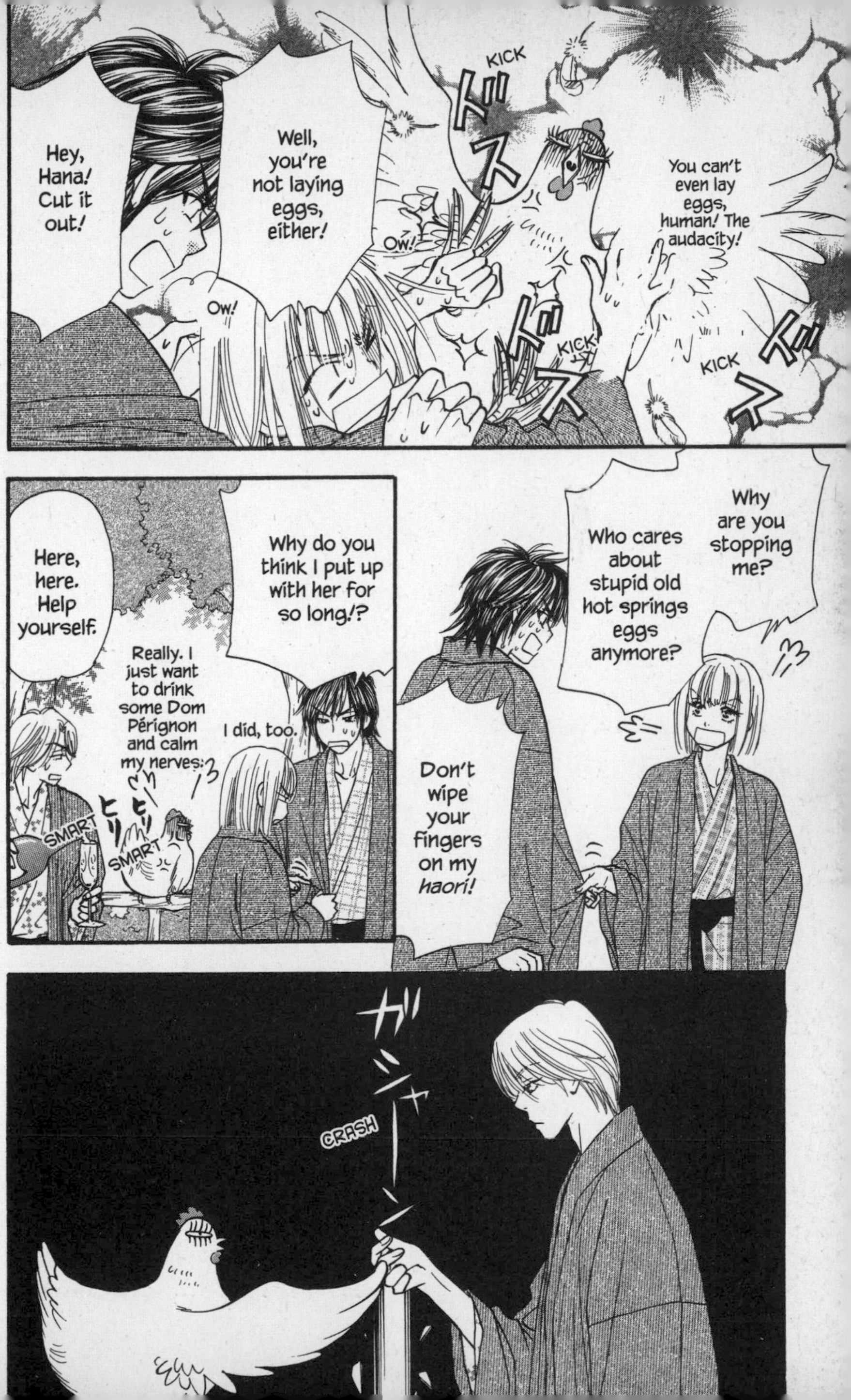
You can't even lay eggs, human! The audacity!
KICK
Well, you're not laying eggs, either!
Ow!
Hey, Hana! Cut it out!
KICK
KICK
Ow!
Why are you stopping me?
Who cares about stupid old hot springs eggs anymore?
Don't wipe your fingers on my *haori*!
Why do you think I put up with her for so long!?
Here, here. Help yourself.
Really. I just want to drink some Dom Pérignon and calm my nerves.
I did, too.
SMART
SMART
CRASH

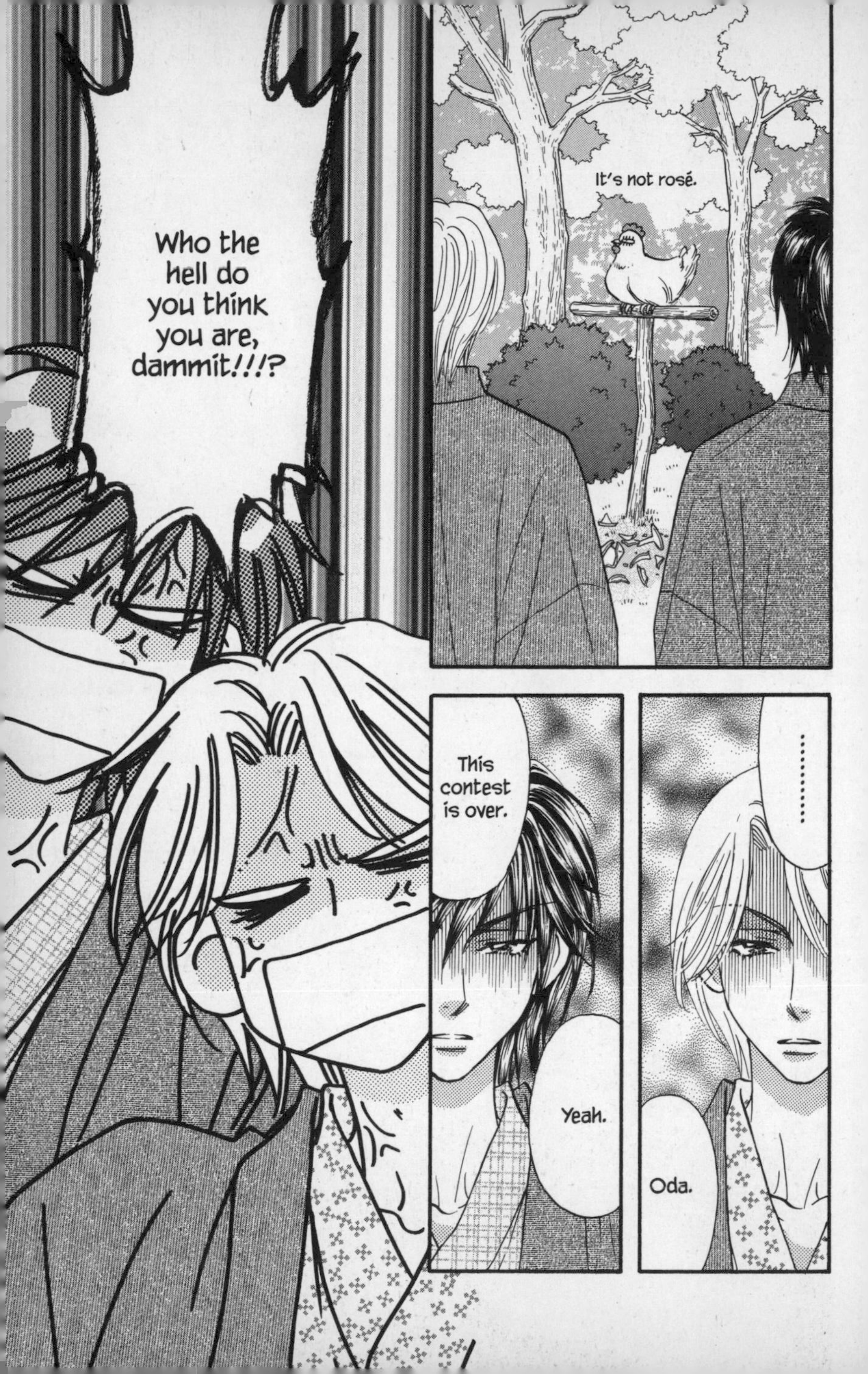
It's not rosé.
....
Oda.
This contest is over.
Yeah.
Who the hell do you think you are, dammit!!!?

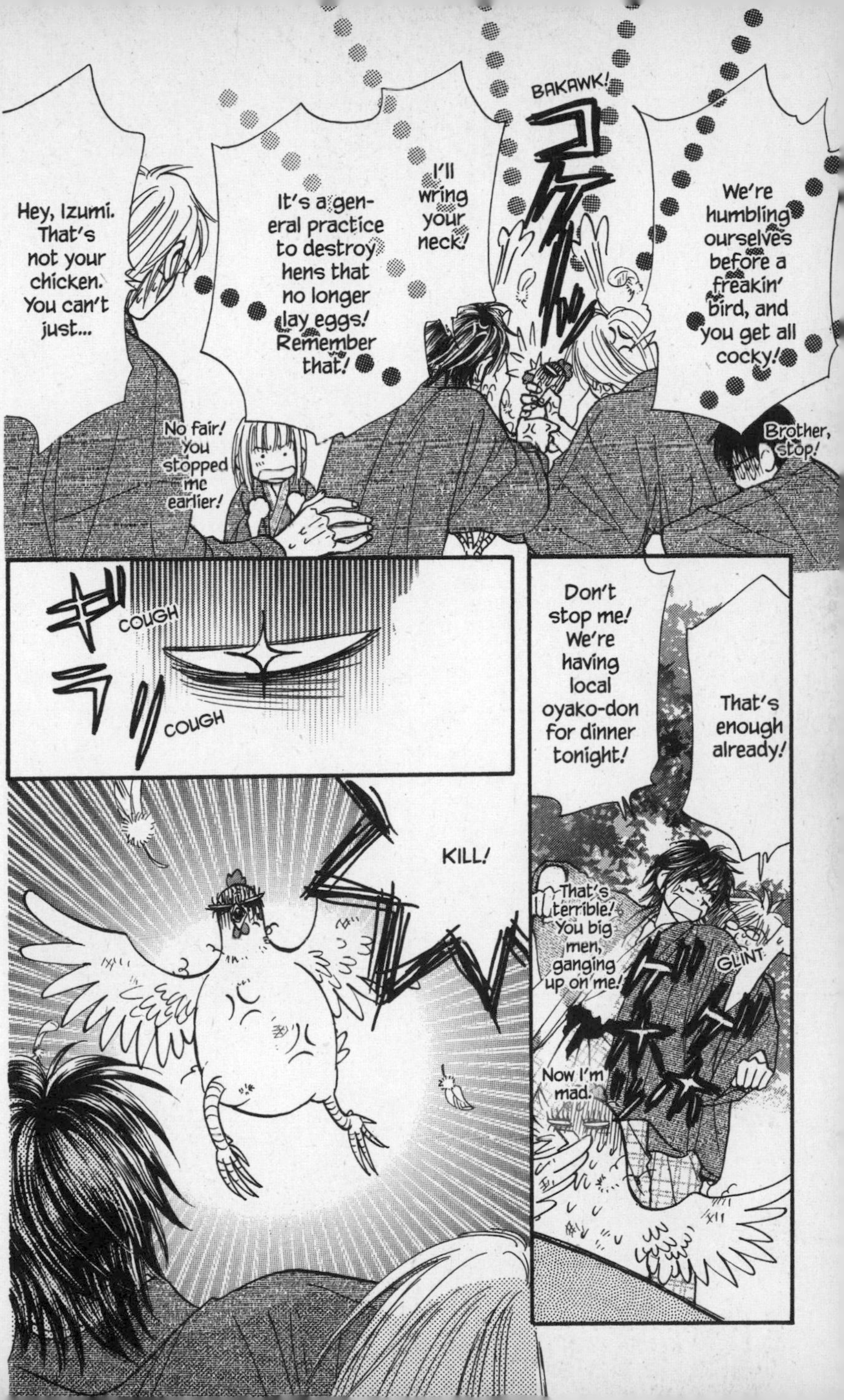
We're humbling ourselves before a freakin' bird, and you get all cocky!
BAKAWK!
I'll wring your neck!
It's a general practice to destroy hens that no longer lay eggs! Remember that!
Hey, Izumi. That's not your chicken. You can't just...
Brother, stop!
No fair! You stopped me earlier!
That's enough already!
Don't stop me! We're having local oyako-don for dinner tonight!
GLINT
That's terrible! You big men, ganging up on me!
Now I'm mad.
COUGH
COUGH
KILL!

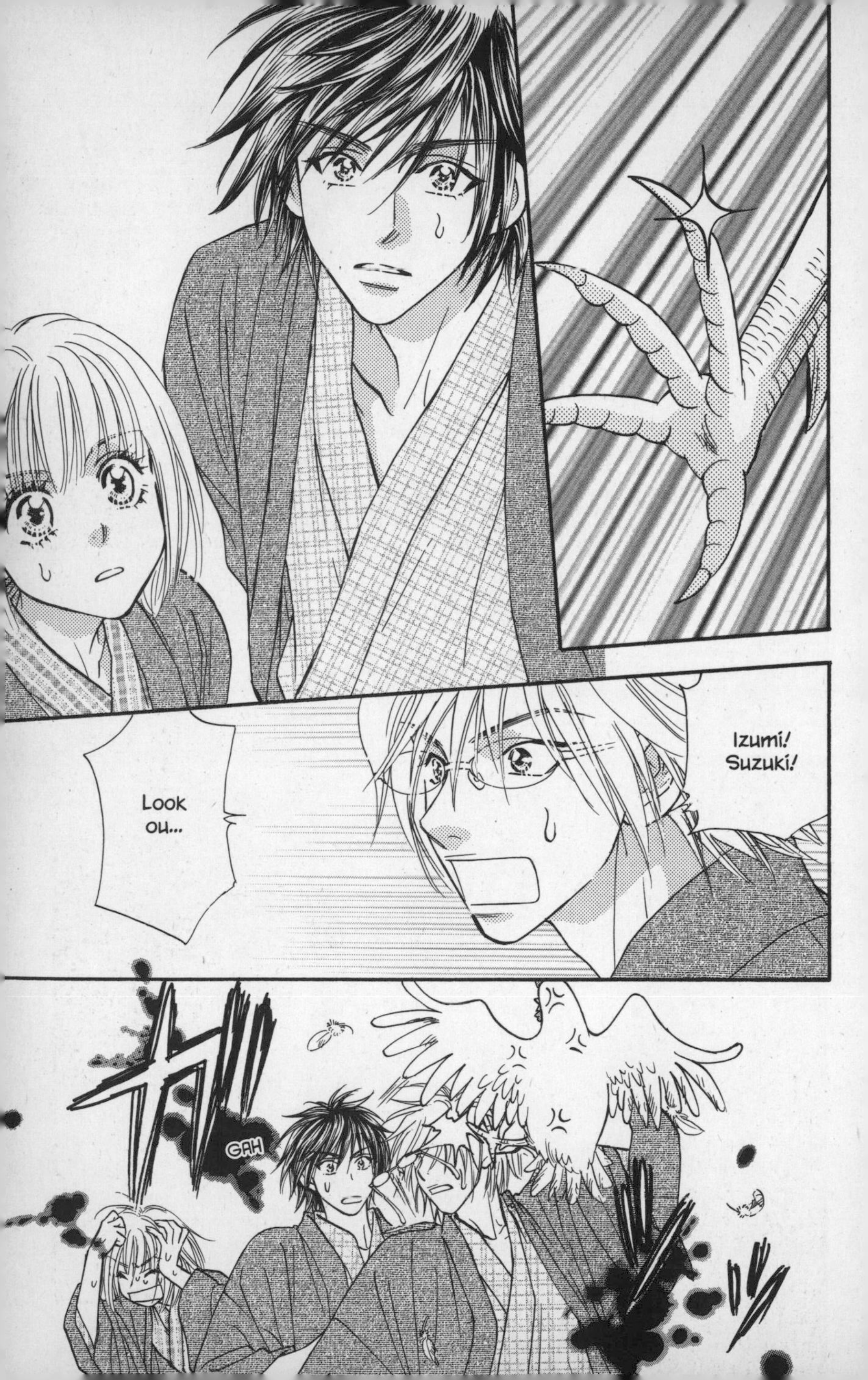
Izumi! Suzuki!
Look ou...
GAH

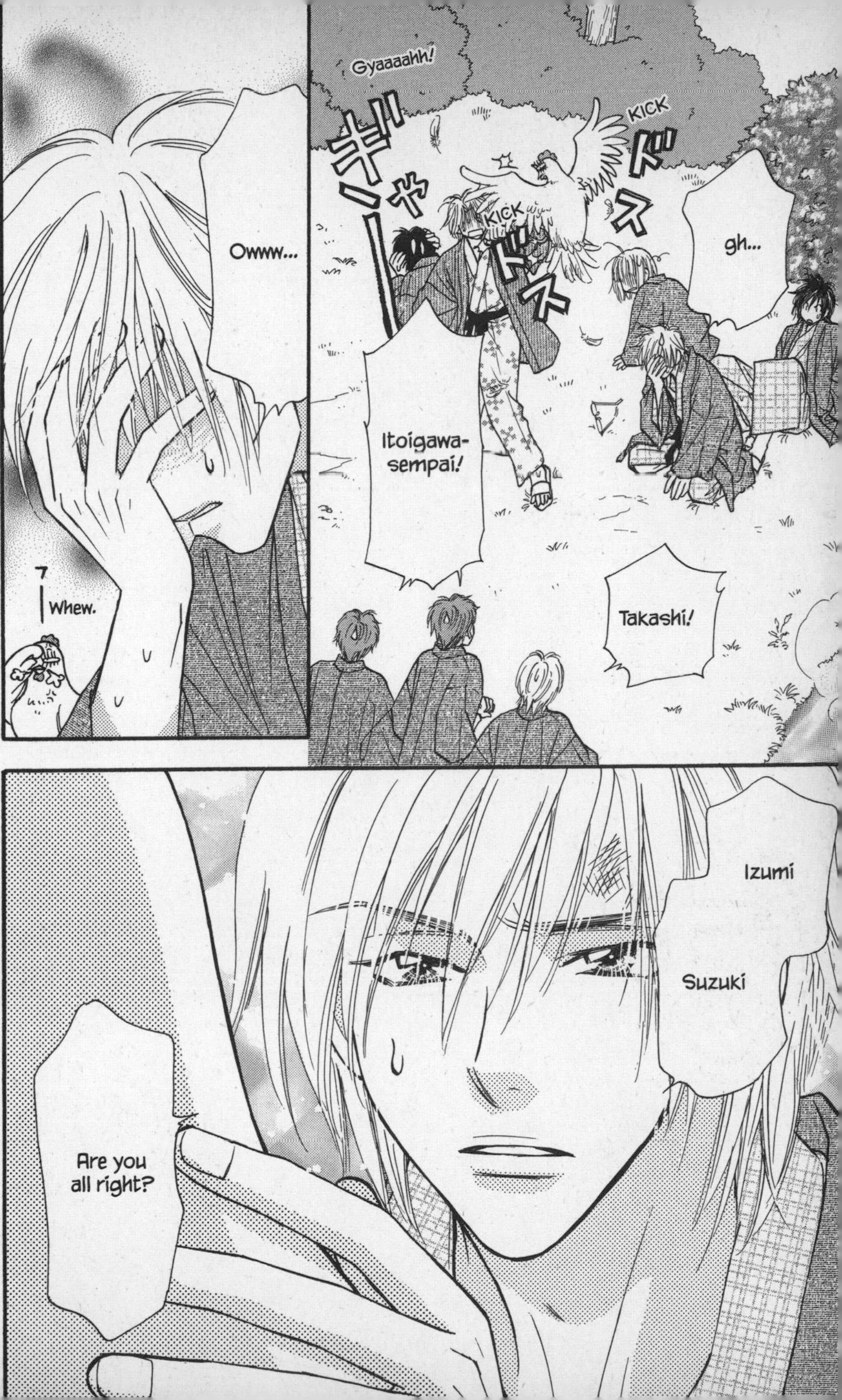
KICK
gh...
Gyaaaahh!
KICK
Itoigawa-sempai!
Takashi!
Owww...
Whew.
Izumi
Suzuki
Are you all right?

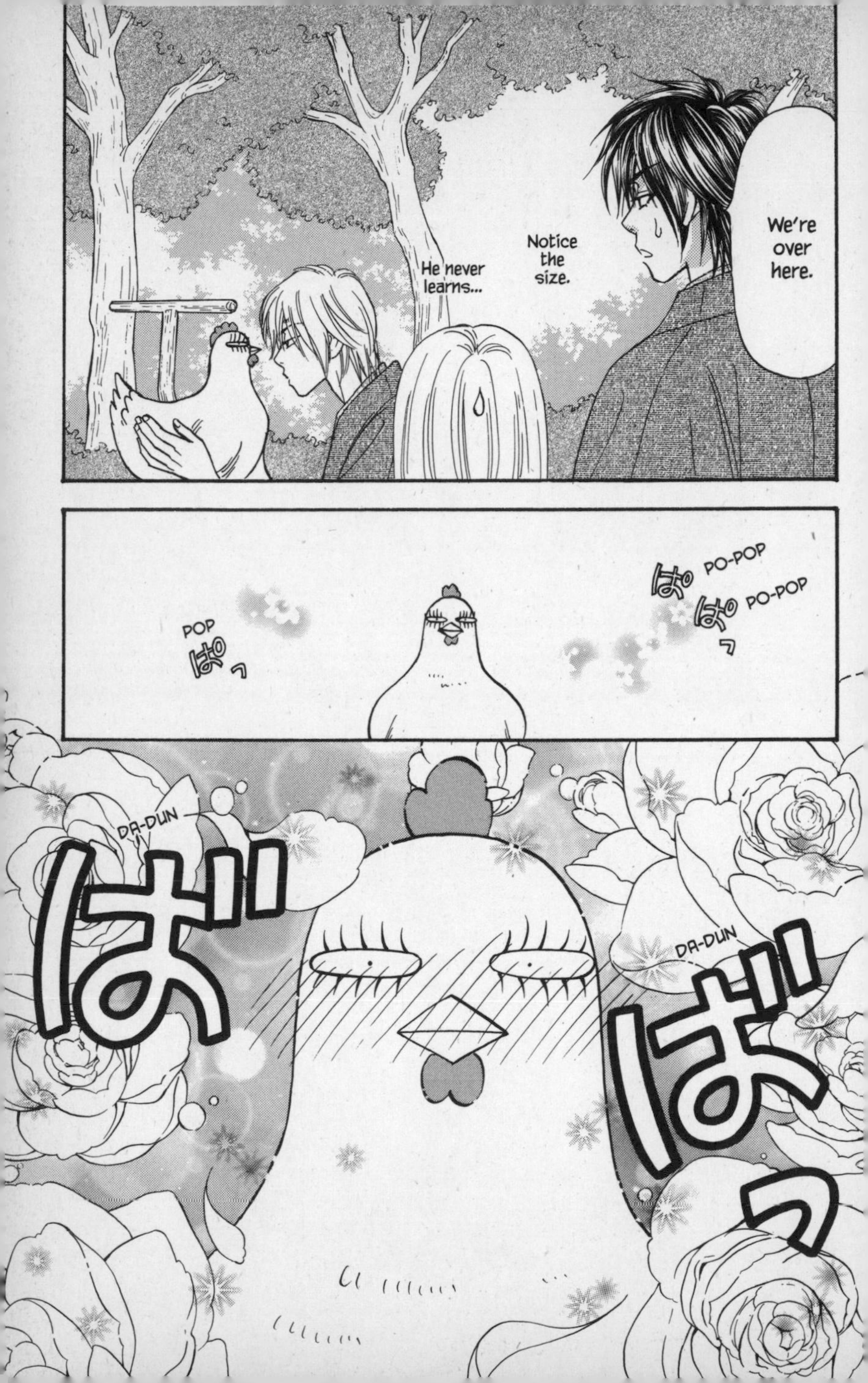
We're over here.
Notice the size.
He never learns...
ぱ PO-POP
ぱっ PO-POP
ぱっ POP
DA-DUN ぱっ
DA-DUN ぱ

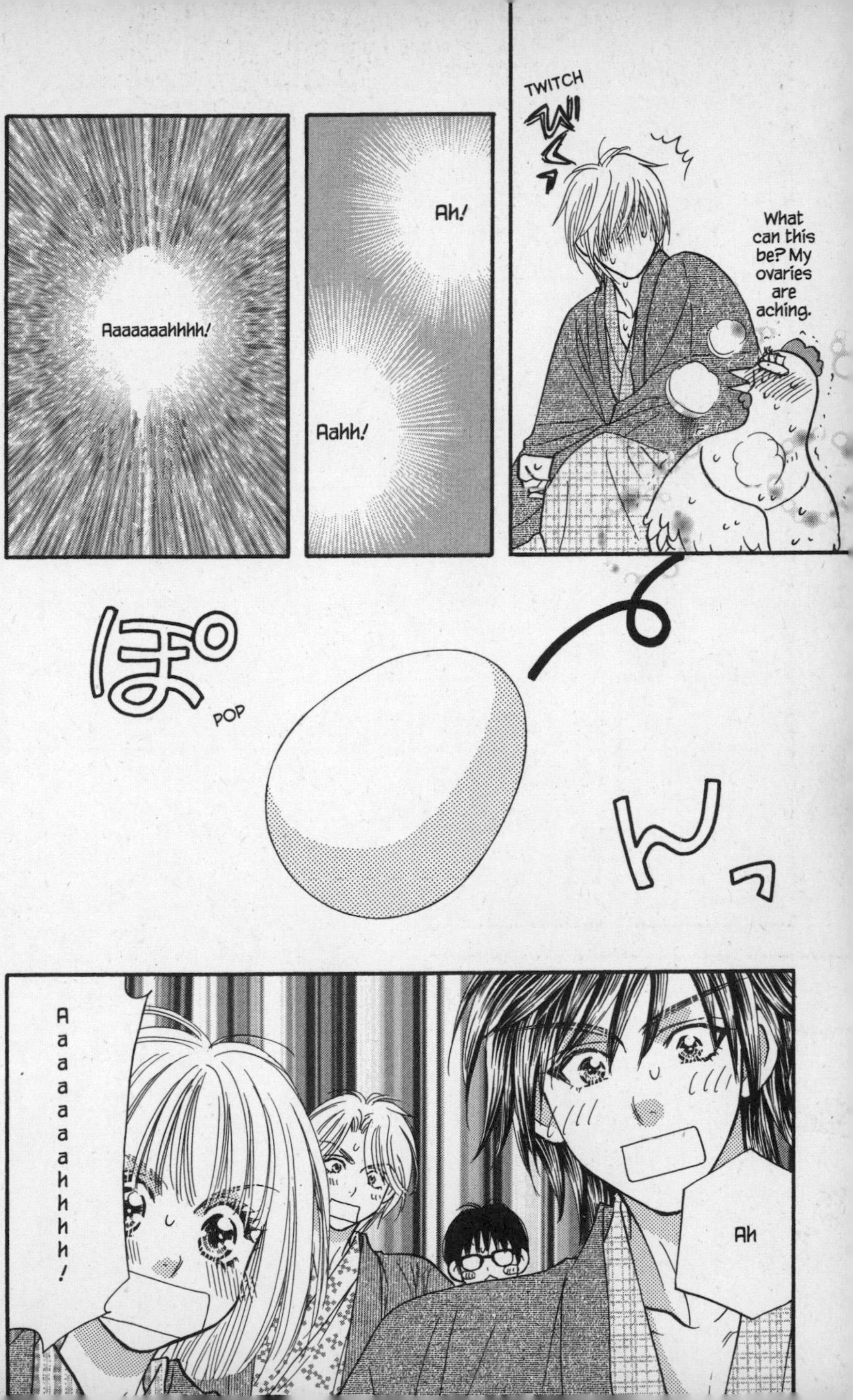
TWITCH
What can this be? My ovaries are aching.
Ah!
Aahh!
Aaaaaaahhhh!
ぽ
POP
ん
Ah
Aaaaaaahhhh!

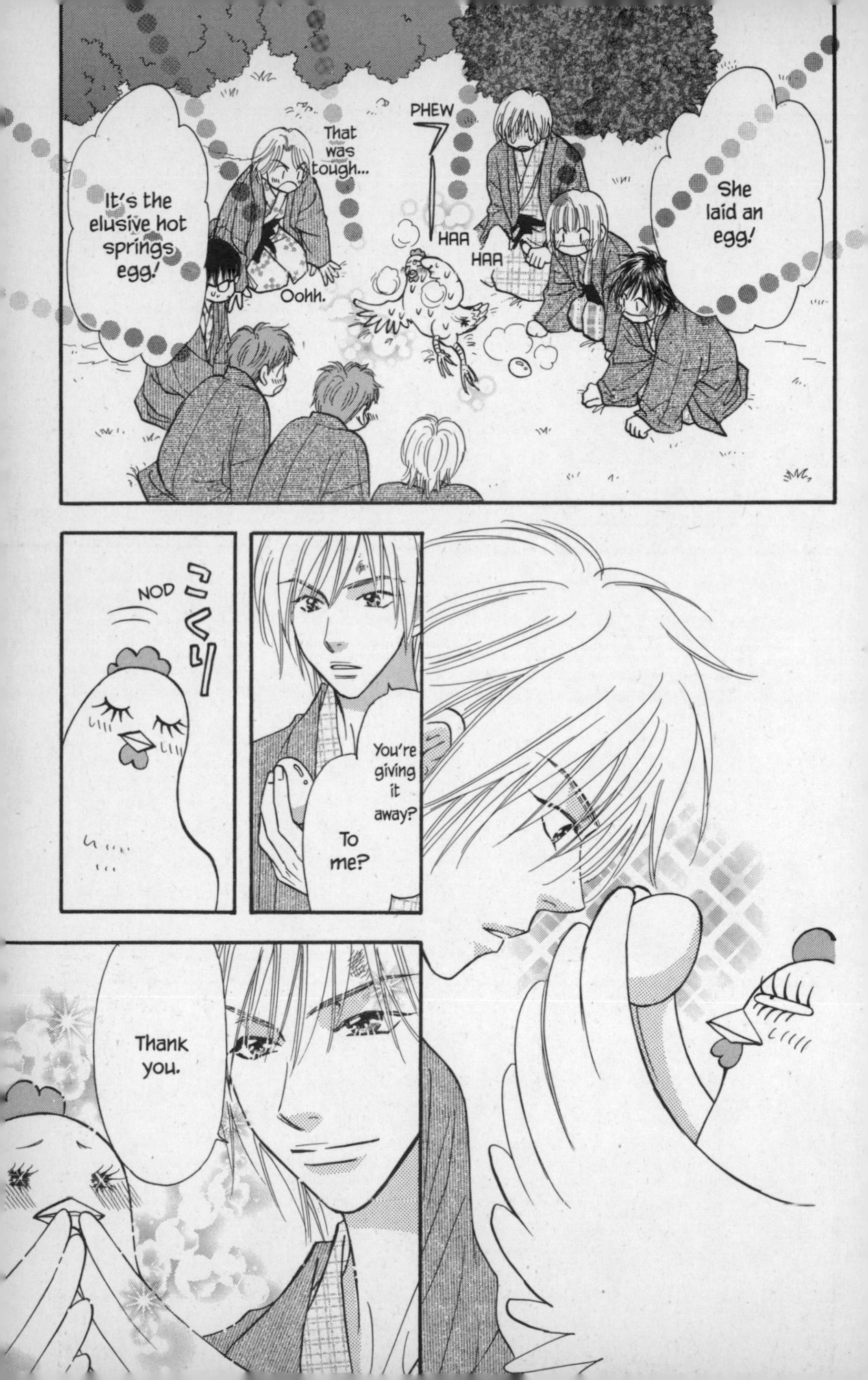
She laid an egg!
PHEW
HAA
HAA
That was tough...
Oohh.
It's the elusive hot springs egg!
You're giving it away?
To me?
NOD
Thank you.

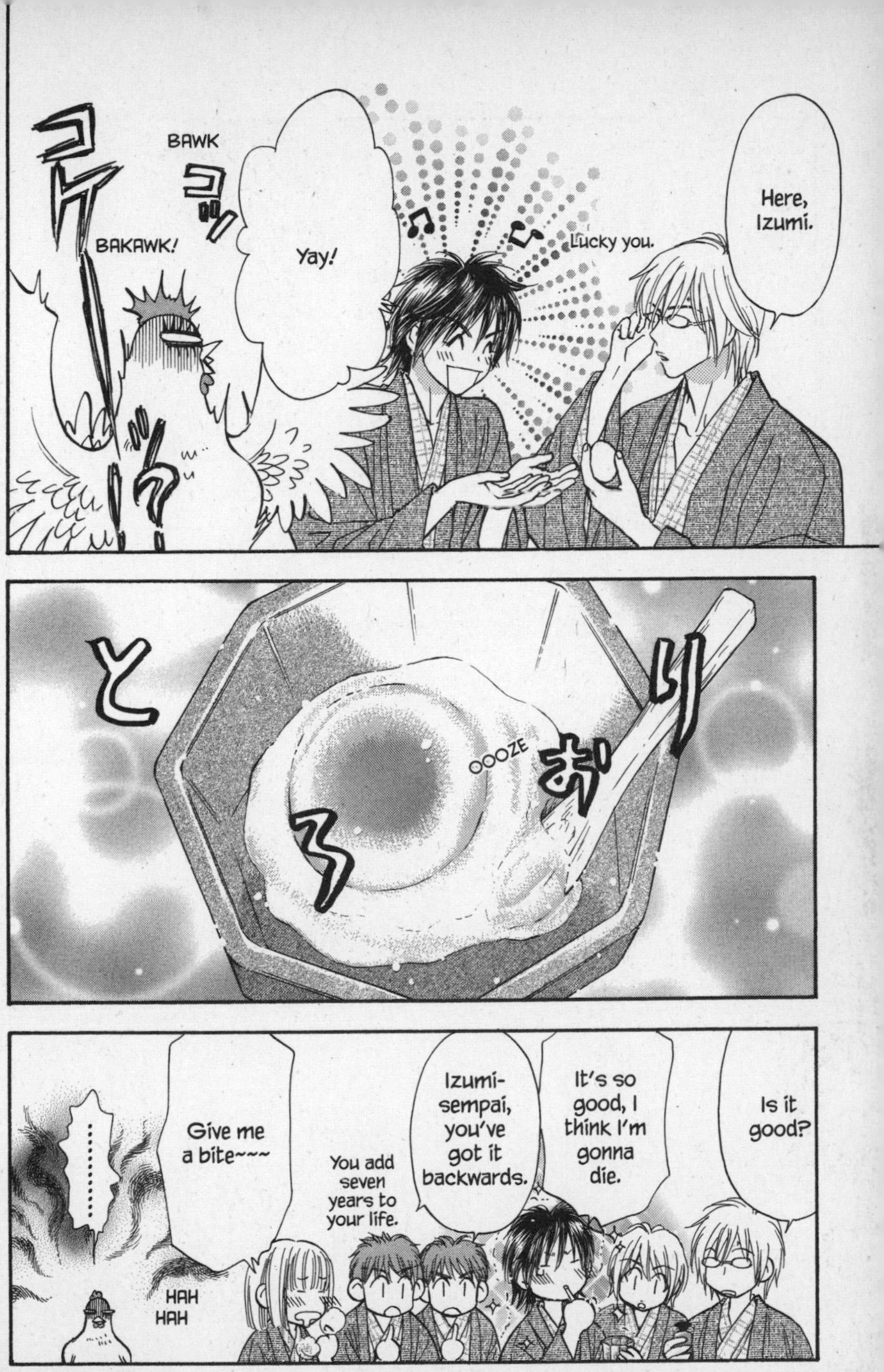
Here, Izumi.
Lucky you.
Yay!
BAWK
BAKAWK!
OOOZE
Is it good?
It's so good, I think I'm gonna die.
Izumi-sempai, you've got it backwards.
You add seven years to your life.
Give me a bite~~~
HAH HAH
......

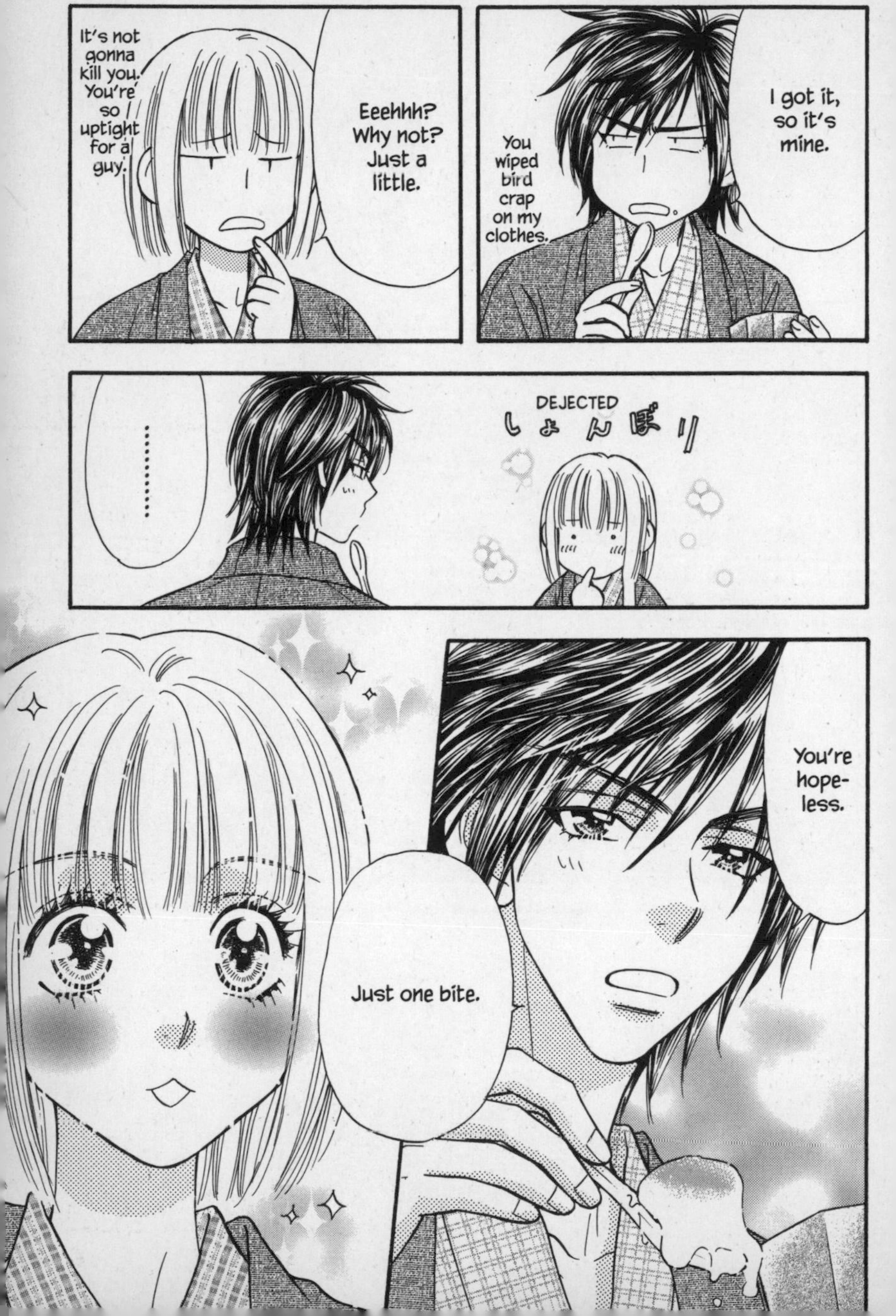
I got it, so it's mine.
You wiped bird crap on my clothes.
Eeehhh? Why not? Just a little.
It's not gonna kill you. You're so uptight for a guy.
DEJECTED
しょんぼり
......
You're hope-less.
Just one bite.

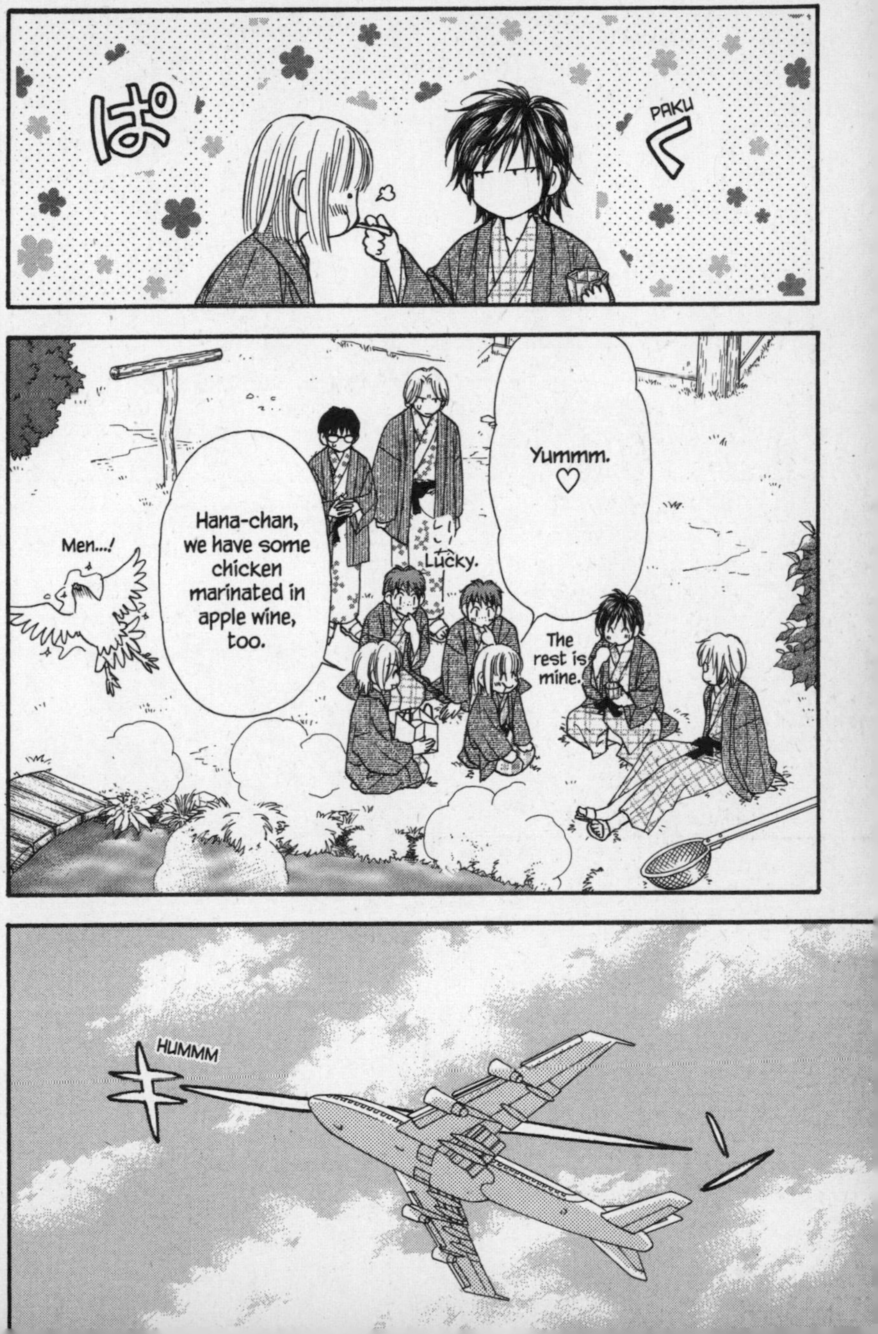
ぱく
PAKU
Yummm. ♡
The rest is mine.
Lucky.
Hana-chan, we have some chicken marinated in apple wine, too.
Men...!
HUMMM
キ

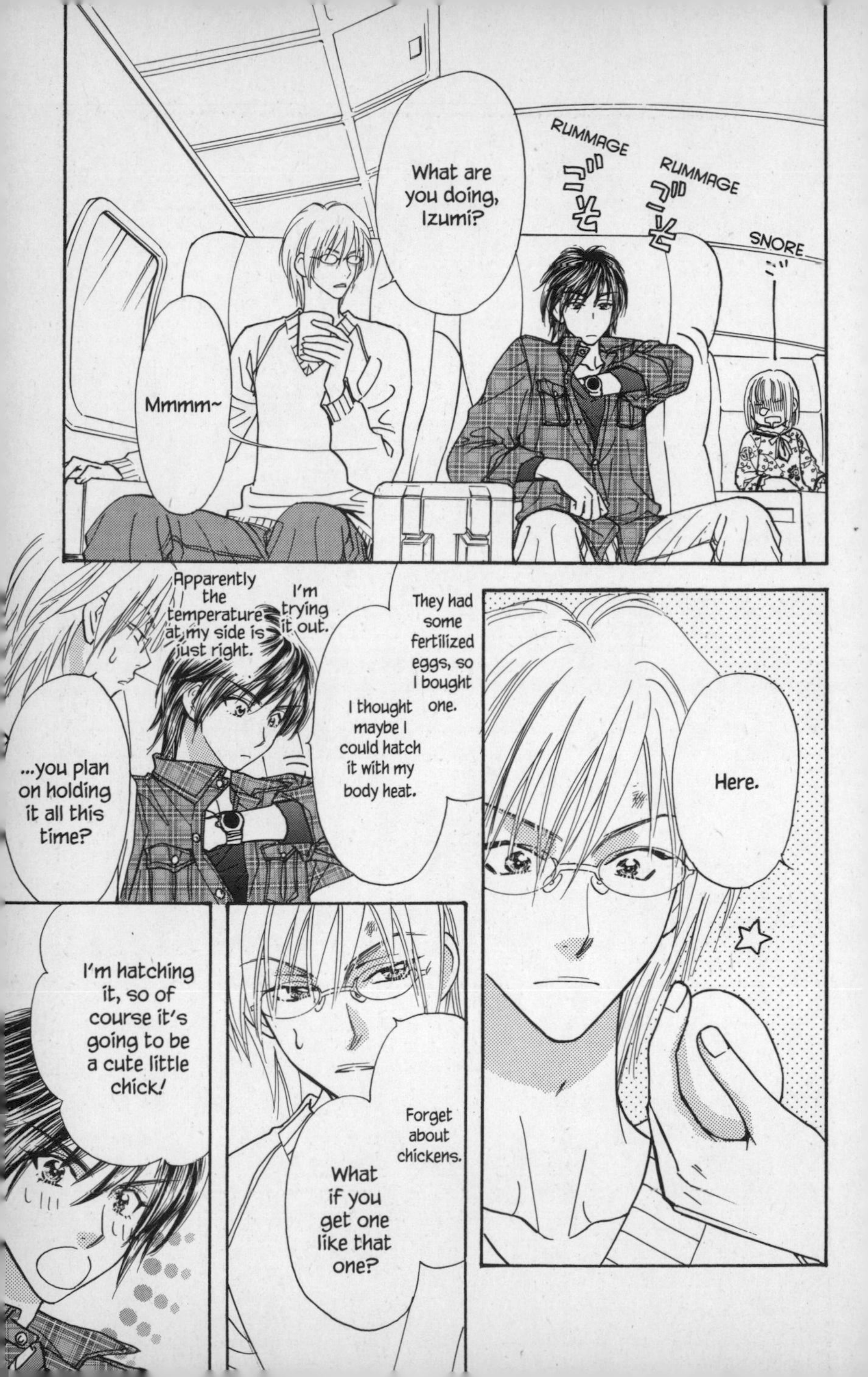
SNORE
RUMMAGE
RUMMAGE
What are you doing, Izumi?
Mmmm~
Here.
They had some fertilized eggs, so I bought one.
I thought maybe I could hatch it with my body heat.
I'm trying it out.
Apparently the temperature at my side is just right.
...you plan on holding it all this time?
Forget about chickens.
What if you get one like that one?
I'm hatching it, so of course it's going to be a cute little chick!

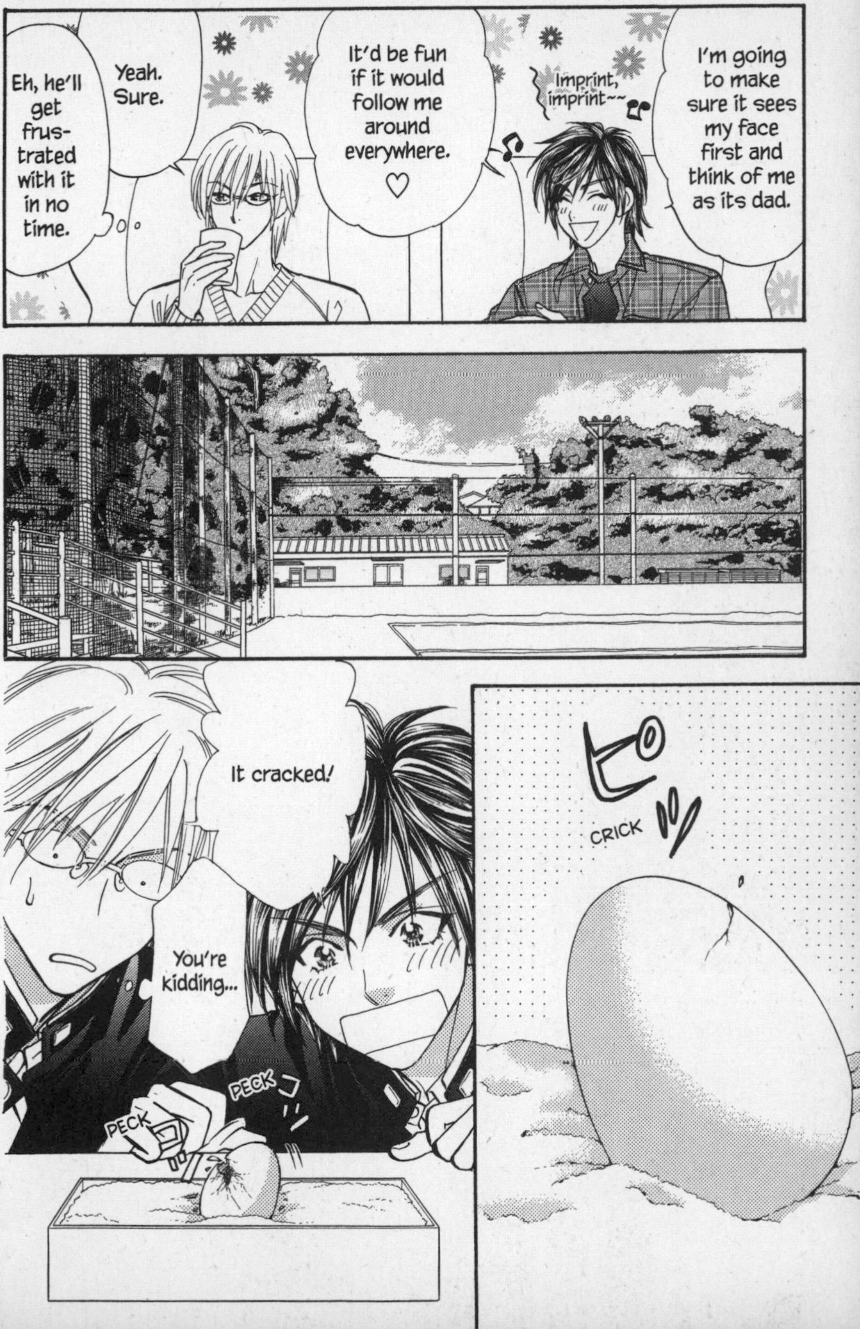
I'm going to make sure it sees my face first and think of me as its dad.
Imprint, imprint~~
It'd be fun if it would follow me around everywhere. ♡
Yeah. Sure.
Eh, he'll get frus-trated with it in no time.
CRICK
It cracked!
You're kidding...
PECK
PECK

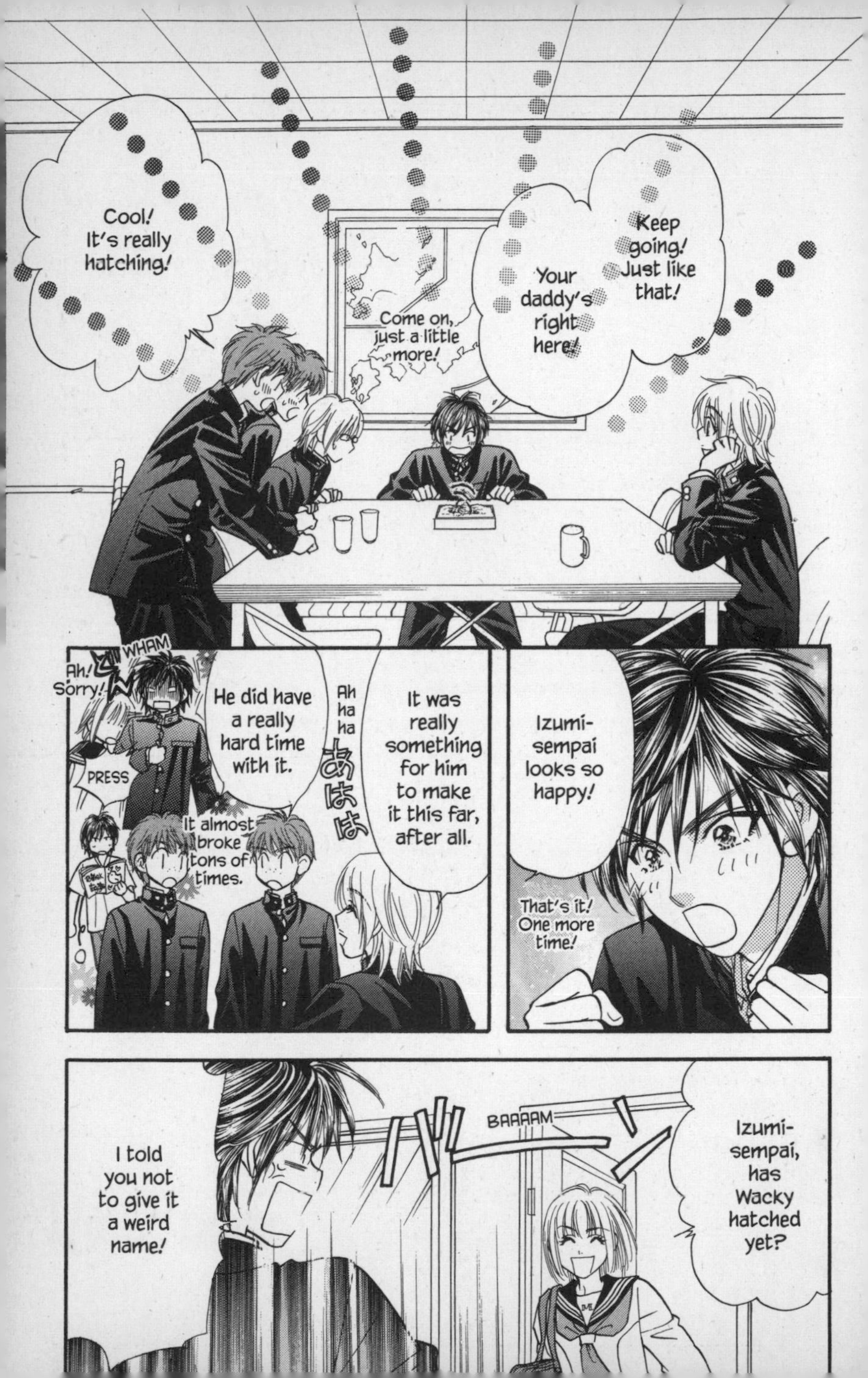
Keep going! Just like that!
Your daddy's right here!
Come on, just a little more!
Cool! It's really hatching!
Izumi-sempai looks so happy!
That's it! One more time!
It was really something for him to make it this far, after all.
Ah ha ha
あはは
He did have a really hard time with it.
It almost broke tons of times.
WHAM
Ah! Sorry!
PRESS
Izumi-sempai, has Wacky hatched yet?
BAAAAM
I told you not to give it a weird name!

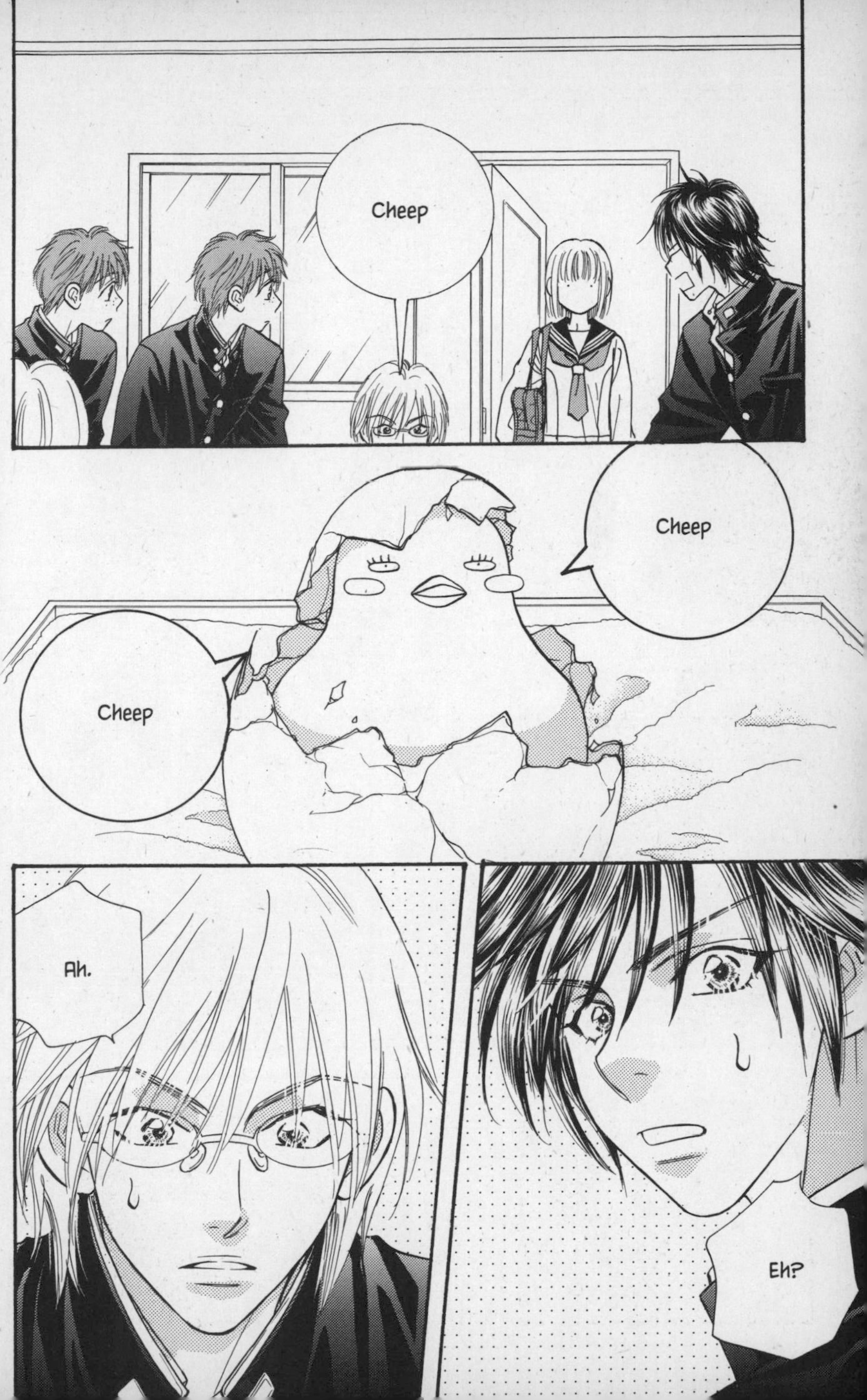
Cheep
Cheep
Cheep
Eh?
Ah.

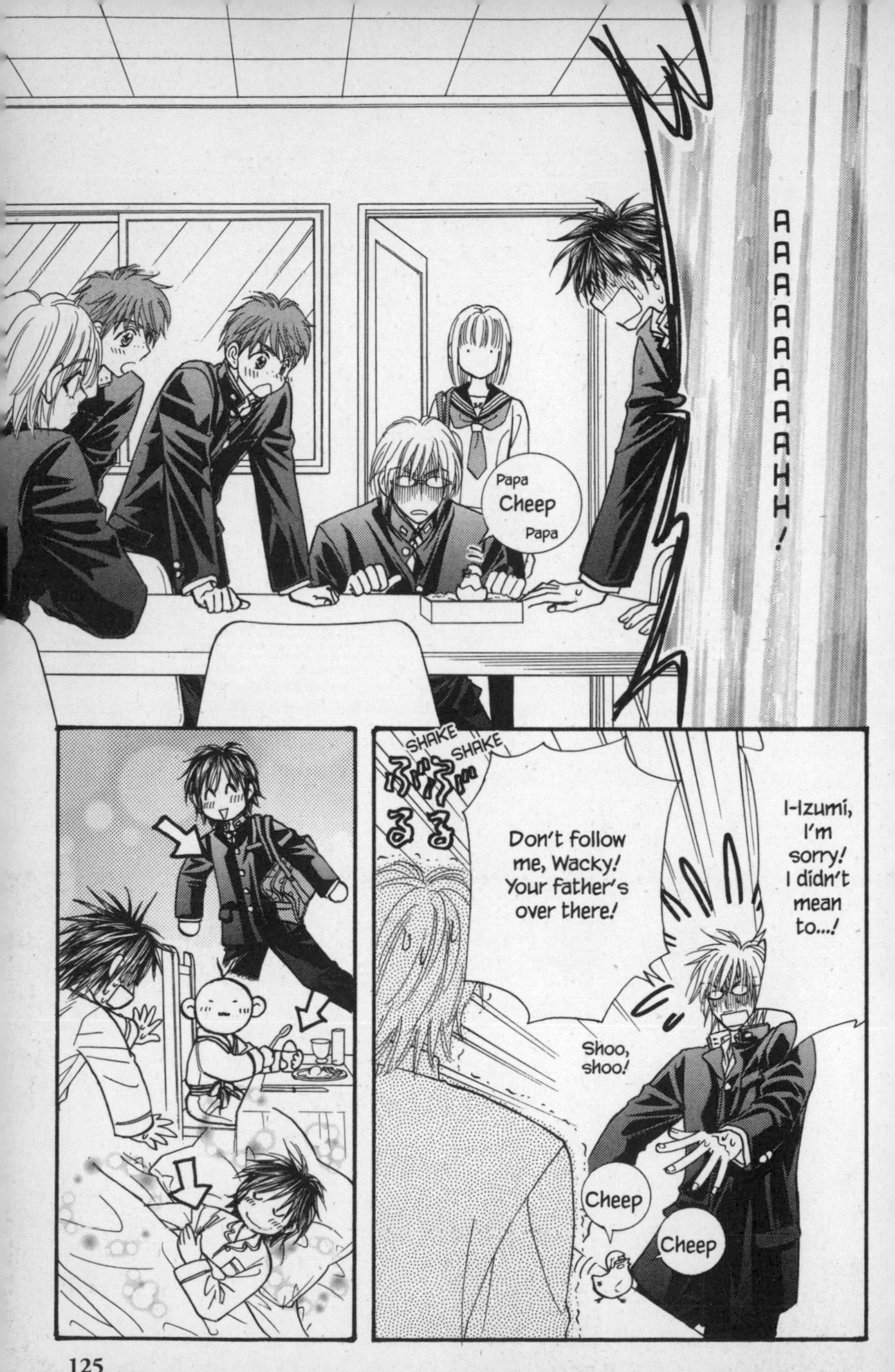
AAAAAAAAHH!
Papa
Cheep
Papa
SHAKE SHAKE
I-Izumi, I'm sorry! I didn't mean to...!
Don't follow me, Wacky! Your father's over there!
Shoo, shoo!
Cheep
Cheep

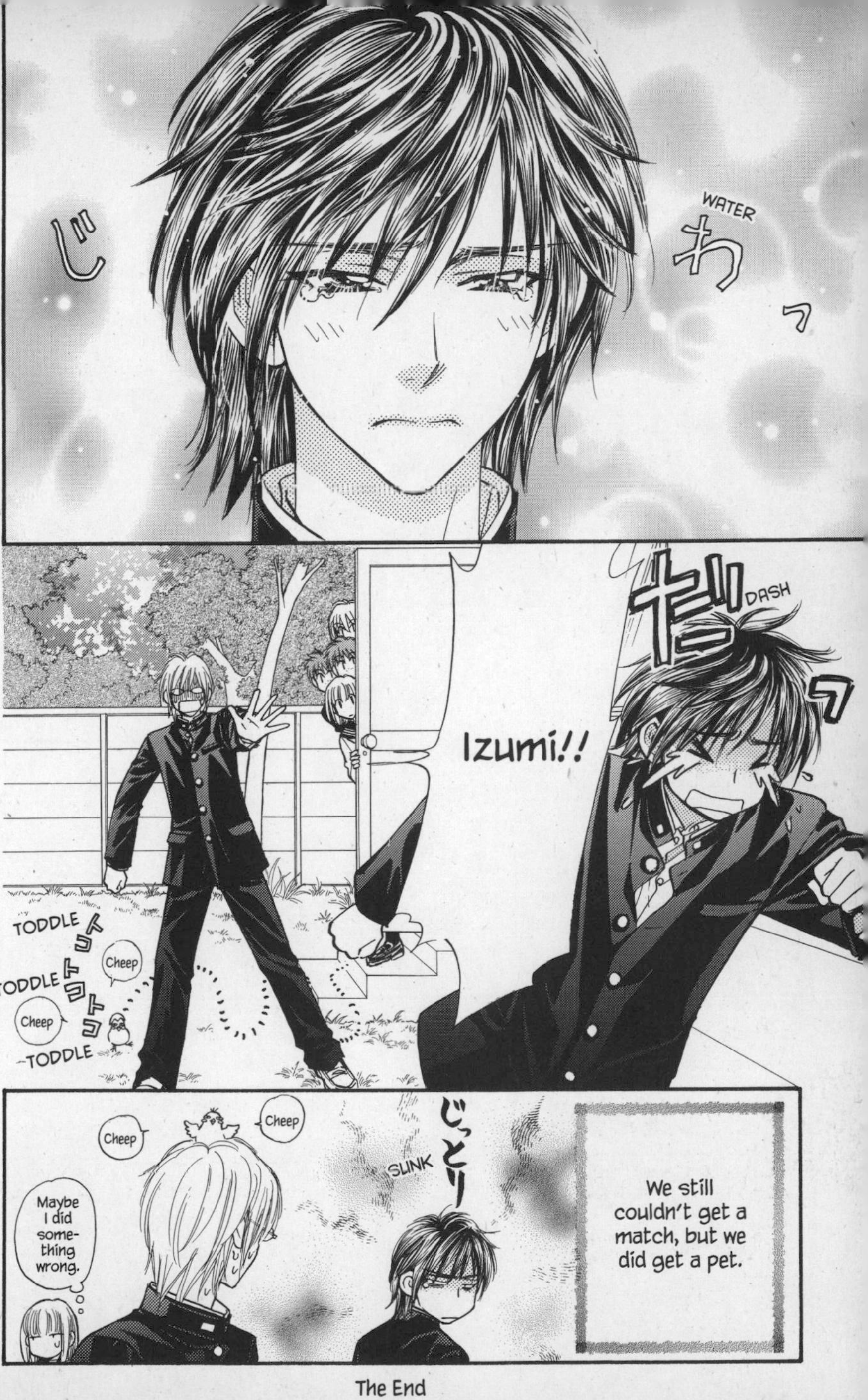

WATER
わっ
じ
DASH
だっ
Izumi!!
TODDLE
トコ
TODDLE
トコトコ
TODDLE
Cheep
Cheep
We still couldn't get a match, but we did get a pet.
SLINK
じっとり
Cheep
Cheep
Maybe I did some-thing wrong.

The End

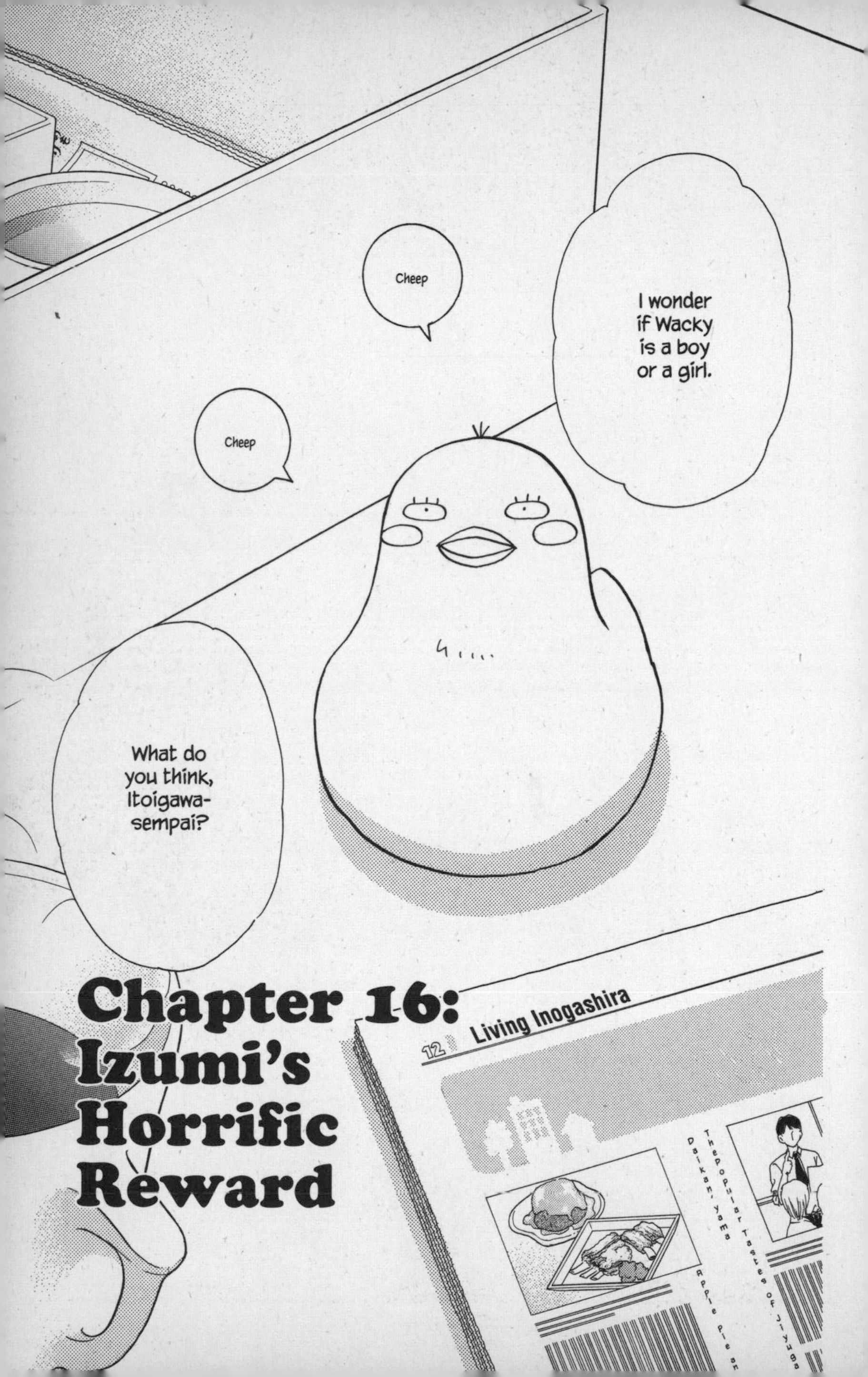
I wonder if Wacky is a boy or a girl.
Cheep
Cheep
What do you think, Itoigawa-sempai?
12
Living Inogashira
Daikanyama

Chapter 16: Izumi's Horrific Reward

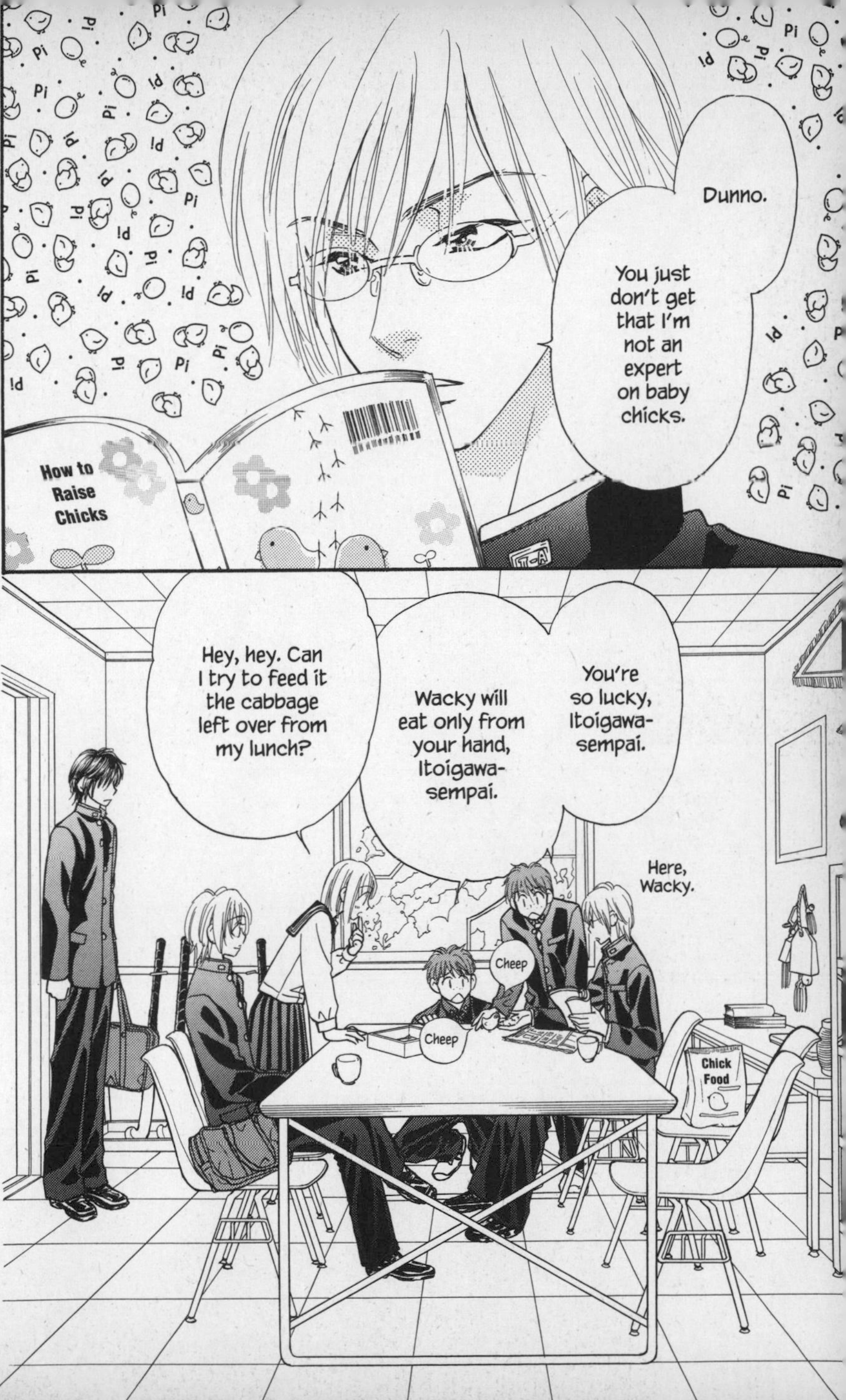
Pi
Dunno.
You just don't get that I'm not an expert on baby chicks.
How to Raise Chicks
You're so lucky, Itoigawa-sempai.
Wacky will eat only from your hand, Itoigawa-sempai.
Hey, hey. Can I try to feed it the cabbage left over from my lunch?
Here, Wacky.
Chick Food
Cheep
Cheep

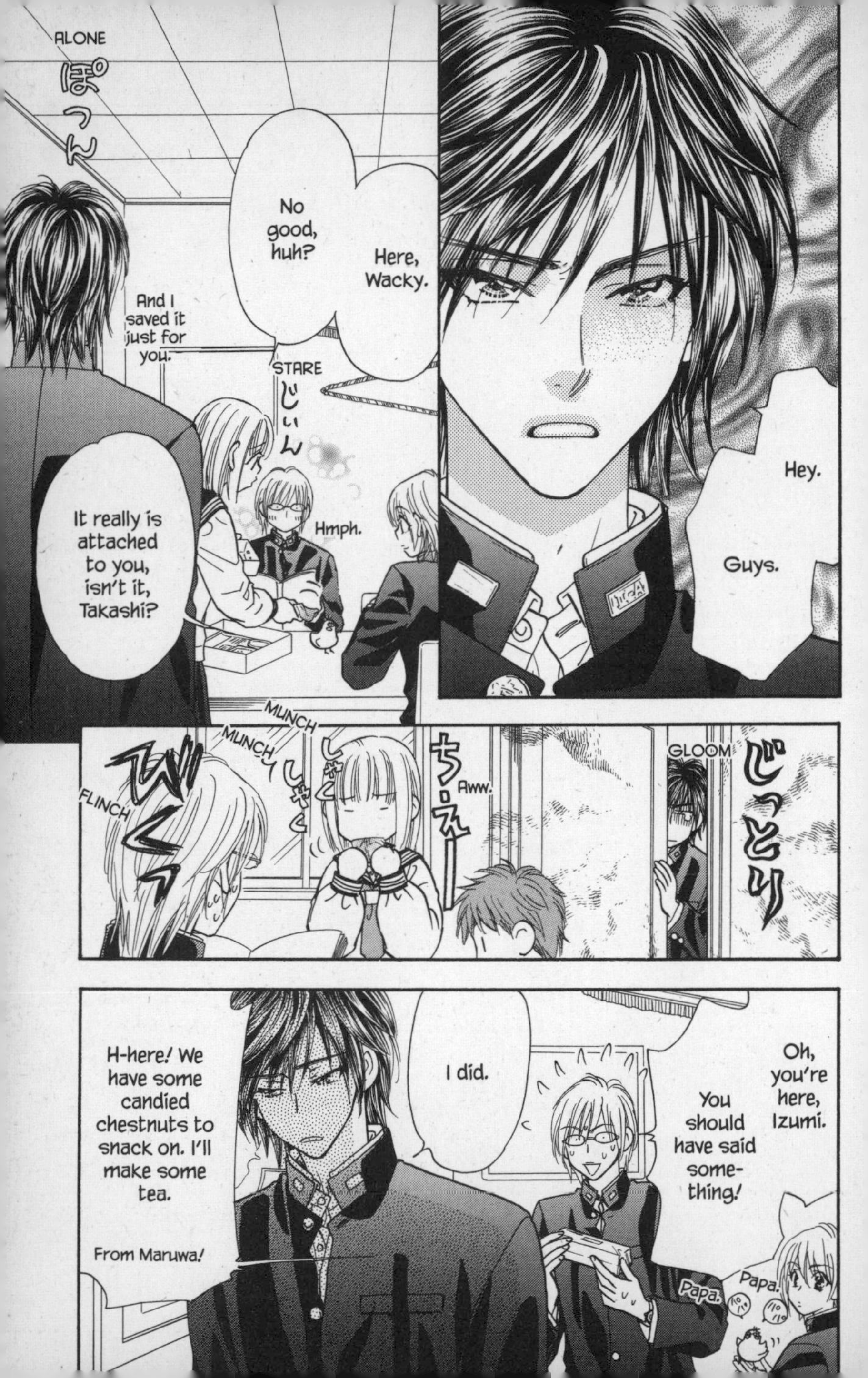
Hey.
Guys.
Here, Wacky.
No good, huh?
ALONE
ぽつん
And I saved it just for you.
STARE
じぃん
Hmph.
It really is attached to you, isn't it, Takashi?
GLOOM
じっとり
Aww.
ちぇー
MUNCH
MUNCH
しゃくしゃく
FLINCH
Oh, you're here, Izumi.
You should have said something!
I did.
H-here! We have some candied chestnuts to snack on. I'll make some tea.
From Maruwa!
Papa.
Papa.

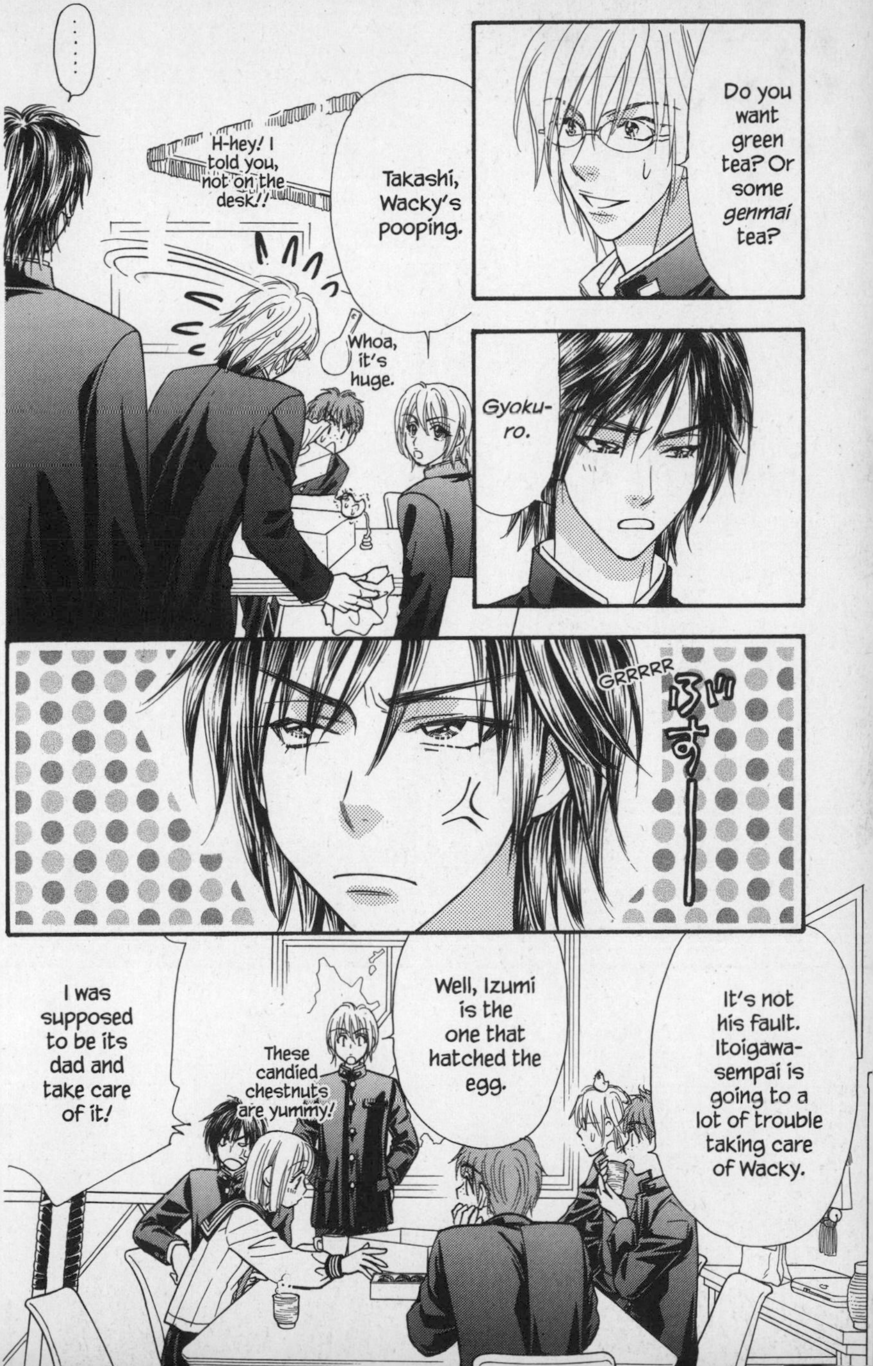
Do you want green tea? Or some *genmai* tea?
Gyoku-ro.
Takashi, Wacky's pooping.
......
H-hey! I told you, not on the desk!!
Whoa, it's huge.
GRRRRR
ふすー
It's not his fault. Itoigawa-sempai is going to a lot of trouble taking care of Wacky.
Well, Izumi is the one that hatched the egg.
These candied chestnuts are yummy!
I was supposed to be its dad and take care of it!

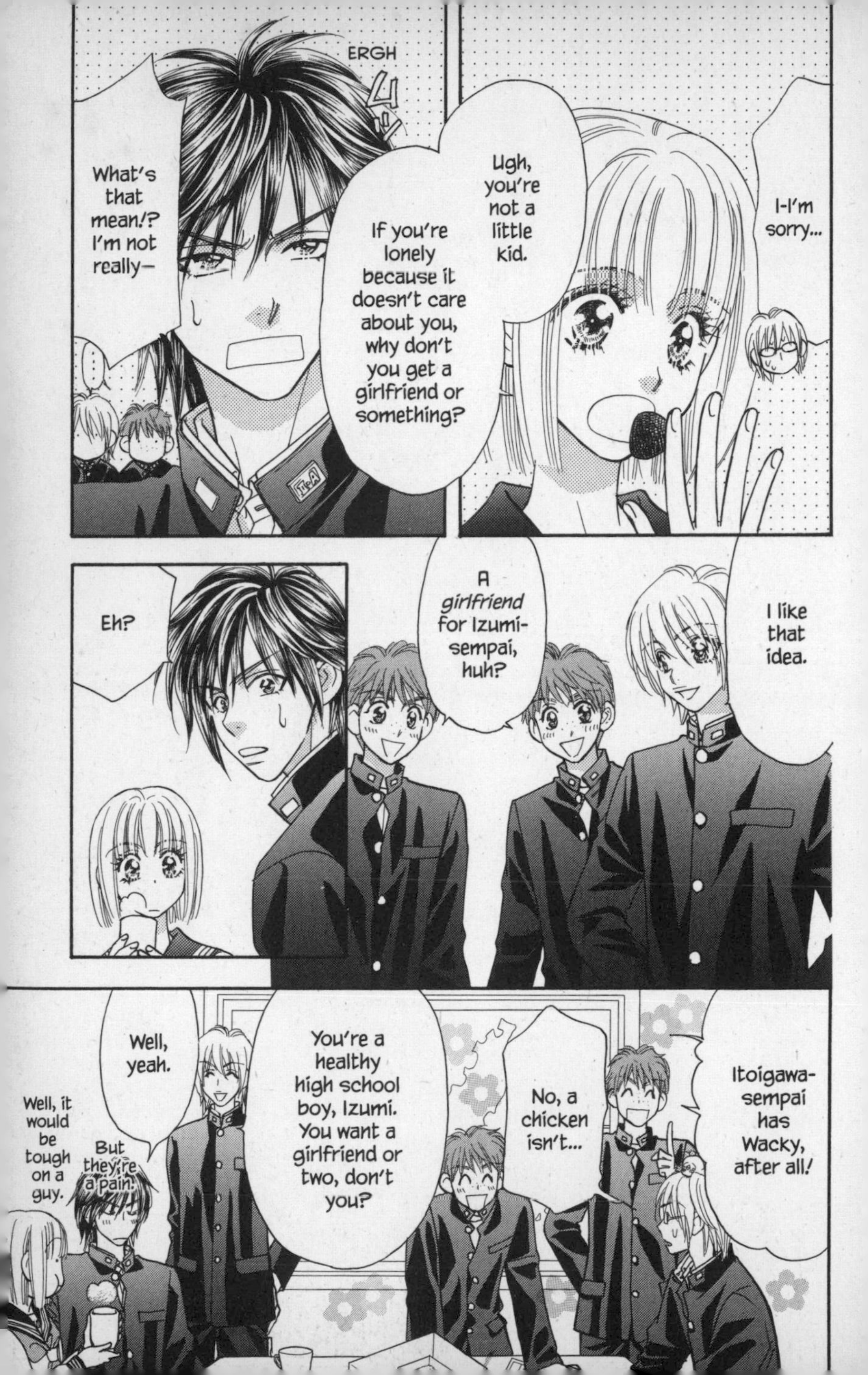
I-I'm sorry...
Ugh, you're not a little kid.
If you're lonely because it doesn't care about you, why don't you get a girlfriend or something?
ERGH
What's that mean!? I'm not really—
I like that idea.
A *girlfriend* for Izumi-sempai, huh?
Eh?
Itoigawa-sempai has Wacky, after all!
No, a chicken isn't...
You're a healthy high school boy, Izumi. You want a girlfriend or two, don't you?
Well, yeah.
But they're a pain.
Well, it would be tough on a guy.

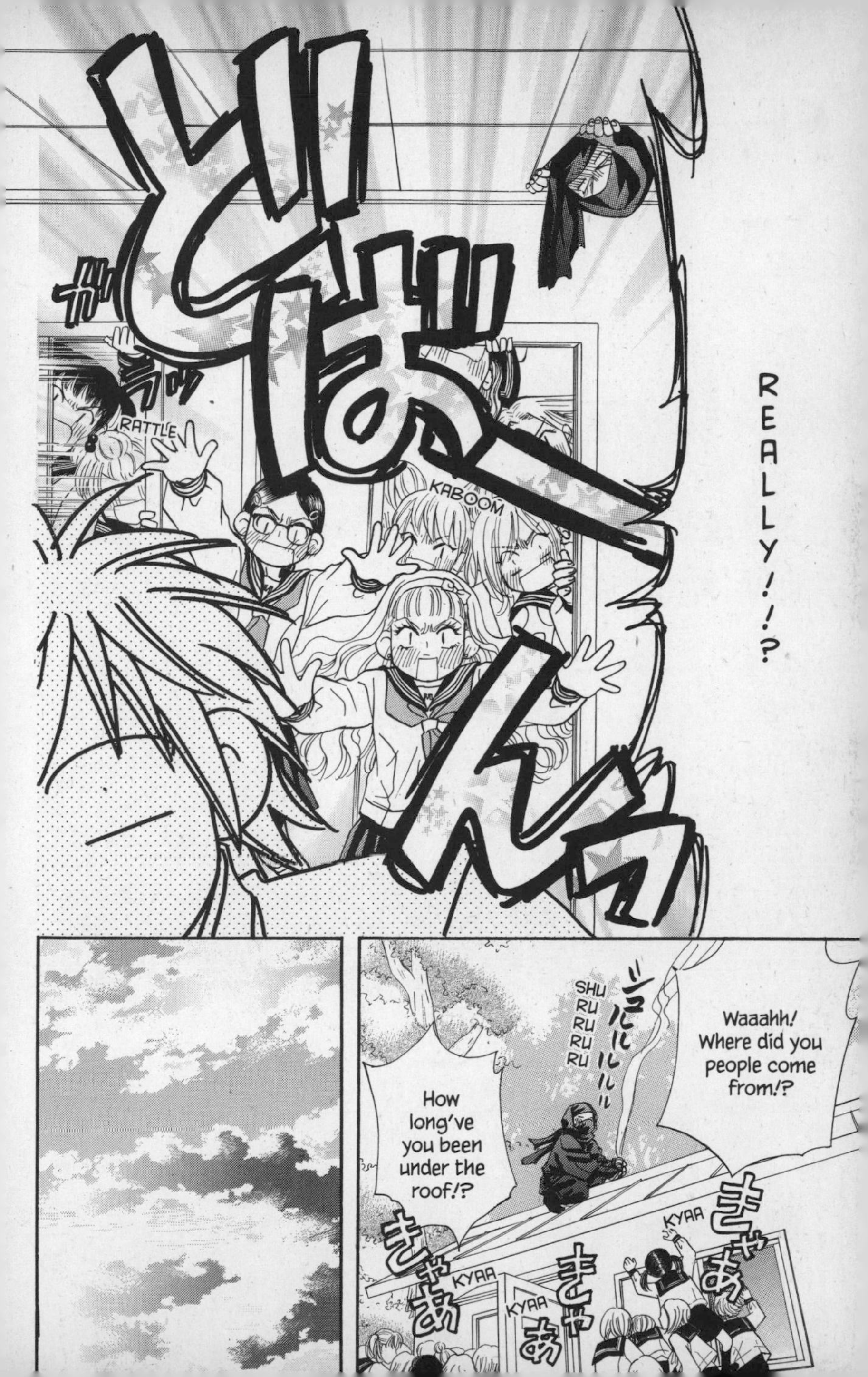

REALLY!!!?
KABOOM
RATTLE
Waaahh! Where did you people come from!?
SHU RU RU RU RU
How long've you been under the roof!?
KYAA
KYAA
KYAA

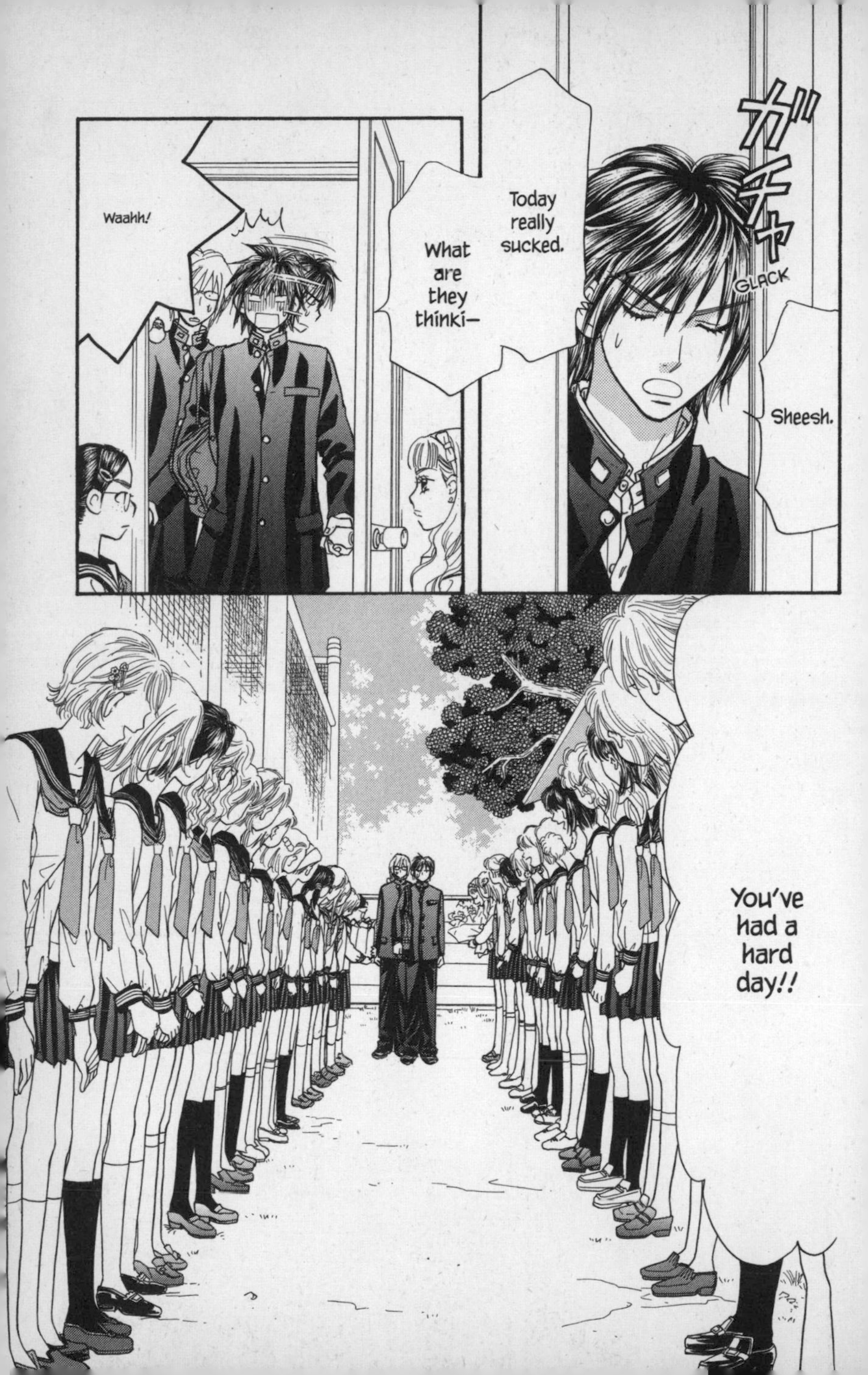
ガチャ
GLACK
Today really sucked.
Sheesh.
What are they thinki—
Waahh!
You've had a hard day!!

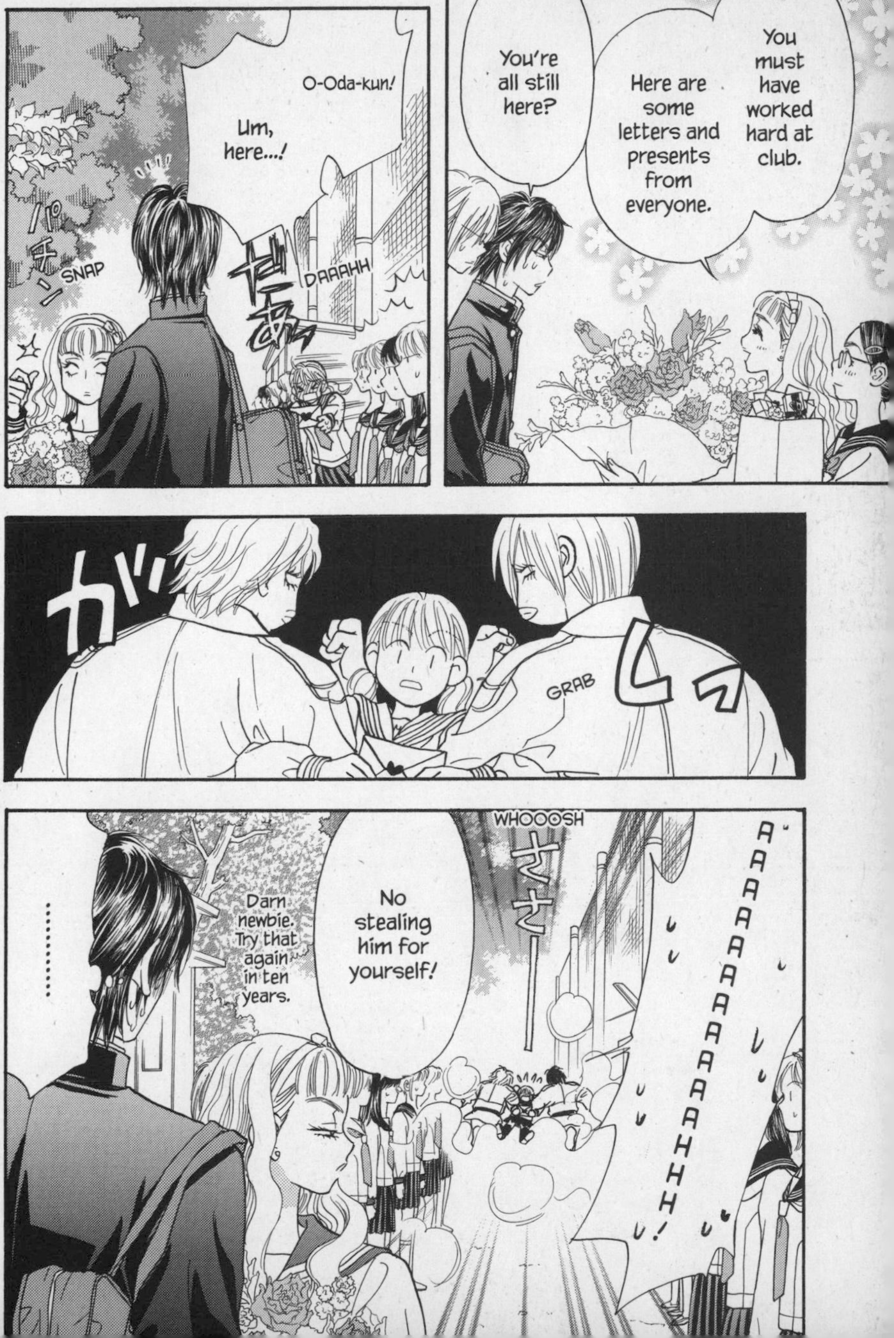
You must have worked hard at club.
Here are some letters and presents from everyone.
You're all still here?
O-Oda-kun!
Um, here...!
DAAAHH
SNAP
GRAB
AAAAAAAAAAAAAAAAHHHH!
WHOOOSH
No stealing him for yourself!
Darn newbie. Try that again in ten years.
......

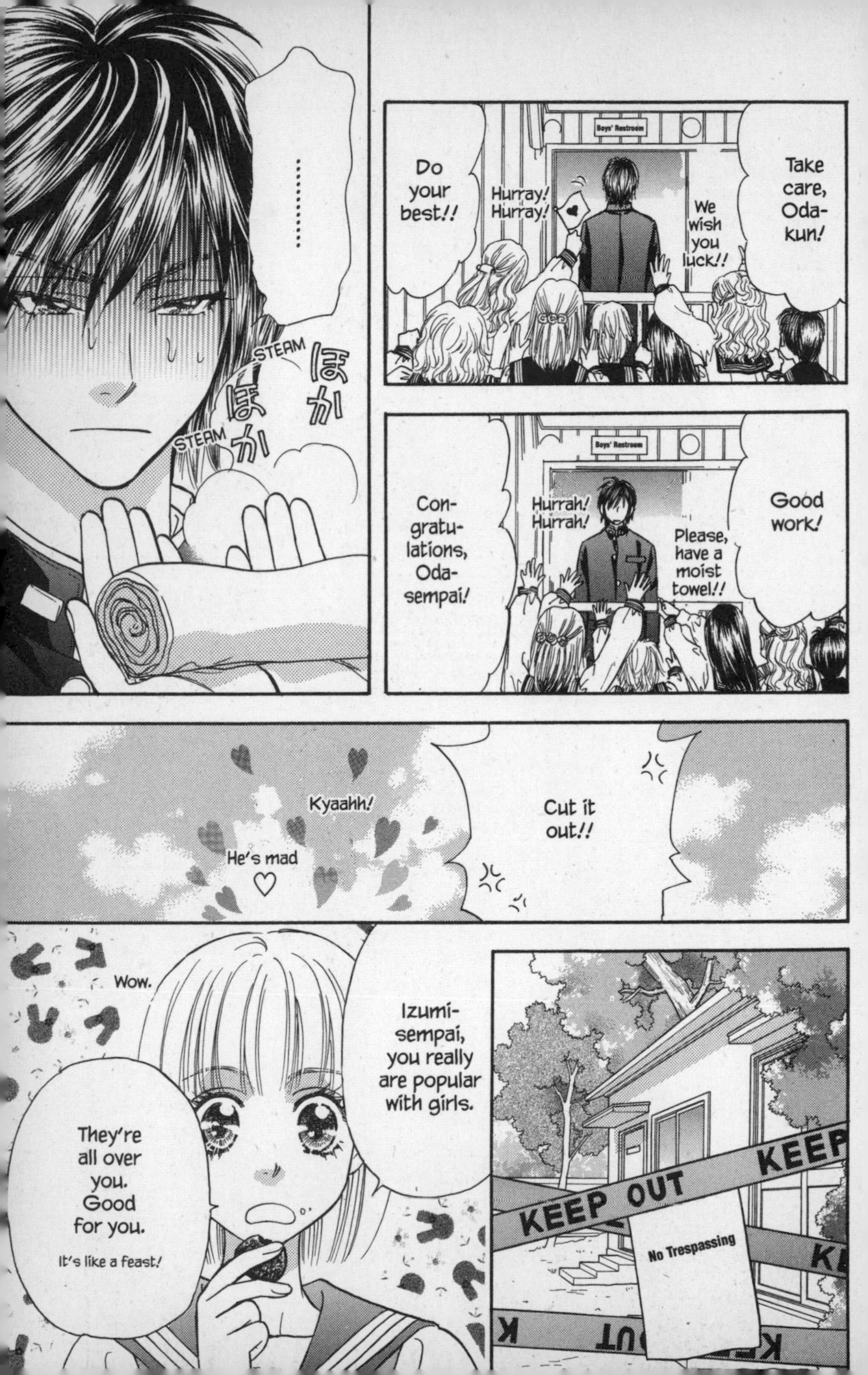
Boys' Restroom
Take care, Oda-kun!
We wish you luck!!
Hurray! Hurray!
Do your best!!
Boys' Restroom
Good work!
Please, have a moist towel!!
Hurrah! Hurrah!
Congratulations, Oda-sempai!
......
ほかほか
STEAM
STEAM
Cut it out!!
Kyaahh!
He's mad ♡
KEEP OUT
KEEP
No Trespassing
Izumi-sempai, you really are popular with girls.
Wow.
They're all over you. Good for you.
It's like a feast!

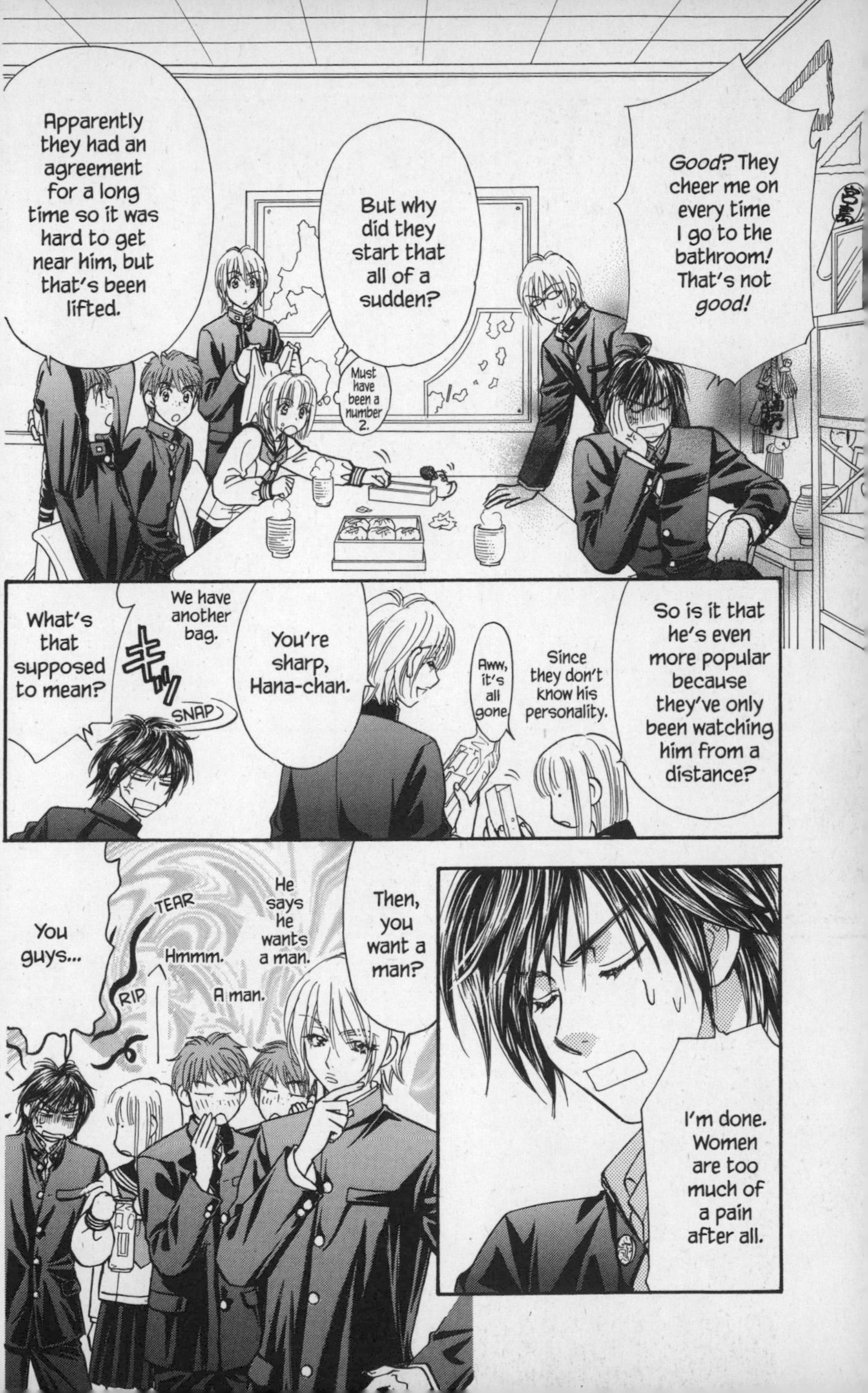
Good? They cheer me on every time I go to the bathroom! That's not good!
But why did they start that all of a sudden?
Must have been a number 2.
Apparently they had an agreement for a long time so it was hard to get near him, but that's been lifted.
So is it that he's even more popular because they've only been watching him from a distance?
Since they don't know his personality.
Aww, it's all gone.
You're sharp, Hana-chan.
We have another bag.
SNAP
What's that supposed to mean?
I'm done. Women are too much of a pain after all.
Then, you want a man?
He says he wants a man.
A man.
Hmmm.
TEAR
RIP
You guys...

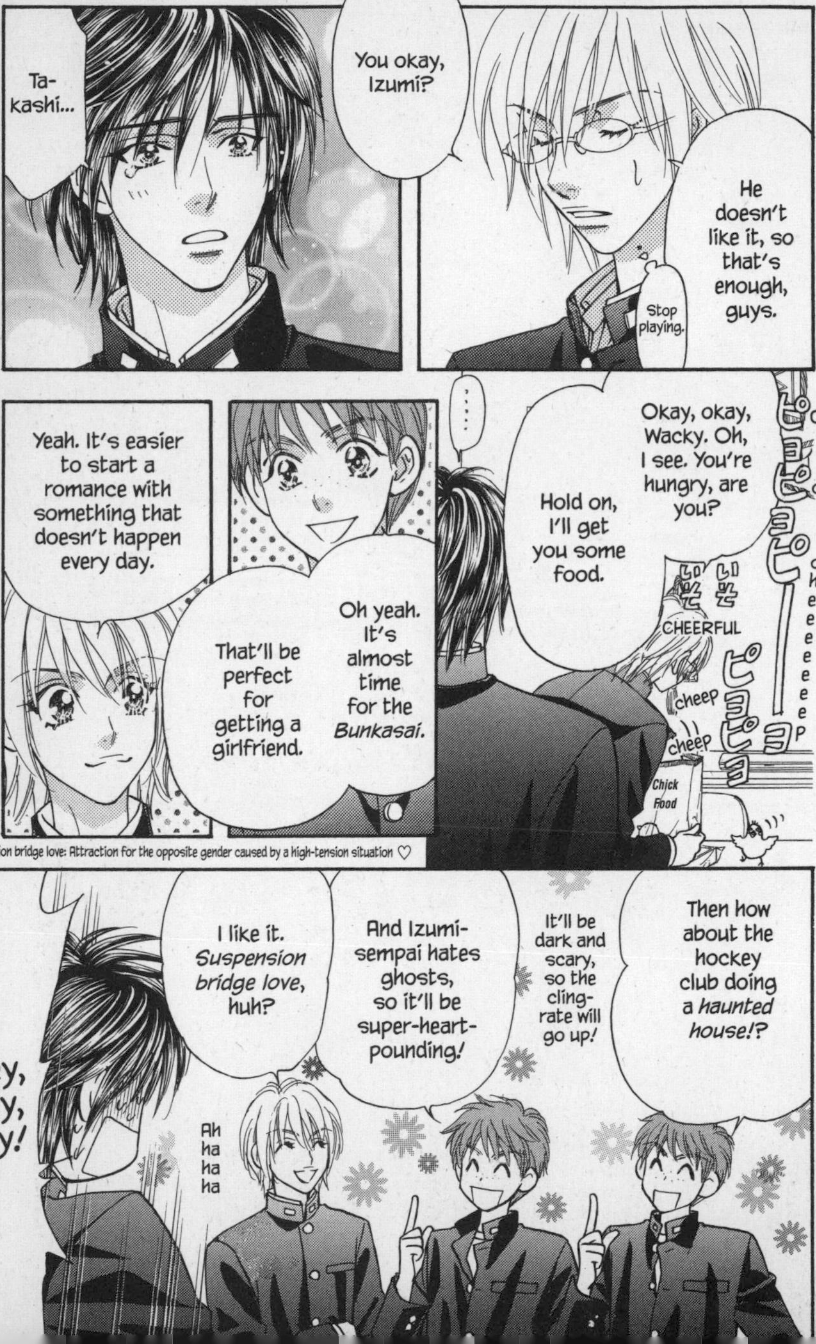
You okay, Izumi?
He doesn't like it, so that's enough, guys.
Stop playing.
Ta-kashi...
Cheep
cheep
Okay, okay, Wacky. Oh, I see. You're hungry, are you?
......
Hold on, I'll get you some food.
cheeeeeeeep
CHEERFUL
cheep
cheep
Chick Food
Oh yeah. It's almost time for the *Bunkasai*.
That'll be perfect for getting a girlfriend.
Yeah. It's easier to start a romance with something that doesn't happen every day.
Suspension bridge love: Attraction for the opposite gender caused by a high-tension situation ♡
Then how about the hockey club doing a *haunted house!?*
It'll be dark and scary, so the cling-rate will go up!
And Izumi-sempai hates ghosts, so it'll be super-heart-pounding!
I like it. *Suspension bridge love*, huh?
Ah ha ha ha
Hey, hey, hey!

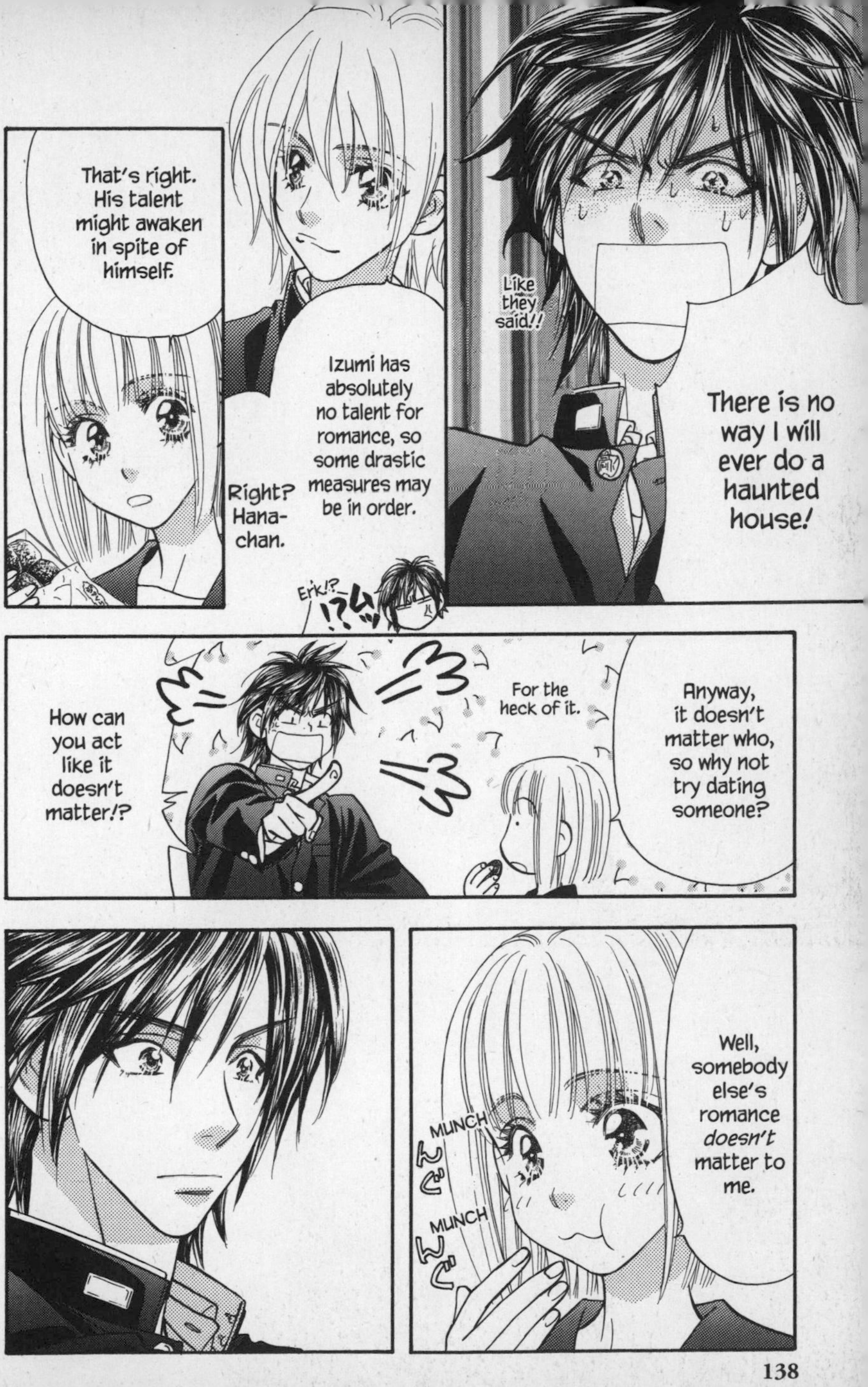

There is no way I will ever do a haunted house!
Like they said!!
Izumi has absolutely no talent for romance, so some drastic measures may be in order.
Right? Hana-chan.
That's right. His talent might awaken in spite of himself.
Erk!?
Anyway, it doesn't matter who, so why not try dating someone?
For the heck of it.
How can you act like it doesn't matter!?
Well, somebody else's romance *doesn't* matter to me.
MUNCH
MUNCH

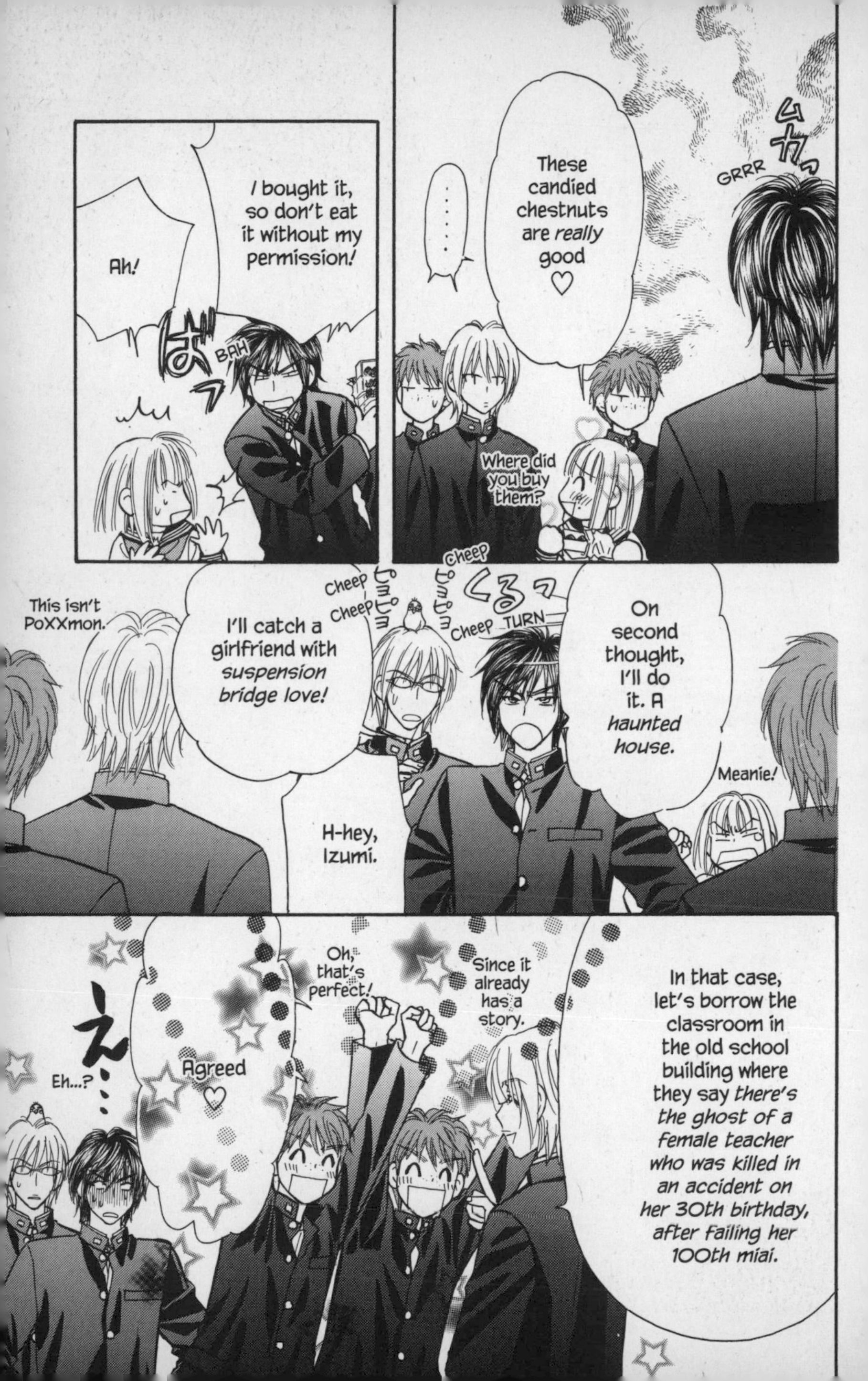
GRRR
These candied chestnuts are *really* good ♡
. . . . .
Where did you buy them?
I bought it, so don't eat it without my permission!
BAH
Ah!
On second thought, I'll do it. A *haunted house.*
TURN
Cheep
Cheep
Cheep
Cheep
I'll catch a girlfriend with *suspension bridge love!*
This isn't PoXXmon.
Meanie!
H-hey, Izumi.
In that case, let's borrow the classroom in the old school building where they say *there's the ghost of a female teacher who was killed in an accident on her 30th birthday, after failing her 100th miai.*
Since it already has a story.
Oh, that's perfect!
Agreed ♡
Eh...?

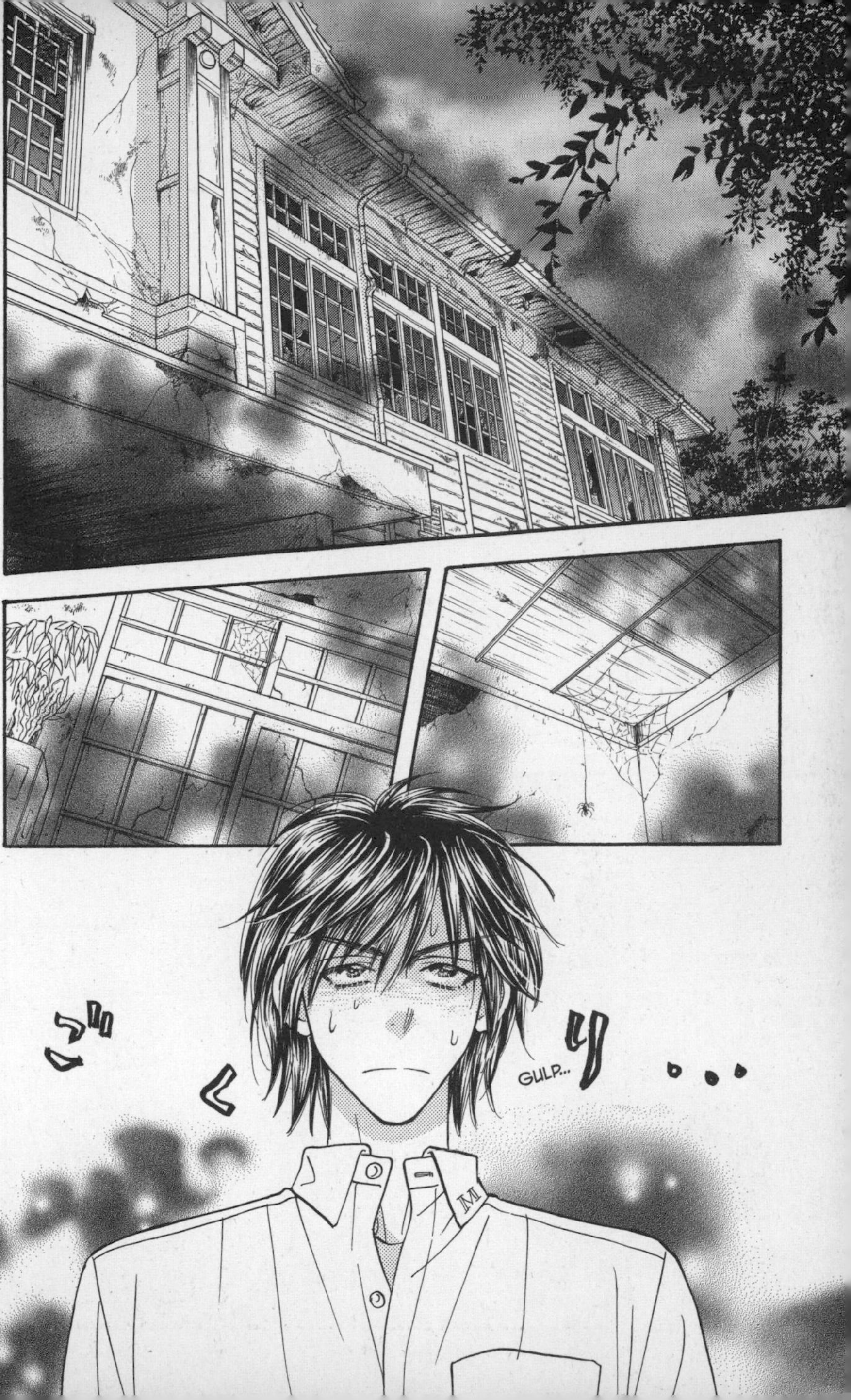
ごくり…
GULP...

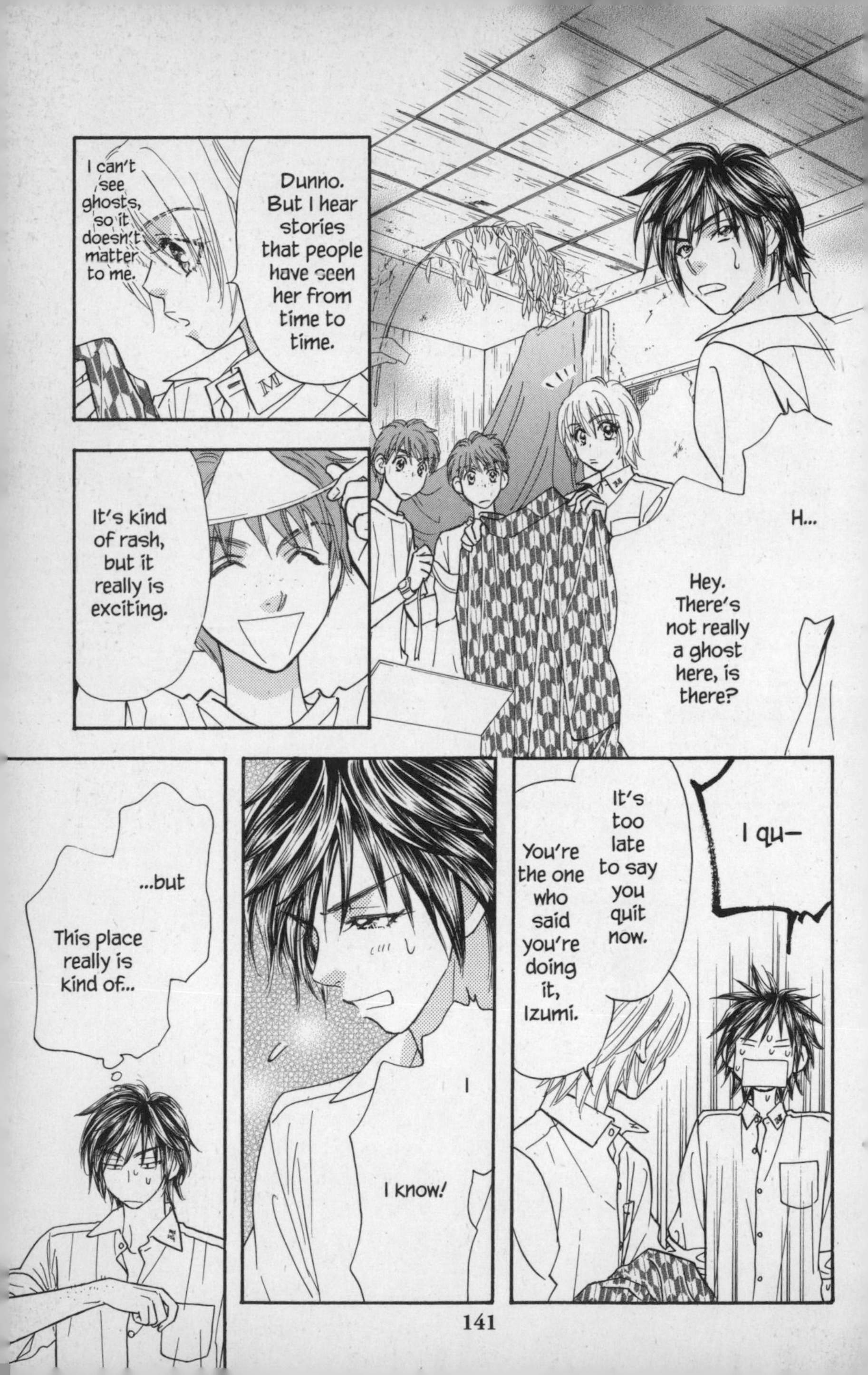
H...
Hey. There's not really a ghost here, is there?
Dunno. But I hear stories that people have seen her from time to time.
I can't see ghosts, so it doesn't matter to me.
It's kind of rash, but it really is exciting.
I qu–
It's too late to say you quit now.
You're the one who said you're doing it, Izumi.
I
I know!
...but
This place really is kind of...

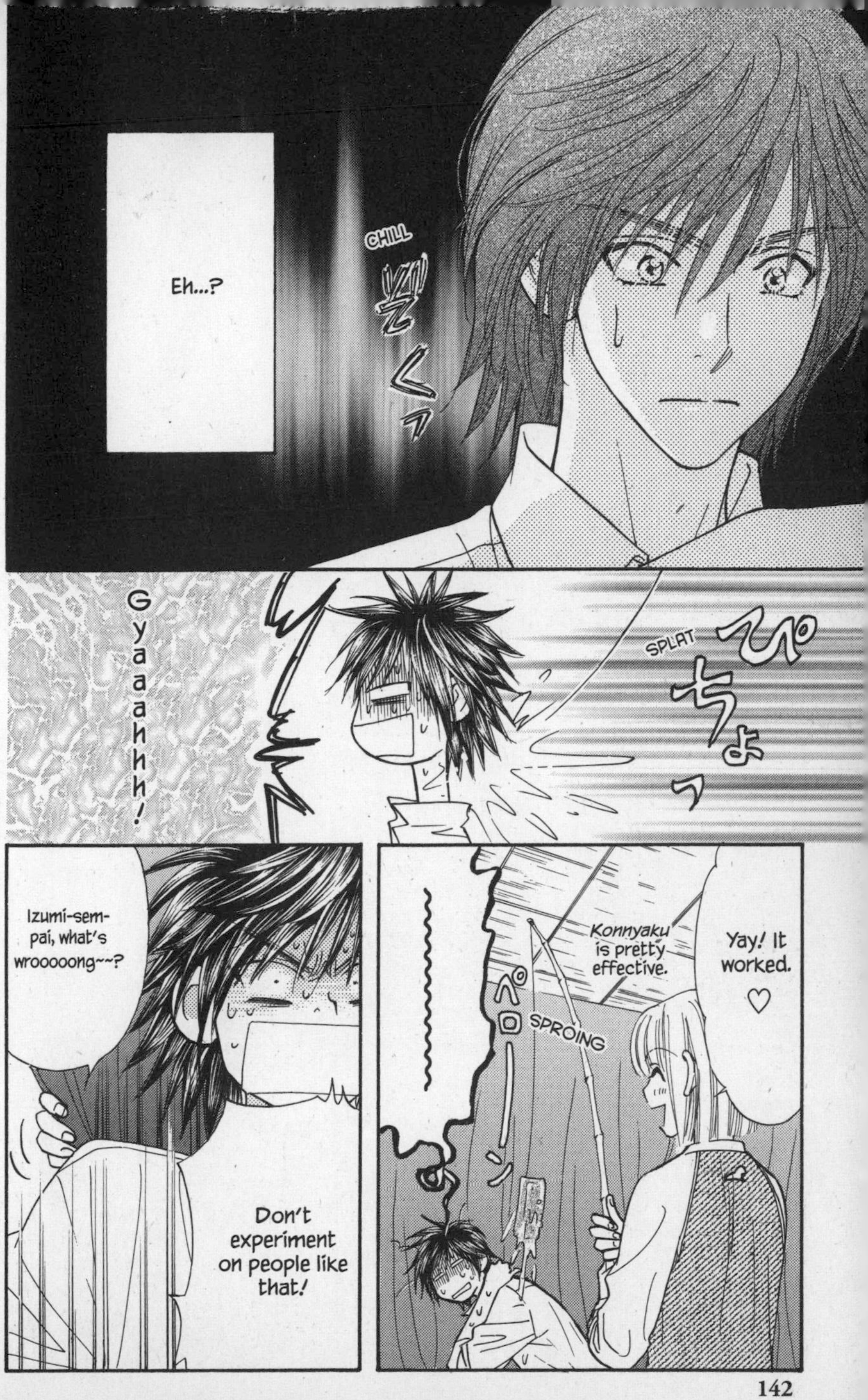
Eh...?
CHILL
ぞくっ
SPLAT
ぴちょっ
Gyaaahhh!
Yay! It worked. ♡
Konnyaku is pretty effective.
SPROING
ぺローン
~~~~~~
Izumi-sem-pai, what's wroooong~~?
Don't experiment on people like that!
~~~~~~

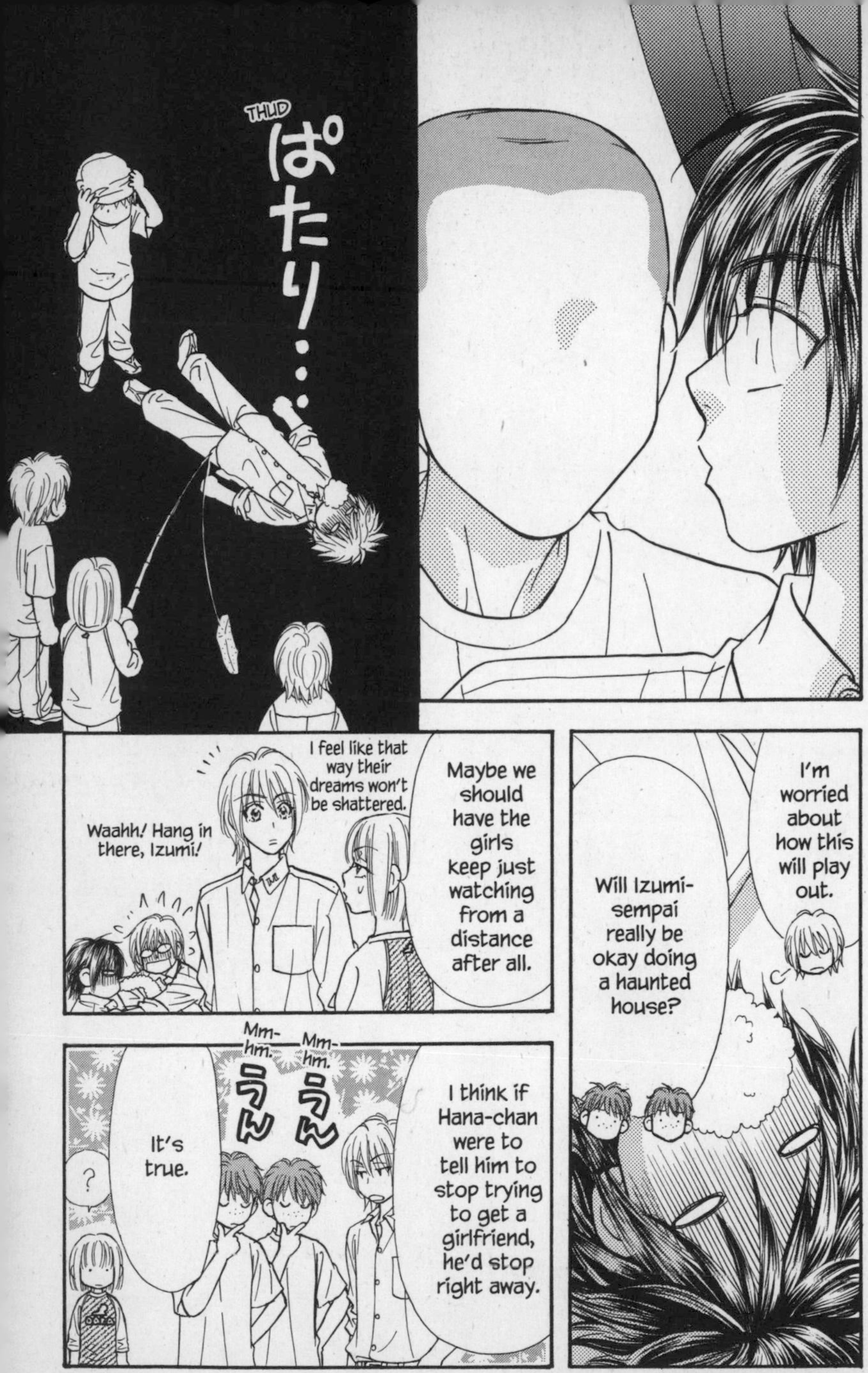
THUD
ぱたり…
I'm worried about how this will play out.
Will Izumi-sempai really be okay doing a haunted house?
Maybe we should have the girls keep just watching from a distance after all.
I feel like that way their dreams won't be shattered.
Waahh! Hang in there, Izumi!
I think if Hana-chan were to tell him to stop trying to get a girlfriend, he'd stop right away.
Mm-hm.
うん
Mm-hm.
うん
It's true.
?

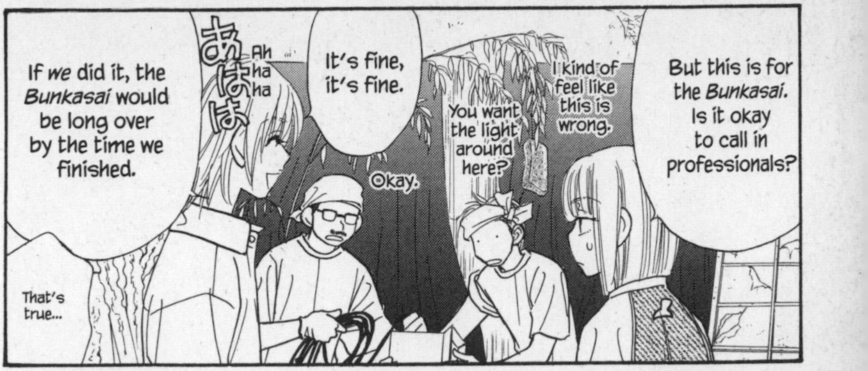
But this is for the *Bunkasai*. Is it okay to call in professionals?
I kind of feel like this is wrong.
You want the light around here?
Okay.
It's fine, it's fine.
あはは
Ah ha ha
If *we* did it, the *Bunkasai* would be long over by the time we finished.
That's true...

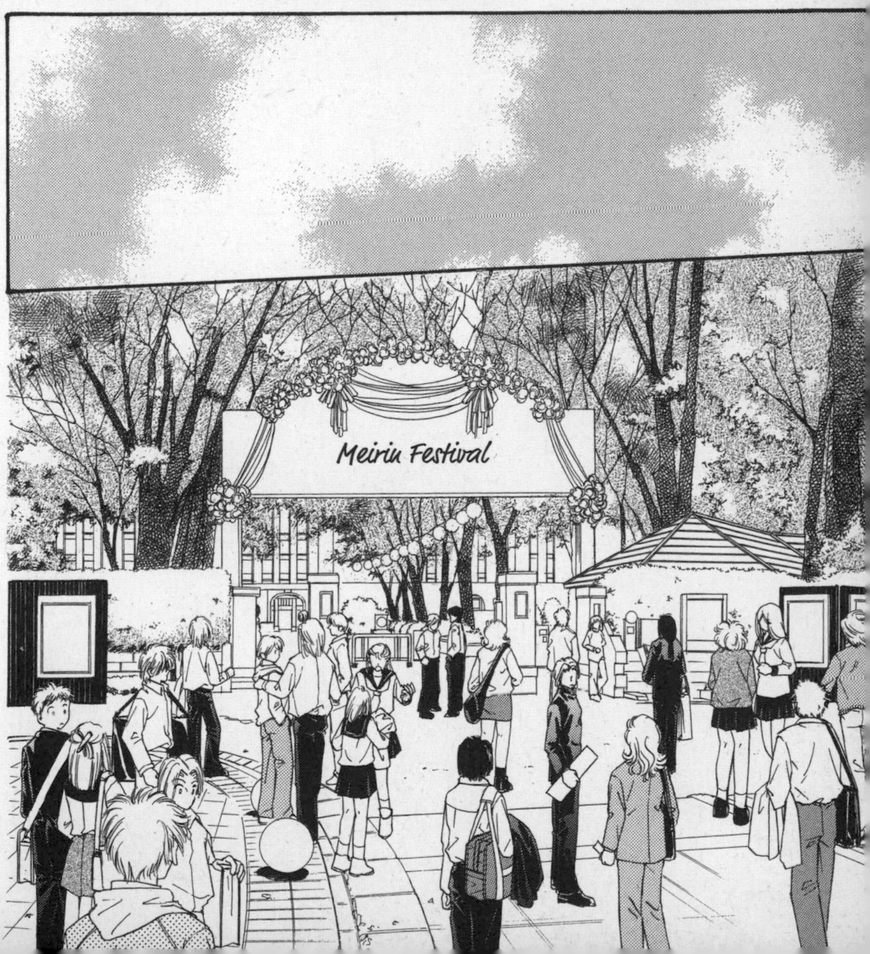
Meirin Festival

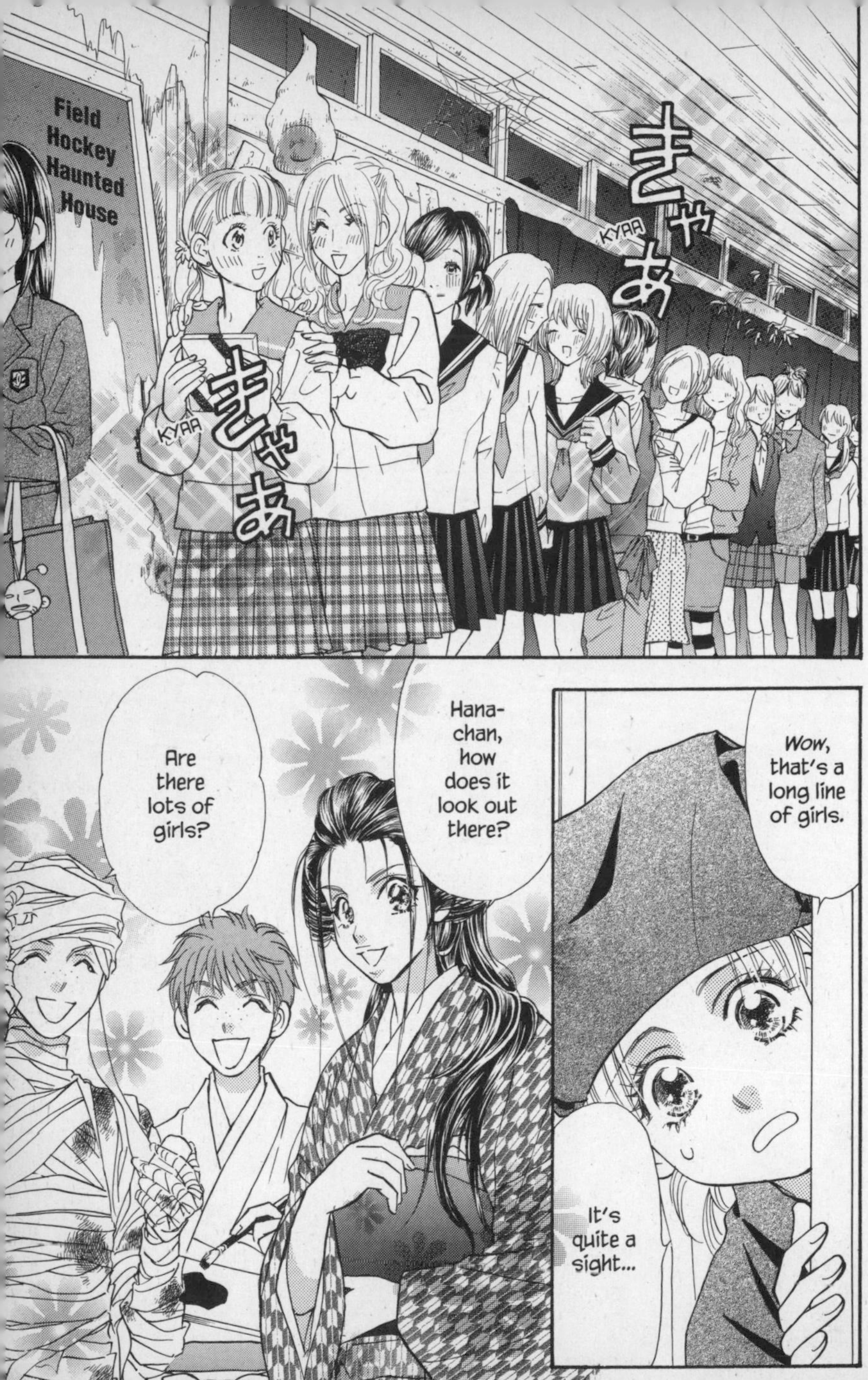
Field Hockey Haunted House
きゃあ
KYAA
きゃあ
KYAA
Wow, that's a long line of girls.
It's quite a sight...
Hana-chan, how does it look out there?
Are there lots of girls?

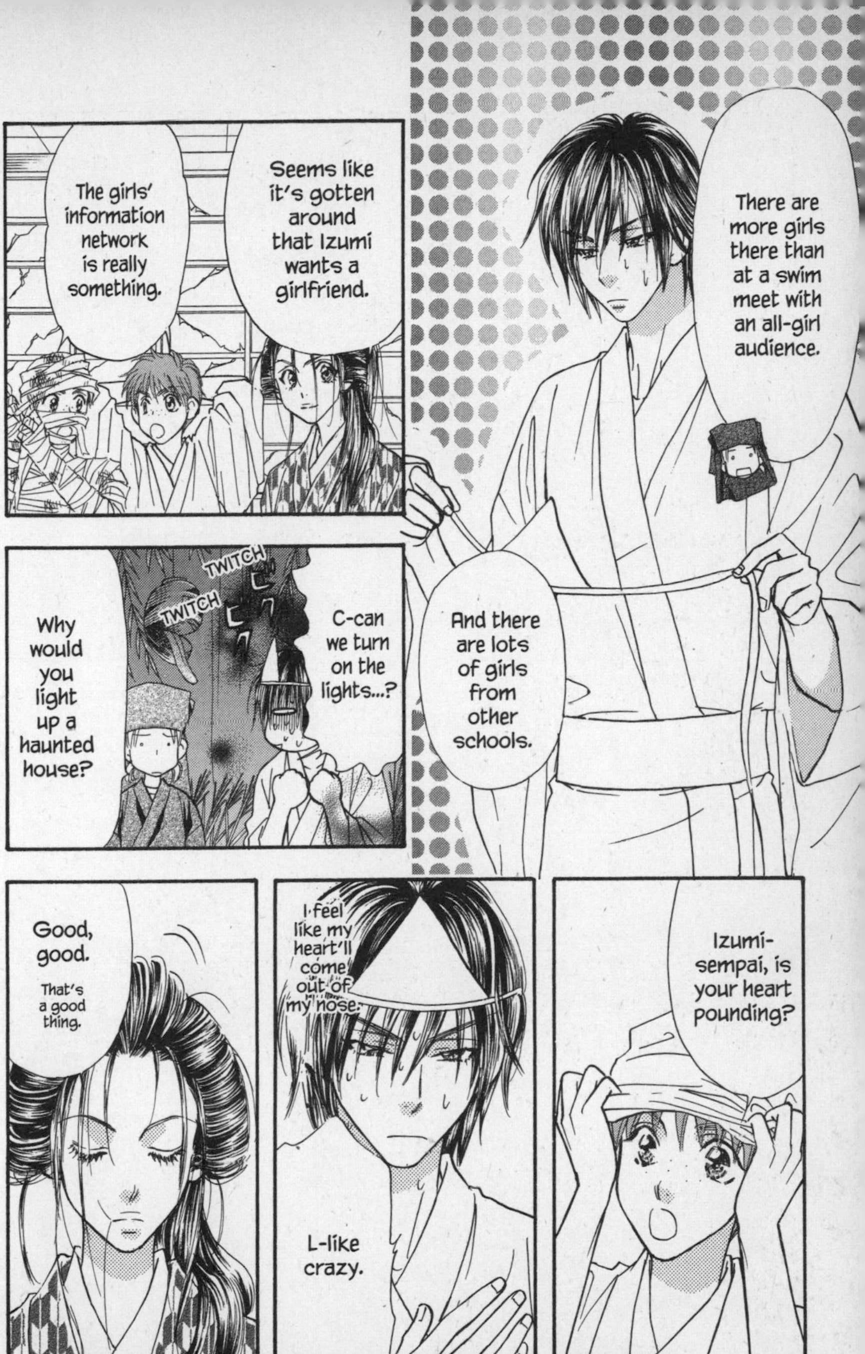
There are more girls there than at a swim meet with an all-girl audience.
And there are lots of girls from other schools.
Seems like it's gotten around that Izumi wants a girlfriend.
The girls' information network is really something.
TWITCH
TWITCH
C-can we turn on the lights...?
Why would you light up a haunted house?
Izumi-sempai, is your heart pounding?
I feel like my heart'll come out of my nose.
L-like crazy.
Good, good.
That's a good thing.

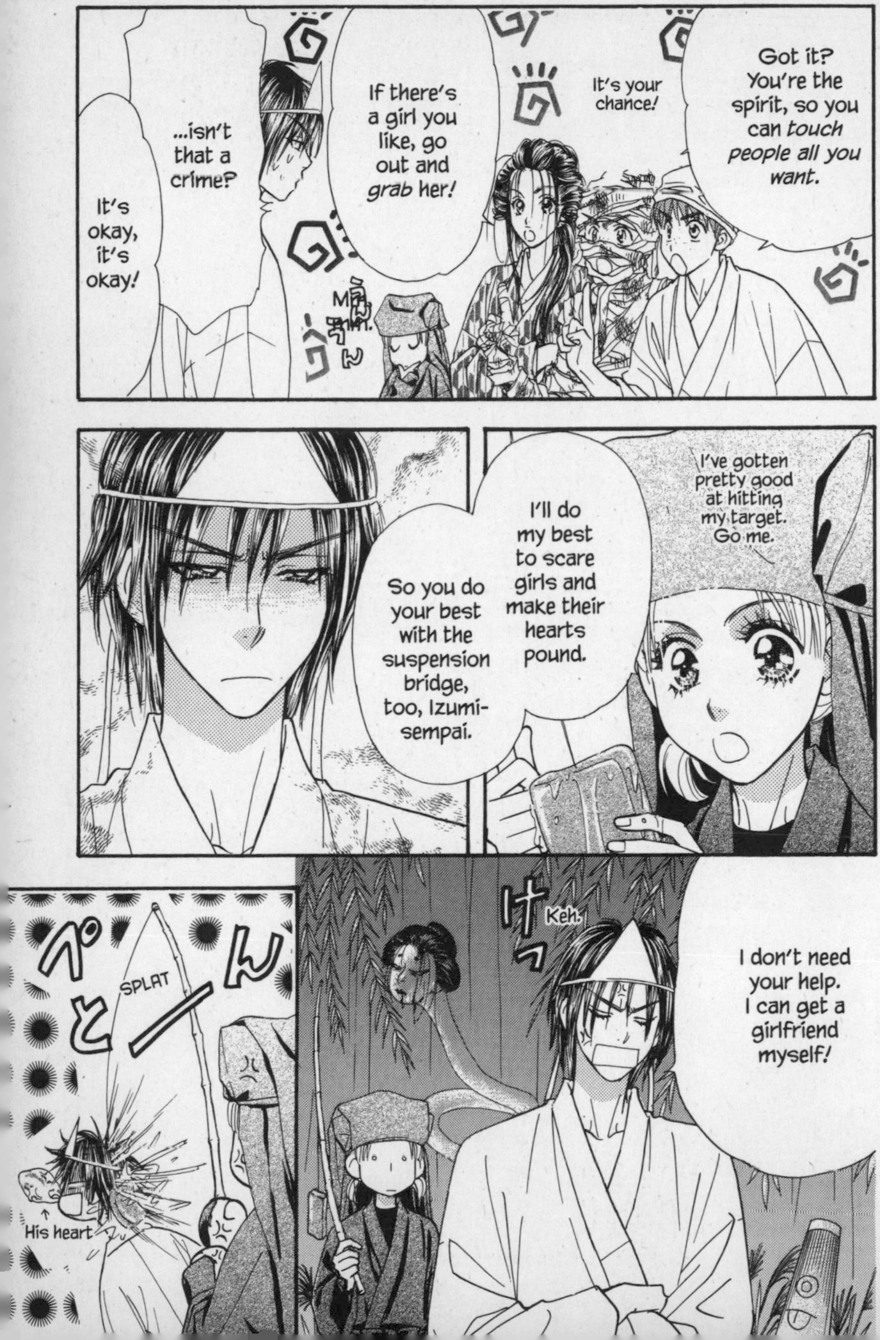
Got it? You're the spirit, so you can *touch people all you want.*
It's your chance!
If there's a girl you like, go out and *grab* her!
Mm-hmm.
...isn't that a crime?
It's okay, it's okay!
I've gotten pretty good at hitting my target. Go me.
I'll do my best to scare girls and make their hearts pound.
So you do your best with the suspension bridge, too, Izumi-sempai.
I don't need your help. I can get a girlfriend myself!
Keh.
SPLAT
His heart

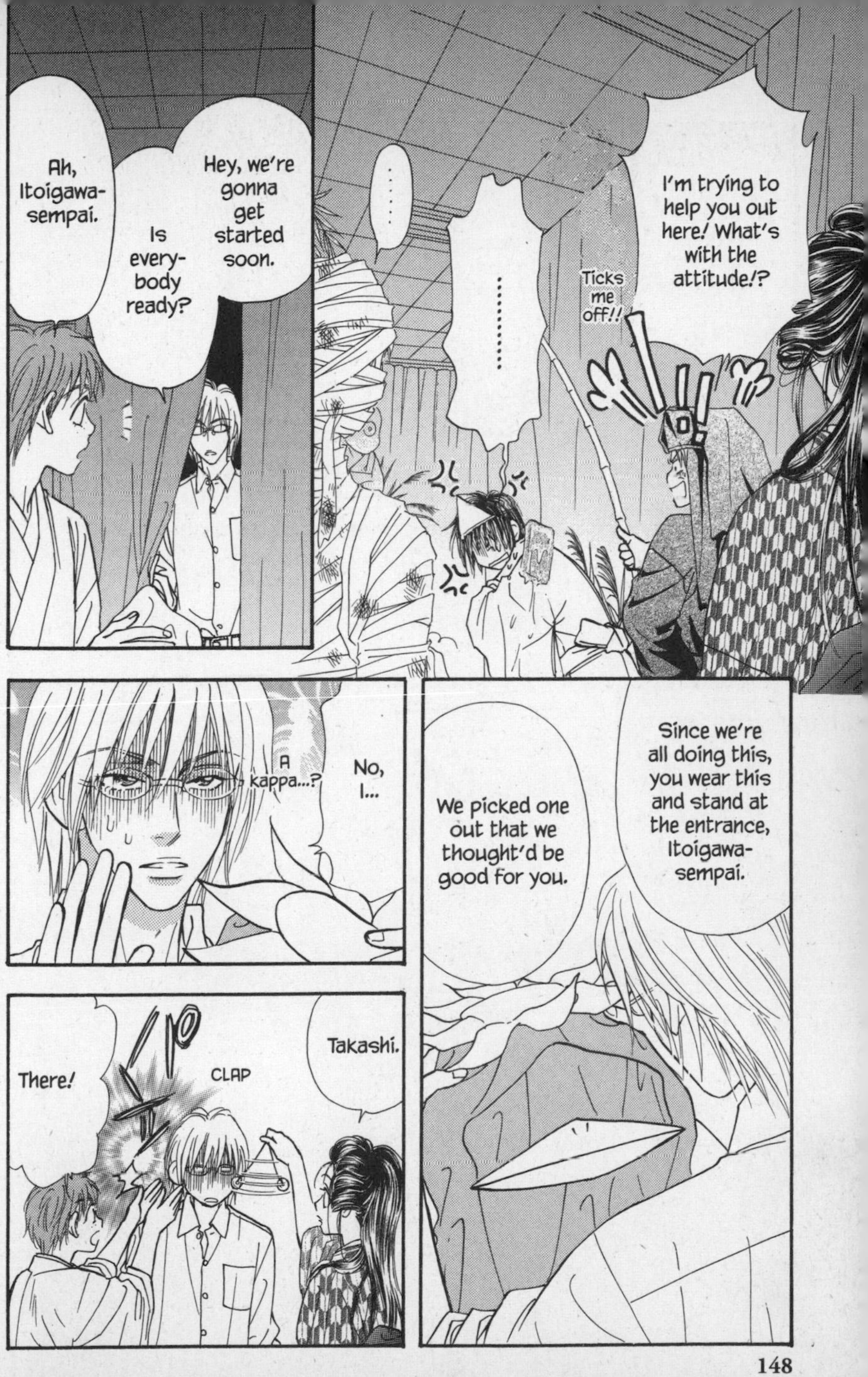
I'm trying to help you out here! What's with the attitude!?
Ticks me off!!
......
......
Hey, we're gonna get started soon. Is everybody ready?
Ah, Itoigawa-sempai.
Since we're all doing this, you wear this and stand at the entrance, Itoigawa-sempai.
We picked one out that we thought'd be good for you.
No, I...
A kappa...?
Takashi.
CLAP
There!

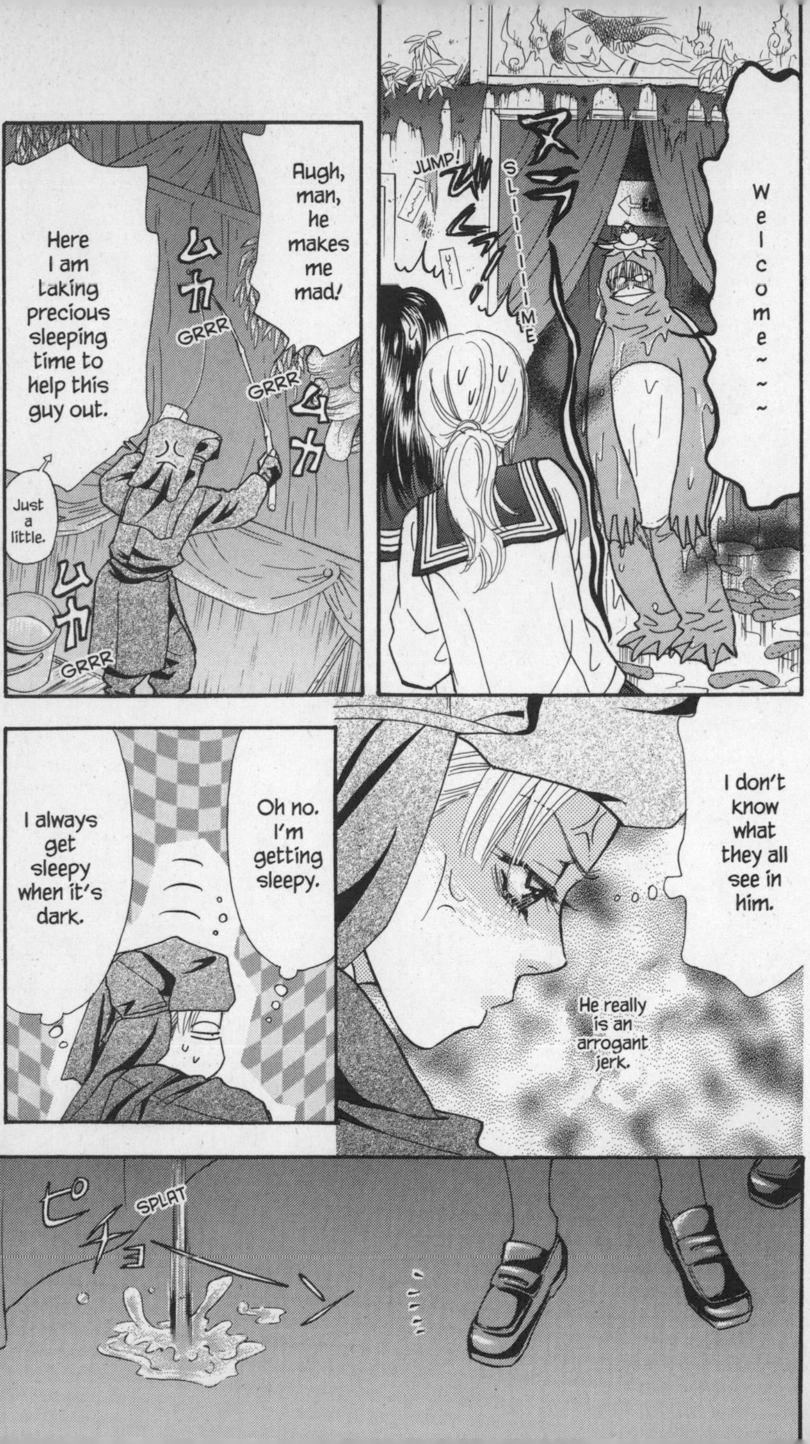
Welcome~~~
JUMP!
SLIIIIIME
Augh, man, he makes me mad!
Here I am taking precious sleeping time to help this guy out.
GRRR
GRRR
GRRR
Just a little.
I don't know what they all see in him.
He really is an arrogant jerk.
Oh no. I'm getting sleepy.
I always get sleepy when it's dark.
SPLAT

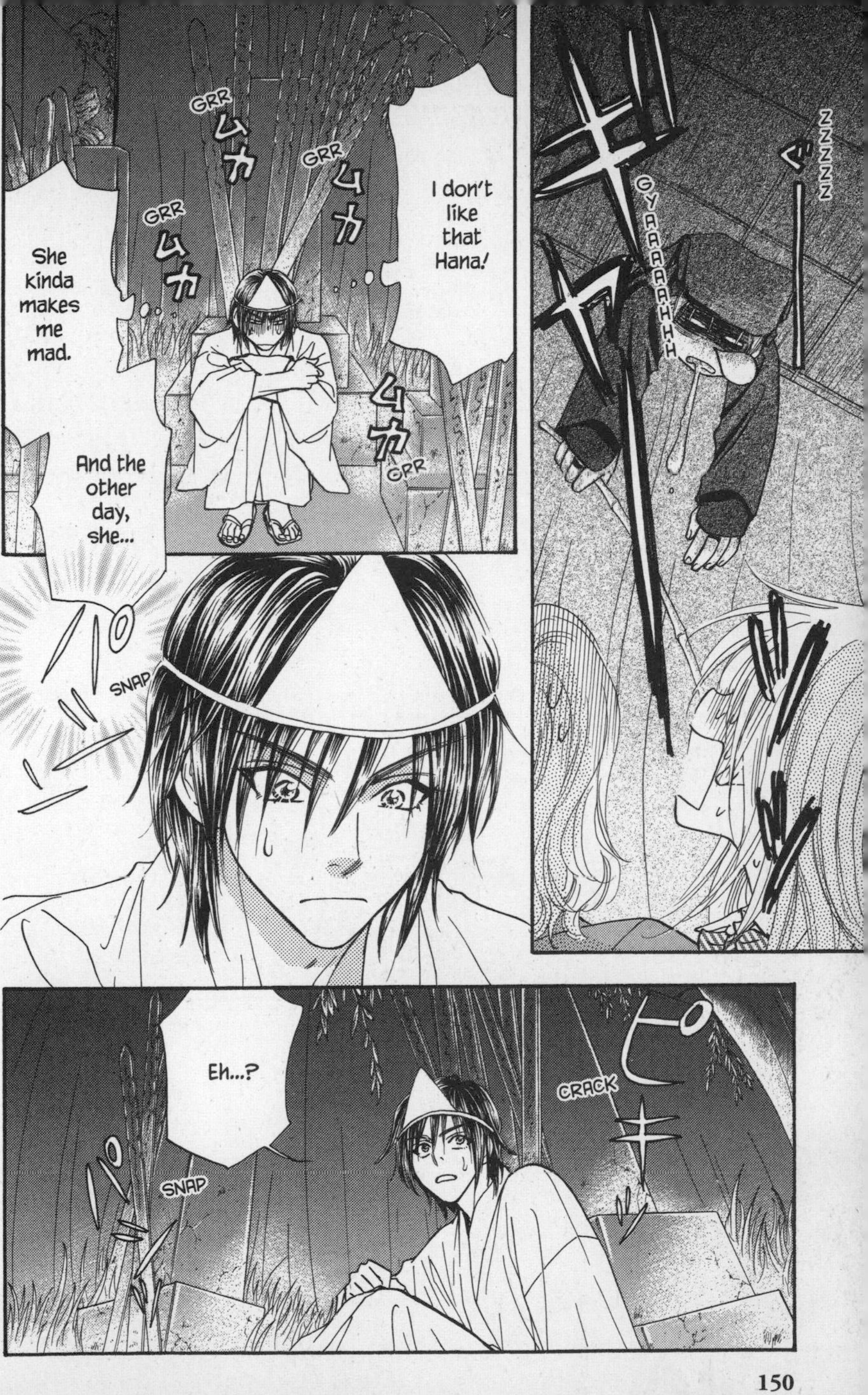
ZZZZZ
GYAAAAAAHH
I don't like that Hana!
GRR
GRR
GRR
She kinda makes me mad.
GRR
And the other day, she...
SNAP
CRACK
Eh...?
SNAP

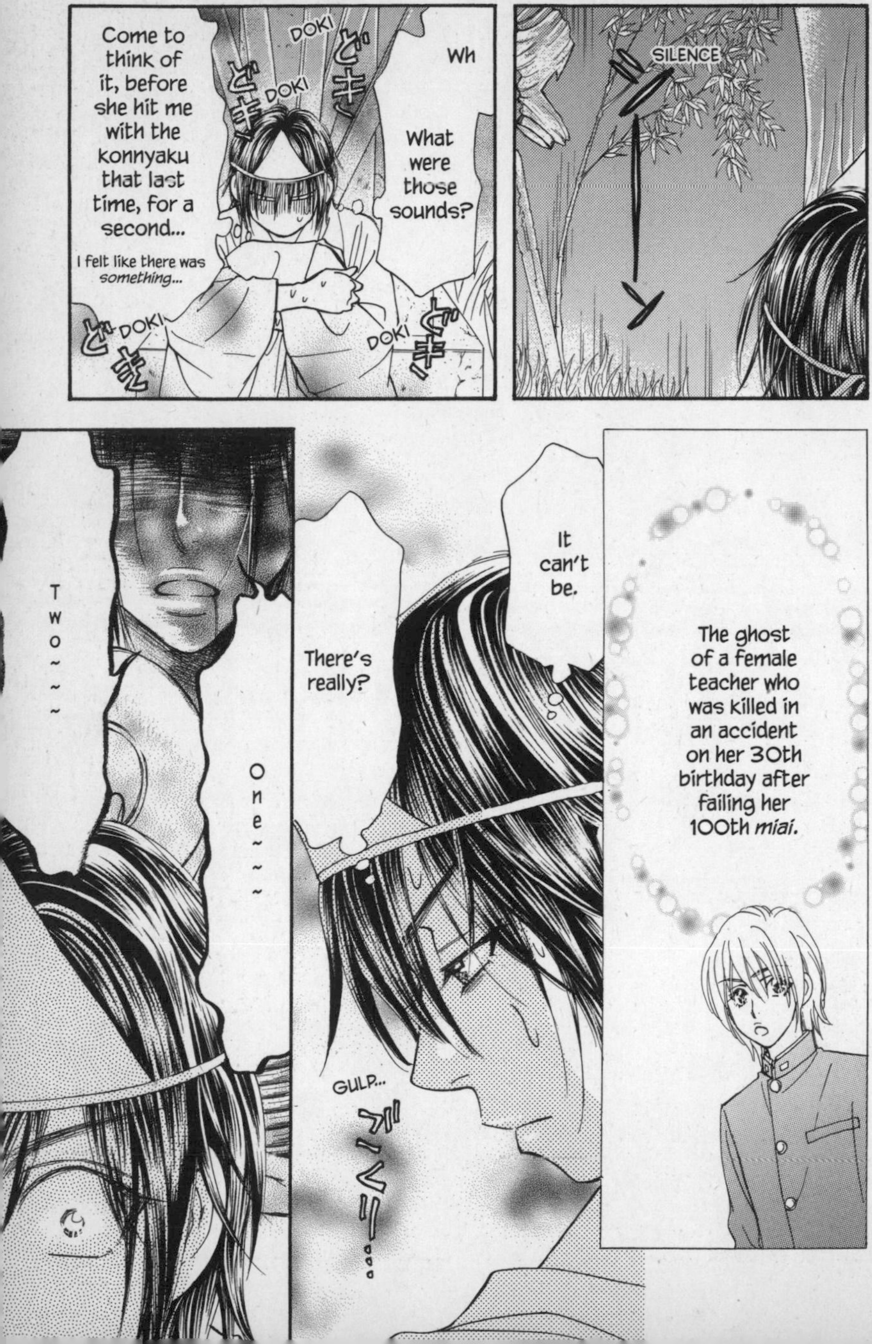
SILENCE
Wh
What were those sounds?
DOKI
DOKI
Come to think of it, before she hit me with the konnyaku that last time, for a second...
I felt like there was *something*...
DOKI
DOKI
The ghost of a female teacher who was killed in an accident on her 30th birthday after failing her 100th *miai*.
It can't be.
There's really?
GULP...
Two~~~
One~~~

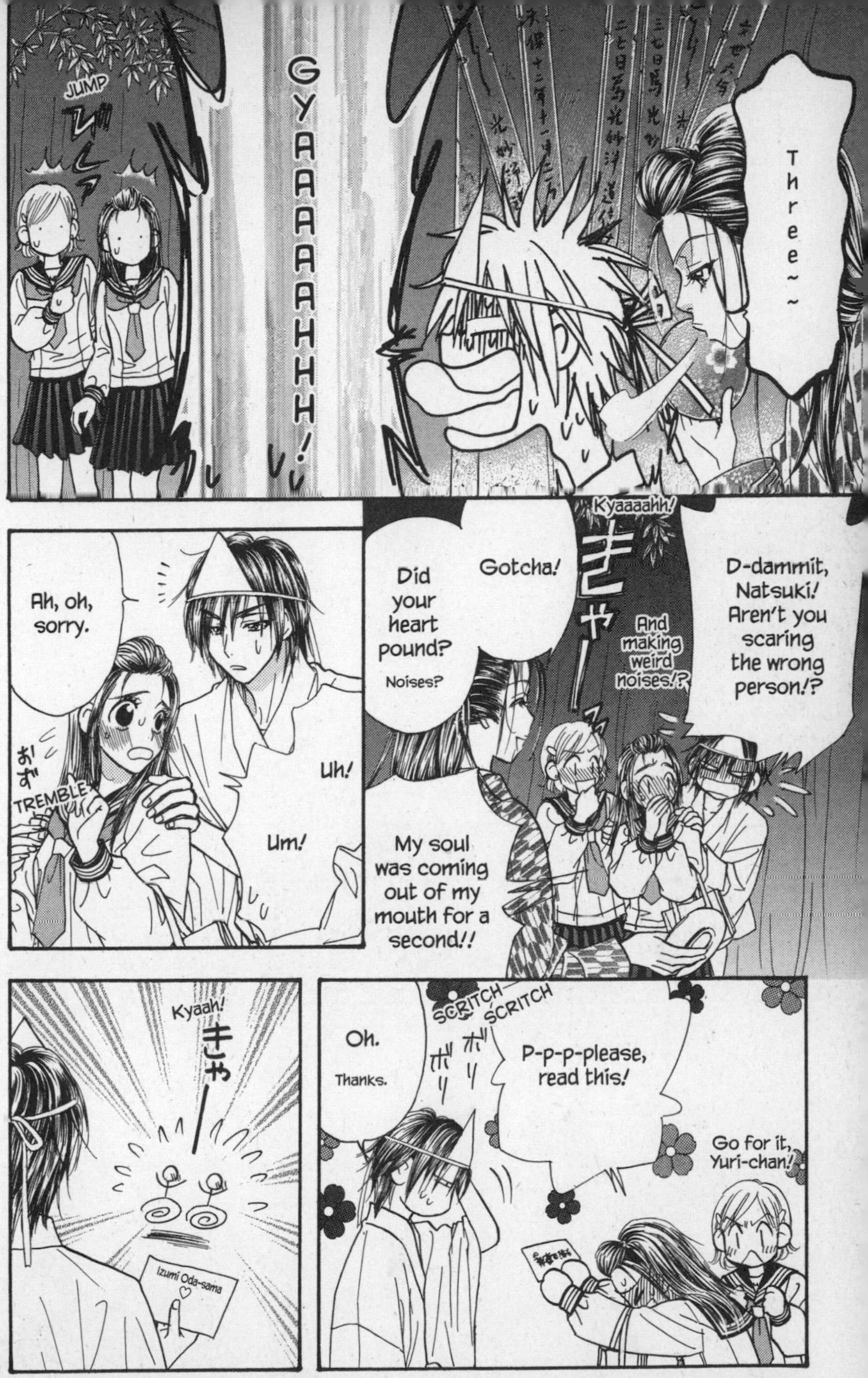
Three~~
GYAAAAAHHH!
JUMP
D-dammit, Natsuki! Aren't you scaring the wrong person!?
And making weird noises!?
Kyaaaahh!
Gotcha! Did your heart pound?
Noises?
My soul was coming out of my mouth for a second!!
Ah, oh, sorry.
Uh!
Um!
TREMBLE
Go for it, Yuri-chan!
P-p-p-please, read this!
SCRITCH SCRITCH
Oh.
Thanks.
Kyaah!
Izumi Oda-sama

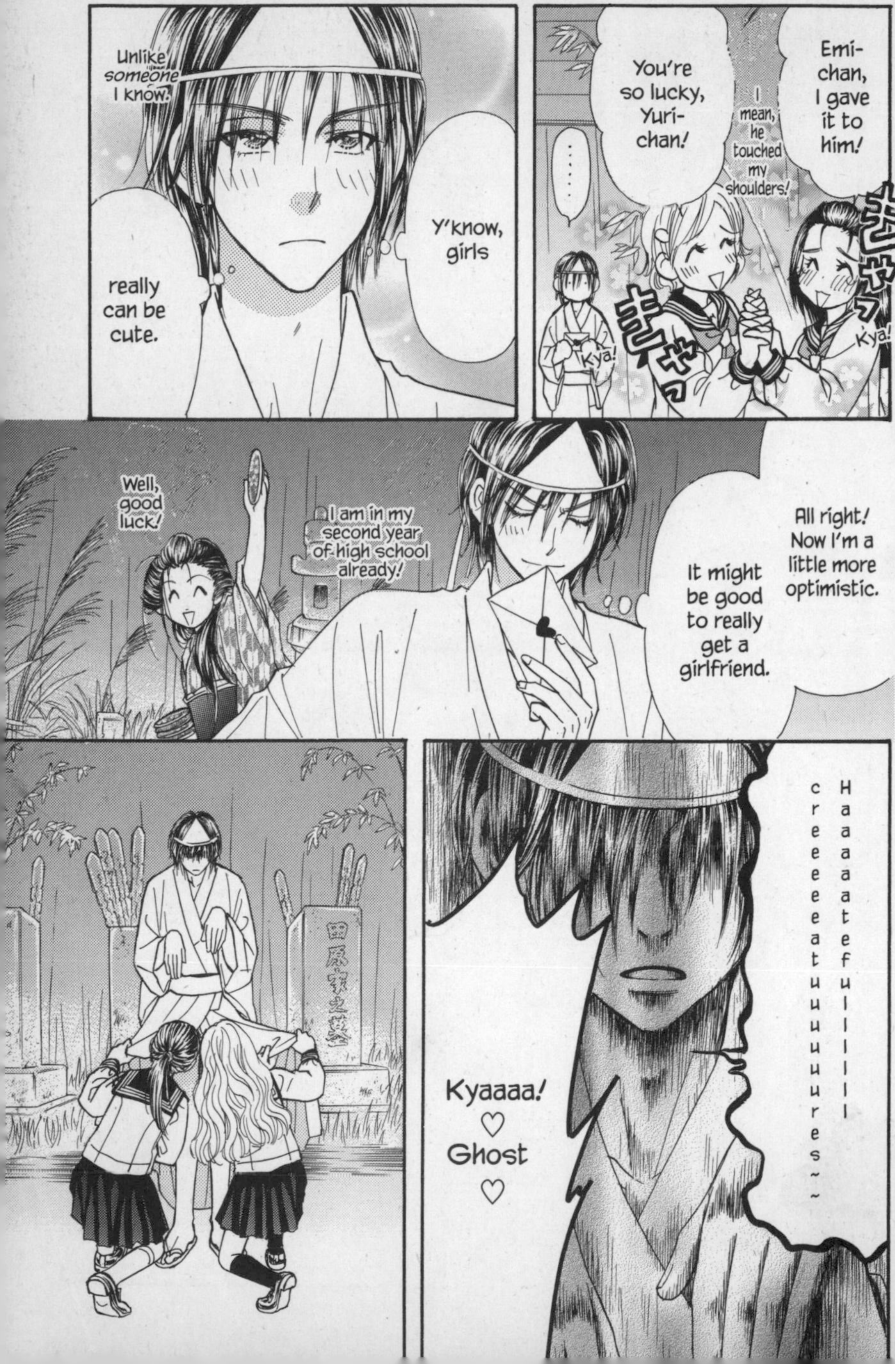
Emi-chan, I gave it to him!
I mean, he touched my shoulders!
きゃっ
Kya!
You're so lucky, Yuri-chan!
きゃっ
Kya!
......
Y'know, girls
really can be cute.
Unlike someone I know.
All right! Now I'm a little more optimistic.
It might be good to really get a girlfriend.
I am in my second year of high school already!
Well, good luck!
Haaaatefulllll creeeeatuuuuuures~~
Kyaaaa! ♡ Ghost ♡

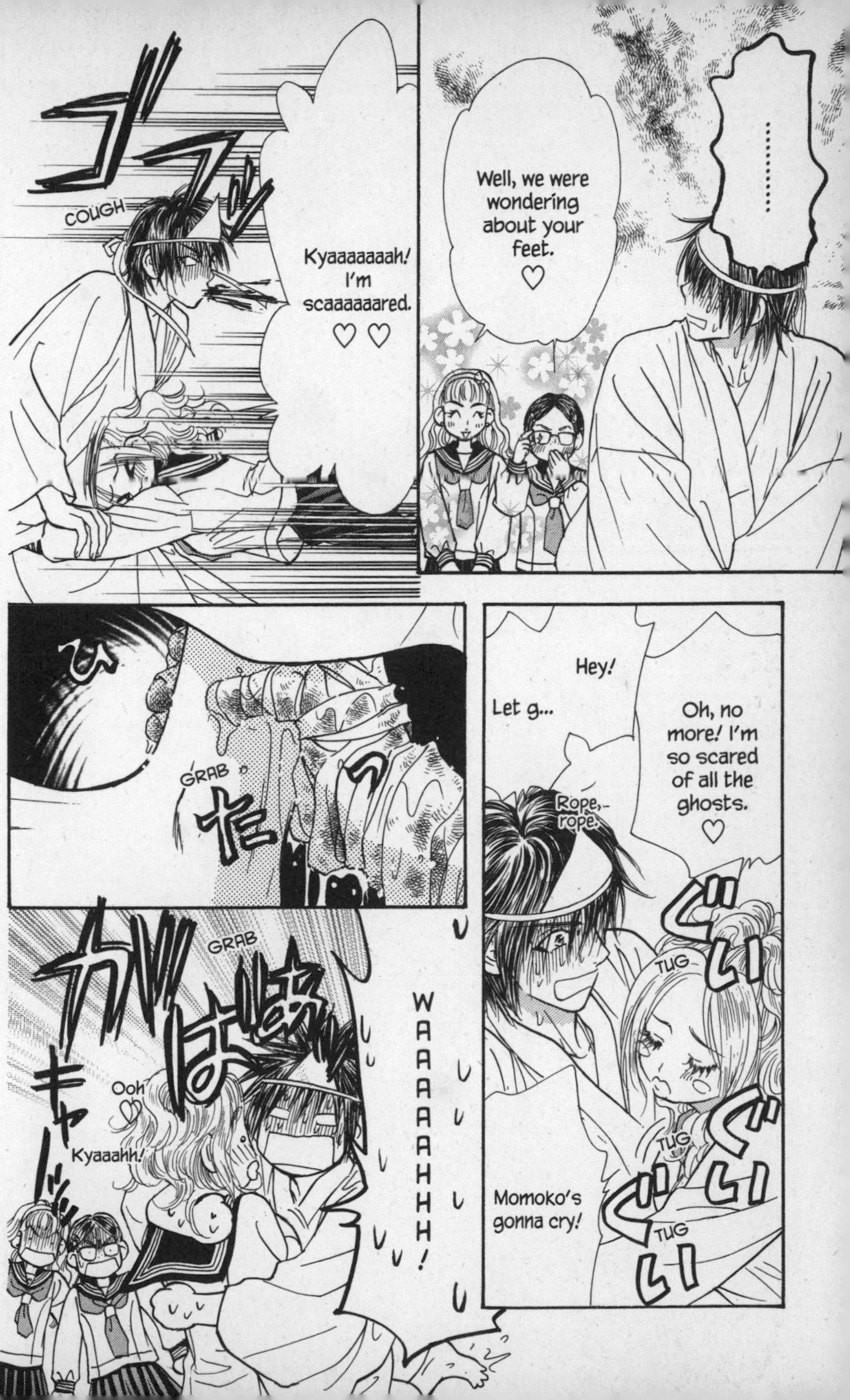
......
Well, we were wondering about your feet. ♡
Kyaaaaaaah! I'm scaaaaaared. ♡ ♡
COUGH
Oh, no more! I'm so scared of all the ghosts. ♡
Hey!
Let g...
Rope, rope.
TUG
TUG
TUG
Momoko's gonna cry!
GRAB
GRAB
WAAAAAAAHHH!
Ooh ♡
Kyaaahh!

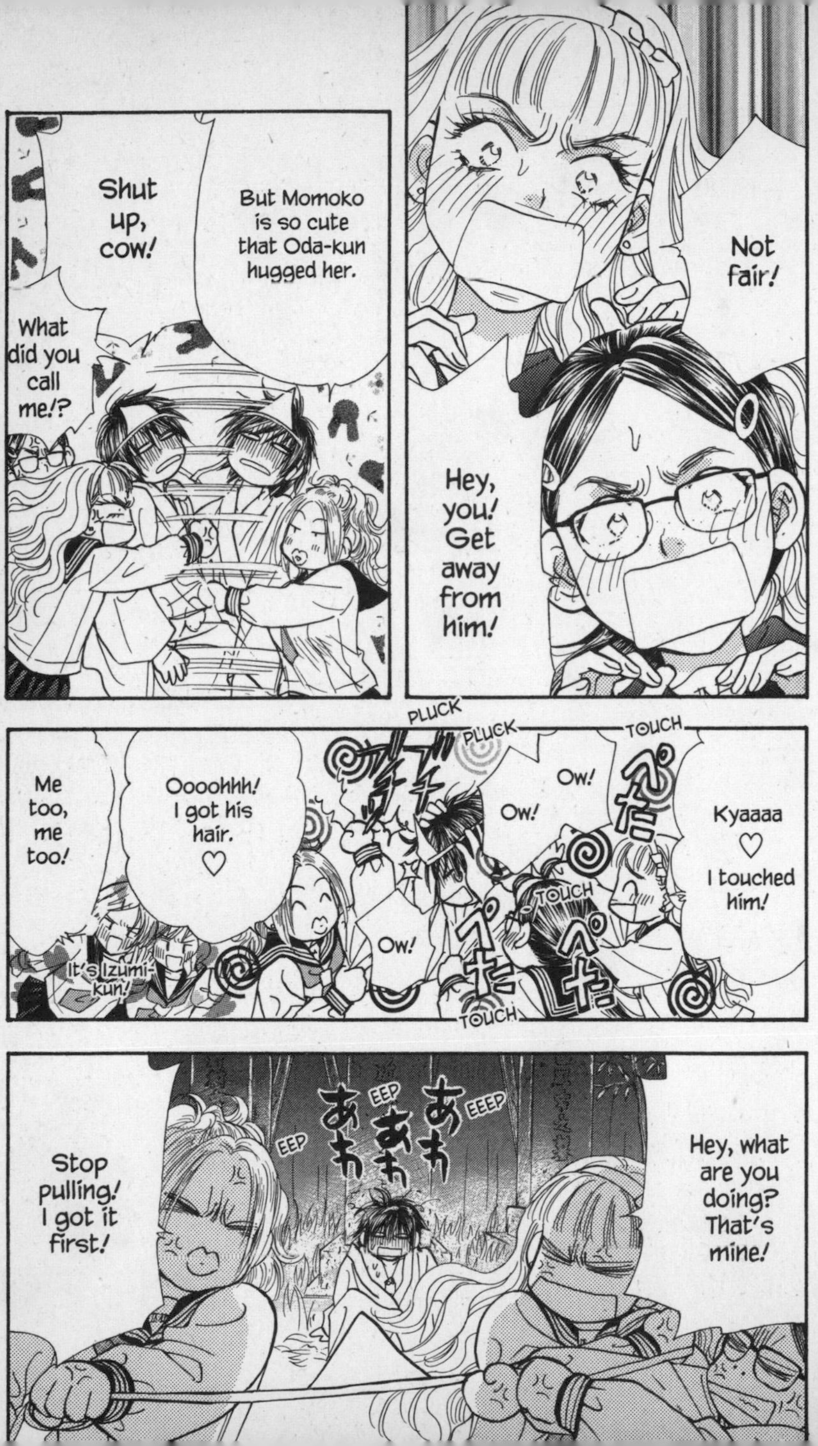
Not fair!
Hey, you! Get away from him!
But Momoko is so cute that Oda-kun hugged her.
Shut up, cow!
What did you call me!?
TOUCH
Kyaaaa ♡ I touched him!
Ow!
Ow!
PLUCK
PLUCK
Ooooohhh! I got his hair. ♡
Me too, me too!
TOUCH
Ow!
It's Izumi-kun!
TOUCH
Hey, what are you doing? That's mine!
EEEP
EEP
EEP
Stop pulling! I got it first!

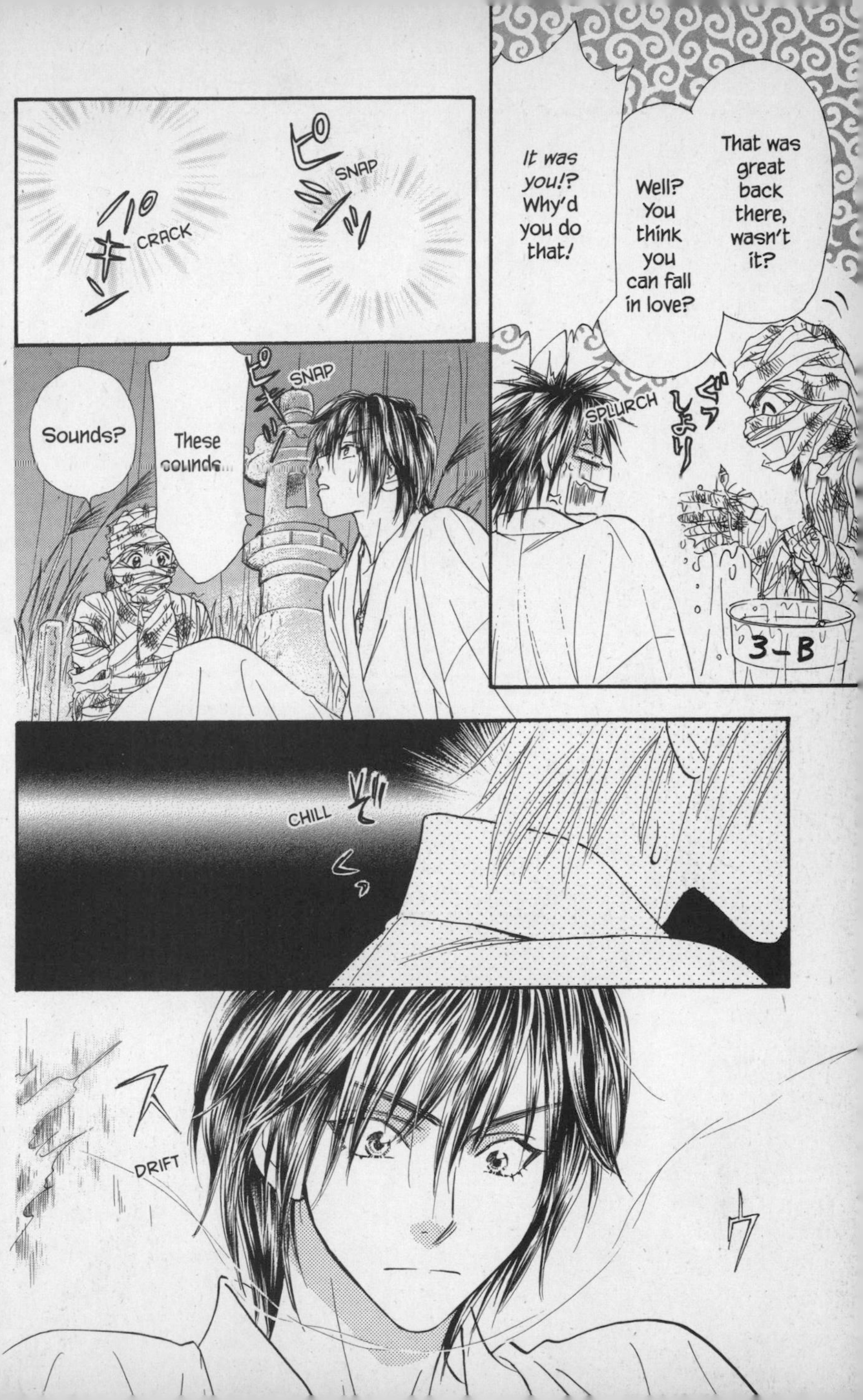
That was great back there, wasn't it?
Well? You think you can fall in love?
It was you!? Why'd you do that!
SPLURCH
3-B
SNAP
CRACK
SNAP
These sounds...
Sounds?
CHILL
DRIFT

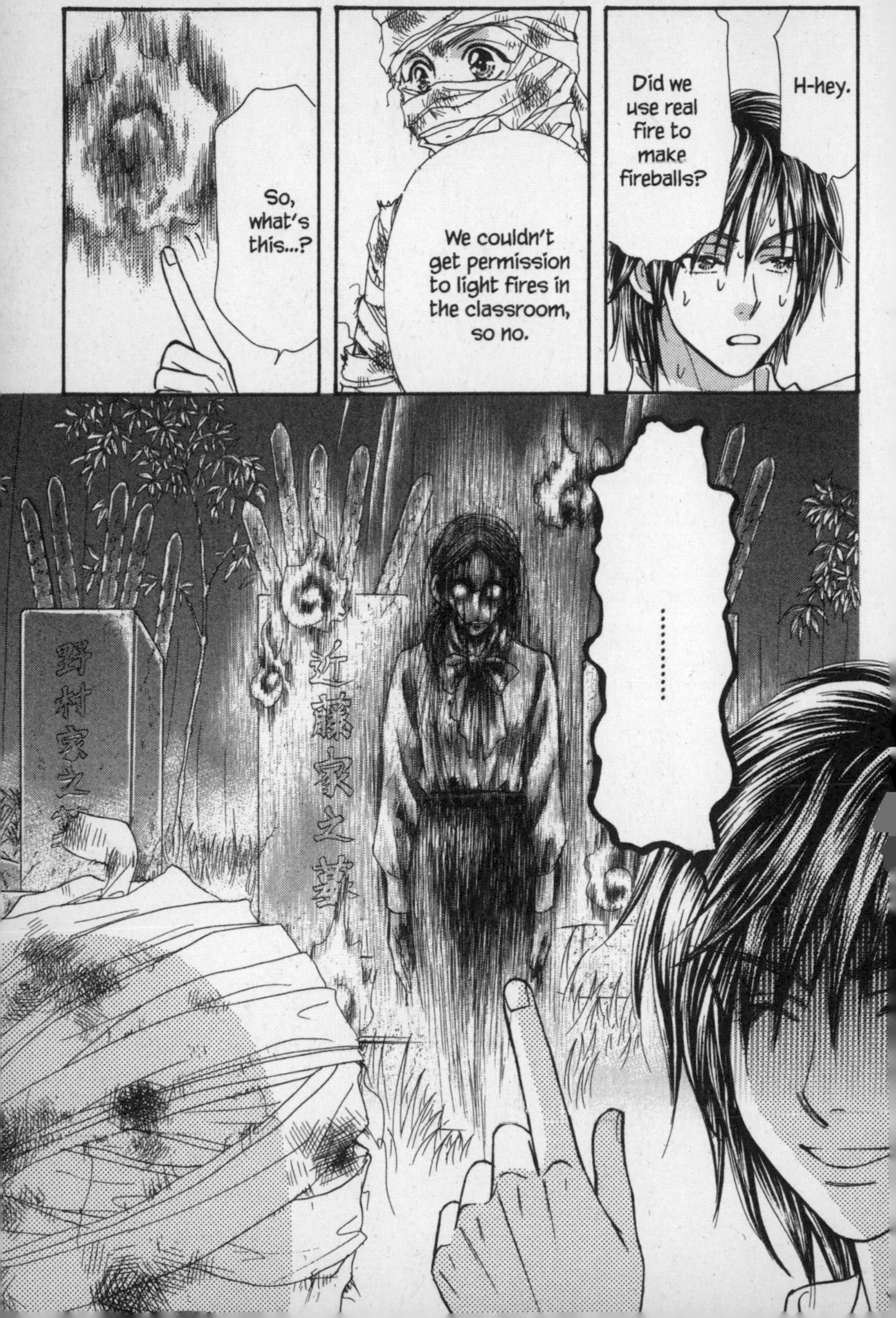
H-hey.
Did we use real fire to make fireballs?
We couldn't get permission to light fires in the classroom, so no.
So, what's this...?
......
近藤家之墓

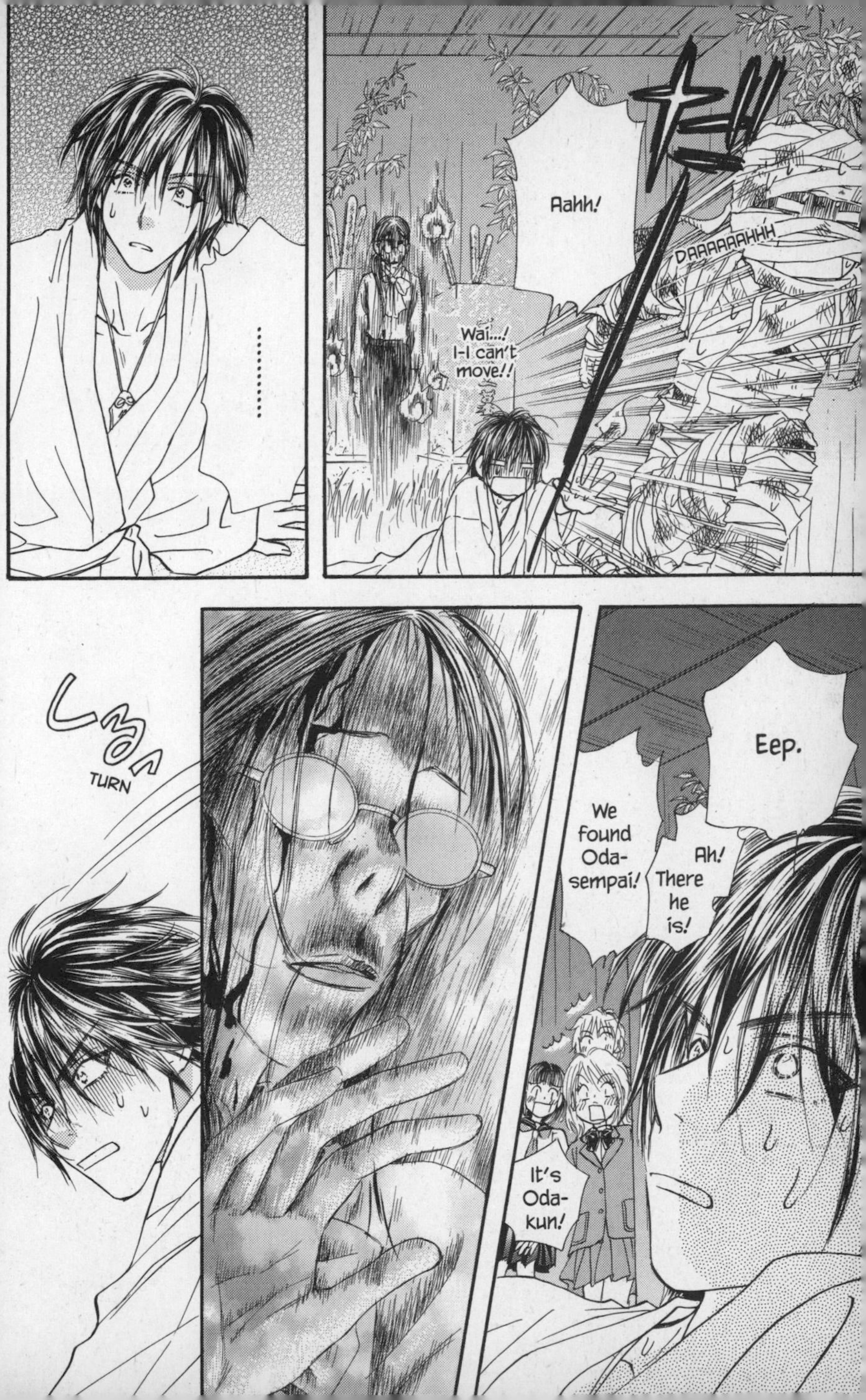
Aahh!
DAAAAAAHHH
Wai...! I-I can't move!!
......
Eep.
Ah! There he is!
We found Oda-sempai!
It's Oda-kun!
TURN

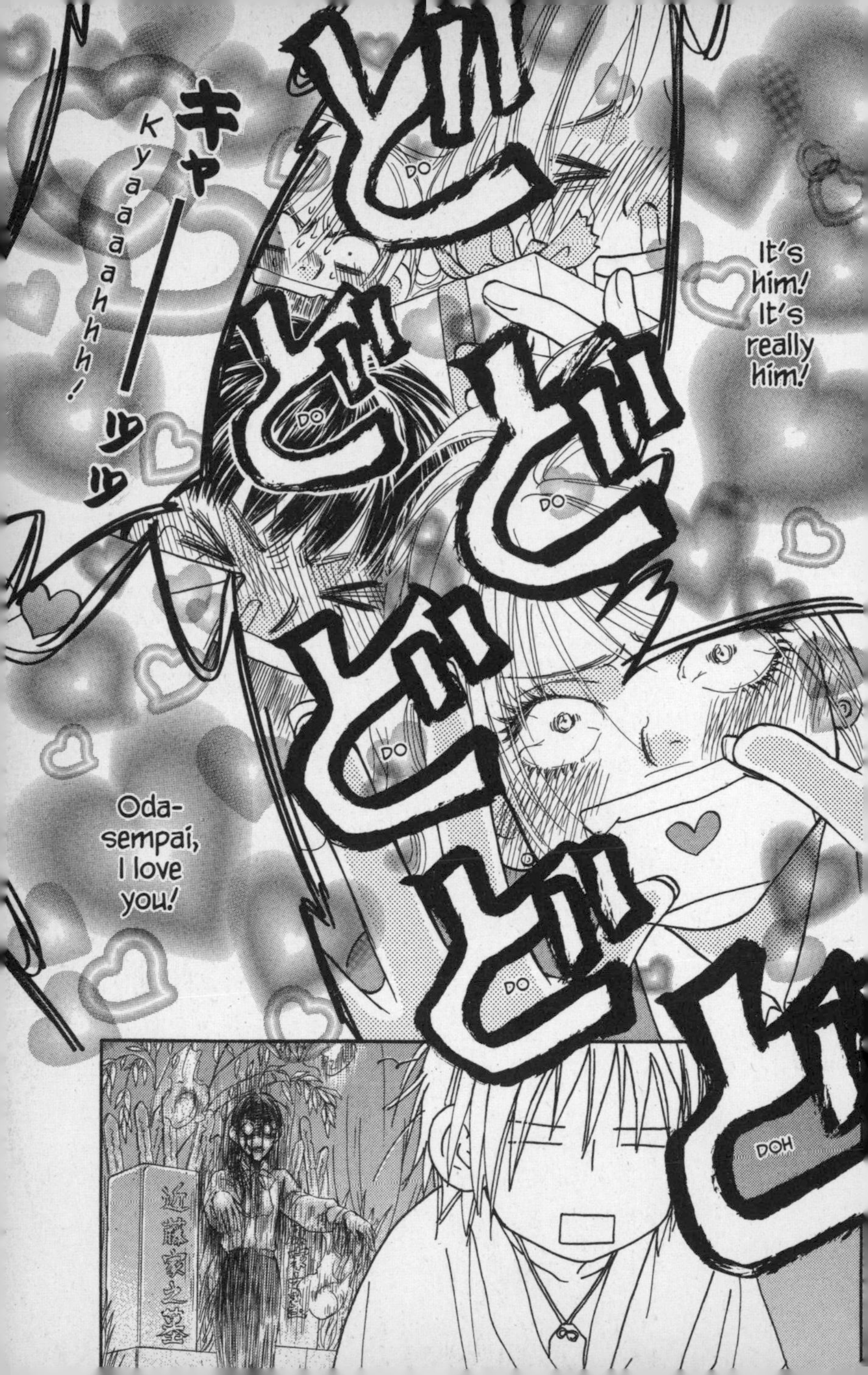

DO
It's him! It's really him!
キャーッッ
Kyaaaaahhhh!
DO
DO
DO
Oda-sempai, I love you!
DO
DOH
近藤家之墓

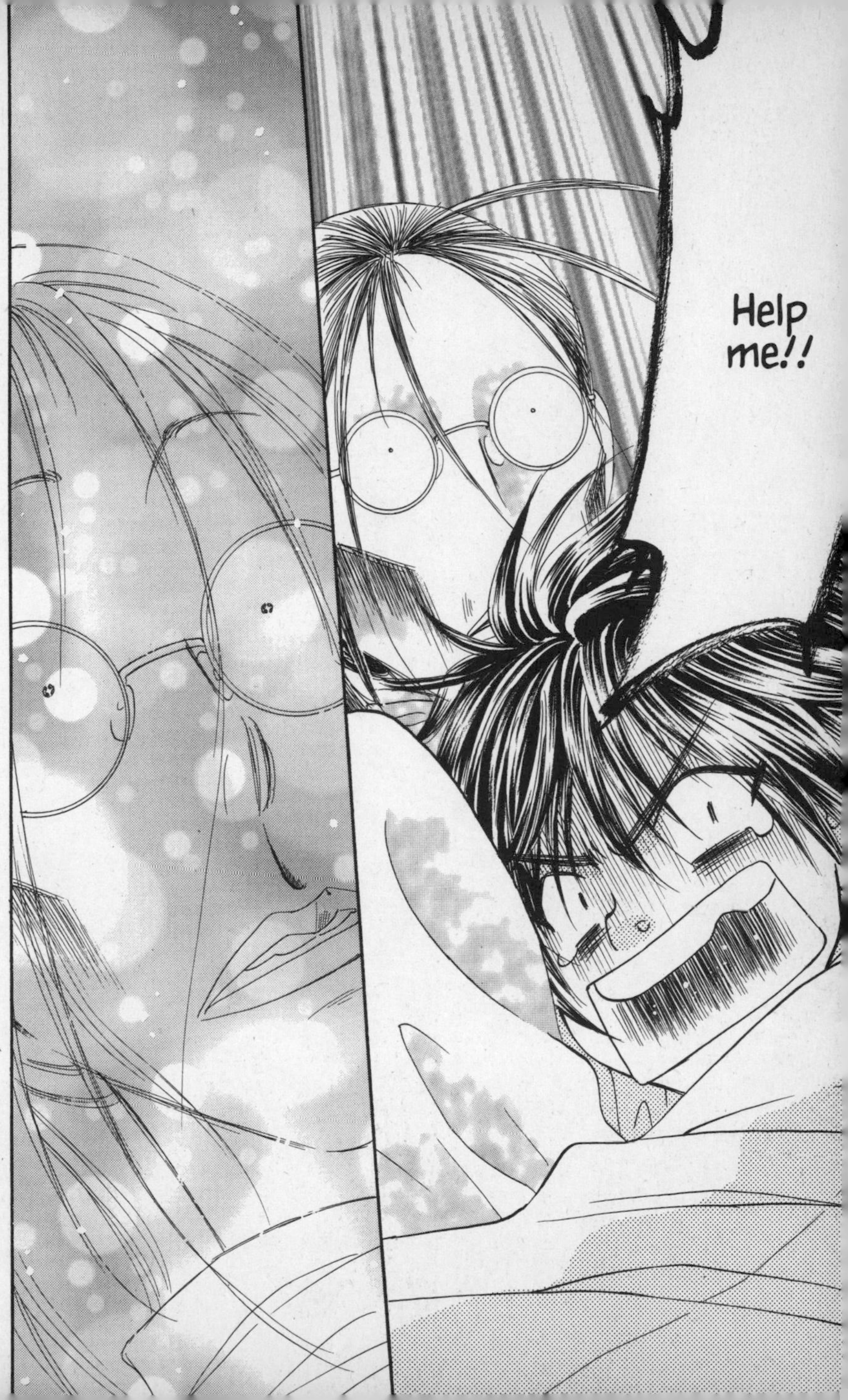
Help me!!

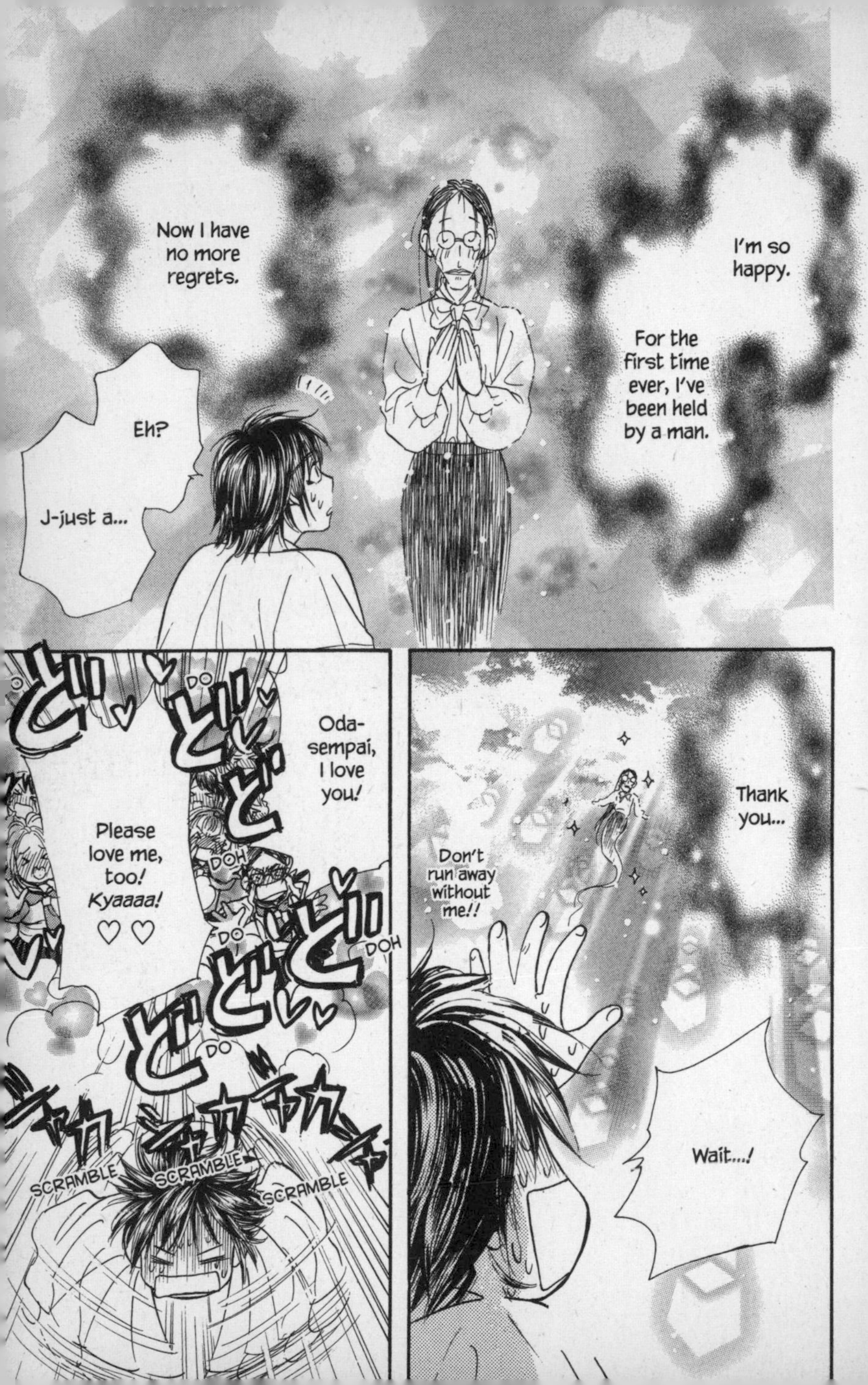
I'm so happy.
For the first time ever, I've been held by a man.
Now I have no more regrets.
Eh?
J-just a...
Thank you...
Don't run away without me!!
Wait...!
Oda-sempai, I love you!
DO
Please love me, too! Kyaaaa! ♡ ♡
DOH
DO
DOH
DO
SCRAMBLE
SCRAMBLE
SCRAMBLE

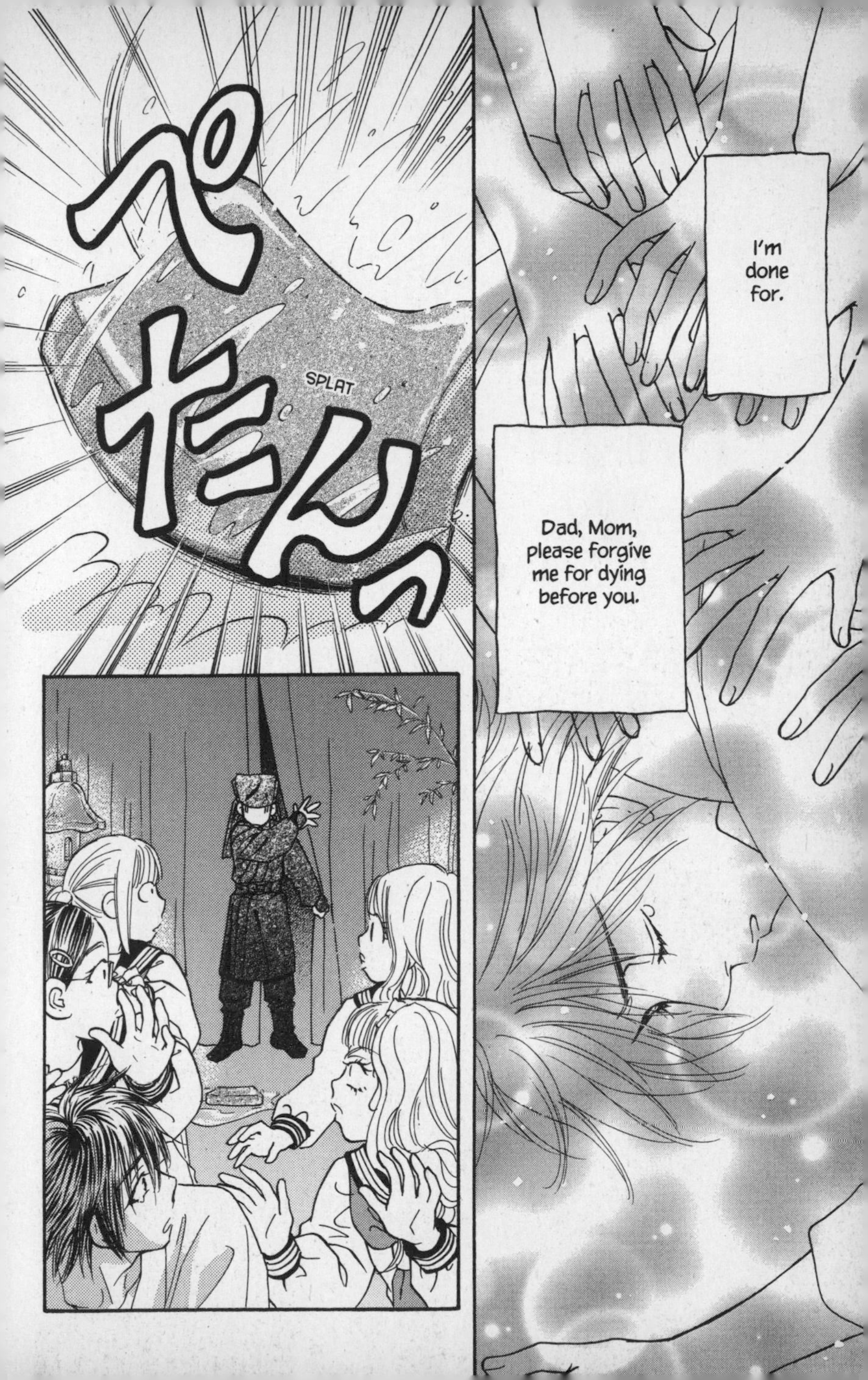
I'm done for.
Dad, Mom, please forgive me for dying before you.
ぺたん
SPLAT

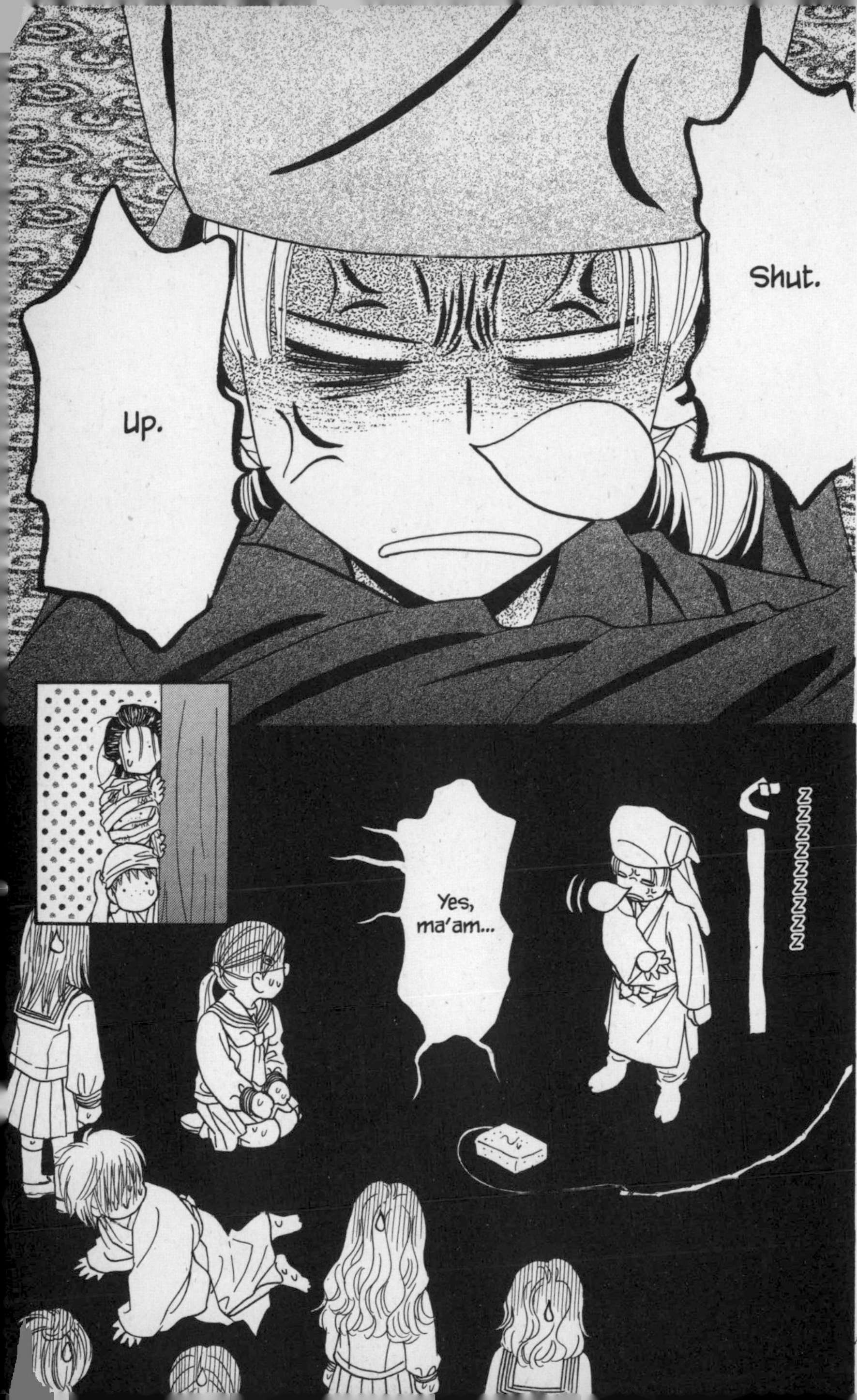
Shut.
Up.
ZZZZZZZZZZ
Yes, ma'am...

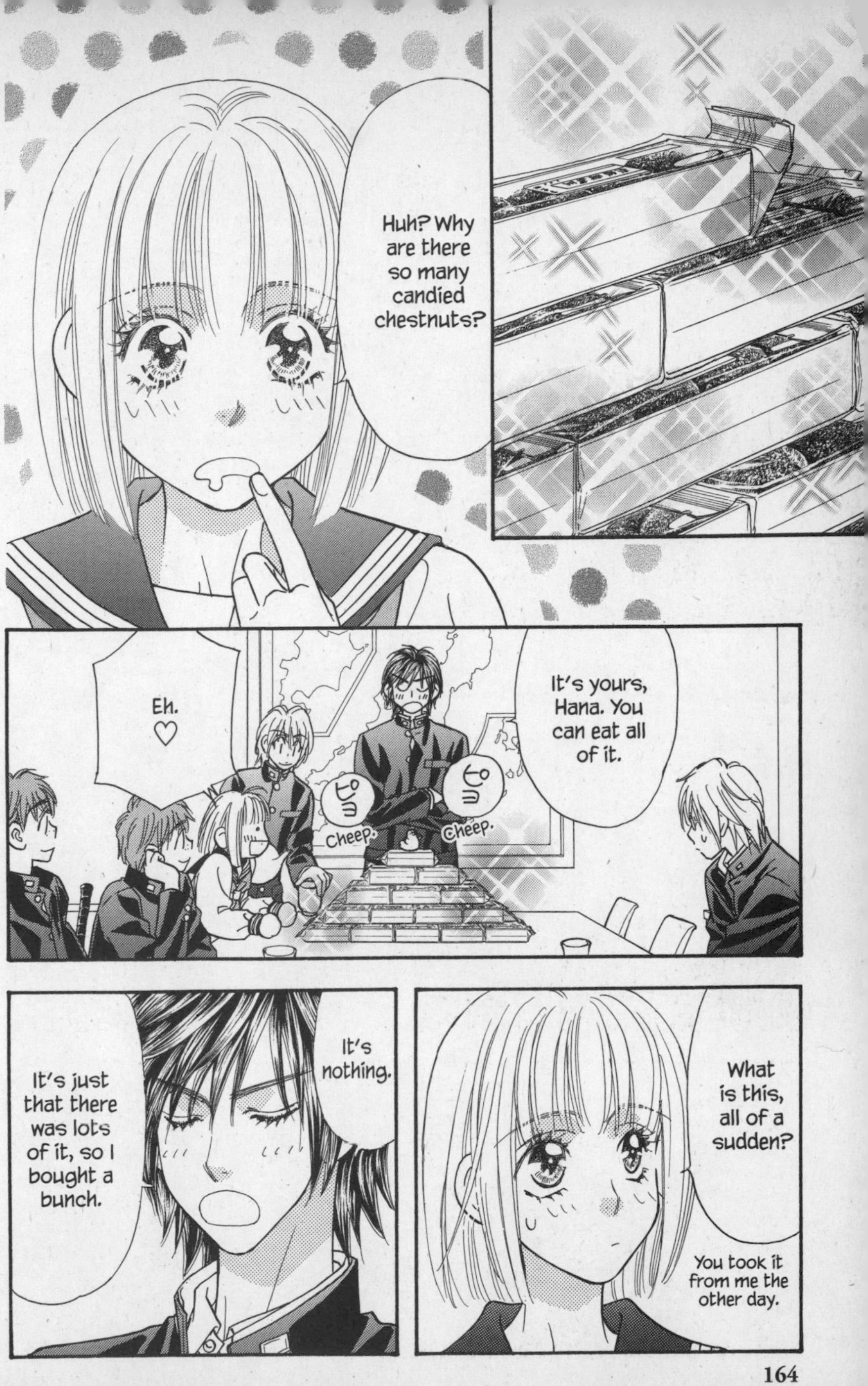
Huh? Why are there so many candied chestnuts?
It's yours, Hana. You can eat all of it.
ピヨ
Cheep.
ピヨ
Cheep.
Eh. ♡
What is this, all of a sudden?
You took it from me the other day.
It's nothing.
It's just that there was lots of it, so I bought a bunch.

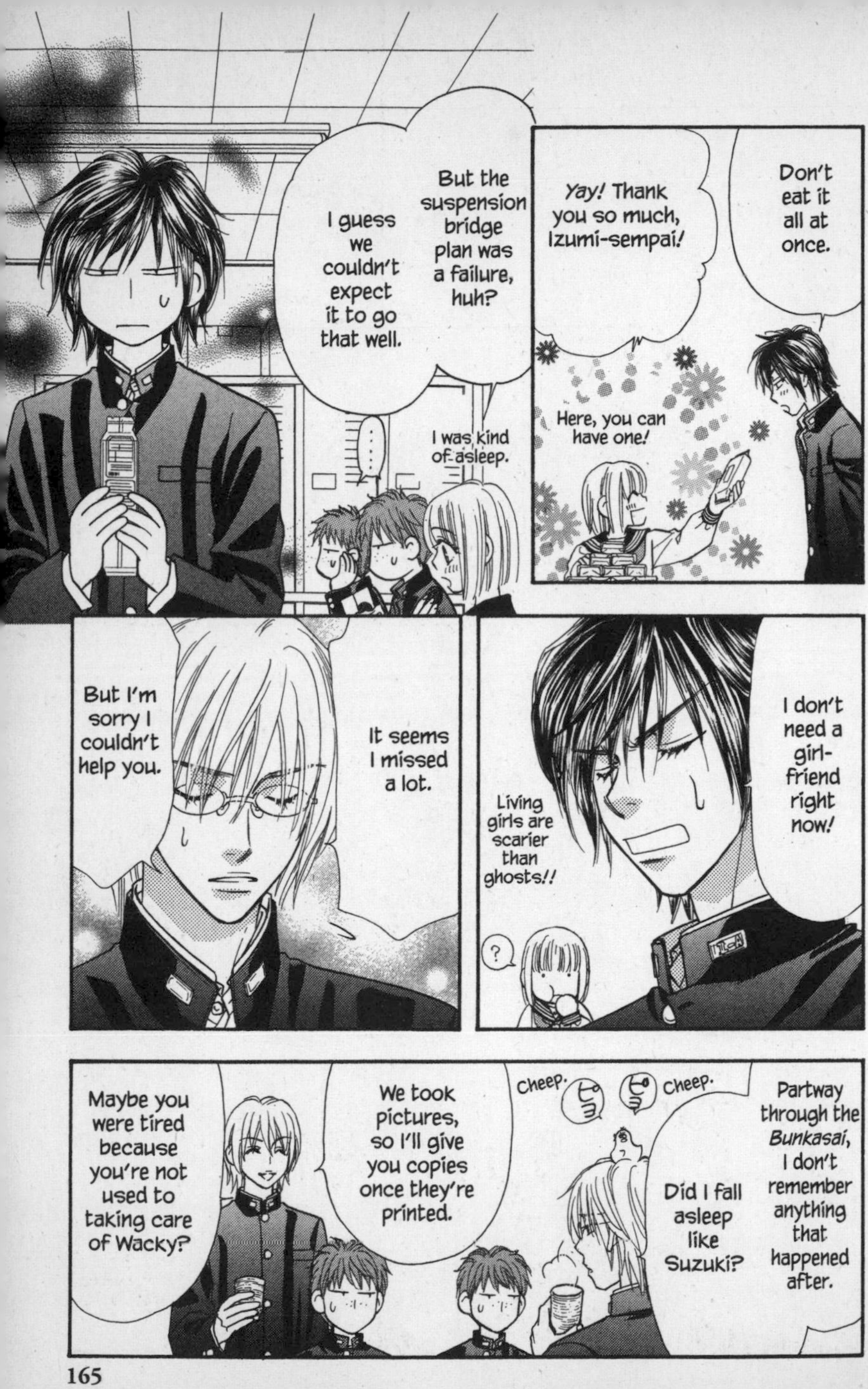

Don't eat it all at once.
Yay! Thank you so much, Izumi-sempai!
Here, you can have one!
But the suspension bridge plan was a failure, huh?
I guess we couldn't expect it to go that well.
I was kind of asleep.
......
I don't need a girlfriend right now!
Living girls are scarier than ghosts!!
?
It seems I missed a lot.
But I'm sorry I couldn't help you.
Partway through the *Bunkasai*, I don't remember anything that happened after.
Did I fall asleep like Suzuki?
Cheep.
Cheep.
We took pictures, so I'll give you copies once they're printed.
Maybe you were tired because you're not used to taking care of Wacky?

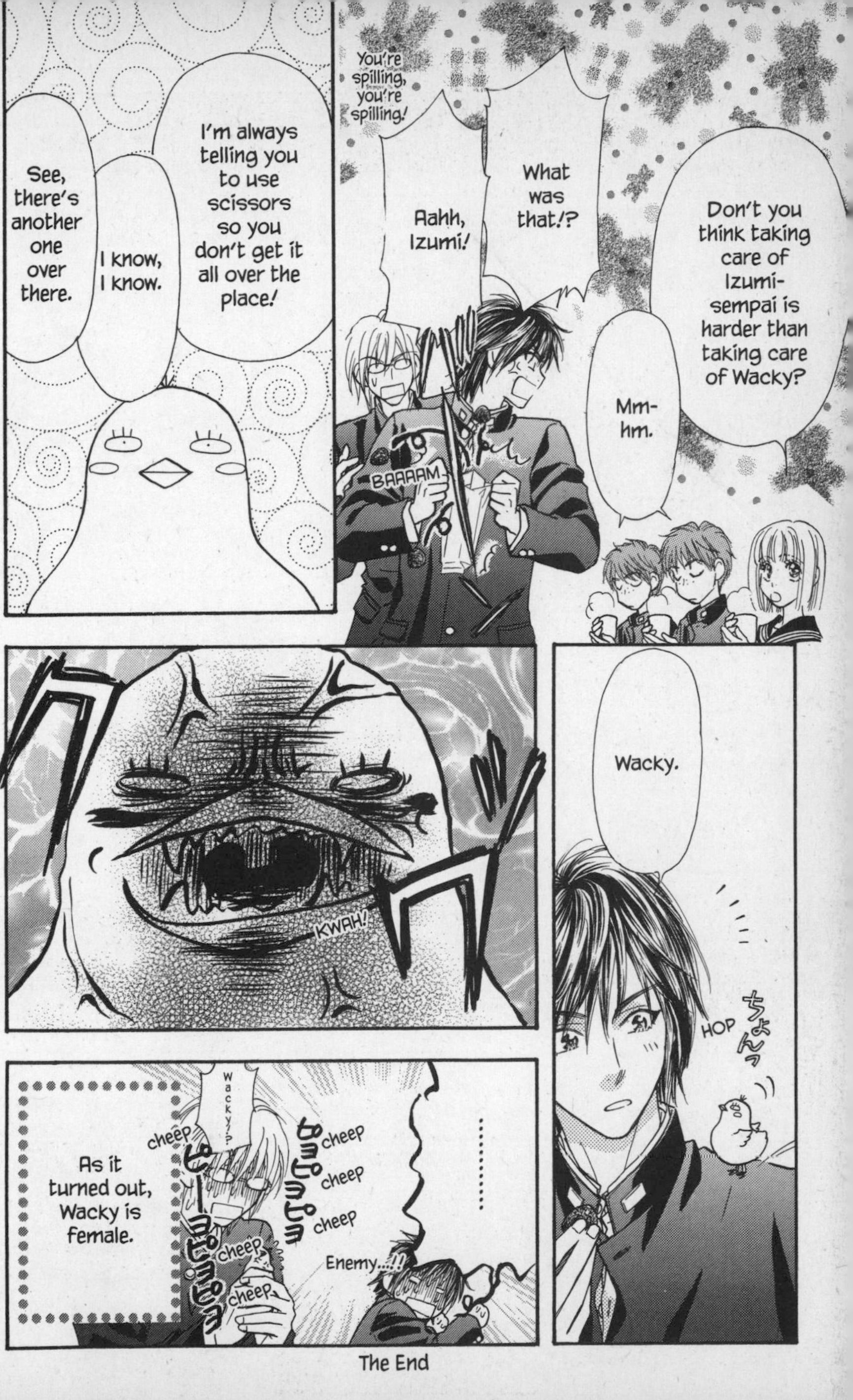
Don't you think taking care of Izumi-sempai is harder than taking care of Wacky?
Mm-hm.
What was that!?
Aahh, Izumi!
You're spilling, you're spilling!
BAAAAAM
I'm always telling you to use scissors so you don't get it all over the place!
I know, I know.
See, there's another one over there.
Wacky.
HOP
ちょんっ
KWAH!
......
Wacky!?
cheep
cheep
cheep
cheep
cheep
cheep
Enemy...!!
As it turned out, Wacky is female.

The End

Hockey Club ♨ Character Profile No.1

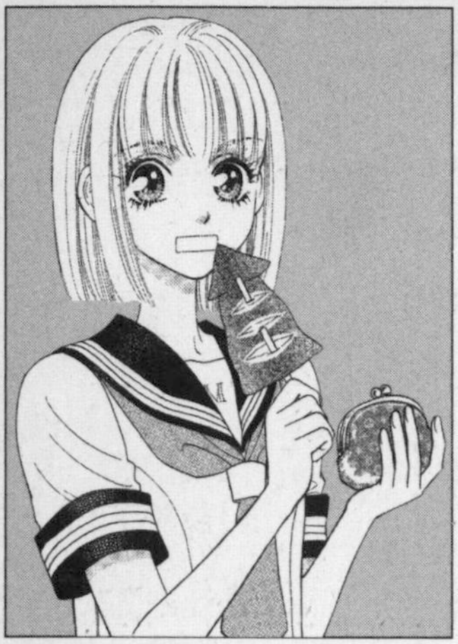

Hana Suzuki

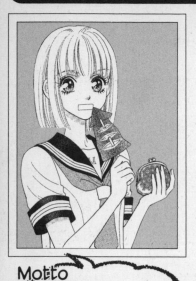

Birthday	May 5th
Blood type	O
Height	5′3″
Hobbies	Sleeping, eating
Special skill	Can go to the bathroom while asleep
Favorite food	Anything yummy
Least favorite food	Anything not yummy
Favorite subject	Cooking
Least favorite subjects	Math, science
Favorite type of guy	None in particular
Other (notes)	Been putting on weight recently

Motto
Good things come to those who sleep!

♨ Famous Scene Selections ♨

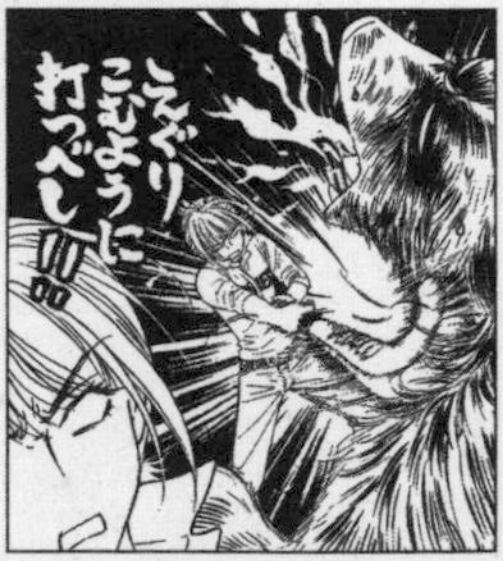
えぐりこむように打つべし!!

▲ More interested in food than the opposite sex. More interested in sleep than food. Hana lives for sleep.

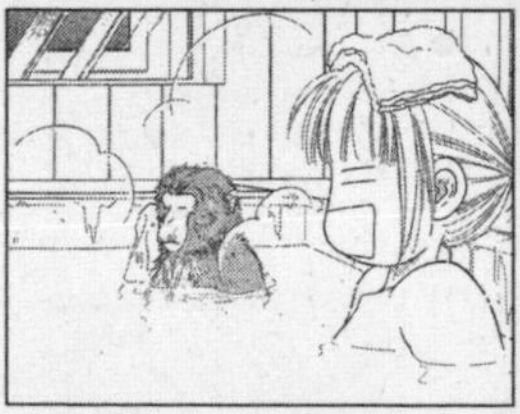

▲ She's so flat that even a monkey laughs at her....

▼ Aim deep, and strike!! Sleeping power awakens...! She even takes out a wild animal in one blow!

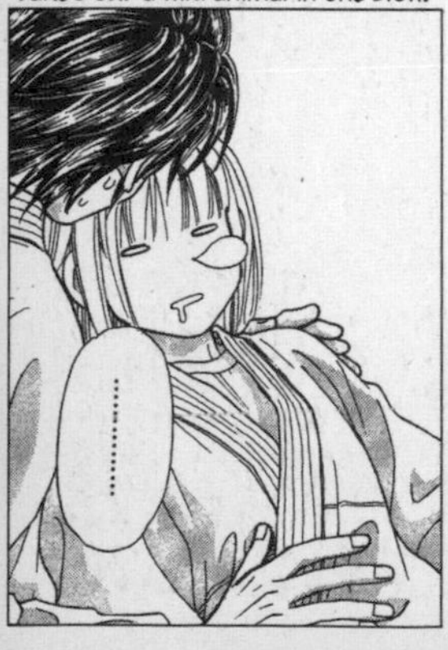

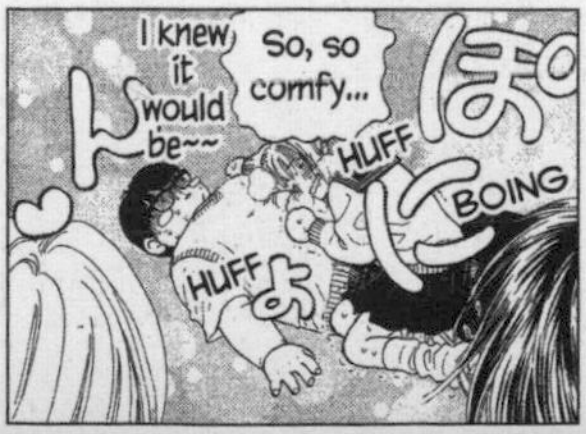
ぽよ
BOING
So, so comfy...
HUFF
I knew it would be~~
HUFF
ト

◀ The stomach pillow to which Hana was once a slave, Ôta the Younger. ♥

Hockey Club ♨ Character Profile No.2

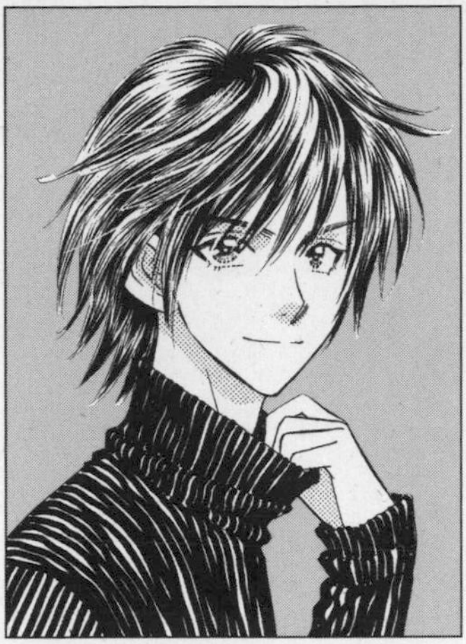

Izumi Oda

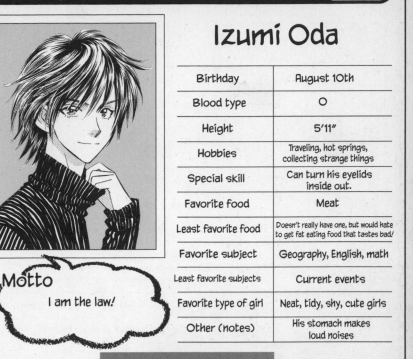

Birthday	August 10th
Blood type	O
Height	5'11"
Hobbies	Traveling, hot springs, collecting strange things
Special skill	Can turn his eyelids inside out.
Favorite food	Meat
Least favorite food	Doesn't really have one, but would hate to get fat eating food that tastes bad!
Favorite subject	Geography, English, math
Least favorite subjects	Current events
Favorite type of girl	Neat, tidy, shy, cute girls
Other (notes)	His stomach makes loud noises

Motto

I am the law!

♨ Famous Scene Selections ♨

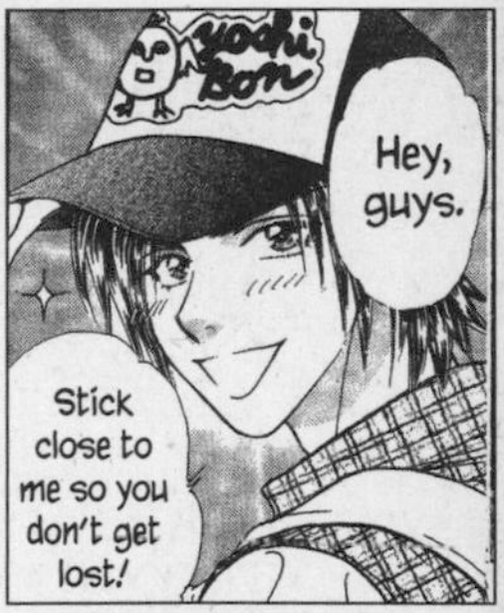
Hey, guys.
Stick close to me so you don't get lost!

▲ Leave leadership to him!... But Izumi is always missing something.

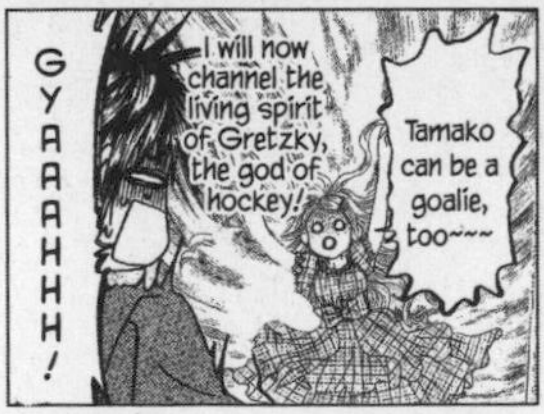
I will now channel the living spirit of Gretzky, the god of hockey!
Tamako can be a goalie, too~~~
GYAAAAHHH!

▲ Self-proclaimed "Izumi's fiancée," Tamako is easily possessed by spirits. Even Izumi is overwhelmed....

▼ In front of Hana, he will show expressions like these.♥

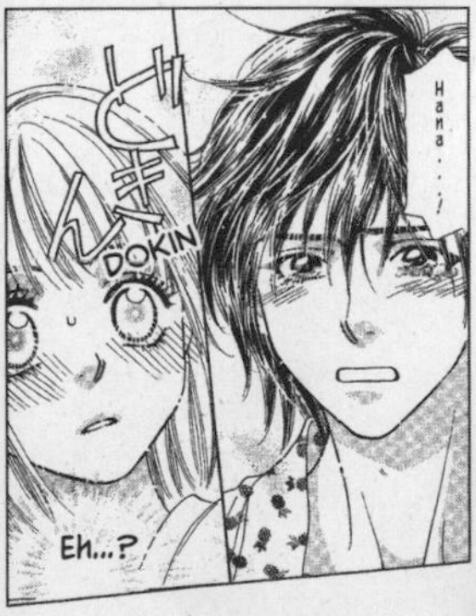
Hana...!
DOKIN
Eh...?

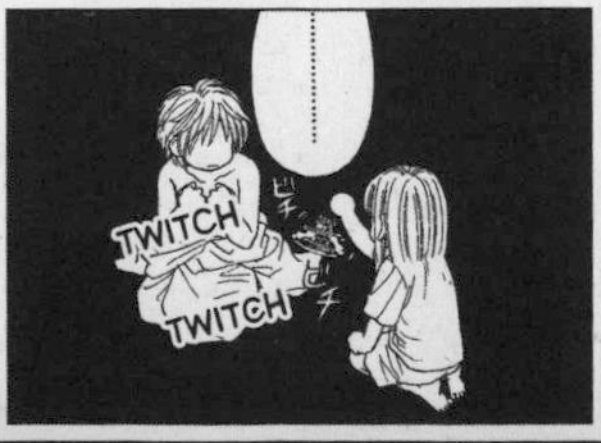
TWITCH
TWITCH

◀ Frightened Izumi-kun. He sees the ghost's true identity, and it's...a gecko.

Hockey Club ♨ Character Profile No.3

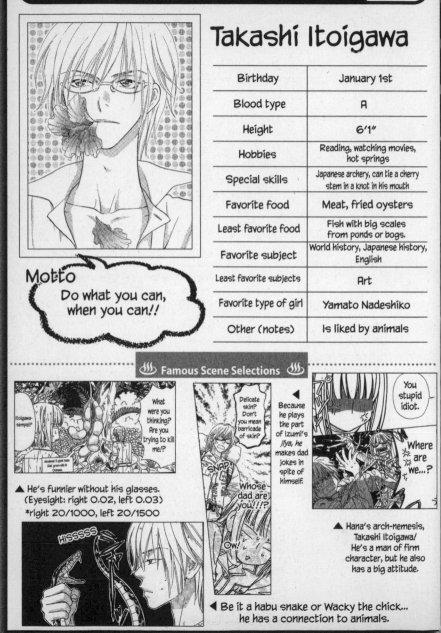

Takashi Itoigawa

Birthday	January 1st
Blood type	A
Height	6'1"
Hobbies	Reading, watching movies, hot springs
Special skills	Japanese archery, can tie a cherry stem in a knot in his mouth
Favorite food	Meat, fried oysters
Least favorite food	Fish with big scales from ponds or bogs.
Favorite subject	World history, Japanese history, English
Least favorite subjects	Art
Favorite type of girl	Yamato Nadeshiko
Other (notes)	Is liked by animals

Motto

Do what you can, when you can!!

♨ Famous Scene Selections ♨

You stupid idiot.
Where are we...?

▲ Hana's arch-nemesis, Takashi Itoigawa! He's a man of firm character, but he also has a big attitude.

Delicate skin? Don't you mean barricade of skin?
SNAP
Whose dad are you!!!?
OW!

◀ Because he plays the part of Izumi's *jiya*, he makes dad jokes in spite of himself.

Itoigawa-sempai?
What were you thinking? Are you trying to kill me!?

▲ He's funnier without his glasses. (Eyesight: right 0.02, left 0.03)
*right 20/1000, left 20/1500

HISSSSS

◀ Be it a habu snake or Wacky the chick... he has a connection to animals.

Translation Notes

Japanese is a tricky language for most Westerners, and translation is often more art than science. For your edification and reading pleasure, here are notes on some of the places where we could have gone in a different direction in our translation of the work, or where a Japanese cultural reference is used.

JAL, page 10

JAL is a common abbreviation for Japan Airlines.

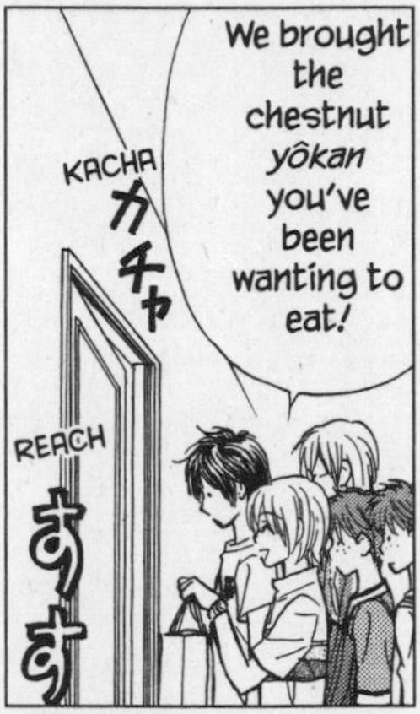
We brought the chestnut *yôkan* you've been wanting to eat!
KACHA
カチャ
REACH

Yôkan, page 24

A jellied sweet made from bean paste.

Jodo Shinshu, page 25

The most common religions in Japan are Shinto and Buddhism, and Jodo Shinshu is considered the most widely practiced sect of Buddhism in Japan. Sunday being the day of rest is a Christian practice, and so would not apply to Hana's family's beliefs.

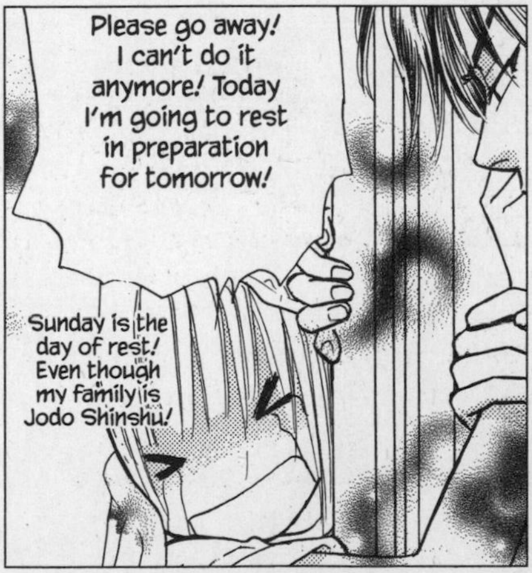
Please go away! I can't do it anymore! Today I'm going to rest in preparation for tomorrow!
Sunday is the day of rest! Even though my family is Jodo Shinshu!

Onigiri, page 33

Kind of like the peanut butter and jelly sandwich of Japan. *Onigiri* literally means "molded" and refers to the fact that this dish is made by molding rice into an oval or triangle shape. Put a salty or sour ingredient in the middle, like a pickled plum or salted salmon, wrap some seaweed around it, and you have a very popular Japanese snack.

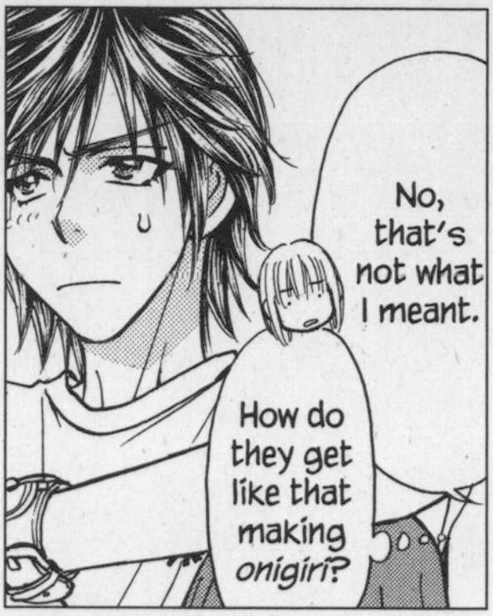
No, that's not what I meant.
How do they get like that making *onigiri*?

Running with bread in your mouth, page 54

Further proof that Izumi is not only a little nuts, but that he watches too much TV. It's an old anime cliché: The show would begin with a character running late to school, holding toast in his mouth because he didn't have time to eat breakfast. Then the character inevitably bumps into someone special, which is usually the start of something big enough to make a whole TV series about.

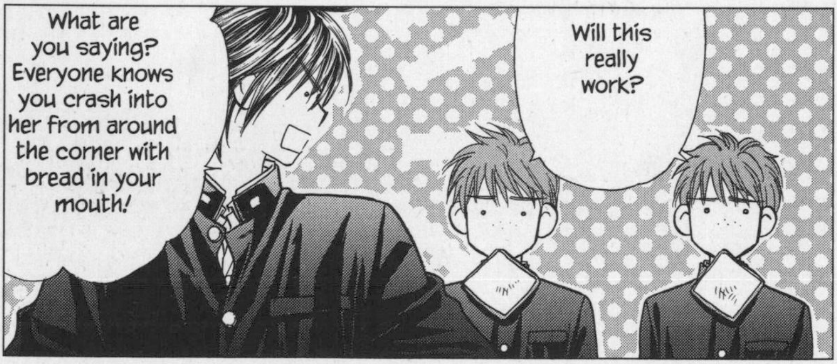
Will this really work?
What are you saying? Everyone knows you crash into her from around the corner with bread in your mouth!

Hana's awkward request, page 69

In Japanese, there are several levels of language that indicate politeness. Hana sounds so awkward because she's trying to use a polite form of the language, but her manners are so unpracticed that she's struggling.

A guy?, page 69

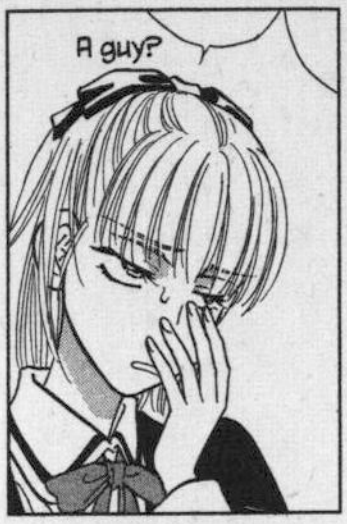
A guy?

Hana wonders if Masumi is actually a guy, because Masumi used the masculine first-person pronoun *boku* in referring to herself.

Masumi-oneesama, page 70

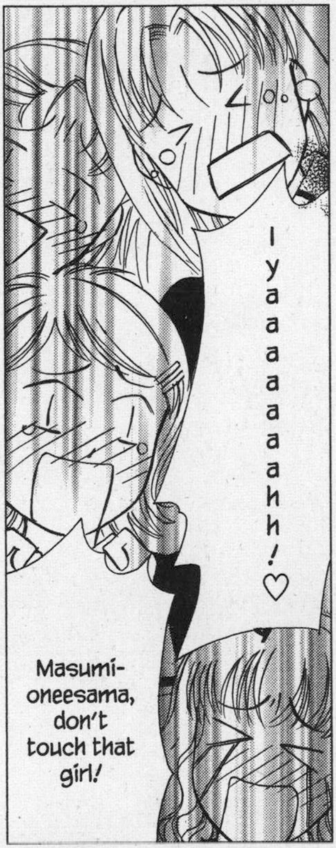
Iyaaaaaaaahh!♡
Masumi-oneesama, don't touch that girl!

"Oneesama" is a very respectful way of referring to your older sister, or someone you respect like an older sister.

Weighs a ton/Stays at home, page 74

Hana first writes "weighs a ton," then crosses it out and replaces it with "stays at home." She made a mistake in writing down the kanji, so that her first attempt meant something more like "prone to chubbiness."

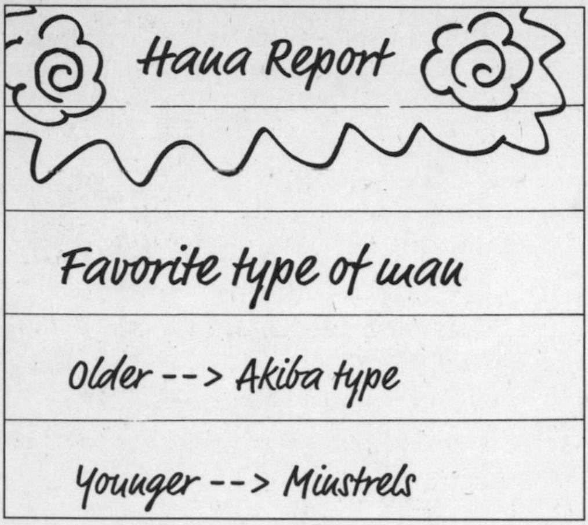
Hana Report
Favorite type of man
Older --> Akiba type
Younger --> Minstrels

Akiba type, page 74

Akiba is short for Akihabara, a district in Tokyo known for selling lots of computer and electronic goods, but also for selling a lot of anime and *otaku* goods. An "Akiba type" is the kind of guy who would frequent Akihabara—in other words, the ultimate fanboy.

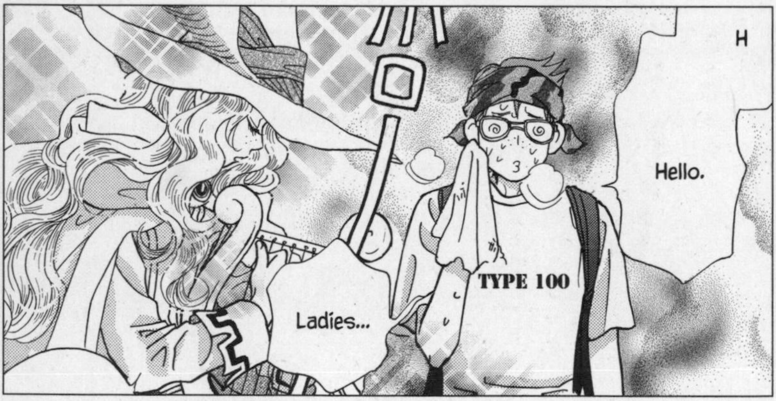
H
Hello.
TYPE 100
Ladies...

Type 100, page 82

Type 100 is a type of Gundam piloted by Char Aznoble, the most infamous villain in the history of the Gundam series.

***Moe moe*, page 83**

Moe is a phrase used by fanboys to describe the type of character from an anime or video game that they have a particular attraction to. *Moe moe* is an emphatic way of saying that someone is just his type.

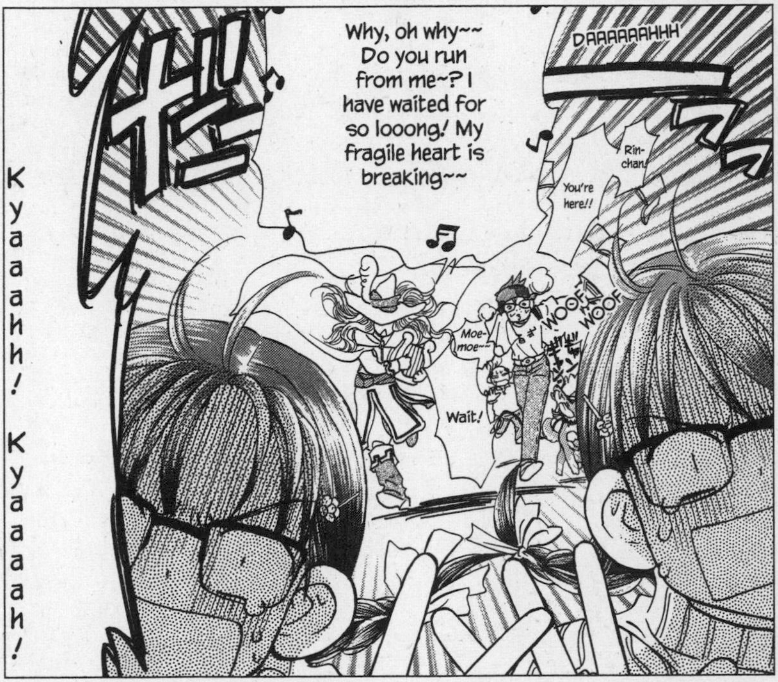
DAAAAAAHHH
Rin-chan!
You're here!!
Why, oh why~~ Do you run from me~? I have waited for so looong! My fragile heart is breaking~~
WOOF WOOF
Moe-moe~~
Wait!
Kyaaahh! Kyaaaah!

Hell tour, page 90

Beppu, where the Hockey Club is currently visiting, is the hot spring capital of Japan and has nine major geothermal hot spots, known as the "nine hells of Beppu" probably because they're so hot. If you toured them all, you would be going on a "hell tour."

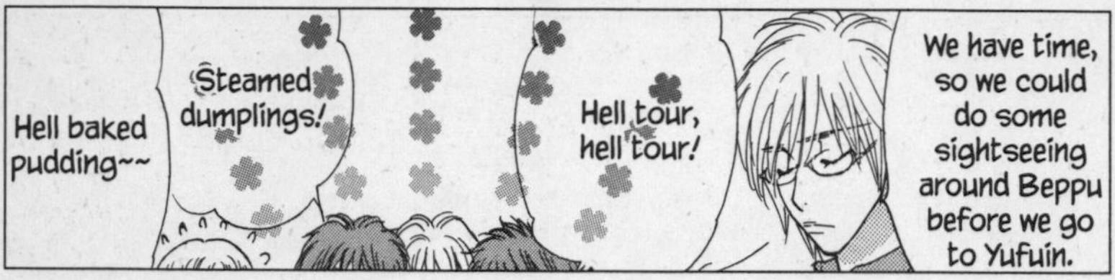
We have time, so we could do some sightseeing around Beppu before we go to Yufuin.
Hell tour, hell tour!
Steamed dumplings!
Hell baked pudding~~

Steamed dumplings, hell-baked pudding, and hot springs egg, page 90

The water in the hot springs at Beppu is so hot it is used to cook various delicacies, either with the steam or by boiling. In the case of the pudding, it is put in a covered pan and cooked.

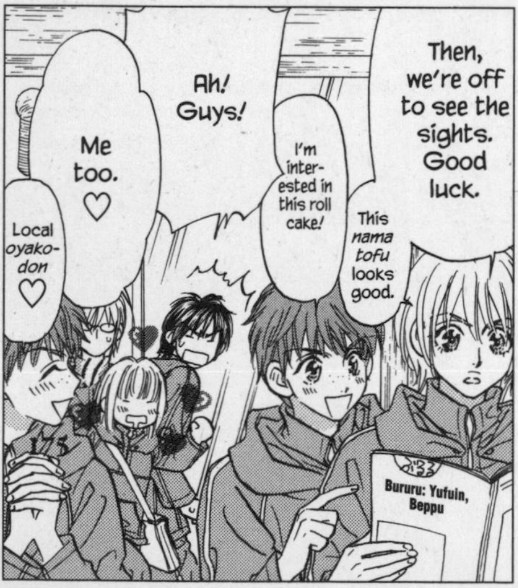
Then, we're off to see the sights. Good luck.
Ah! Guys!
I'm interested in this roll cake!
This nama tofu looks good.
Me too. ♡
Local oyako-don ♡
Bururu: Yufuin, Beppu

Nama tofu and *oyako-don*, page 98

Nama tofu is fresh, cold tofu. *Oyako* literally means "parent and child," and *oyako-don* gets its name from having chicken (the parent) and egg (the child) in a bowl of rice.

WaT, page 101

WaT stands for "Wentz and Teppei." They are the Japanese pop duo Eiji Wentz and Teppei Koike. Clearly, Elisabetta has a crush on Koike-san, who is about 5'6".

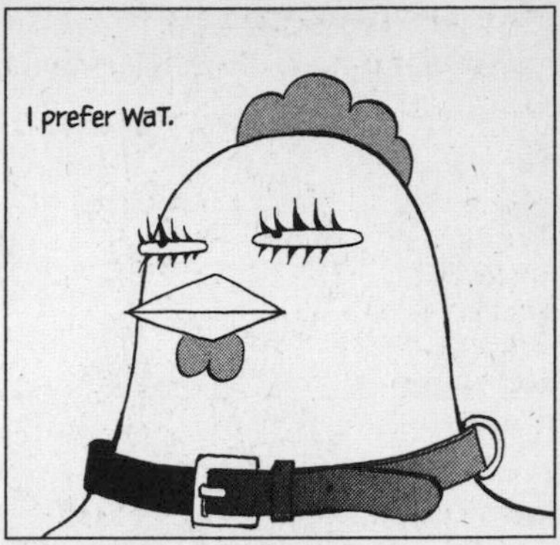
I prefer WaT.

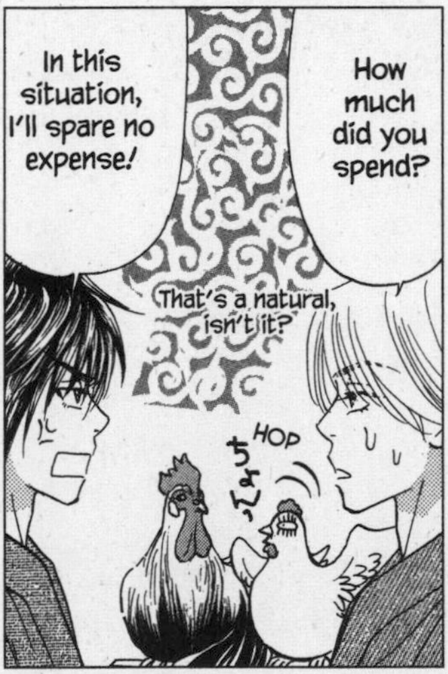
How much did you spend?
In this situation, I'll spare no expense!
That's a natural, isn't it?
HOP

Natural monument, page 106

The rooster that Izumi had brought over is so rare and beautiful that it is protected by law as a natural monument or treasure.

Haori, page 110

A short, kimono-like coat worn over a long kimono.

Dom Pérignon, page 110

A very expensive brand of champagne.

Maruwa, page 129

Maruwa is a high-class supermarket chain in southern Japan.

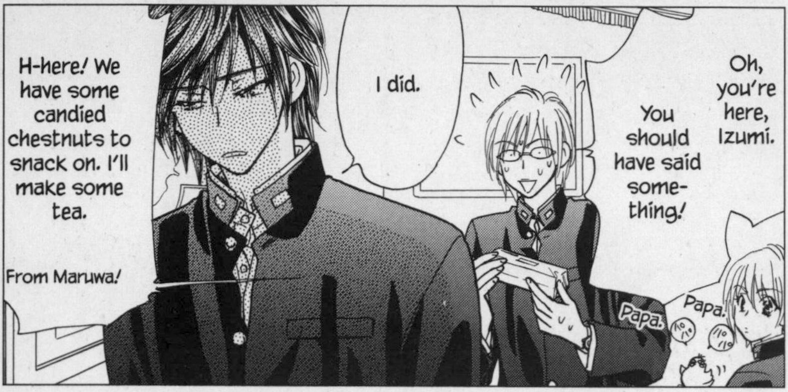
Oh, you're here, Izumi.
You should have said something!
Papa.
Papa.
I did.
H-here! We have some candied chestnuts to snack on. I'll make some tea.
From Maruwa!

Bunkasai, page 137

A *bunkasai*, or culture festival, is held every year by schools in Japan. Students all work together to create attractions, put on plays, and/or sell food.

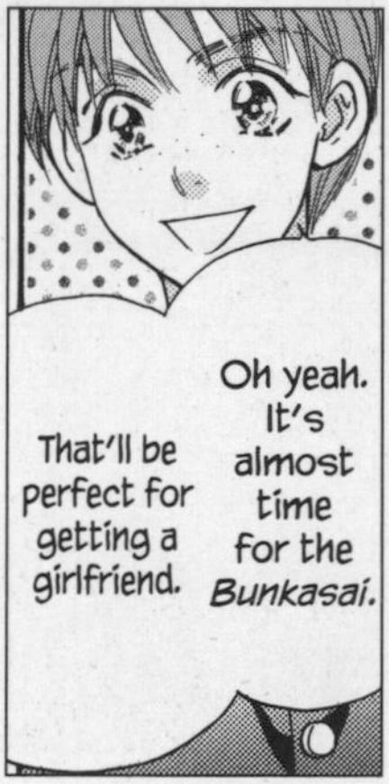
Oh yeah. It's almost time for the *Bunkasai*.
That'll be perfect for getting a girlfriend.

PoXXmon, page 139

It's a common practice in Japanese editions of manga to partially censor the titles of copyrighted material. You can probably guess what "PoXXmon" stands for!

Miai, page 139

A *miai* is a formal interview to arrange a marriage, during which the man and woman in question decide whether or not the other party would be a suitable spouse. Usually, the man and woman in question have not met before, but extensive research has been done on both sides.

***Konnyaku*, page 142**
Jelly made from a pressed vegetable.

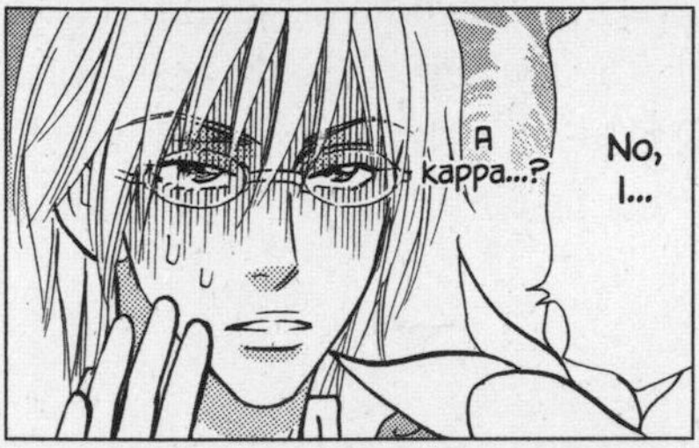
No, I...
A kappa...?

***Kappa*, page 148**
A *kappa* is a Japanese water demon that lurks in rivers and lakes, performing all sorts of misdeeds ranging from looking up women's kimonos to eating children.

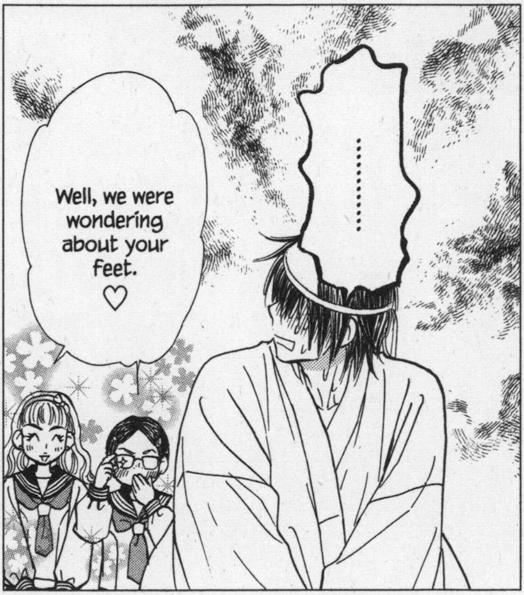
....
Well, we were wondering about your feet. ♡

Wondering about your feet, page 154
According to Japanese legend, ghosts don't have feet.

***Yamato Nadeshiko*, page 169**
The term *yamato nadeshiko*, the name of the Japanese pink flower, has come to refer to a woman who displays all the traditional feminine virtues of old Japan.

***Jîya*, page 169**
A jîya is an elderly servant, kind of like a nanny but male.

Preview of Volume 5

We're pleased to present you a preview from volume 5. Please check our website (www.delreymanga.com) to see when this volume will be available in English. For now you'll have to make do with Japanese!

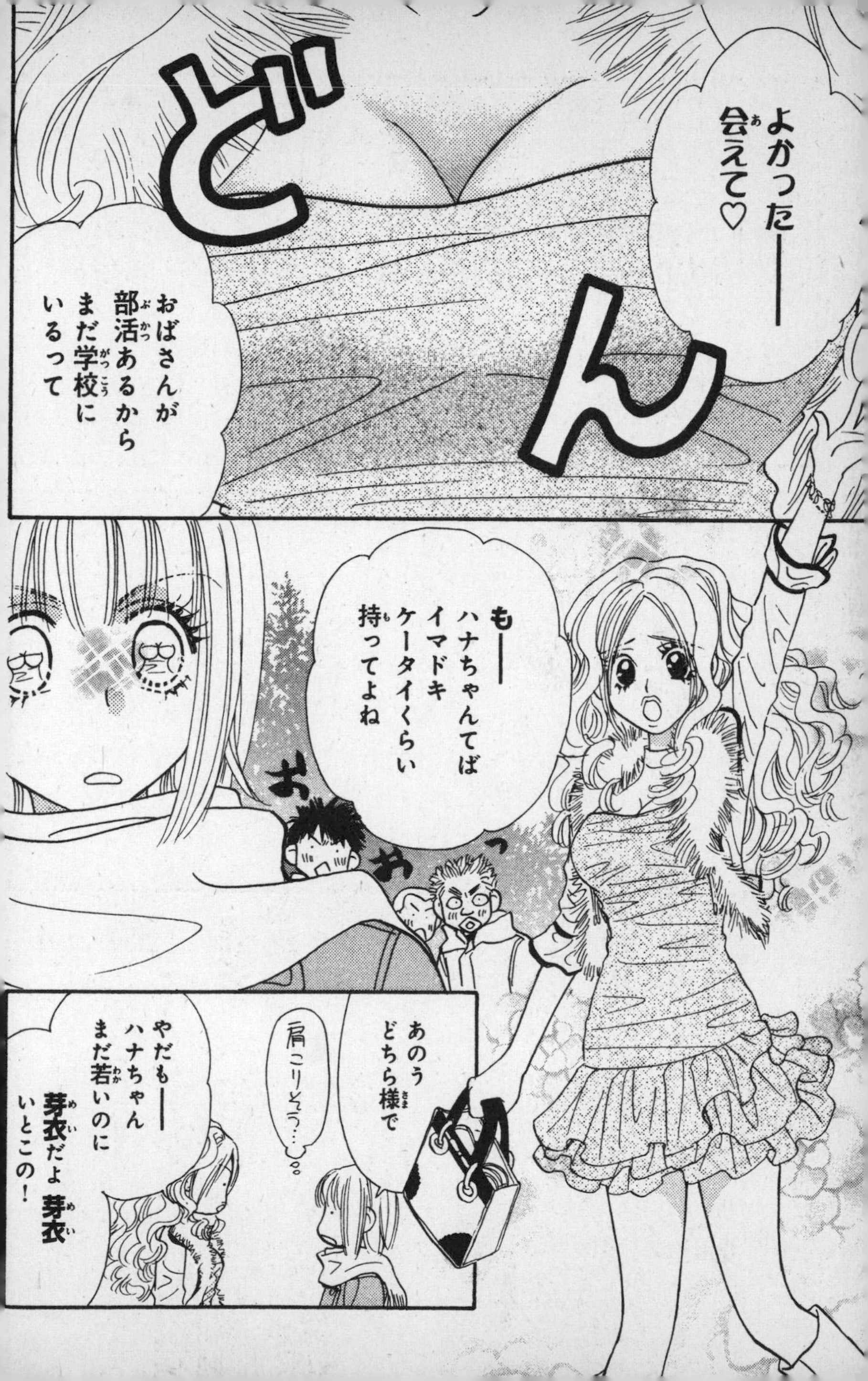
よかったーー
会えて♡
どん
おばさんが部活あるからまだ学校にいるって
もーー
ハナちゃんてば
イマドキ
ケータイくらい
持ってよね
おおっ
あのう
どちら様で
肩こりそう…
やだもーー
ハナちゃん
まだ若いのに
芽衣だよ 芽衣
いとこの！

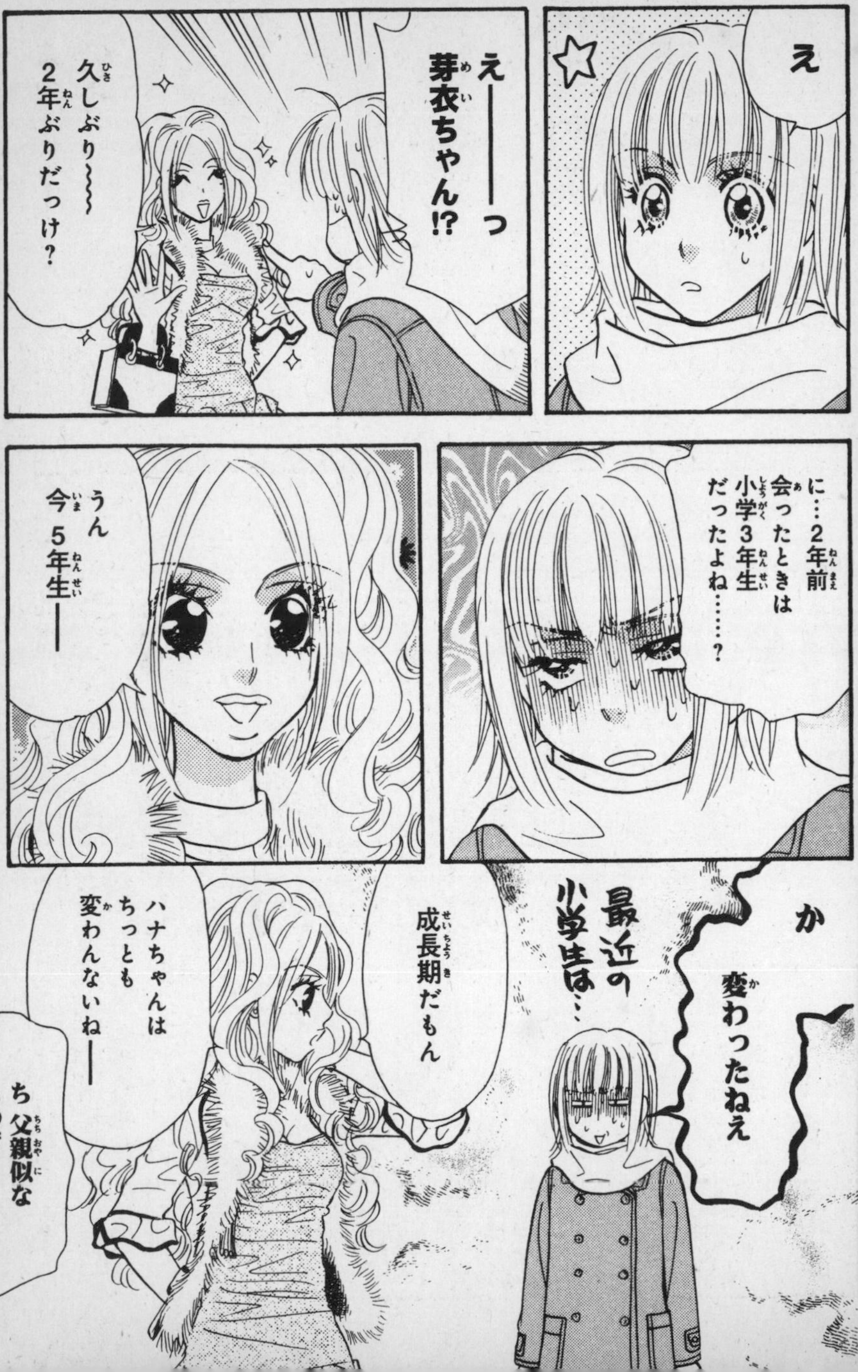

え
え——っ 芽衣ちゃん!?
久しぶり~~~ 2年ぶりだっけ？
に…2年前 会ったときは 小学3年生 だったよね……？
うん 今 5年生——
か 変わったねえ
最近の 小学生は……
成長期だもん
ハナちゃんは ちっとも 変わんないね——
ち 父親似な もので……

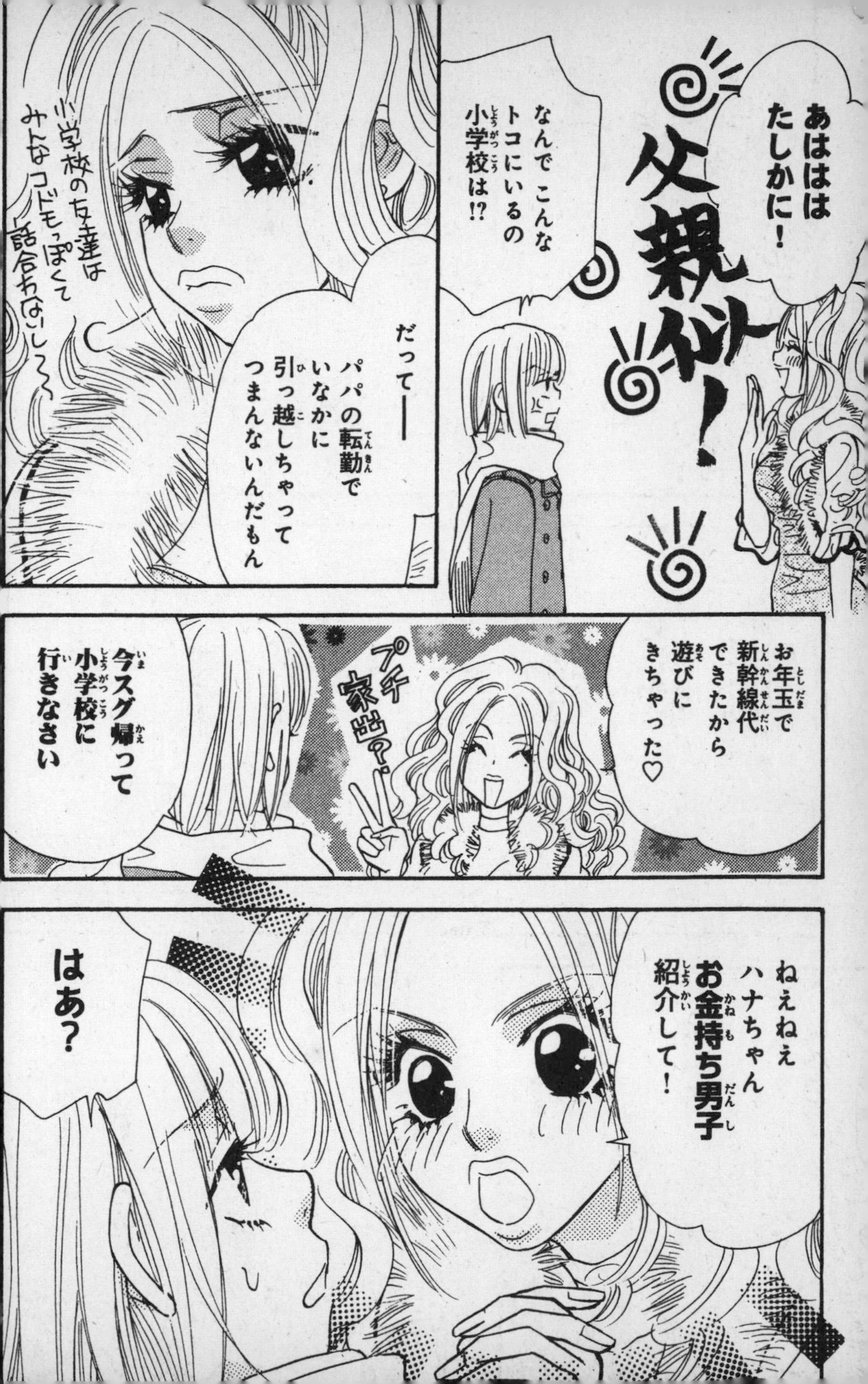
あははたしかに！
父親似！
なんでこんなトコにいるの小学校は!?
だってーー
パパの転勤でいなかに引っ越しちゃってつまんないんだもん
小学校の友達はみんなコドモっぽくて話合わないし〜
お年玉で新幹線代できたから遊びにきちゃった♡
プチ家出?
今スグ帰って小学校に行きなさい
ねえねえハナちゃんお金持ち男子紹介して！
はあ？

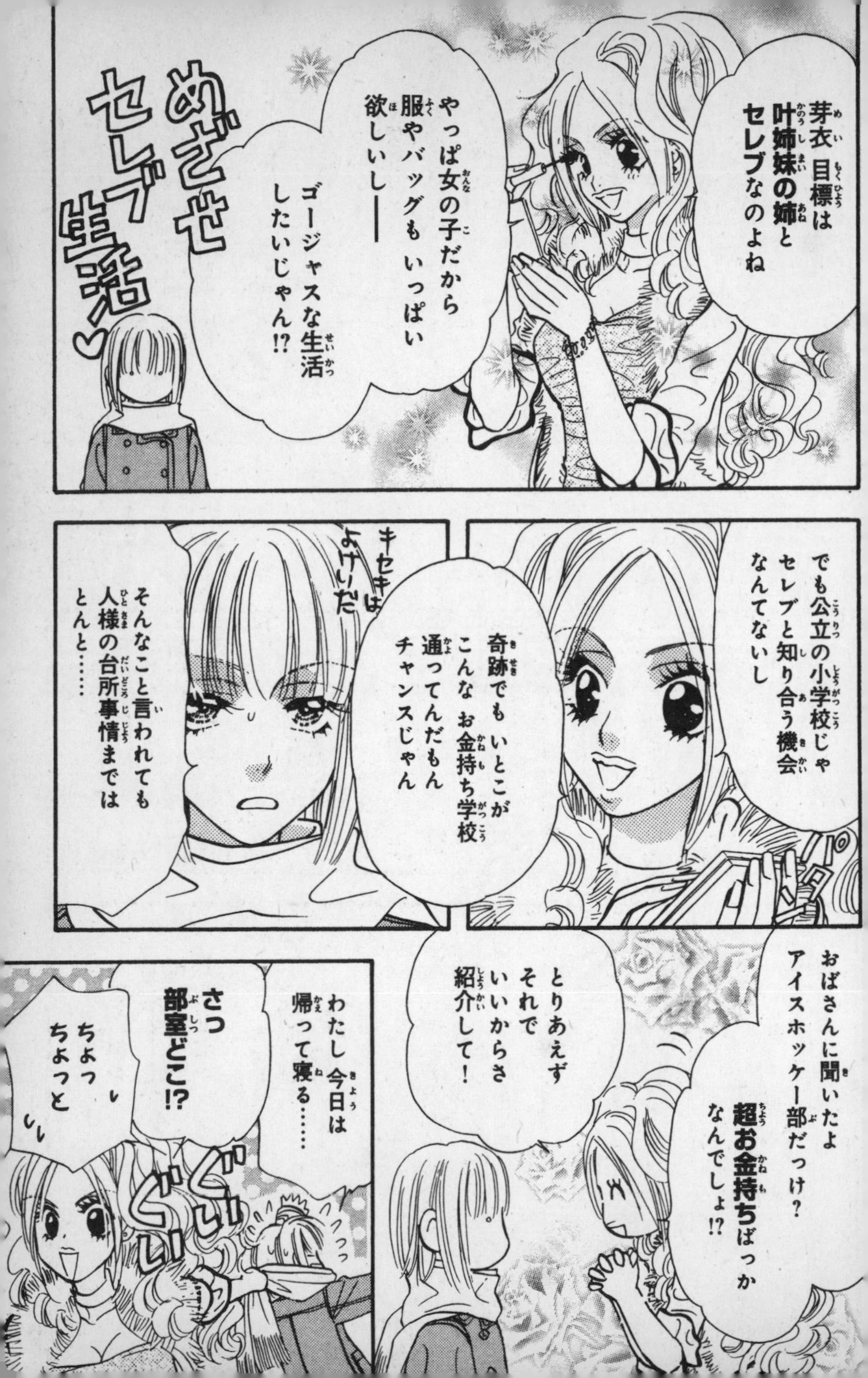
芽衣 目標は 叶姉妹の姉と セレブなのよね
やっぱ女の子だから 服やバッグも いっぱい 欲しいし—— ゴージャスな生活 したいじゃん!?
めざせ セレブ生活♡
でも公立の小学校じゃ セレブと知り合う機会 なんてないし
パタン
奇跡でも いとこが こんな お金持ち学校 通ってんだもん チャンスじゃん
キセキは よけいだ
そんなこと言われても 人様の台所事情までは とんと……
おばさんに聞いたよ アイスホッケー部だっけ? 超お金持ちばっか なんでしょ!?
とりあえず それで いいからさ 紹介して!
わたし 今日は 帰って寝る……
さっ 部室どこ!?
ちょっ ちょっと
ぐい ぐい

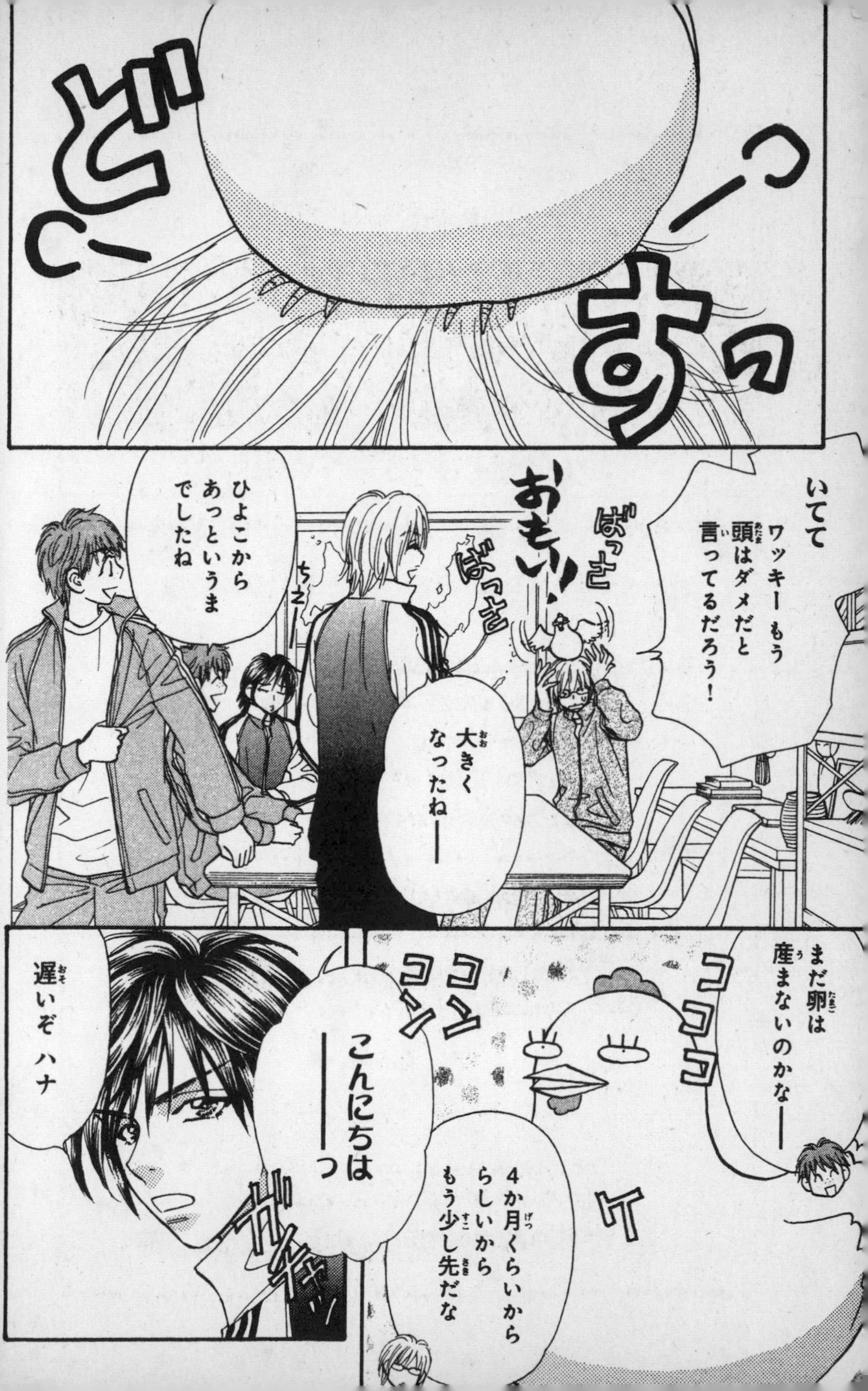
どごーっ
すっ
いてて ワッキー もう頭はダメだと言ってるだろう！
おもいっ！
ばっさ ばっさ
大きくなったね——
ちぇー
ひよこからあっというまでしたね
まだ卵は産まないのかな——
コココ
ケ
4か月くらいからしいから もう少し先だな
コンコン
こんにちは——っ
遅いぞ ハナ
ガチャ

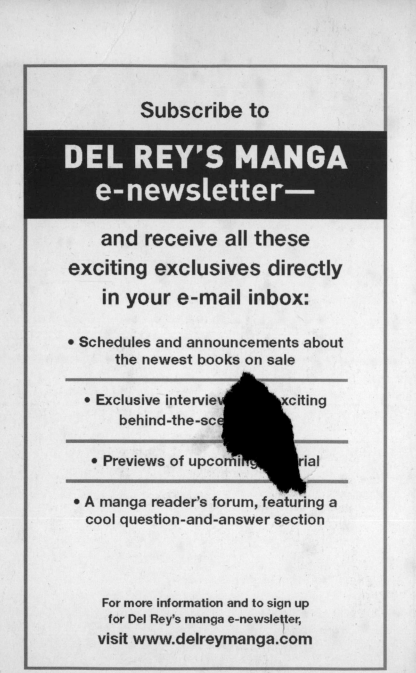

TOMARE!

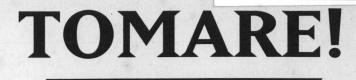

止まれ

[STOP!]

You're going the wrong way!

Manga is a completely different type of reading experience.

To start at the *beginning*,
go to the *end*!

That's right! Authentic manga is read the traditional Japanese way—from right to left. Exactly the opposite of how American books are read. It's easy to follow: Just go to the other end of the book, and read each page—and each panel—from right side to left side, starting at the top right. Now you're experiencing manga as it was meant to be!